WARLORD
POLITICS
▼ A N D ▼
AFRICAN
STATES

William Reno

LYNNE
RIENNER
PUBLISHERS

BOULDER
LONDON

Paperback edition published in the United States of America in 1999 by
Lynne Rienner Publishers, Inc.
1800 30th Street, Boulder, Colorado 80301

and in the United Kingdom by
Lynne Rienner Publishers, Inc.
3 Henrietta Street, Covent Garden, London WC2E 8LU

Published in hardcover in 1998

ISBN 1-55587-883-0 (pbk. : alk. paper)

Printed and bound in the United States of America

The paper used in this publication meets the requirements
∞ of the American National Standard for Permanence of
Paper for Printed Library Materials Z39.48-1984.

5 4 3

CONTENTS

ILLUSTRATIONS

TABLES

FIGURE

▼ ▼ ▼ ▼ ▼ ▼ ▼ ▼ ▼ ▼ ▼ ▼ ▼ ▼ ▼

PREFACE

This book examines alternative, usually clandestine economic systems to offer a new approach to understanding politics in weak states and warlord organizations. As with most countries, African societies have their share of tax evasion, barter deals, illicit production, smuggling, and protection rackets. I argue here that these phenomena have become widespread and integral to building political authority in parts of Africa, which challenges existing assumptions about how political actors calculate their interests. My argument also makes clear the limitations of the liberalizing reforms of the World Bank and the International Monetary Fund (IMF) by showing in detail how weak-state and warlord political economies restrict and manipulate bank and IMF prescriptions.

Official reports and statistics usually ignore these activities, forcing the researcher to look elsewhere for data. Such information is also lacking because many of these activities are covert; they take place outside the law and are thus difficult to investigate. Furthermore, informants may suspect that a researcher who asks about these activities harbors hidden motives. Because much of this kind of information involves activities integral to political and commercial competition, it can be difficult to convince informants that the researcher is not working for a rival. And when the cast of characters includes mercenaries, rogue generals, nervous civil servants, buccaneer foreign entrepreneurs, and people trying to stay out of the limelight, claims that one is seeking data for an academic study can appear far-fetched.

Nonetheless, in these societies political authority and command over resources come mainly through the decisions of specific individuals who act to serve their private interests, largely without regard for formal government institutions, rules, and processes. Likewise, those who resist these actions cannot call upon a shared authority to settle conflicts with their adversaries; their security and prosperity depend on their own power, tactical advantage, and alliances. In situations in which no effective government is present to impose order, contacts with individuals and detailed personal knowledge of local conditions uncover what is invisible from the capital, unwritten in law books, and unmentioned in legislative debates.

Thus, networks of personal contacts, usually involving repeated interviews, underlie much of this study of warlord politics. For example, part of the research for the chapter on Liberia took me to West Africa in mid-1994, where I was able to follow up on contacts made during a prior extended stay in Sierra Leone and during previous trips to Liberia. These contacts led to Liberians associated with warring factions and involved in regional trade. Visits to Sierra Leone, Liberia, and Guinea at various times since 1989 provided me with a range of contacts from which to gather data and analyze and verify information. In the case of Liberia and to some extent Sierra Leone, bank records, documents from warlord factions and recognized governments, business files, and personal correspondence offered additional points from which to evaluate information. Data from these sources—produced to keep track of organizations' internal activities and finances—offer a valuable glimpse into the inner workings of warlord factions, groups of state officials who oppose them, and businesses associated with both.

Many of these contacts demanded confidentiality as a precondition for their assistance. Given the recent major conflict in three of the four countries examined in detail here, this is a sensible precaution, and it has been observed.

Local newspapers also provide valuable information. At first glance, many appear to be little more than gossip sheets that report outrageous allegations and are unduly influenced by warlord factions or state officials. Some journals are in fact owned by prominent strongmen and are used as broadsheets to slander and threaten opponents. The poor technical quality and irregular publication of some papers heighten suspicions about their credibility. Nonetheless, careful attention to such sources of data—even from highly biased journalistic sources—can yield important information. Ways particular Monrovia papers attack or praise specific individuals help one to map political cliques and informal but highly relevant personal associations.

For example, the *Patriot* serves as a mouthpiece for Charles Taylor and his National Patriotic Front of Liberia (NPFL), Liberia's largest warlord faction. Yet the newspaper's content provides valuable clues to NPFL alliances and associations, particularly when it attacks allies who have fallen out of favor. Kinshasa's *Le Soft* counts journalists, government officials, economists, and businesspeople among its editorial board. When substantiated by other reliable sources, this newspaper yields important information about conflicts among Congolese elites and their commercial and political activities.

Alternatively, Monrovia's *Inquirer*, Freetown's *For Di People*, and Lagos's *Guardian* have attracted praise from human rights organizations, international journalist groups, and local readers for their often respectable independent reporting. The fact that their offices and personnel have been targets of armed attacks and official harassment by many sources gives one further confidence in their journalistic quality.

Ownership is not a definitive indicator of journalistic slant. The Nigerian government is one of the owners of the weekly *West Africa*, which is widely considered a journal of record with regard to the Liberian war even as a Nigerian expeditionary force has been embroiled in that conflict. In the early days of the war, reporters from *West Africa* were among the few journalists sending dispatches from outside the capital. But one must read carefully: The publication's reporting on Nigerian politics hews closely to an official version of events.

In sum, my choice of sources of information and my judgments about their validity reflect the locations of power in warlord and weak-state politics. The most useful information focuses on commercial enterprises and personal networks of rulers, which are usually, though not always, constructed behind the facade of formal statehood. That the pursuit of power in Africa's worst-off states is essentially a matter of private gain becomes clear in my examination of Liberia, Sierra Leone, Congo (formerly Zaire), and Nigeria.

▼ ▼ ▼

Major credit for this project goes to Florida International University (FIU), which has employed me for the three-year duration of this project. While writing the book, I benefited from several research grants from the FIU Arts and Sciences dean's office. I am also grateful to successive chairs of my department, Mary Volcansek, Chris Warren, and John Stack, for their tolerance of my frenetic travel schedule. I also thank them for their support, particularly for their acceptance of outrageous telephone charges for frequent calls to Africa. I assure them that my phone mail message no longer says that "this number accepts collect calls from Liberia, Nigeria, Sierra Leone, and Zaire."

While writing this book, I also benefited from the help and hospitality of Stephen Ellis and the librarians of the Afrika Studiecentrum at Leiden in the Netherlands and from Wayne Nafziger and Raimo Vayrynen at the United Nations University in Helsinki, Finland. Richard Joseph at the Massachusetts Institute of Technology, Dan Smith at the University of Denver, Thomas Callaghy at the University of Pennsylvania, Michael Chege at the University of Florida, Jeff Herbst at Princeton,

Thomas Spear at the University of Wisconsin, and Leo Villalón at the University of Kansas gave me opportunities to present and discuss portions of this book at their institutions. I am also grateful for the hospitality of John Sharpless of the University of Wisconsin History Department during critical phases of the writing of this book. I acknowledge the advice and guidance of Chris Dietrich, Janet Fleischman, Herb Howe, Bruce Magnusson, and Elizabeth Rubin. I also recognize the patience of Lynne Rienner and the careful work of Cheryl Carnahan, whose efforts made this book easier to read. I am ever grateful to the numerous people in government, industry, academia, and at war who shared their insights and concerns on this controversial subject. At their insistence, and due to the dangers that tyrants pose, they remain anonymous. The views expressed in this book are mine alone and should not be ascribed to any of the persons or institutions mentioned above.

William Reno

INTRODUCTION

Ex Africa semper aliquid novi [There is always something new out of Africa]
> —*Pliny the Elder,* Historia Naturalis[1]

In a seminal 1989 report, World Bank officials wrote that "Africa needs not just less government, but better government—government that concentrates its efforts less on direct interventions and more on enabling others to be productive."[2] Most reformers aim to build a state that acts as a neutral institution under the rule of law and that is engaged in promoting compromises and resolving conflicts among individuals and groups. Yet in the four cases in this study—Liberia, Sierra Leone, Zaire,* and Nigeria—less government has contributed not to better government but rather to warlord politics.

In these cases, rulers reject the pursuit of a broader project of creating a state that serves a collective good or even of creating institutions that are capable of developing independent perspectives and acting on behalf of interests distinct from the rulers' personal exercise of power. Economic development is abjured when it threatens to put resources into the hands of those who might use them to challenge the rulers' position. Consequently, anxious rulers contract a wide array of economic roles to outsiders, in part to deny resources to internal rivals and to use outsiders' skills and connections to gather as much wealth as possible. Rulers then convert wealth into political resources, buying the loyalty of some and buying weapons to coerce others and thus gather more resources and so on. More significantly, the virtual total absence of bureaucratic state institutions, or "state collapse," means outsiders also take on a wider range of political roles conventionally reserved for state institu-

---

*In May 1997, Zaire became the Democratic Republic of Congo. I refer to that country as Congo (not to be confused with Congo-Brazzaville) throughout.

1

tions, such as providing internal security for rulers and diplomatic relations with other outsiders.

Warlord rulers and their allies also disrupt authority in other states. They ignore the significance of frontiers if they obstruct efforts to control markets, clandestine or visible. Alternatively, the more expansive pursuit of power is not necessarily repeated within those frontiers if efforts to control populations or territories are deemed to outweigh the potential benefits of direct control.

To many, this behavior seems to continue the politics of the bureaucratically weak and internally insecure African states of the postcolonial era; it is distinguished by its intensity and moves further along a spectrum of (bureaucratic) state weakness but is really nothing new. Indeed, each of the four countries examined in detail in this book was marked by intense patronage politics after independence. Rulers in each country found themselves presiding over diverse societies in states colonial rulers had not created with the intention that they would become sovereign states. But central to my notion of weak-state capacity and the change in warlord politics is Jean-François Bayart's notion of "elite accommodation."[3] That is, to sustain a meaningful semblance of sovereignty—the exclusive control over territory and people—rulers needed to cut informal deals with individuals who exercised power in their own right. Elsewhere I call this a "shadow state," a very real, but not formally recognized, patronage system that was rigidly organized and centered on rulers' control over resources. This control bound rulers' potential rivals to them in exchange for largesse without the need to create strong bureaucracies they feared would heighten independent tendencies among elites.

The external dimension of this accommodation involved close ties to powerful non-African states that provided patronage to rulers in exchange for Cold War diplomatic or strategic support. Robert Jackson, who used the term *quasi-states* to describe this combination of external dependency and internal institutional weakness, nonetheless recognized that foreign patronage permitted rulers to pursue two projects simultaneously.[4] They used foreign patronage to finance their own networks of clients. Rulers also used money to provide some benefits to wider constituencies of supporters—even if inefficiently—through weak, politically emasculated, and foreign-funded state bureaucracies. Thus, the term *weak state* signifies a spectrum of conventional bureaucratic state capabilities that exists alongside (generally very strong) informal political networks. This condition is not particularly novel, as these features can be said to exist in many parts of the world.

But critical to my distinction between weak states and the warlord politics that follows in some cases is another feature of this spectrum, that of collective versus private interests. In principle, the triumph of informal (shadow state) networks to the near exclusion of state bureaucracies, or state collapse in political science literature, could leave rulers in a condition in which they pursue power through purely personal means and that pursuit becomes synonymous with and indistinguishable from their private interests. Rulers thus would jettison all pretenses of serving the interests of a public that may contain dangerous rivals or unruly citizens. Certainly, liberalism and its threatening ideas of political and economic individualism would undermine such rulers' notions of political order. At this extreme, rulers and their associates resemble a mafia rather than a government if one thinks of the latter as necessarily serving some collective interest, however faint and by whatever means, to be distinguished from the mafia. This absence of collective, versus private, interest is a major distinguishing feature of warlord politics.

Collective authority and private authority may, by coincidence, resemble one another on occasion. For example, inhabitants of a collapsed (bureaucratic) state may enjoy security because of the presence of an armed organization seeking mineral resources for its members and its shareholders. But the critical difference between this style of organization and a conventional state, even if very weak, lies in the fact that the inhabitants do not enjoy security by right of membership in a state. Security is coincidental; it is reliant on the venture's profitability and the degree to which it satisfies the shared interests of the members of the organization (a foreign firm and a warlord, for example). When either or both conditions no longer pertain, local security may cease unless inhabitants take it upon themselves to provide this collective good in a way that does not threaten the ruler.

How does one distinguish a ruler of a very weak state from a warlord? Obviously, this calls for a judgment as to where to draw a line along a continuum of informal versus bureaucratic and collective versus private. I suggest here that a partial answer lies in revisiting the notion of elite accommodation, examining how accommodation has changed in weak states, especially since the end of the Cold War. Since the mid-1980s, resources that underwrote old accommodations have undergone a major shift. The World Bank, for example, reported a 1.2 percent annual decline in per capita output in sub-Saharan Africa from 1985 to 1994.[5] Declining internal resources and new conditions for external patronage receive considerable attention in this text. Most important, these shifts undermine the attractiveness of serving a collective interest in weak-state rulers' pursuit of power. Seen slightly differently, these changes signal the end of broad-based patronage politics in Africa and the end of a Cold War elite accommodation that politics sustained. The next chapter explains why this old arrangement is falling apart at the same time building strong bureaucracies is becoming more difficult and dangerous.

Some might wonder if the disruptions of crisis might entice rulers to pursue the risky but rewarding task of building viable bureaucracies. I argue later that this is indeed an option but that the combination of risks and often unanticipated rewards of the warlord strategy encourages rulers to go down the warlord path. In the separate country studies, we will see the specific features of state weakness in those cases that make this outcome more likely. This is not to say that warlord politics is the fate of all weak states. Some argue, for example, that a stateless public order is emerging in Somalia and has characterized local authority there.[6] Outcomes are not preordained, and the cases in this book show considerable experimentation among rulers. But one must also keep in mind that the actions and choices of outside actors play a considerable, often unforeseen role in shaping the calculus of choice in weak states.

THE DILEMMA OF REFORM

Liberalization of markets is a major external factor affecting weak-state rulers' pursuit of authority. All but one of Africa's forty-seven sub-Saharan states borrow from the World Bank and are thus forced to acknowledge its advice, which focuses on the wholesale dismantling of economically inviable political networks based on patronage.[7] But as the World Bank envisions a new role for government in which "foreign investors would be welcomed as partners," it brings to rulers new nonstate allies with access to important sources of wealth—including those beyond the frontiers of the state—and, more critically, new means of coercion. Reformers envision that "the state would no longer be an entrepreneur, but a promoter of private producers, and the informal sector would be valued as a seedbed for entrepreneurs, not a hotbed of racketeers."[8] In fact, this situation hastens the privatization of state assets into the hands of essentially private commercial networks of politicians on which rulers base their personal power.

A central paradox of this book is that in this context reform that emphasizes economic and political liberalization further undermines weak-state rulers' incentives to pursue conventional strategies for maximizing power through generating economic growth and, hence, state revenues. At the same time, new entrepreneurial opportunities may become available to individual officials and other strongmen whose broader interests run counter to those of the ruler. Rulers cannot mobilize popular support against strongmen from within the population, since most weak states long ago ceased helping people to meet their needs or building up a sense of legitimacy among them. Reform in this direction would require much more government and much stronger (and expensive) institutions, which are precluded by threatening strongmen and fiscal austerity of reforms. These developments go a long way toward explaining why some states in Africa continue to weaken and why politics in those states increasingly resembles warlord politics. This is why I look at how warlords really work rather than dwelling on the collapse of state institutions that are a consequence, rather than a cause, of those politics.

Weak-state rulers' dilemmas are acute. They must analyze their need to provide effective responses to creditor demands in order to continue to receive loans they need to stave off threats to their survival. These threats emerge from enterprising elements within patronage networks, but the reforms seem to require that those elements be cast off. One could imagine plowing ahead with reform and countering threats to regime security with coercive force, but even the exercise of such power is in doubt if shrinking state resources cut into soldiers' salaries and independent commanders use the lack of patronage as an excuse to mobilize disgruntled soldiers to pursue private interests. Furthermore, creditor insistence that rulers give bureaucrats administrative autonomy raises fears that even successful reform will weaken their patronage base long before they reap the benefits of legitimacy from an appreciative population. Meanwhile, efficient bureaucrats who command the distribution of state resources would be in a position to directly mobilize supporters at the expense of even a reform-minded ruler's authority.

In the following pages I explore relations between the end of state-based patronage politics and weak-state rulers' efforts to continue to exercise political authority. How do rulers of states in which patronage politics is becoming unsustainable, through external pressure or an internal lack of resources, actually change the way they govern? Even in remote corners of sub-Saharan Africa, official and popular assumptions about the role of state authority have changed. Why have the contours of state power not been redrawn as reformers envisioned? Political actors in the four cases described in this book show equivocation, hedging, and backtracking, which Henry Bienen and Jeffrey Herbst identified as characteristic of reform across the continent.[9] Extending their observation, the cases in this book show an entirely different model of political authority—one that rejects liberal assumptions of reform and that is characterized by a lack of many functions statehood is supposed to provide.

Thus, the focus of this book is not on the formal role of institutions; instead, it looks at rulers' efforts to manage external challenges and reconfigure old patron-client politics. My definition of state thus borrows from Max Weber's observation that states vary in their degree of resemblance to an ideal type in which they enforce regulations, backed up with a monopoly of violence.[10] I find throughout the four case studies that the exercise of political authority in these countries represents nearly the opposite of the Weberian ideal. But throughout the book I explain how rulers in Africa find that an additional, outward-looking perspective that defines statehood in part by mutual recognition with other states in the international system, in contrast to Weber's emphasis on internal capacity, is difficult to abjure.

Liberalizing reforms also offer warlord politicians valuable resources and bring important incentives that shape political choices, even if formal statehood is a facade behind which a political-commercial network operates. Even such states have the capacity to enter into the full range of international relations reserved for those who possess globally recognized sovereignty over a piece of territory, regardless of whether weak states exercise control on the ground.[11] Here, too, actual behavior can stray considerably from the ideal type the mutually constitutive definition of states projects.

To look solely at formal institutions and shifts in output, the classic indexes of reform policy impact, would miss important aspects of changing relationships between rulers and their political networks. One might observe that the Abacha regime in Nigeria holds numerous anti-corruption tribunals and thus conclude that fiscal transparency and efficiency constitute the intended aim. On the contrary, we find in Chapter 6 that the tribunals accomplish no such thing but instead serve as vehicles through which the president reins in powerful associates and roots out enemies or simply pares down expensive patronage networks. A Nigerian religious scholar has criticized fake banking "reforms," rigged "privatization" of state-run companies, ever changing electoral timetables, and constant promises to create new government jurisdictions. He has argued that these changes merely reveal how Nigeria's ruler has manipulated state institutions, using a "struggle against fraud" to struggle against factions and centralizing his political authority against a wide array of rivals.[12] Yet these actions have strengthened Nigeria's external face, convincing some outsiders of Abacha's supposed seriousness about reform.

I will look at how changes in the elite accommodation of patronage politics affect weak-state rulers' capacities to govern and will explore the nature of resistance among some former clients and how that resistance greatly complicates rulers' efforts to manage change. This broader view of political change renders notions of statehood and global recognition of sovereignty as independent variables, as the tools and resources manipulated by one side or another in the struggle to create the new political arrangements that are the subject of this book. The calculations of political relations in Africa's weak states change, causing forces that operate outside formal state boundaries and functions to play increasingly important roles in the exercise of local political authority.

All reformist rulers face compromises between powerful groups and their own capabilities and goals. Economic and political reform in Japan, an effectively organized bureaucratic state, faces stiff resistance from individual political patrons and cadres of civil servants who are graduates of Tokyo University.[13] As noted previously, the constraints on formal state institutional capabilities to manage demands of informal political networks have been especially acute among already weak states in Africa.

EXTERNALIZING POLITICAL STRUGGLE

This book highlights two paradoxes that appear in the vast literature on political reform, particularly the paradox regarding shortcomings in African states and other weak states such as Burma, Haiti, and the formerly Soviet Central Asia taken up in Chapter 1. A closer look at the actual management of change reveals that rulers often pursue strategies that operate on principles at odds with those conceived by foreign advocates of reform. Paradoxically, rulers of the institutionally weakest states, which face the most severe threats from strongmen and the most intense pressures from outsiders, are the most consistent and thorough in destroying remaining formal state institutions—the very tools advocates of reform regard as the key to regime capabilities.

The second paradox is even more surprising. Outsiders such as creditors, foreign firms and even some officials of strong states participate in or tacitly support hard-pressed rulers' desperate attempts to manage change in this unexpected fashion. These outsiders not only replace collapsing formal state institutions but also play critical roles in local factional politics, helping rulers push aside and discipline old political networks and strongmen. In fact, over half of about $20 million in private capital inflows to sub-Saharan Africa (excluding South Africa) in 1994–1995 went to the four countries in this study despite their ongoing factional quarrels, widespread violence, and extremely weak state institutions.[14] Even larger projects are in the works. The Canadian-Swedish firm Eurocan, for example, has proposed $300 million in start-up funding for the world's largest copper mine in Congo's Shaba province.[15] Meanwhile, more bureaucratic African states such as Kenya are suffering losses of foreign investment.[16] This situation reflects a decisive shift in the nature of foreign investment in Africa, with significant implications for weak-state rulers.

Outside commercial interest in weak states is not unique to Africa. Companies promoting a multibillion dollar gas pipeline from Turkmenistan to Pakistan through Afghanistan proposed creating a "pipeline council." "They are prepared to make millions of dollars in bonus payments to various factions in Afghanistan," reports the *Financial Times*, "but only in the form of humanitarian aid whose distribution will be overseen by a non-governmental aid organization."[17] It is through such means that new nonstate global actors and the pressures and opportunities of global markets come to play important roles in the political economy of weak-state–warlord transitions. In such cases, one finds that political actors innovate, borrowing selectively from past practices—for the sake of efficiency, out of fear of change, or to satisfy outsiders' expectations of how they should behave—and combining them with new techniques.

A major innovation of the present study lies in its examination of this new partnership between rulers of weak states and foreign nonstate actors centered on the political struggles over markets in places where formal state institutions have collapsed. It is in this partnership that the innovative ruler in the very weak state bears a striking resemblance to the "warlord" politics that marks places such as Somalia and Liberia outside of Monrovia, where political power is pursued almost exclusively through control over markets and accumulation and state institutions play little, if any, role in regulating political competition. Violence, however, is needed to control the distribution of wealth and the building of political alliances. Leaders of these political units seek external patronage opportunistically, usually through commercial opportunities they carefully control.[18] As a visitor to Liberia observed, "All these [mining] businesses were operated by rebels. For them to talk of opening the roads or uniting with the Monrovia-based government only remained an illusion because their business was at stake if that happened."[19] The analysis of the Liberian case in Chapter 3 includes a detailed account of this politics, which threatens weak-state rulers in the other three cases.

The political strategies of these warlords and the innovations of weak-state rulers facing internal threats bear more than a passing resemblance to one another. In the cases of Sierra Leone, Congo, and Nigeria, rulers address the internal threat of warlord politics by transforming their own political authority into an effective means of controlling markets without reliance on formal state institutions. As a corollary to market control without institutions, weak-state rulers use new and strengthened alliances with outsiders to shed old clients and discipline those who remain, which results in a strategy that deals with the threat of warlord politics by mimicking the political innovations of warlords. This noninstitutional strategy, which stresses closer collaboration with foreign firms, fits nicely into the neoliberal economic ideas of outsiders who see these strategies promoting their ideal notions of a state as a minimalist organization, relieved of overstaffed, corrupt bureaucracies.[20] The continued claim of weak-state rulers to a globally recognized sovereign status, however, gives those rulers additional outside resources to discipline unruly strongmen. Rulers manipulate definitions of sovereignty and statehood to protect their personal authority, unhitching it from the dangerous and cumbersome exercise of building effective bureaucracies that could challenge the rulers' private interest. Fortunately for these rulers, outsiders' recognition of their claim to supreme authority over a given jurisdiction is absolute and recognizes no intermediate or contrary category.[21]

As it happens, the empirical reality of political control in weak states diverges increasingly from this absolutist definition. No distinct domestic politics as commonly understood is seen in the weak states in this study, since the new political alliances with nonstate global actors take on functions usually reserved for formal state institutions, such as warfare and coercion of populations. Tacit acceptance or outright collaboration by outsiders with new weak-state political alliances gives weak-state rulers and outsider partnerships the capacity to use global recognition of sovereignty to serve their own private interests. This coincidence of interest creates constituencies in strong states outside of Africa that continue to recognize the sovereignty of extremely weak states and tolerate their rulers' transitions to warlord politics.

WHY WEAK STATES ARE IMPORTANT

Recent literature on political change in weak states that stresses state-society relations has been helpful for framing complex processes in the case studies in this book. But much of this literature contains serious flaws by failing to consider how rulers manage change outside formal institutional channels. Much recent commentary on African states also focuses on their performance, taking states as given and rarely paying attention to the organization of political authority. This study challenges teleological unilinear assumptions that rulers face clear choices between reform of state institutions and "state failure," that collapse into factionalized competition among strongmen as political power at the center dissolves is the cost of failure to adapt to a particular model of state-society relations. Much recent literature contains prescriptions for rebuilding institutions and shortchanges analysis of clandestine compromises rulers make with opponents or the informal role powerful new allies play in convincing a ruler that compromise is avoidable. I emphasize the impact of politics on fragmenting patronage networks, bringing into focus the ways strongmen utilize new techniques and resources to resist rulers' efforts to reassert central control.

This study also challenges analyses of weak-state security that emphasize rising internal security threats at the expense of examining regime innovations for managing those threats. Kalevi Holsti, for example, explains that the end of the Cold War left weak-state rulers not only bereft of internal legitimacy but also unable to eliminate or manage military challenges from armed strongmen. He accurately describes the fate of state rulers who failed to adapt to this threat in places such as Liberia, Somalia, and Afghanistan.[22] But in showing how rulers in Sierra Leone, Congo, and Nigeria managed these threats, my conclusions are at odds with those who see strongmen as an overwhelming threat to political order itself.[23]

My approach also relies on some conceptions developed in world systems theory, but tendencies in that approach fail to look at the dynamics of dissolving state institutions as a result of processes in core countries. As Chapter 2 and the case studies make clear, rulers who appear to be victims of weakening formal state institutions exercise surprising autonomy to shape political relations with outsiders and manage unruly clients. Rulers and their rivals use alliances with outsiders to shape important aspects of core-periphery relations, which suggests that Africa's apparent marginalization does not automatically determine how politics in weak states will be structured. My analysis helps to uncover a new, informal regional integration of economies and political networks as others who are dealing with new pressures following the end of the Cold War team up with warlords.

This book breaks new ground in analyzing the character of relations between reconfigured weak states and the global political economy. Since political change in Africa's weak states does not conform to a dichotomous choice between stronger state institutions and dissolution, it becomes apparent that global society accommodates new political authorities that stray considerably from conventional notions of what states should be. Global recognition of sovereignty is pivotal to explaining the politics of weak states in permitting agencies such as the World Bank, supposedly designed to enforce a standard of behavior in global economic matters, to deal with these new political authorities. The resulting political authorities, heavily reliant on nonstate global actors and nearly bereft of formal state institutions, also fail to fit into realist notions that predict that rulers will maximize their political authority through self-sufficiency and building an autonomous bureaucratic capacity to act. Too often, literature on political change in Africa takes conventional notions of state organization for granted and applies them indiscriminately to weak-state cases. For example, populations not served by state institutions may be seen to be exercising an "exit" option to escape predation. This may be so when producers of wealth can withhold that wealth from rulers, but marginalization may be a consequence of an intentional strategy by rulers to abandon people who could contribute little to a political alliance and would make demands on scarce political resources.

My model of changing politics in weak states focuses on the experiences of Liberia, Sierra Leone, Congo, and Nigeria. These cases provide a basis for illustrating the relationship between internal and global change in the politics of already weak states, the role of political choice, and a similarity of outcomes. My purpose is not to provide definitive political histories of each case; rather, the four countries are used to highlight the character of change in weak states.

Why these four countries? I sought a range of cases along a spectrum of the collapse of patron-client politics, each with variations in external pressures to change. All four countries show remarkably weak formal state institutions. We find in Chapter 5 that state spending for health and education in Congo is officially close to zero, for example. All four cases contain examples of strongmen who are capable and desirous of exercising power in their own right and who threaten rulers. Together, all four weak states show different ruler strategies for dealing with formal state recession, external pressure, and internal security threats to regimes. Two states—Liberia and Sierra Leone—are very small and have long been recognized for their extremely weak bureaucratic capacity. The other two—Congo and Nigeria—are among Africa's most populous and politically influential states.

The selection of the four cases was also influenced by the variable importance of colonialism in structuring patron-client relationships. Sierra Leone and Nigeria were greatly affected by British colonial administrative policies, which influenced the later fragmentation of state control and the rise of strongmen. Congo's Belgian colonial rulers initially built their authority in partnership with a private corporation. Elements of past strategies of political control resurface in that case. Liberia, which gained independence in 1847, became sub-Saharan Africa's first globally recognized self-ruling state but was heavily influenced thereafter by U.S. economic and political interests.

Each case also shows substantial variation in Cold War reliance on patronage from foreign states. U.S. aid and diplomatic support were pivotal in sustaining the regimes of Presidents Mobutu of Congo (1965–1997) and Doe of Liberia (1980–1990). The rapid cutoff of aid in each case created sudden pressures for rulers to create new political strategies. Nigerian rulers relied less on support from Cold War patrons, whereas Sierra Leone's rulers desperately sought assistance from all quarters but received only limited support. Thus, each case shows variation in the extent and speed of change in the character of external support and pressures for innovation.

ORGANIZATION OF THE STUDY

The book begins with an explanation of internal features of Cold War–era patron-client politics and shows how those features translated into vulnerabilities for rulers amid external pressures to change and the collapse of domestic economies at the end of the Cold War. Significant elements of past strategies were reworked into elements of new strategies. These features of collapsing patronage politics played key roles in the conversion of patronage politics into warlord politics.

The second chapter examines changes in the global political economy that not only created pressure for change, such as demands by creditors, but also brought new resources to help weak-state rulers develop new strategies to manage change. Specifically, this chapter charts the appearance and organization of Executive Outcomes and other private military service firms that arose as a consequence of recent changes in South African politics. This firm and other private companies, which would be vulnerable in more competitive areas of the global economy, have teamed up with hard-pressed weak-state rulers to conquer and exploit resources in those states. In turn, these new partnerships are driving strongmen and citizens away from valuable resources and are replacing old patronage networks with a new, more politically reliable commercial partnership that (for rulers) replaces the old Cold War state.

Chapter 3 traces the collapse of Liberia's patronage politics. Focusing on the development of warlord Charles Taylor's Greater Liberia, this chapter illustrates key features of the organization of warlord politics. Whereas Liberia is an example of state "failure," this case also allows me to compare the strategy of President Samuel Doe in Liberia with that of Sierra Leone's president Valentine Strasser (1992–1996) in Chapter 4 as Strasser reacted to the spread of warlord competition within his country. On the brink of dissolution in 1995, Strasser saved his regime through the intervention of Executive Outcomes mercenaries and their mining firm partners. These soldiers, skilled in anti-insurgency warfare, removed disgruntled clients from the country's resources, thereby enabling the president to establish a new partnership among his new commercial allies, aid agencies, foreign governments, and creditors. This case demonstrates the pivotal role of globally recognized sovereignty, which largely accounts for the Sierra Leone president's superior ability to secure outside patronage in contrast to Liberia's Charles Taylor, who had yet to achieve sovereign status. It also illustrates the dangers of extreme dependence on self-interested outsiders to manage internal politics.

Chapter 5 is about the politics of Congo. This case illustrates how President Mobutu managed the sudden and thorough cutoff of external resources. At the same time, his regional rivals found favorable access to new resources after 1990, especially when political change in South Africa brought new commercial operators into the area. In many ways the dissolution of patronage networks resembles the collapse of Liberia's central regime, yet Congo did not break up. This chapter highlights the factors that mitigated against a breakup. Congo shows the importance of variables such as the geographic distribution of resources and the nature of involved external actors in influencing strategies for managing change, as well as the unexpected importance of formal sovereignty in influencing internal actors' strategies, even when this status has virtually no empirical basis. Mobutu's style of rule also marks the regime of his successor, Laurent Kabila.

Chapter 6 is devoted to Nigeria. The Abacha regime (1993–) began with a revision of customary patronage strategies. Events in Abacha's first year of power demonstrated the futility of old strategies and the prospects for a new, more narrowly based political network. His associates became more heavily reliant on independent contacts to gather resources. At first, this policy seemed to free Abacha from having to support a huge patronage network, but it also raised the danger that strongmen—including military officers—would translate economic entrepreneurialism into informal political autonomy. Abacha now directly attacks these strongmen, but he must do so in ways that appear to promote private enterprise to appease creditors and foreign investors. This case adds to the examples of ways in which rulers use market reforms to further externalize their political relations and destroy troublesome state institutions.

The final chapter explains why warlord politics has developed in weak states. I seek to explain the evolution of political authority in Africa's weak states in tandem with changes in the global political economy. Why, even after pressures to conform to a model of development increased during the 1990s, have many weak states continued to evolve in a divergent fashion? This chapter returns to variables highlighted in the case studies to provide a guide for determining likely outcomes in other weak-state transformations. Which factors promote dissolution into factional struggle, as occurred in Liberia, and which generally help weak-state rulers to reassert their political authority through warlord means?

Overall, I find African economies and weak states are still engaged in the global economy and politics, only now in increasingly unexpected, direct, and violent ways. Rather than being cut off from changes in the global economy, Africa's weak states have emerged as a new form of authority suited to operating on the margins of that economy. Formal imperial rule was the primary outcome of the last great age of African insolvency. Likewise, at the end of the twentieth century, something new is coming out of Africa. The weak states in this study shed light on a new organization of global capital that exploits commercial opportunities previously out of reach, and it does so from a stance in which the exercise of political authority is almost indistinguishable from private commercial operations.

NOTES

1. Burton Stevenson, *The Home Book of Quotations,* 10th ed. (New York: Dodd, Mead, 1967), 1415.

2. World Bank, *Sub-Saharan Africa: From Crisis to Sustainable Growth* (Washington, D.C.: World Bank, 1989), 5.

3. Jean-François Bayart, *L'État en Afrique* (Paris: Fayard, 1989).

4. Robert Jackson, *Quasi-States: Sovereignty, International Relations, and the Third World* (New York: Cambridge University Press, 1990).

5. World Bank, *World Development Report, 1996* (New York: Oxford University Press, 1996), 189.

6. Virginia Luling, "Come Back Somalia? Questioning a Collapsed State," *Third World Quarterly* 18:2 (June 1997), 287–302; Anna Simons, *Somalia: Networks of Dissolution* (Boulder: Westview, 1995).

7. World Bank, *Adjustment in Africa* (New York: Oxford University Press, 1994), xvii.

8. World Bank, *Sub-Saharan Africa,* 5.

9. Henry Bienen and Jeffrey Herbst, "The Relationship Between Political and Economic Reform in Africa," *Comparative Politics* 29:1 (Oct. 1996), 23–42.

10. Max Weber, *The Theory of Social and Economic Organization* (New York: Free Press, 1964), 324–373.

11. James Crawford, "The Criteria for Statehood in International Law," *The British Yearbook of International Law 1976–1977,* vol. 48 (Oxford: Oxford University Press, 1978), 111–119.

12. John Sigo, *Political Jesus* (Enugu, Anambra State, Nigeria: Snaap Press, 1995).

13. Quansheng Zhao, *Japanese Policymaking: The Politics Behind Politics* (New York: Oxford University Press, 1996).

14. "Resource Flows," *Africa Recovery* 10:2 (Oct. 1996), 14–15.

15. "Decisive Decision on Tenke-Fungurume," *Africa Energy and Mining,* 4 Dec. 1996.

16. "Is the UK Pulling Out of Africa?" *Africa Economic Digest,* 28 Aug. 1995, 10–11.

17. Robert Corzine, "Aid to Pave Way for Pipeline," *Financial Times,* 4 Oct. 1996, 3.

18. Clapham defines this as warlord politics. Christopher Clapham, *Africa and the International System* (New York: Cambridge University Press, 1996), 212; Roger Charlton and Roy May, "Warlords and Militarism in Chad," *Review of African Political Economy* 45–46 (Winter 1989), 12–25.

19. Bayo Ogunleye, *Behind Rebel Line: Anatomy of Charles Taylor's Hostage Camps* (Enugu: Delta, 1995), 138.

20. Mamadou Dia, *Africa's Management in the 1990s and Beyond* (Washington, D.C.: World Bank, 1996).

21. Alan James, *Sovereign Statehood: the Basis of International Society* (London: Allen and Unwin, 1986), 48.

22. Kalevi Holsti, *The State, War, and the State of War* (New York: Cambridge University Press, 1996).

23. Robert Kaplan, *The Ends of the Earth* (New York: Random House, 1996); Mohammed Ayoob, *The Third World Security Predicament* (Boulder: Lynne Rienner, 1995).

1

▼ ▼ ▼ ▼

THE DISTINCTIVE POLITICAL LOGIC OF WEAK STATES

The Kalashnikov lifestyle is our business advantage.

—NPFL fighter[1]

The new strategy presupposes a better understanding of the role of capitalism in development. . . . It must increasingly be seen as a developmental force whose historical task is far from completed on the continent.

—Gordon Hyden[2]

WARLORDS AND INTERNATIONAL RELATIONS

A central premise of this study of the transformation of weak states to warlord politics lies in recognizing how rulers control markets to enhance their own power. The way this is accomplished is at odds with most views about the relation between weak states and markets, insofar as rulers do not base their control on bureaucratic institutions or accepted concepts of legitimacy. Which weak-state rulers follow a warlord course of action? Certainly, the prior degree of privatization of ruler alliances with external and domestic partners in efforts to control internal rivals weighs heavily on subsequent calculations. Further privatization of political power is thus likely in states that are already institutionally weak and in which rule is highly personalized, such as the Central African Republic, Chad, Guinea, Guinea-Bissau, and Congo-Brazzaville.

Paradoxically, external pressures that seem to require that rulers strengthen state institutions in order to survive press in the opposite direction if considered in the context of existing state weakness. This factor recognizes that interstate and domestic actors influence one another. True, the end of the Cold War allowed some external patrons, creditors, and foreign firms to demand that rulers implement policies designed to strengthen state institutions, following from the recognition that rulers in powerful countries are dependent on investors and employers for revenue. State institutions are thus seen as properly supporting economic growth and efficiency, on which revenues are dependent.

From the position of the World Bank, a major source of loans to economically bankrupt regimes and facilitator of loans and grants from other sources, market-supporting state institutions underlie the economic success of once corrupt and inept East Asian states.[3] From a critical perspective, Anthony Giddens noted that rulers pursue accommodations with autonomous business classes, since that is the most effective way to generate revenues. This arrangement has the virtue of disciplining domestic populations by punishing those who reject market competition with poverty and unemployment.[4] Furthermore, the success of other states at protecting such alliances forces all state rulers to contend with one another to accommodate capital, since they all compete for investments.[5]

Students of the neorealist school of international relations make a similar point, noting that the global system of states is organized according to principles of constant competition. That is, rulers rationally maximize their power through self-sufficiency, thereby minimizing their reliance on others.[6] To do this, rulers try to build an independent state capacity to act. Competition in global society, wrote Kenneth Waltz, is comparable to the pursuit of advantage in markets. The most efficient organization—the organization best able to generate revenue to carry out regime interests and cultivate popular legitimacy, to effectively manage external influences—makes the rules for all the rest.[7] States that fail to conform to this standard, especially as foreign aid declines or comes with new demands, can be expected to collapse. These arrangements suggest that just as a manager who acts at variance with the norms of efficiency and competition risks being eliminated from the economic scene, the inability to perform sovereign duties risks the collapse of political authority into anarchy and the constant strife of warlordism.

Yet this book takes as analytically significant not only this collapse but also the rise of warlord alternatives such as Liberia's Charles Taylor, Angola's Jonas Savimbi, and Somalia's Mohamed Aideed, as well as rulers in weak states who so thoroughly privatize their pursuit of power as to mimic their counterparts who do not enjoy recognition as heads of sovereign states. "International relations" in this context goes beyond relations between states that are assumed to conform to a given (and ahistorical) set of internal structures and behavior.

The argument presented here is also at odds with neo-marxist variants of structural explanations of how states emerge, which regard the nature of political units as reflecting the pressures and possibilities within a global capitalist system. The autonomy of action and capacity to innovate that we find in the four cases in this book would be denied or dismissed as irrational behavior. For Immanuel Wallerstein, for example, the operation of the world economy and a political unit's place in that economy determine the nature of the political unit. "The states," he wrote, "created institutions reflecting the needs of class forces operating in the world economy."[8] As with other explanations that stress the disciplining nature of external structures, this view overlooks divergent, seemingly dysfunctional features in the politics of individual African weak states. Consequently, this literature does not accurately identify the external pressures that explain change in weak states or how and why some rulers of weak states in Africa consciously chose alternatives to expected responses to global pressures. An accurate account of Africa's political evolution in the post–Cold War world needs to explain how these alternatives arose and displaced the pursuit of conventional sovereignty over fixed territories.

Much of the literature on political change in Africa also accepts the proposition that the evolution of political authority is a universal process from which many postcolonial African rulers stray at considerable peril. Many who write about governance in Africa blame "bad policies" for the failure of African governments to rule effectively since independence.[9] This philosophy reverses effect and cause, since these writers explain the withering of state institutions as a consequence of popular withdrawal from ineffective and predatory rulers. Some also posit a progression of stages from which many African regimes deviate, a condition from which "cure and remission are possible."[10] That is, the combined need to base the exercise of political authority on a domestic revenue base, commerce with foreigners, and popular acceptance permits only one set of rational responses, which includes strengthening and streamlining a set of state institutions that perform core functions.[11]

Given the continuing divergence of outcomes from a model of long-term rationality, it is not surprising that much of the literature that focuses on weakening formal state institutions in Africa is prescriptive. For example, World Bank proposals recommend "capacity building," or enhancing the efficiency of state institutions and accommodating them to the interests and opportunities of global capital.[12] Like Giddens, these proposals regard the structure of global economic competition as forcing African rulers to consider universal strategies of "shrewd states" capable of using revenues efficiently to manage global economic pressures and seize opportunities.[13]

What about states in which bureaucracies have already collapsed and faction leaders are fighting one another for political power? When state collapse occurs, it is taken as evidence of a failure to learn or an incapacity to act. One analyst has blamed collapse on the accumulated environmental and social consequences of misrule. Overpopulation, collapsing political authority, and sudden urbanization, wrote Robert Kaplan, enforce "natural" limits on African governments that are overwhelmed by or that neglect this wider set of rules when it comes to ruling states. Kaplan even includes Côte d'Ivoire, one of Africa's most bureaucratized states, as a state that could potentially fail, noting "there was no economy here. . . . Innumerable settlements such as these throughout West Africa were emptying out so that slums . . . could expand."[14] This approach also returns to a need (or inevitability) to impose an international standard of behavior on African political leaders.[15]

WEAK-STATE CAPACITY TO MANIPULATE EXTERNAL ACTORS

But Robert Jackson showed that during the Cold War rational rulers of weak states in Africa did not always pursue conventional institutional methods of building political authority to compensate for weak-state capabilities. He adduced that patrimonial postcolonial African states show the limits of a strict application of assumptions that global structures enforce a ruler's exercise of globally recognized sovereignty. Such expectations of a universal standard of behavior fail to capture the logic of weak-state organization. Instead, Jackson identified a contrary "quasi-state" logic in which rulers possess sovereignty by virtue of a globally recognized people's right to a particular territory. Regimes bolstered their internal power with entitlements to aid from former colonial powers and interested superpowers engaged in Cold War competition in efforts to attract diplomatic and strategic supporters. They did not gain political authority primarily from internal legitimacy, bureaucratic efficiency, nurturing of local revenue sources, or attractiveness to foreign investors. Instead, the possession of globally recognized sovereignty, with its access to international organizations and creditworthiness, allowed rulers to claim resources from powerful outside patrons.[16]

The subordinate position of Africa's weak states in the Cold War global political economy did not restrict African rulers to a single code of behavior. Jackson pointed out that Africa's weak states essentially constituted a different species of state organization. Unlike classic state-building rulers elsewhere, quasi-state rulers did not hold power by virtue of effective internal control and capacity to mobilize citizens but recognized that decisions made in strong states empowered those who inherited African colonies as rulers of states, whereas rival claimants such as secessionist insurgents were denied that status. Thus, external decisions and constraints played a huge role in shaping the numbers and configurations of African states. Colonial administrations that employed local intermediaries created classes of strongmen who came to exercise proprietary control over sections of the state bureaucracy and who commonly used their new official powers to exercise local political authority in their own right.[17] Eager to limit this fragmentation of internal social control and rein in the strongmen, rulers of weak states discovered that outsiders' recognition of their sovereign status could be used to attract aid from outsiders that filled in for absent domestic political resources.

Jackson's observation of the simultaneous existence of strong states and quasi-states reinforces John Ruggie's notion that sovereignty is contextual.[18] Hence, the structure of Africa's states is not simply derivative of Africans' relations with non-African states. Further, as Jackson's illustration of the import of external support shows, the structure of African political units is not simply the aggregate of formal state organization. While external structure offers opportunities and imposes constraints, agents—rulers, strongmen, external actors—interact with one another to pursue their own interests. By imposing their own domestic priorities on those interactions, rulers of weak states redefined patronage from strong states during the Cold War to meet internal threats.

Mohammed Ayoob's focus on the internal security threat to African rulers posed by local strongmen reinforces the importance of rulers' manipulating the material benefits of sovereignty to build political authority. State officials in Africa, he argues, have had difficulties insinuating a distinct definition of state interest into popular identities. The rival power centers strongmen build continue to play a large role in people's lives and to provide them with identities such as clan and ethnicity that clash with the state's effort to shape popular definitions of identity.[19] The threats this struggle poses to rulers are considerable. An actuarial calculation showed that as of 1991 the 485 postcolonial African rulers faced a 59.4 percent chance of dying, being imprisoned, or being exiled as a consequence of holding office.[20] Rulers of weak states risk having strongmen appropriate bureaucracies that are effective at accumulating resources and using them to build their own power bases from which to challenge the regime.

Rulers who face threatening internal behavior intentionally cripple the arms of the state, which weakens the agencies that outsiders prescribe as the best means to mobilize resources to alleviate pressure from the international economy, such as debts, balance-of-payments imbalances, and instruments to enhance state revenues.[21] Rulers confront this contradictory situation with strategies that diverge even farther from ideal notions of state sovereignty, since the threat posed by unruly strongmen precludes what they, along with their critics, recognize as a long-term rewarding course of action. During the Cold War, for example, external resources went into patronage networks aimed at reining in unruly strongmen at the expense of development. This scenario describes how rulers make rational choices for reasons other than state-building efficiency and how in weak states institutions and political relations are adapted for unorthodox functions.

This quasi-state alternative, characterized by an internal milieu threatening to weak-state rulers, offers a conceptual way out of unilinear perspectives that see political behavior that is hostile to formal state institutions as inherently dysfunctional. Attention to internal security threats to rulers shows how rulers of weak states have used resources and relations for means other than those Cold War patrons initially intended.

In Chad, for example, vulnerable rulers have used foreign military aid and elaborate diplomatic exercises to garner resources to fight internal opponents. French assistance during the 1980s provided as much as 70 percent of Chadian government expenditures, but dependence was not absolute. Chad's politicians used rivalries among French, Libyan, Nigerian, and U.S. interests to manipulate patrons. Here, divisions between external and internal politics dissolve as the resources and actions of foreigners are used to fill in for missing bureaucracies while rulers struggle to shift political resources to the disadvantage of rivals.[22] Thus, internal weakness need not render African political actors incapable of exercising choice in relations with outsiders. Indeed, limited autonomy to manipulate outsiders while facing an internal crisis exerts strong pressure on rulers to find new sources of external aid without the benefit of strong state institutions.

This Cold War logic in which external support for sovereign rulers was fairly dependable helped to sustain a dual standard of state behavior. External pressure to conform to one standard of diplomatic behavior—choosing sides in Cold War conflicts—helped to widen the gulf in internal capabilities between states approaching a sovereign ideal and Africa's weak states. During the Cold War, global society tolerated behavior that patently did not conform to conventional notions of sovereignty, accepting deviations from conventional rules such as maintaining enough administrative capacity to control all territory within a state's borders or to force (or convince) substantial portions of a population to accept their citizenship in a particular state. The weak state's limited legitimacy among citizens (including strongmen) left few people to carry out rulers' directives. Mirroring future warlord politics, some rulers hired mercenaries, pitted factions against one another, and sought foreign advisers to control populations. In contrast, strong-state rulers can rely on a coherent national security force to coerce compliance if legitimacy is lacking.

Rulers of weak states continued to compensate for their failures by mobilizing resources in the external environment. All sorts of opportunities appeared under the shield of external guarantees to weak-state regimes. Israelis offered military and financial aid to rulers who promised diplomatic recognition in return. Private Lebanese and Greek commercial networks traded political protection from individual state rulers for a share of profits from regional trade.[23] In these cases, weak-state rulers used aspects of formal sovereignty, such as the right to define a legal order, for purposes other than those intended by conventional standards of sovereignty. The trappings of sovereignty—such as the capacity to manipulate enforcement of laws, to generate globally accepted documents, and to hide clandestine activity behind diplomatic immunity—also gave many of those rulers the capacity to meld commercial opportunities with political alliances.[24]

Violence and militarization of commerce were central to adapting the functions and forms of state sovereignty to the pressing task of building political authority in heavily divided postcolonial African societies.[25] These methods were not new in Africa; they looked back to colonial strategies that had manipulated markets to supply scarce revenues to finance the alien bureaucracies, which local people regarded as an imposition. Later, the coercive power of colonial armies, occasional emergency subventions from overseas, and Colonial Office oversight strengthened the autonomy of bureaucracies. But even then, colonial rulers cut deals with local strongmen, tolerating their use of delegated state authority for private gain in return for their loyalty and help in reining in administrative costs. Foreign companies were also good partners for colonial regimes, not only for the revenues they generated but also for taking over local administrative tasks in return for privileged access to resources or markets.

Contemporary rulers who lack capable administrations find markets to be useful for controlling and disciplining rivals and their supporters. Intervening in markets enables rulers to accumulate wealth directly, which is then converted into political resources they can distribute at their discretion. This strategy directly contradicts liberal principles of private markets, since it is designed to block entrepreneurial activity among threatening rivals. But it is not state action, since the intervention can occur through the agency of individual commercial partners rather than formal state institutions.

This commercialization of political control is compatible with formal prerequisites for reform. Rulers of weak states learn that as with sovereignty, economic reform programs outsiders insist on in return for aid can be manipulated to gain access to resources and thus enhance a vulnerable ruler's political authority. Rulers can then intrude into "private" markets through the agency of preferred cronies or compliant foreign firms and limit their rivals' access to wealth. Most important, rulers can still forego the creation of expensive and potentially threatening formal state institutions, which most reformers reject as hopelessly corrupt or, at best, inefficient. Rulers continue to provide for essential allies, whereas large numbers of state officials—such as teachers, health care workers, statisticians, and accountants—who consume scarce resources and do little to strengthen rulers' capacity to control rivals (while documenting their disregard for pronouncements) can be safely jettisoned. Reforms that emphasize cutting state expenditures help rulers to justify to external audiences their internal efforts to weaken and even attack threatening strongmen.

Weak-state rulers use such strategies to weather what outsiders and citizens who expect development recognize as the withering of formal state structures. The bureaucratic apparatus of the state can be allowed to decay even as a ruler's patronage network extends into spheres of activity farther removed from the purview of conventional states. Whether these activities take place in separate spheres of state or as societal activity is especially relevant. Notions such as those of state or society and public or private become blurred as regimes presiding over patronage systems focus increasingly on controlling all kinds of accumulation and translating resources into political power. This strategy permits elites in Africa's most heavily patrimonialized economies to avoid relying on citizens' support to rule, since it denies citizens autonomous control over resources the regime needs to manage strongmen.

Jean-François Bayart has termed this invasion of informal political networks into ever wider spheres of economic activity a "criminalization of the state." An alliance of state officials and nominally private commercial networks has manipulated state prerogatives in global society to combine the alliance's capacity to create disorder for rivals with its private business acumen to expand its commercial reach. This partnership cemented an elite accommodation that helped to mitigate rulers' internal security threats without needing to build politically unreliable bureaucracies. Compliant strongmen profited from this alliance.[26] But this strategy did not totally erase dangers that enterprising strongmen would take over elements of the alliance when the end of the Cold War reduced rulers' centrality as the distributors of resources.

In fact, Cold War superpower support was central to underwriting this nonbureaucratic strategy. As long as foreign backers supported a version of the rules of the game that rejected irredentist or separatist claims and armed and financed incumbent regimes, the costs to strongmen of not accepting a ruler's patronage were much higher than the weak internal capabilities of the state alone would suggest. External aid helped weak-state rulers to reward loyalty and cooperation. This external guarantee—the global recognition of sovereignty—gave those rulers the autonomy to experiment with strategies that diverged from the sovereign state ideal. So whereas Africa may have become less significant to the global economy and foreign backers in the 1970s and 1980s, weak-state regimes became progressively more enmeshed in informal networks. This is the reason the loss of external support for weak-state rulers at the end of the Cold War suddenly rendered old strategies that combined maintaining minimal bureaucratic capacity with extensive informal networks of clients not just unsustainable but also dangerous to those rulers' regimes.

Does the sudden loss of external support for weak-state regimes force rulers to confront that crisis by conforming to a single standard of behavior former patrons are now free to define? The end of the Cold War cut off easy access to aid and loans, the lifeblood of the old patron-client politics. As the old strategies that had been used to manage strongmen now gave those strongmen the tools to challenge weak-state rulers, would those rulers be forced to cultivate a broader base of legitimacy, to seek support from citizens to whom they would provide services, security, and growing economic opportunity?

Instead, World Bank agents and officials of non-African states took advantage of the new vulnerability of the rulers of weak states to impose conditions for loans and aid. The agents proposed that "good governance" and neoclassical economic policies would limit the exercise of power to the formal state institutions. With the end of the Cold War, they expected rulers to promote economic efficiency because the external support that had helped to underwrite the gutting of bureaucracies, rent-seeking behavior, and the intrusion of state officials into private and clandestine economies no longer existed. Consistent with Waltz's predictions, rulers were assumed to have no choice but to try to nurture economies that would be able to compete in global markets and to boost state revenues by catering to the interests of a competitive indigenous business community.[27] This scenario envisioned a whole new social alliance. Rulers would jettison costly but unproductive clients. Reminiscent of early modern Europe's development of capitalism, the rulers were expected to join the power of the state with the interests of a rising middle class.

Yet in the cases in this book, weak-state rulers have managed elite power struggles with even more informal invasions into commercial activities at the expense of formal state institutions, and they have done so as strongmen have posed a growing threat to their regimes and against the warnings of external actors. They have proved capable of successfully managing disapproving creditors such as the World Bank while facing all of the other demands and pressures of a competitive global economy from which they need resources to fend off increasingly unruly strongmen. The question of how rulers devise innovative strategies that are contrary to expectations about how political authority is built is central to whether the political forms described in this study are sustainable alternatives to conventional state sovereignty, a matter to which I turn next.

COMMERCIAL ADVANTAGES OF WEAK STATES

It would seem that rulers must promote and protect markets with state institutions if they wish to attract investment. In Iran, for example, Prime Minister Mir Hussein Mussavi doubted Islam's capacity to generate an original form of economic organization.[28] India's rulers swept aside "Nehru socialism" as they tried to mimic the methods of rapidly developing market economies. South Africa's Nelson Mandela abandoned the egalitarian promises of the organization that brought him to power and instead talked to Western financiers and Johannesburg businessmen.

So, too, for quasi-states the structure of the global economy appears to exert competitive pressure on participants, limiting the range of effective action for state rulers.[29] A related reason one might expect quasi-state exclusion from the post–Cold War political economy has to do with the patronage system's tendency to impose political criteria on commercial transactions. Since rulers who enjoyed external backing did not have to confine their authority to demarcations between public and private interests or limit their use of coercion, both domestic and foreign holders of capital were reluctant to risk investing in such an uncertain environment, with its unpredictable informal costs of doing business and the risk of confiscation by unruly politicians.

These fears appear to privilege noninterventionist, market-facilitating states. Although this may weaken states vis-à-vis their capital, some argue that it will enforce a uniform standard of behavior that includes a capacity to make and abide by agreements that protect the autonomy of that capital.[30] In Africa, this apparent interest in capital and the abandonment of quasi-states by Cold War patrons strengthen international organizations such as the World Bank and the International Monetary Fund, which certify and enforce conformity with prescribed state policies. Such a development would seem entirely inimical to maintaining informal networks that rely on manipulating all resources, public and private, to counter centrifugal internal politics. Such a standard of "governance" leaves no room for informal patronage networks, much less mercenaries and privateers.[31]

Nonetheless, some investors do make deals with Liberian warlords; others regard mercenaries as critical to their operations in Sierra Leone, Angola, and Congo. Nigeria's military rulers attract respectable foreign partners while ignoring outside calls for reform. This is not to ignore the fact that Africa's weak states are subject to external realities, such as the French devaluation of the CFA and declining global demand for Africa's raw materials, but translating these pressures into local political action is not so easy. Some prescribe "capturing" peasants and other producers and forcing them into taxable formal markets; others see crises as favoring the technocratic elements of bureaucracies, which will be prized for suddenly valuable skills.[32]

Although most analysts recognize that peasants and individual state officials may already collaborate with (or confront) one another in informal markets, the flexibility of that behavior is often overlooked, especially when it is seen as a consequence of bureaucratic incapacity or weak attachment to the "modern" notion of national identity. In fact, this behavior, which is so characteristic of weak states and declining formal economies, is observed to be engaged in by individuals who pursue mobility, exhibit individual initiative, and value self-aggrandizement.[33] Further, informal markets built on these social ties tend to put a premium on displaying and dispersing wealth, which undermines investment and exerts debilitating inflationary pressures.[34] But external challenges may transform domestic informal networks, thereby privileging "positive" social values that promote accumulation. In meeting external challenges, is it more important to satisfy personal interests or conform to a specific organizational model?

Max Weber's observations about the nature of capitalism help to broaden our focus beyond the organization of some state structures to the role accumulation plays in strategies of weak-state rulers. Weber noted that a Protestant ethic is one of many (and at one time seemingly irrational) routes to prosperity. "The ideal type of the capitalist entrepreneur," Weber wrote, "gets nothing out of his wealth for himself, except the irrational sense of having done his job well."[35] Weber's point is that a Protestant ethic incorporates capitalism, not the other way around. His analysis shows that capitalism can be manipulated to accord with the priorities and values of the entrepreneur, be they those of Protestant asceticism or of the acquisitive lifestyle of the francophone African *sapeux* (from SAPE [Societé des Ambienceurs et des Personnes Eligantes]), who value fine clothing, comportment, and refined appearance. So although old patronage political arrangements may become unsustainable, elements may be reincorporated into a new arrangement better suited to competition in global markets.

This point is relevant to African weak states insofar as it helps to explain the continent's failure to conform to teleological assumptions that African rulers and clients (both loyal and unruly) will reject their private interests and hand over control of resources to rivals. Just as Weber regarded capitalist accumulation as compatible with and supportive of changing notions of Protestant asceticism, markets in weak states remain part of ongoing political struggles. In the context of Cold War weak states that lack effective bureaucracies, these struggles continue to follow the same market vectors as now unsustainable patronage politics. Enterprising strongmen focus on controlling accumulation, which may now mean collecting aid, seizing natural resources, and manipulating calls for reform. Political struggle continues through a contest to control and benefit from these market connections to the outside world, a realm weak-state rulers once controlled more effectively with help from their Cold War patrons. Overall, recognizing that the often violent contest to control commerce is a way politics functions in the post–Cold War quasi-state allows one to see that global markets serve a variety of internal po-litical functions that neorealist and structuralist analyses of Africa's weak states do not consider.[36]

Warlord Capitalism

Manipulating markets to achieve noneconomic and nonbureaucratic aims is not unique to Africa. Direct selling organizations in the United States, for example, provide platforms for highly charismatic leaders who use commercial networks to attract followers who exhibit transcen-dent devotion to the products they sell. These organizations actively dis-courage competitive behavior and promote strong organizational ide-ologies that address distributors' social needs in ways that at first seem contrary to success in a competitive economy as members pursue noneconomic goals.[37] Living room parties and self-improvement classes serve an important social role for members.[38] The "Beauticon family of products" becomes a distinctive lifestyle, much as the Liberian fighter's "Kalashnikov lifestyle" noted in the epigraph at the start of this chapter, as it mobilizes entrants into the market and develops its own techniques for dealing with suppliers, competitors, and consumers.

We also see elsewhere that local political relationships link global markets with elite authority. Japanese politicians and businesspeople have created a social alliance based on manipulating markets for the pri-vate good of an alliance of elites. *Yakusa* organizations bind business and government officials in congenitally politically corrupt networks to pro-tect elite privilege in ways that at times promote Japanese economic effi-ciency and competitiveness. Karel van Wolferen has argued that this cal-culus of interest is so intense that it undermines the independent definition of state interest separate from the interests of powerful cliques and networks, which is why Japanese politicians negotiate trade treaties in good faith but agreements go unimplemented.[39] The subtitle of his 1990 book, "People and Politics in a Stateless Nation," belies no-tions that states must perform in a particular way to be successful in a capitalist global economy.[40]

Van Wolferen's model shows a case of development in which elite cliques and networks undermine the autonomy of state action. In Japan, one encounters a far higher degree of interelite consensus and bureaucratic administration than is found in Africa. Nonetheless, the rules for Japan's success in the global economy stray from neoliberal notions of how to maximize economic and political power. Moreover, traditions of the "family state" are incorporated into a uniquely Japanese style of capitalism, thereby reinforcing Weber's notion that markets are compatible with a variety of "styles of life." Thus, Meiji reformers could label their reconfiguration of social alliances a "restoration," reinterpreting local traditions and culture to respond to but not mimic nineteenth-century European capitalism. So, too, in Africa responses to external pressures incorporate and may even intensify features drawn from past weak-state politics.[41] Although they are hardly candidates for economic superpower status, the cases in this book also show that features of weak-state politics can be rearranged as part of an economically sustainable post–Cold War political realignment.

Comparisons with non-African weak states also show how clandestine markets are used similarly to exclude and incorporate political players. The failure of state institutions allows nonstate organizations to take advantage of economic opportunity and create new political alliances. The disorder of collapsing elite accommodations opens new, unorthodox vectors for accumulation.[42] In Iran, networks of *bazzari* businesspeople have used capital expropriated from the Pahlavi regime and now held in religious foundations to take advantage of disorder in neighboring countries. Earlier, Iran was a conduit for trade of goods looted from Kuwait, and Iraqi Kurds still sell humanitarian food aid in Iran. Weapons trading in Baluchistan and Afghanistan offers new opportunities for profit and for establishing ties to new political actors, including Kurdish rebels and Iraqi officials. To the north, changes in the former Soviet republics have opened new frontiers of commerce and political relations with Baku mafias, which have recently been implanted among the Tabriz and Teheran ethnic kinsfolk.[43]

Trade in drugs in Nigeria, Colombia, Peru, and Burma figures heavily in rulers' strategy of holding onto power while compensating for their lack of bureaucratic autonomy and capacity, regardless of the clandestine nature of activities to achieve that goal.[44] Some see that even strong states such as the United States manipulate elite involvement in violent, illicit commerce to advance foreign policy goals when the use of bureaucracies would expose the covert nature of the operations.[45] For example, rebel groups involved in drugs and arms trade in Afghanistan made common cause with U.S. officials who were eager to harass Soviet forces but were unable to emerge with a decisive victory.[46]

Meanwhile, elites in Iran's northern neighbors have parlayed connections to inherited Communist Party organizations into positions that allow them to benefit from the marketization and increasing extroversion of their economies.[47]

This struggle is as much about shaping new elite alliances, about who will exercise power in the future, as it is about wealth. Communist parties were once an obstacle to capitalism; now they are an asset in the scramble to adapt to it. As in Africa, external pressure for freer access to global markets energizes "private" groups that are in fact part of the political establishment on which the economic crisis is blamed. Free from Moscow, local elites are fighting among themselves to determine the direction of the flow of goods. According to Stephen Handelman, this "mafiya economy" is the result of a criminalization of commerce—the grafting of weapons trades, money laundering, and drug trafficking onto all of the other economic assets and opportunities that membership in old political networks offers new "reformers."[48]

As do their counterparts in Moscow, Iranian officials rightly fear that these commercial activities may be part of a reordering of elite power that is not directly controlled by Teheran officials. Economic globalization and the end of the Cold War may undermine and topple rulers who fail to control internal politics. But existing structures of global society and the intractability of internal politics alone do not lead to state failure; other contributing factors include the level of prior destruction of bureaucracies, the concentration and accessibility of material resources, and the availability of external partners.

Thus, a turn away from conventional state structures, or warlordism, is a rational response to globalization in weak states. Rulers of these states must consider more than global economic or diplomatic changes in their struggle to survive; they must also respond to dramatic increases in internal security threats. The real question for these rulers is how to manage elites who discover a dramatically wider scope for personal gain through the manipulation of global political and economic changes. Incumbent rulers accordingly subordinate external pressure to conform to a particular standard in attempts to resolve this internal crisis.

REGIONAL IMPACT OF POLITICAL EXPERIMENTATION

The way this political experimentation works out in one region or country influences the way adaptation to new conditions occurs elsewhere. The breakup of the Soviet Union and the marketization of power struggles there affect the calculus of weak-state rulers in Africa as former

Soviet elites sell Red Army arsenals at bargain prices. Disorder along borders has changed the calculus of rulers in Teheran, who are anxiously watching Afghan and Caucasian dealings with an increasingly assertive business group that provided crucial social support for the 1979 revolution.

Regional shifts in the scramble for markets that can be converted to political resources are also occurring in Africa. In his quest for power, Liberian warlord Charles Taylor, for example, recognizes the advantages of grafting on Casamance separatists, Burkinabe and Gambian dissidents, Washington insiders seeking public relations contracts, and traders from all around the region. Liberia's President Doe (1980–1990) died as a consequence of his failure to find new ways to manage unruly associates, including Charles Taylor. Taylor managed to take over most of Doe's domestic sources of patronage. Prince Johnson, another Doe rival, kidnapped the weakened president and murdered him in 1990.

Nigeria's military ruler has used alliances with Liberian warlords to advance his regional goals. He has used Nigerian dominance in regional groups such as the Economic Community of West Africa (ECOWAS) to exercise informal control over the flow of resources outside Nigeria's borders. Nigeria's army has become a major actor in conflicts over resources in Liberia and Sierra Leone through this institution, for example.

Conventional distinctions such as those between state and society and public and private, which are so central to transformative expectations of African states, are difficult to discern in these cases. It is also difficult to label challenges to a particular regime as internal or external. Regime attempts to deny resources to rivals also tend to ignore formal frontiers. Angola's Uniõ Nacional para a Independencia Total do Angola (UNITA) rebels, for example, figured highly in former Congo President Mobutu's efforts to control diamond markets in Congo while grafting UNITA's Angolan mining operations to his own commercial network. Likewise, rebel insurgents from Liberia have posed a major security threat to Sierra Leone regimes throughout the 1990s as the insurgents have sought cross-border alliances and opportunities.

Olivier Roy has explained the regionalization of elite struggle to manage informal markets in Afghanistan in a way that could also describe weak states in Africa.

> As long as the conflict remained internationalized . . . the possession of power within a political party gave access to a new asset—arms, sometimes accompanied by the arrival of humanitarian and financial aid from abroad. Often a right-hand man jealous of his chief would open a front as one might open a shop. Then, to attract a "clientele," he had to give not just arms, but also humanitarian aid: the "French doctor," for example, became a political medium of exchange.[49]

Roy noted that warlordism is not simply an implosion or disintegration of a state but is also a technique for building new political authority. Heads of factions emerge when it is easy to become a military or commercial entrepreneur. From their regional bases, these entrepreneurs try to assemble and control resources and convert them to their own political advantage. Rulers of weak states confront these elites on this terrain.

The result is a reflexive "criminalization of the state," or, more precisely, of weak-state regimes, and a militarization of the economy that is the target of political struggle. This reconfiguration of political struggle is rooted in the Cold War–era tendency for rulers of weak states to tolerate and manage elite independence in patronage systems through such unconventional means as clandestine trafficking in diamonds, ivory, and petroleum.[50] Another feature of Cold War weak states that becomes generalized among regimes and opponents is the proliferation of gangsterism, both "official" and unauthorized. Rival security forces with foreign funding, multiple party militias, and "action forces" that enjoy the patronage of individual politicians—all recognizable from Cold War weak states—continue as instruments of disorder, as strongmen and rulers vie with one another for power. The reality of formal economic decline, bureaucratic decrepitude, and the collapse of the rule of law—all consequences of regime reluctance to support strong bureaucracies in the face of internal security threats during the Cold War era—leaves rulers with few options except to battle opponents in markets, which are the foundation of political authority.

To the extent that rulers and challengers use foreign firms to help them gain access to and control of markets, can their violent and unpredictable actions more strongly consider their partners' interests in profit and efficiency? In the four cases described in this book, control over markets is compatible with sustainable accumulation, even as contenders battle each other. Challengers to weak-state rulers also learn to use foreign partners to mutual advantage, further drawing global commerce into the dynamic of warlord politics. The joining of political struggle and accumulation—even as a violent Kalashnikov lifestyle of protection rackets, forced labor, and fencing of stolen goods—is as much a candidate for a Weberian capitalist style of life as is a Protestant ethic or a Japanese way of doing business.

HOW REFORM WORKS IN WEAK STATES

Proponents of reform, especially creditors such as the World Bank, attribute bureaucratic collapse in Africa's hardest-pressed weak states to state ownership of enterprises, control of prices, and manipulation of exchange rates and foreign trade to the benefit of entrenched privileged groups. It is well known that these policies promote the interests of self-serving state officials, benefiting regime favorites and urban consumers at the expense of producers.[51] In contrast, reform policies aim to reorganize the social basis of political authority in Africa to mimic the type believed to have led to the development of capitalism in Europe.

No alternative to reform appears to exist for hard-pressed rulers in Africa, so creditors are insisting on what Thomas Callaghy and John Ravenhill called a "back to the future" strategy in exchange for more loans, a policy intended to return African states to the relative prosperity of the 1960s. World Bank officials especially want "to start the development process over and do it right this time,"[52] to create a social structure that will be propitious for the development of capitalism. The first priority is to rehabilitate primary product exports, which will generate revenues and reclaim foreign markets. Privatization, devaluation, deregulation, and enticements to foreign investors will entice foreign firms to produce products locally, export those products, pay revenues on profits, and help to reclaim market shares African exports have lost since independence. Meanwhile, local reformers will use revenues from growing trade to slowly and carefully reconstruct bureaucracies, cutting unproductive employees in the process and creating an "enabling environment" that will promote additional local entrepreneurial talent.[53]

Political liberalization is crucial to support this risky offensive against entrenched groups by giving voice to beneficiaries of reform policies who are expected to call for even more economic reform. World Bank officials have identified this mutually supportive coalition as a major factor in promoting economic growth and administrative efficiency in once poor and corrupt Asian states, a lesson World Bank literature cites for Africa.[54]

Some critics of this neoliberal reform strategy point to structural obstacles to reform, arguing that simultaneous export promotion will drive down world market prices for Africa's products.[55] But a more serious flaw lies in outsiders' assumptions about rulers' interests and the relative strengths and cohesion of social groups. First, the neoliberal model presupposes a domestic social shift akin to that which seemed to underlie Europe's modernization. That is, rising commercial and manufacturing classes forced regimes to heed their interests in return for supplying revenues. Some rulers allied with strongmen (nobility); others posed as protectors of subjects against the socially disruptive individualism and competitiveness of new classes. Ultimately, the most successful states were those in which rulers protected economic autonomy and heeded the political interests of producers in exchange for revenue and political backing. But in contemporary weak states, where local sources of accumulation are the front line for battles for control between strongmen and rulers (and where no significant new class has arisen as a consequence of economic transformation), beneficiaries of reform are unlikely to arise who will be capable of defending an autonomous political interest.

It is far more likely that strongmen-turned-warlords will crowd out new entrepreneurs. One alternative is to accept enterprising warlords as the positive development of a commercial class, hoping this class will eventually be interested in efficiency and economic growth for their own sake. But the cases in the chapters that follow show that this commercial style places heavy emphasis on violence and cultivates disorder to promote accumulation. Its disregard for interstate frontiers and conventions disrupts enterprise and destabilizes politics elsewhere. A third difficulty lies in the significant role foreign firms play in weak-state–warlord political economies, which undermines incentives for local actors to strike compromises and causes rulers to worry that entrepreneurs will ally with foreign partners and weaken their political authority.

In fact, the record of reform in Africa since the mid-1980s is not encouraging. Significantly, some nonreformers with weaker macroeconomic indicators have registered higher growth rates than some committed reformers with stronger indicators.[56] This finding implies that accumulation may occur in a larger variety of conditions, including warlord and weak-state politics, than was previously suspected. This is not to reject wholesale the potential of neoliberal reforms. Ghana and Uganda, both of which have grown at about 5 percent annually since 1985, present a positive contrast to their own earlier records of economic decline. But as fancy hotels in dilapidated capitals such as Freetown in Sierra Leone or Monrovia, Liberia, illustrate, even war does not deter a surprising array of foreign businesspeople, con artists, and crooks. Freetown's Mammy Yoko Hotel, for example, hosted a steady stream of mining executives—many from firms listed on major stock exchanges—until it was severely damaged in a May 1997 naval bombardment. Likewise, the lounge at the Ducor Hotel in Monrovia housed a collection of businesspeople eager to exploit the country's "untapped" resources; they counted decades of corruption and recent wars as constituting a competitive advantage since, as one declared, such an environment creates a "frontier mentality of opportunity" and leaves local people desperate to make deals.

The real story of reform lies in how it is molded to fit local political purposes rather than in its transformative possibilities. In 1995, World Bank officials were mystified by the Sierra Leone government's close adherence to reform while devoting over half its revenues to fighting rebels. This situation was at odds with predictions that the hard-pressed regime would abjure harsh austerity to avoid domestic criticism during the crisis. How do rulers of weak states avoid having powerful outsiders force them to adhere to a universal standard? How does manipulation of reform contribute to a political strategy to manage internal security threats?

Nicolas van de Walle's analysis of reform in Cameroon puts at center stage the elite politics that is the basis of the regime's hold on power. He has noted that President Biya was eager to keep his elite political alliance together but faced creditor pressure to change his policies. Biya had to figure out how to implement reform to both appease creditors and minimize threats from his patronage networks. "Reform and economic austerity can be imposed in the general population," wrote van de Walle. "It is the state elite that will not tolerate the end of a system of prerogatives and privileges that is the glue that keeps the system together."[57] Pressure to conform to a visible standard of behavior caused Biya to refashion, rather than cast aside, informal patrimonial arrangements since he recognized that true political liberalization would give strongmen independent access to economic resources and threaten his authority.

Creditors consistently underestimate the extent to which the entrenchment of patronage politics into centers of accumulation hobbles attempts to mobilize those resources. A "civil society" of independent entrepreneurs may consist of the very same people a ruler regards as menacing rivals or local people identify as warlords. As I noted earlier, equating entrepreneurs with an independent commercial class can betray an ahistorical, universal understanding of the role of markets in patronage politics. Goran Hyden wrote that "early phases of class formation in industrial society may contain more important leads to an understanding of African development today than contemporary parallels from other parts of the world, be it India, China, the Soviet Union."[58]

Yet in Cameroon, Biya and his associates (like apparatchiks-turned-businesspeople in Russia) have shifted the costs of appeasing creditors to citizens, whether "captured" in formal markets or not, while distributing the benefits of reform—privatized state assets, for example—to favored supporters. Most citizens are the victims of reform, whereas elements of the pared-down patronage network benefit. Nonetheless, creditors may acquiesce in such an arrangement, especially when they are anxious about a regime's stability and its capacity to pay its debts.

Tying expectations of reform to good governance may be unrealistic in states where rulers place their highest priority on managing unruly patronage networks to the extent that this priority overshadows citizen critics who generally receive more sustained attention from researchers.[59] Unruly strongmen represent a far more immediate threat if they are firmly entrenched in the country's areas of wealth. The hoped-for bourgeois transformation comes only if a broader social class controls sufficient resources to force rulers to heed their interests in the first place. But how can such a class arise when no real autonomous "state" exists to offer protection to that group and to political elites who vie for access to resources? This degree of state weakness is tied, but not limited, to bureaucratic incapacity, since the latter is most often a manifestation of a more fundamental political balance that favors strongmen over small producers who are capable of organizing and calling for state protection and support. In this context, neoliberal reform does not necessarily strengthen this group (and, in fact, may do the opposite), especially when the group is small and disorganized to begin with.

This amendment to the definition of a weak state beyond merely considering bureaucratic incapacity permits us to refine our spectrum of state weakness (and possibilities for warlord politics) beyond bureaucratic collapse alone. For instance, during the 1970s Ghana's presidents Acheampong and Limann distributed state assets to associates to the almost total exclusion of the definition of an interest of state. But that economy was fairly reliant on small cultivators who could—and did—withhold resources and exercise an exit option that diminished the rulers' capacity to distribute rewards to loyal allies. In spite of massive corruption, a civil society exercised power in Ghana. Small producers of cocoa smuggled over 70 percent of their production out of the country.[60] Equally important, presidential rivals had difficulty accumulating resources on their own, since to do so would have required protecting small producers, at least long enough to allow them to harvest a crop. Such an enterprise would have seemed like an attempt to build government administration—at least to provide security, which itself is a collective good.

One should not overstate the success of subsequent reform in Ghana, however. Elements of elite networks still scramble to manipulate new policies to their benefit. Jeffrey Herbst has shown that even the task of building a political coalition willing to back reform from which it benefits has been a slow process that shows few signs of overwhelming long-standing ethnic and clan political networks.[61] But more careful attention to the political context of civil society not only illustrates the limits of reform-minded governance and civil society approaches (while anticipating positive results within these bounds) but also shows that resource distribution is yet another independent variable that influences the degree of state weakness and warlord politics in the context of changing patronage politics.

The weak-state regimes studied in this book can reap alternative resources that are outside the reach of the general population. In Nigeria, oil helps the regime to create an elite accommodation. A near total popular exit from the formal economy in Congo has not seriously disturbed the rival elite groups' grip on power and on the major sources of foreign exchange. Warlords in Liberia battle for resources and commerce against the continual and vocal protests of the majority of the population. The distinctive social constitution and distribution of resources in Africa's weakest states are at the heart of their vulnerability to warlord politics. This condition is closely related to the capacity of rulers, their elite associates, and their rivals to use political influence over markets to control access to wealth both inside and outside globally recognized state borders.

Regime efforts to control resources recall some compromises made by colonial states, which were forced to choose between *Afrique utile* (areas that produced revenues sufficient to pay for administration) and *Afrique inutile* (areas abandoned by the state as too costly to administer). Whereas the contemporary version of *Afrique utile* is delineated in terms of controlling salable resources rather than of colonial concerns with labor, its *inutile* counterpart still denotes regions and people that are best governed lightly, if at all, rather than waste scarce revenues in attempts to control them. So, too, rulers may now prefer an "integral state" of strong bureaucracies and an autonomous purpose of development.[62] But if they are unable to redirect society to this task, rulers use ties to creditors, foreign firms, and clandestine trading networks to control resources and build political authority. This situation also mirrors struggles of precolonial rulers who used ties to European trading houses to buy guns to conquer more people, forcing them to produce exports to trade for guns, and so on.[63]

In contemporary weak states in Africa, Joel Migdal has observed rulers trapped in a "politics of survival" in which the pursuit of stability and security undermines the pursuit of legitimacy through the promotion of economic development.[64] Vulnerable rulers in the cases in this book have turned creditor insistence on privatizing state assets—increasing exposure to global markets and using partnerships with foreign firms—to militarize commerce, discipline compliant strongmen, and chase others out. If a resurgent civil society cannot effectively contest political power on terrain that is unconstrained by formal state institutions or globally recognized state boundaries, then the popular action supporters of reform find so promising can be circumvented by rulers of weak states who fight their battles in these spheres. Rulers who face immediate threats from increasingly independent and unruly strongmen focus on this wider array of economic and political action. In fact, they may permit citizens of *Afrique inutile* to engage in "reform" politics, since elections, new laws, and new declarations might attract money from well-intentioned foreigners to which rulers of states would have access. This shift, the commercialization of political struggle and jettisoning of obligations to citizens and former clients, lies at the heart of the warlord politics that follows patronage politics.

Recycling Colonial
Innovations in Warlord Politics

Three of the weak-state rulers examined in this study have been surprisingly successful at satisfying and playing external actors against one another while managing their own internal threats. But one, President Samuel Doe of Liberia, failed in his attempt to do so. His example shows that the political arena has become more open to strongmen challenging rulers. This political fluidity simultaneously gives some rulers of weak states greater latitude in their responses to threats.

Paradoxically, this precept is most true in cases where patrimonial structures were less effective at controlling strongmen before the end of the Cold War. Each case examined in this book shows how efforts of rulers and strongmen to shape changes bring new external actors into the arena of local political struggle. Warlords and weak-state regimes integrate these actors by intensifying patrimonial ties to cross-border commerce, trading diasporas, and clandestine trades. Individuals vying for political power incorporate mercenaries, foreign firms, arms traders, money launderers, and the like, along with elements of the old patron-client alliance, into their new political networks to strengthen their positions. Advocates of reform such as the World Bank hasten this shift as they insist on greater economic extroversion and slimmer bureaucracies. Their calls to mobilize people and resources with a minimum of corrupt bureaucracy and with the help of foreigners have been interpreted locally as an opportunity to use foreigners as stand-ins for unreliable local allies.

Foreign firms pursue different but compatible interests within this political arrangement. Clandestine and small diamond marketers perform in ways the giant De Beers cartel cannot, taking advantage of the commercial benefits that come with rulers' abilities to manipulate laws and provide cover for clandestine activities. Drug cartels and money launderers bring visible physical might, which, in partnership with politicians, is important in shaping local politics. This view of the connection between local political struggle and global economic ties resembles Ronald Robinson's idea of "imperialism by invitation." In his analysis, those who control these ties acquire proportionally greater power vis-à-vis local rivals.[65] The problem for post–Cold War leaders of weak states is that internal rivals can now more easily invite collaboration with outsiders, especially if liberalization measures are implemented. Thus, whereas commerce has long been a tool of political control in de-bureaucratized weak states, the struggle over continued control has become increasingly violent.

The shape of partnerships with foreigners is, as with markets, a dependent variable in a broader task of asserting political authority in post–Cold War weak states. It makes sense in this context to pursue what Migdal has called an "anthropology of the state" in which the political unit "is not a fixed ideological entity. Rather, it reflects an ongoing political dynamic, a changing set of goals, as it engages other societal groups."[66] Boundaries of conventional state-society relations have limited meaning here, since they are defined in reference to an ideal that is not dominant among Africa's weak states. Conventions of sovereignty, such as uniform internal hegemony and clearly defined functions and borders, have a more contingent meaning in these instances of warlord politics, which is subordinated or manipulated in the pursuit of political authority. When rulers or their rivals abjure the political risks of directly mobilizing subjects through strong bureaucracies, development is not a goal or a function of political authority. Contrary to Samuel Huntington, rulers of weak states seek stability and security by destroying state institutions and contracting indispensable functions out to foreign partners. These partners appeared with globalization and the end of the Cold War, which was supposed to—but did not—enforce a standard of behavior on weak-state rulers.[67]

Recognition of political units in Africa that stray from state ideals brings us back to the related question of how the global political economy tolerates the existence of dissimilar units. Clues lie in the convergence of interest between key external actors and warlord politicians. African rulers and warlords who strive to exercise more exclusive control over accumulation match the goals of some state and nonstate actors outside of Africa. Some foreign firms are seeking partnerships with rulers who use their sovereign powers in clandestine or informal ways to maximize commercial advantage. Meanwhile, these African partners are subjected to the foreign firms' expectations of profit and maximization of efficiency. The more coercive winnowing features of competition fit well with rulers' agenda of paring down the numbers and demands of clients and denying enterprising strongmen economic opportunity and assets. Markets discipline in ways that are compatible with, but that go beyond, incentives for profit and efficiency. What critics condemn as exploitative behavior by "buzzards in uniform" and actions of a "vampire state" can be reconfigured to attract new partners, obey dictates of competition, and create new political authorities—although those authorities will still be alien to the norms and values of most of the societies they rule.

The danger for those living in weak states is that external actors and local competitors for political power will collaborate to squeeze them out of politics and marginalize their efforts to resist. The cases of Congo and Sierra Leone in this book show how warlord strategies help rulers pay off creditors, thereby gaining backing for more loans and attracting foreign firms. The targets of legitimacy are foreign firm shareholders and anxious creditors who have a short-term interest in increasing accumulation in weak states, which simultaneously increases the political rewards of exploiting local resources and people who receive no reciprocal benefits from this arrangement. More powerful states and aid organizations appreciate the stability and order this new extroverted social alliance can create. Politicians in strong states avoid being squeezed politically by constituents who call for intervention in cases of state failure. In the case of Sierra Leone, some aid organizations happily accept the protection of South African mercenaries, since they facilitate delivery of relief supplies. Some even prefer the new arrangement to the decrepit but more statelike previous political arrangements with which they were impatient and which they blamed for the country's slide into anarchy.

Nineteenth-century parallels can be found. As with today's warlords and weak-state rulers, Belgian king Leopold II abjured the expensive and politically formidable task of building transformative state agencies in his Congo Free State. It was easier and more profitable to run the state as a business, using its status as a sovereign entity and manipulating global interest in further integrating the Congo Basin into world markets to boost profits and more effectively exploit the local population and resources and co-opt local and regional trade networks.[68] Then as now, the rest of the world was willing to pretend the Congo Free State was a state at least until abuses there could no longer be ignored. No market was struggling to break free, since then as now the exercise of power did not permit the creation of an economic class capable not only of autonomous local accumulation but also of threatening the elite accommodation that would convert control over commerce into violence and insecurity for the rest of the population.

The feature that most distinguishes the building of political authority in weak states and warlord political units in Africa from the early modern European experience is the absence of an indigenous social alliance with which rulers must bargain in exchange for resources. The use of external actors as stand-ins for mobilizing local populations makes violence in warlord strategies rather different from that in early modern European state building. Charles Tilly identified the state role in early modern Europe as one of selling protection to a class of independent entrepreneurs whose activities political authorities needed and could not duplicate.[69] He and others have observed that this unconquerable division of social power determined the terms of political alliances between princes and towns.[70] The contemporary African weak-state and warlord trajectory to building political authority is more akin to strategies of sixteenth-century Venetian authorities or private chartered companies of the seventeenth and eighteenth centuries such as the East India Company and Hudson's Bay Company. Mercenaries, pirates, and privateers all bolstered a political authority built on control of commerce for the profit of both the political unit and the private individuals who stood in for bureaucracy.[71]

Some European princes built states, whereas others built leagues, empires, and city-states; similarly, one finds different responses to changing global conditions in Africa. As in Europe, the social and spatial distribution of resources, the availability of external partners, and the success of earlier efforts to implant a popular idea of state all play critical roles in shaping the options available to rulers who must innovate in efforts to survive. Rulers in Congo, Benin, Côte d'Ivoire, and Senegal, among other places, have dealt with very tense post–Cold War situations. But exit by populations in these relatively stronger bureaucratic states can undermine rulers, because some sense of shared national identity exists among popular and elite social groups or no easy alternative exists to cultivating legitimacy among the population, whose efforts as workers or small producers provide the bulk of internal resources. In these cases, rulers face conditions that resemble the dilemma of hard-pressed rulers in early modern Europe who were forced to bargain with significant segments of the population to get resources with which to fight for the regimes' survival. Reform programs and integration into the global political economy will likely have significantly different outcomes than in situations where rulers can more easily jettison troublesome former clients and broad segments of the population.

As Max Weber wrote, the routines of capitalist accumulation are diverse and do not exist in a fixed relation to states or to the global state system:

> At all periods of history, wherever it was possible, there has been ruthless acquisition, bound to no ethical norms whatever. Like war and piracy, trade has often been unrestrained in its relations with foreigners and those outside the group. The double ethic has permitted what was forbidden in dealing with brothers.[72]

It is improper, he wrote, to speak of capitalist economic activity as an inevitably pacific process.[73] It is not inevitable that Africa's increasingly intense commercial ties with the rest of the world will favor the building of sovereign, territorial states. Indeed, rulers of other political units take advantage of opportunities conventionally organized states would be incapable of seizing. This conclusion avoids the reductionism of agentless history that characterizes many accounts of weak states and state failure. In contrast, my analysis attributes these struggles to a rational adaption to a sudden shift in the calculus of opportunity. This shift away from a sovereign state ideal in an attempt to cope with global capitalism and internal struggle violates teleological assumptions about the nature of existing capitalism, especially the state system.[74] It concludes that forces of the global economy give rulers tools with which they can respond to political struggle by acting in their own interest.

This point has been made in recent writing about the perceived weakening of the state system in an increasingly global economy. This approach modifies neorealist approaches that assert the continued dominance of the global state system.[75] Evidence shows that warlord politicians and their commercial allies are not in the business of replacing states; in fact, the success of the collaboration lies in manipulating existing conventions of sovereignty. But this situation does change state-to-state relations and offers new options to rulers of weak states who are constrained by their inheritance of postcolonial patronage politics.

The analysis in Chapter 2 explains how and why different types of political units emerge. From there, in the case studies I address whether it is likely that all or some of these units will substantially modify Africa's system of states or whether sovereign state organizations will eventually triumph over the synchronic alternatives.

NOTES

1. Interview with NPFL fighter in Cotonou, Benin, 29 July 1994.
2. Goran Hyden, *No Shortcuts to Progress* (Berkeley: University of California Press, 1983), 53.
3. World Bank, *World Development Report 1996* (New York: Oxford University Press, 1996).
4. Anthony Giddens, *A Contemporary Critique of Historical Materialism: Power, Property and the State* (Berkeley: University of California Press, 1981), 214–217.
5. Anthony Giddens, *The Nation-State and Violence* (Berkeley: University of California Press, 1985), 282.
6. Kenneth Waltz, *Theory of International Relations* (New York: McGraw-Hill, 1979), 88.
7. Ibid., 89; Kenneth Waltz, "Reflections on *Theory of International Politics:* A Response to My Critics," in Robert Keohane, ed., *Neorealism and Its Critics* (New York: Columbia University Press, 1986), 339.
8. Immanuel Wallerstein, *The Politics of the World Economy* (New York: Cambridge University Press, 1984), 33.
9. For example, Goran Hyden, "Governance and the Study of Politics," in Goran Hyden and Michael Bratton, eds., *Governance and Politics in Africa* (Boulder: Lynne Rienner, 1992), 23.
10. I. William Zartman, "Introduction: Posing the Problem of State Collapse," in I. William Zartman, ed., *Collapsed States: The Disintegration and Restoration of Legitimate Authority,* (Boulder: Lynne Rienner, 1995), 8.
11. World Bank, *World Development Report, 1996,* 110–122.
12. World Bank, *Adjustment in Africa* (New York: Oxford University Press, 1994).
13. John Stopford and Susan Strange, *Rival States, Rival Firms: Competition for World Market Shares* (New York: Cambridge University Press, 1991).

14. Robert Kaplan, *The Ends of the Earth* (New York: Random House, 1996), 27.

15. Peter Lyon, "The Rise and Fall and Possible Revival of International Trusteeship," *Journal of Commonwealth and Comparative Politics* 31:1 (March 1993), 96–110; Paul Johnson, "Colonialism's Back—and Not a Moment Too Soon," *New York Times Magazine*, 18 April 1993, 22–26; William Pfaff, "A New Colonialism?" *Foreign Affairs* 74:1 (Jan.–Feb. 1995), 2–6; Ali Mazrui, "The Blood of Experience," *World Policy Journal* 12:1 (Spring 1995), 28–33.

16. Robert Jackson, *Quasi-States: Sovereignty, International Relations, and the Third World* (New York: Cambridge University Press, 1990).

17. Basil Davidson, *The Black Man's Burden* (New York: Times Books, 1992); Steven David, "Explaining Third World Alignment," *World Politics* 43:2 (Jan. 1991), 233–256; Mahmood Mamdani, *Citizen and Subject* (Princeton: Princeton University Press, 1996).

18. John Ruggie, "Territoriality and Beyond: Problematizing Modernity in International Relations," *International Organization* 47:1 (Winter 1993), 139–174.

19. Mohammed Ayoob, *The Third World Security Predicament: State-Making, Regional Conflict, and the International System* (Boulder: Lynne Rienner, 1995).

20. John Wiseman, "Leadership and Personal Danger in African Politics," *Journal of Modern African Studies* 31:4 (Dec. 1993), 657–660.

21. Joel Migdal, *Strong Societies and Weak States* (Princeton: Princeton University Press, 1988), 207–213.

22. Sam Nolutshungu, *Limits of Anarchy: Intervention and State Formation in Chad* (Charlottesville: University of Virginia Press, 1996).

23. Stephen Ellis, "Les prolongements du conflit israélo-arabe: le cas du Sierra Leone," *Politique Africaine* 30 (June 1988), 69–75.

24. Pierre Péan, *L'argent noir: corruption et sous-devellopement* (Paris: Fayard, 1988).

25. Achille Mbembe, "Pouvoir, violence et accumulation," in Jean-François Bayart, Achille Mbembe, and Comi Toulabor, eds., *Le politique par le bas en Afrique noire* (Paris: Karthala, 1992), 233–256.

26. Jean-François Bayart, "Une criminalisation de l'economie?" in Fariba Adelkhah, Jean-François Bayart, and Olivier Roy, *Thermidor en Iran* (Paris: Éditions Complexe, 1993), 40–41; Kuyu Mwissa, "La privatisation de la violence institutionnalisée," in Etienne le Roy and Trutz von Trotha, eds. *La violence et l'état: formes et évolution d'un metropole* (Paris: Harmattan, 1993), 165–181.

27. A scenario outlined in Richard Sandbrook, *The Politics of Africa's Economic Recovery* (New York: Cambridge University Press, 1993); World Bank, *Adjustment in Africa*.

28. Olivier Roy, *The Failure of Political Islam* (Cambridge: Harvard University Press, 1994), 88.

29. The proposition that interdependence enhances sovereignty is found in Giddens, *The Nation-State and Violence*, 255–285, Raymond Aron, *Peace and War: A Theory of International Relations* (New York: Anchor Press, 1973), 742.

30. Hendrik Spruyt, *The Sovereign State and Its Competitors* (Princeton: Princeton University Press, 1995); Hedley Bull, ed., *The Expansion of International Society* (New York: Oxford University Press, 1984).

31. Janice Thomson, *Mercenaries, Pirates, and Sovereignties: State-Building and Extra-Territorial Violence in Early Modern Europe* (Princeton: Princeton University Press, 1994).

32. Hyden, *No Shortcuts to Progress;* Merilee Grindle, *Challenging the State: Crisis and Innovation in Latin America and Africa* (New York: Cambridge University Press, 1996).

33. See especially Janet MacGaffey, ed., *The Real Economy of Zaire* (Philadelphia: University of Pennsylvania Press, 1991); Stephen Ellis and Janet MacGaffey, "Le commerce international informel en Afrique sub-saharienne," *Cahiers d'Études Africaines* 37:1 (1997), 11–37.

34. Sara Berry, "Social Institutions and Access to Resources," *Africa* 59:1 (1989), 40–55.

35. Max Weber, *The Protestant Ethic* (London: Allen and Unwin, 1948), 71.

36. This can be seen in reference to Chad in William Foltz, "Reconstructing the State of Chad," in Zartman, *Collapsed States,* 15–31; Roger Charlton and Roy May, "Warlords and Militarism in Chad," *Review of African Political Economy* 45–46 (Winter 1989), 12–25.

37. Nicole Biggart, *Charismatic Capitalism: Direct Selling Organizations in America* (Chicago: University of Chicago Press, 1989).

38. Allen Myerson, "The Death of Some Salesmen," *New York Times,* 28 April 1996, sect. 4, 14.

39. Karel van Wolferen, "The Japan Problem Revisited," *Foreign Affairs* 69:4 (Fall 1990), 42–55.

40. Karel van Wolferen, *The Enigma of Japanese Power: People and Politics in a Stateless Nation* (New York: Vintage Books, 1990).

41. A point made in James Rosenau, *Turbulence in World Politics: A Theory of Change and Continuity* (Princeton: Princeton University Press, 1990), 143.

42. Peter Geschiere, "Kinship, Witchcraft and 'the Market': Hybrid Patterns in Cameroonian Society," in Roy Dilley, ed., *Contesting Markets: Analyses of Ideology, Discourse and Practice* (Edinburgh: Edinburgh University Press, 1992), 86–104; Théophile Dzaka and Michel Milandou, "L'entrepreneuriat congolais à l'épreuve des pouvoir magiques," *Politique Africaine* 56 (Dec. 1994), 108–118.

43. Bayart, "Une criminalisation de l'economie?" 40–41.

44. José Gonzales, "Guerrillas and Coca in the Upper Huallaga Valley," in David Scott Palmer, ed., *Shining Path of Peru* (New York: St. Martin's Press, 1994), 123–143; Axel Klein, "Trapped in the Traffick: Growing Problems of Drug Consumption in Lagos," *Journal of Modern African Studies* 32:4 (Dec. 1994), 657–677.

45. Alfred McCoy, *The Politics of Heroin: CIA Complicity in the Global Drug Trade* (New York: Lawrence Hill Books, 1991).

46. Barnett Rubin, *The Fragmentation of Afghanistan: State Formation and Collapse in the International System* (New Haven: Yale University Press, 1995).

47. Olivier Roy, "En Asie centrale: kolkhoziens et entreprenants," in Jean-François Bayart, ed., *La réinvention du capitalisme* (Paris: Fayard, 1994), 73–86.

48. Stephen Handelman, *Comrade Criminal: Russia's New Mafiya* (New Haven: Yale University Press, 1995); Olga Kryshtanovskaia, "Illegal Structures in Russia," *Russian Social Science Review* 37:6 (Nov.–Dec. 1996), 44–64; Tom Hunter, "Russia's Mafiyas: The New Revolution," *Jane's Intelligence Review* 9:6 (June 1997), 247–254.

49. Olivier Roy, *Afghanistan: From Holy War to Civil War* (Princeton: Darwin Press, 1995), 109.

50. William Reno, *Corruption and State Politics in Sierra Leone* (New York: Cambridge University Press, 1995).

51. Robert Bates, *Markets and States in Tropical Africa* (Berkeley: University of California Press, 1981).

52. Thomas Callaghy and John Ravenhill, "How Hemmed In?" in Thomas Callaghy and John Ravenhill, eds., *Hemmed In: Responses to Africa's Economic Decline* (New York: Columbia University Press, 1993), 524.

53. World Bank, *Adjustment in Africa*.

54. World Bank, *The East Asian Miracle* (New York: Oxford University Press, 1993).

55. Michael Barrett-Brown and Pauline Tiffen, *Short-Changed: Africa and World Trade* (Boulder: Pluto Press, 1992), 28–32.

56. Sayre Schatz, "Structural Adjustment in Africa: A Failing Grade So Far," *Journal of Modern African Studies* 32:4 (Dec. 1994), 679–692; Sayre Schatz, "The World Bank's Fundamental Misconception in Africa," *Journal of Modern African Studies* 34:2 (June 1996), 239–248.

57. Nicolas van de Walle, "The Politics of Non-Reform in Cameroon," Callaghy and Ravenhill, *Hemmed In,* 359. Similar analyses are found in Bernard Contamin and Yves-A Fauré, *La Bataille des enterprises publiques en Côte d'Ivoire: L'histoire d'un ajustement* (Paris: Karthala, 1990); Bogumil Jewsiewicki, "Jeux d'argent et de pouvoir au aire: la 'bindomonie' et le crépuscule de la Deuxieme Republique," *Politique Africaine* 46 (June 1992), 55–70.

58. Hyden, *No Shortcuts,* 22.

59. Hyden and Bratton, eds., *Governance and Politics in Africa*.

60. Naomi Chazan, *An Anatomy of Ghanaian Politics: Managing Political Recession, 1969–1982* (Boulder: Westview, 1983).

61. Jeffrey Herbst, *The Politics of Reform in Ghana, 1982–1991* (Berkeley: University of California Press, 1993).

62. Crawford Young, "Zaire: The Shattered Illusion of the Integral State," *Journal of Modern African Studies* 32:2 (June 1994), 247–264.

63. Jack Goody, *Technology, Tradition and the State in Africa* (London: Hutchinson, 1971), 39–56.

64. Migdal, *Strong Societies,* 214–226.

65. Ronald Robinson, "The Excentric Idea of Imperialism, with or Without Empire," in Wolfgang Mommsen and Jurgen Osterhammel, *Imperialism and After: Continuities and Discontinuities* (Boston: Allen and Unwin, 1986), 267–89.

66. Joel Migdal, "The State in Society: An Approach to Struggles for Domination," in Joel Migdal, Atul Kohli, and Vivienne Shue, eds., *State Power and Social Forces* (New York: Cambridge University Press, 1994), 7–34.

67. Samuel Huntington, *Political Order in Changing Societies* (New Haven: Yale University Press, 1968).

68. Catherine Coquery-Vidrovitch, *Le Congo au temps des grandes compagnies concessionaires* (Paris: Mouton, 1972).

69. Charles Tilly, "War Making and State Making as Organized Crime," in Peter Evans, Dietrich Rueschemeyer, and Theda Skocpol, eds., *Bringing the State Back In* (New York: Cambridge University Press, 1985), 169–191.

70. Charles Tilly and Wim Blockmans, eds., *Cities and the Rise of States in Europe, A.D. 1000 to 1800* (Boulder: Westview, 1994).

71. Frederic Lane, *Venice: A Maritime Republic* (Baltimore: Johns Hopkins University Press, 1973); Sir Percival Griffiths, *A License to Trade: The Histories of English Chartered Companies* (London: Ernest Benn, 1974). See also Frederic Lane, *Profits from Power: Readings in Protection Rent and Violence Controlling Enterprises* (Albany: State University of New York Press, 1979).

72. Weber, *Protestant Ethic*, 57. See also Pino Arlacchi, *Mafia et Compagnies: L'éthique mafieusse et l'espirit du capitalisme* (Grenoble: Presses Universitaires de Grenoble, 1986).

73. Max Weber, *General Economic History* (New York: Collier Books, 1961), 227–228.

74. Criticism of the teleological approach is found in Alexander Wendt, "The Agent-Structure Problem in International Relations Theory," *International Organization* 41:3 (Summer 1987), 335–370.

75. James Rosenau and Mary Duffee, *Thinking Theory Thoroughly* (Boulder: Westview, 1995).

2

▼ ▼ ▼ ▼ ▼

AFRICA'S WEAKEST
STATES AFTER
THE COLD WAR

France made it clear . . . that democracy is relative and that Paris would
not support chaos over stability. The British seemed to prefer stability
as well. U.S. Ambassador Smith Hempstone's relentless three-year
drive for multiparty democracy in Kenya had British diplomats irate
over its "naivete."

—*Marguerite Michaels*[1]

A FASTER TEMPO OF CHANGE

The end of the Cold War shifted the distribution of opportunities available to African rulers, whose old strengths and vulnerabilities were al-
tered as they responded to these changing external conditions. Some patronage techniques opened opportunities for accumulation through new
ties to the global economy. Other aspects of the rulers' political authority had to be jettisoned or entirely reworked. These shifts have been
played out amid major changes in the character of African economies.
These internal and external pressures to change and new opportunities
that prompted the shift toward warlord politics in some weak states constitute the subject of this chapter.

This recent political shift resembles what natural scientist Stephen
Jay Gould has called a "punctuated equilibrium."[2] That is, fossil records
show a series of catastrophic changes. Entire faunas are wiped out, and
new species suddenly appear. Gould hypothesized that these rapid
changes occur when reinforcing mechanisms break down, thus weakening a previous equilibrium. Applying this conception to recent African
politics, declining strategic importance weakens outside support for
Jackson's quasi-state model of interstate relations (discussed in Chapter
1). This loss of external economic and diplomatic support, coupled with
changes in global markets, leaves internal patronage politics unsustain-

able. These pressures also act as incentives, especially in places that are the most diplomatically and economically marginal. As in Africa's weakest states, it is in such places that the greatest reward can be found in experimentation (since to do nothing would be to accept extinction) and experimentation encounters the least sanction.

Applied to social relations, this view contrasts with the gradualist assumptions of reformist governance models of change examined in Chapter 1. Those models adopt static equilibrium assumptions that are at the heart of neoliberal economics. This simplified assumption about behavior tends to ignore change and fails to account for it when it occurs.[3] In this chapter, however, we find that actors (strongmen, rulers, and investors) change the criteria they use to calculate their maximum utilities. Likewise, behavior does not follow a specific set of rules, since the heterogeneous microworld of changing individual behavior among rulers, rivals, and outsiders contributes to the shift in the macroworld of regularities actors face. Additionally, the structure of ruler-society relations (examined in Chapter 1) has a critical bearing on this pace and direction of change. Rulers who are not compelled to address significant social groups as a condition for access to resources find more leeway to experiment and seize new opportunities, although at the price of abandoning the project of economic development through state institutions. Internally, the ruler's urgency to experiment will be reinforced if local strongmen learn they can grab opportunities to challenge their superiors.

For rulers of weak states, the end of the Cold War signaled the demise of old forms of politics. Creditors and aid donors quickly discovered that they could impose a growing list of conditions in return for cash. Old external patrons either pressed for major changes in the manner of rule—demanding elections, for example—or simply disappeared, as in the case of the Soviet Union. Meanwhile, the Soviet collapse and the Eastern bloc successor states' need to boost export earnings turned Soviet military aid into a private arms market. Cheap weapons gave strongmen new opportunities to arm themselves and to directly challenge vulnerable rulers. Rulers learned that they could also afford these surplus weapons, even as their revenues grew tighter.

Creditors insisted that hard-pressed African rulers rely more heavily on private firms to boost exports. At the same time, the dismantling of apartheid-era security establishments in South Africa left numerous military officers and entire units searching for new ways to support themselves. These former government agents, who were familiar with clandestine trades and boasted of covert political and commercial ties to many African rulers, built private business syndicates. South African officials, anxious about their own bureaucratic constituencies and economic reform programs, have allowed these former agents of apartheid to translate their old privilege into private gain.

As heirs to an old security establishment, some South African firms possess connections and skills that give them advantages over foreign rivals in the search for profits in Africa. These firms offer a range of services rulers of weak states can manipulate for political gain, as we see in this chapter with Executive Outcomes, a South African firm. For example, mining and engineering firms might also offer private military protection, reflecting the common origins of these entrepreneurs in South African military units that were once clandestinely involved in trades; this scenario represents a new commercial "lifestyle" that selectively incorporates elements of both previous practice and ideology. These services are very attractive to cash-strapped and politically vulnerable weak-state rulers who need both capital investment to satisfy creditors and reliable fighters to battle rivals and control access to resources. Alliances with foreign firms of this sort allow rulers to jettison politically unreliable military officers, marginalize units that have become essentially private militias of strongmen, and use new commercial allies to defend their power. Other firms bring opportunities to profit in criminal networks in drugs, money laundering, and other contraband trades they developed under the protection of Cold War politicians in strong states who tolerated such behavior for the greater good of strategic aims. Thus, weak-state rulers and their private foreign-firm partners can actually profit from commercial opportunities created by disorder and collapsing authority in weak states.

This punctuation upsets old calculations of benefit. Should rulers risk cultivating popular legitimacy by providing services to citizens and thereby marginalize threatening rivals? Should they complete the privatization of state power, perhaps selling the benefits of their globally recognized sovereignty to drug traffickers and money launderers seeking safe havens? Or should they adopt intermediate strategies, such as becoming heavily dependent on new foreign investors who leave rulers free to wage war against internal enemies? Herein lies the element of choice, although it is constrained by changing exogenous conditions. Nonetheless, actors have a variety of ways of calculating their interests.

VARIABILITY OF NEW
POLITICAL ARRANGEMENTS

The sudden post–Cold War increase in the pace of change opened uncharted paths for building political power. Although many outsiders saw new constraints on rulers of weak states after the Cold War as an opportunity to force those rulers to change their behavior, we saw in Chapter 1 that change gave some rulers unexpected leeway to innovate and to manipulate external demands. Stephen Krasner has applied Gould's notion of punctuated equilibrium to help explain how speedier change produces variety in new political arrangements. Such change is concentrated in relatively instantaneous events in which "geographically isolated groups may then displace their ancestral populations."[4] This phenomenon occurs because the underlying conditions that supported old arrangements no longer exist. For rulers of weak states in Africa, this means rewards for mimicking old models of political development disappear, whereas pressures and potential rewards of innovation grow.

The possible variation in local responses to crisis and change in Africa's weak states provoked by rapid change recalls Fernand Braudel's observation of how a new capitalist global economy prompted European rulers to experiment with city-states, leagues, empires, and chartered companies. States eventually won out as the dominant political unit, but it was not evident during the initial rush to manage rapid change that states would emerge as the most stable result.[5] Only in hindsight can we see the comparative advantages of states as the rational and efficient response to that global change, and significant variation remains. Barrington Moore has pointed out that democratic and authoritarian regimes differ in their internal strategies to compete against other states. Moore also noted that the power of specific social groups and their previous political arrangements shape experimentation and choice in new political alignments, even when external variables are fairly constant across cases.[6]

Africa's rulers must choose arrangements that respond to a variety of pressures. They may face immediate threats—from warlord neighbors, unruly strongmen, or demanding subjects. The opinions of creditors and officials of strong states who insist that their prescriptions for efficiency receive highest priority are usually less important to African weak-state rulers than are success in competition against rivals, personal or family profit, or concern about the fate of ethnic kinsfolk if the regime should fail. Those who vie for political power in weak states, however, may stumble on new arrangements to handle internal priorities while coincidentally addressing growing external pressures. For example, weak-state ruler alliances with global firms underwrite greater regime autonomy in novel ways that need not accord with the notions of state politics developed from European experiences in which political authority was derived from clearly defined bargains between politicians and indigenous entrepreneurs.[7]

Disaggregation of external and internal changes shows how weak-state actors actually make choices.[8] From this we can inductively determine individual or group preferences and the impact they have had on those choices. In contrast, labeling a particular type of behavior as always rational (or dysfunctional) implies that actors make calculations according to a universal cost-benefit ratio. Yet rulers in weak states may advance private commercial interests of their own and of their partners, even when their original aim might have been to recruit new political partners, manipulate clashing interests of external actors, or strike new bargains among old political associates. This does not mean such rationalities vary in unpredictable or unknowable ways. Rather, my aim is to illuminate variations in interests among actors and show how they interact in a weak-state context.

Greater tolerance by global society for experimentation by African rulers in the 1990s has also promoted diversity within political units. Domestic repression, coups, and insurgencies are hardly new phenomena in weak states. Discontinuity, however, appears in the extent to which outsiders have tolerated the intensification and internationalization of unorthodox strategies of control. To take an extreme case, the extent to which the planners and executioners of genocide in Rwanda—many of whom were state officials—escaped interference from abroad is remarkable, despite widespread, public condemnation of the tragedy in foreign capitals.[9] More generally, as in Africa's weakest states, economic predation has played a more significant role in ruler strategies to address internal security threats and the problem of accumulation. Hence, new opportunities have appeared for some rulers (and for rivals too) in the context of nearly permanent warfare. The diversity of clandestine and illicit networks in old patronage systems has also given rulers and challengers numerous types of interactions to choose from, intensifying some and restricting others in efforts to exercise political authority and accumulate resources.[10]

This enhanced political role for informal and clandestine channels of accumulation has transformed interstate relations in a variety of ways that are closely related to new strategies for exercising internal control. Three cases in this book—Liberia, Sierra Leone, and Congo—are situated in zones of regional conflict that are largely products of intensified and militarized battles for control of cross-border commerce for conversion into political resources. Drug trafficking by Nigerians, for example, has complicated that country's interstate relations. Nigerians supply 70 to 80 percent of Burmese heroin imports into the United States and 35 to 40 percent of the U.S. heroin market from other sources. They accounted for 90 percent of cocaine trafficking arrests in South Africa in 1994.[11] Some suspect that key Nigerian army and government officials are involved in this trade, although no concrete proof has been found.[12] Nigeria's military is also bogged down in conflicts in Liberia and Sierra Leone and has become involved in clandestine commerce there.

What is important here is whether rulers or their rivals seize these and other new opportunities and the extent to which rulers can oppose, control, or speed up privatization of commerce. Meanwhile, the choices political actors make in these situations impose their own pressures and attractions on hard-pressed rulers elsewhere in Africa. To the extent that neighbors pursue warlord politics, the chance that political units in Africa will develop along a common path that created strong states elsewhere is reduced. It is important to recognize, however, the extent to which global changes—particularly outsiders' confidence that deregulated markets and minimal state administration are cures for corruption and inefficiency—offer new opportunities for warlord politics.

UNINTENDED CONSEQUENCES OF "REFORM"

Creditors point out correctly that corruption and economic mismanagement have chased foreign investors from Africa. The continent accounted for 1.4 percent of world trade in 1994, down from 3 percent in the early 1960s. Foreigners invested a mere $830 million annually in the period 1990–1995, compared with $38 billion invested in China in 1995 alone.[13] Except in South Africa, African rulers cannot generally tap private bond markets to finance government expenditures. Proponents of reform can also point to the disastrous drop in Africa's share of global agricultural exports, from 17 percent in 1970 to 8 percent in 1990.[14]

Meanwhile, loans and aid from creditors and foreign governments remained consistent at 5 percent of sub-Saharan Africa's gross product in the first half of the 1990s, partially buffering declines in private foreign investment.[15] Creditors need Africa: As one field contractor said, "little shit countries cannot be allowed to show the rest that irresponsibility is rewarded with debt cancellation,"[16] arguing that debtors elsewhere will note with interest any evidence of creditor disengagement from Africa that seems to signal an abandonment of loans. For example, if World Bank officials discounted Liberia's $4 billion debt (valued at four cents on the dollar in commercial markets) or Somalia's almost $3 billion debt (no commercial value) with no reciprocal concession, politicians in Russia or Brazil might stress their greater strategic importance to the global economy and press to renegotiate terms of their nearly $200 billion in collective loans.

But rulers of weak states in Africa remain desperate to attract foreign private investment as creditors prescribe, if only to provide economic opportunities for powerful clients and to continue to make loan payments. Creditors are using this leverage to impose conditions for new loans and aid, holding out as a sanction the fact that bilateral creditors and many official foreign aid organizations use World Bank and IMF certification as a criterion for committing resources to debtor states. As Julius Nyerere, former president of Tanzania, noted, "When we reject IMF conditions we hear the threatening whisper: 'Without accepting our conditions . . . you will get no other money.'"[17]

Despite the continued presence of creditors and their demands for political and economic liberalization in African debtor states, economies have not significantly revived. Failure to adopt policies is not the main culprit. By 1993, government spending in Africa, for example, had fallen 25 percent from highs in 1981, despite the high population growth and popular clamor for services that accompanied political liberalization in the 1990s. Privatization of state-owned firms has continued apace with World Bank reform programs since the 1980s. Thirty states have significantly changed their mining investment codes since 1987.[18] Yet these changes have not attracted substantial foreign investment or radically reversed the economic decline.[19] Paradoxically, mining investment in the mid-1990s focused on Congo and Angola. The former has suffered from extreme bureaucratic incapacity and one of the most predatory regimes on the continent, a regime that made no serious attempt to implement new investment codes. The latter has been the site of nearly continuous war since independence in 1975.

Despite these outcomes, World Bank analyses in the mid-1990s attribute policy failure to the persistence of patron-client networks that hobble even the most reform-minded African rulers.[20] Even the major state layoffs creditors prescribe do not end the irresistible demands of still powerful patronage networks. In very weak states, former bureaucrats and military units may remain organized and lay claims to resources at the expense of the regime's favorites. Even following formal deregulation, bureaucrats face pressures to manipulate financial markets and give preferential access to credit to the "private" enterprises in politicians' hands, which further discourages the emergence of a truly autonomous private sector.[21] Remaining state-run enterprises such as utilities that provide inputs for former state-run firms continue to face demands for credit (that goes unpaid) from political elites who now own former state enterprises, thus generating more debt. Even reform-minded rulers find it difficult to force those strongmen to pay their bills to the state.[22]

Creditors suspect that political liberalization reinforces this political gridlock, since even the most committed reformers face pressure to hand out resources both to head off electoral challenges from entrenched elites who grab state resources for themselves and to cultivate followings. Even in Ghana, which is hardly among Africa's weakest states, President Rawlings raised civil service salaries by 80 percent and loosened credits to state-run and private enterprises before the 1992 election.[23] The election itself resulted from creditor pressure for political liberalization.

Paradoxically, creditors that press African rulers to expose themselves to challenges from rivals risk undermining the individuals most able or likely to undertake the political risks of directly confronting rent-seeking activities among strongmen. One way to manage this situation is to force regimes to adopt more efficient administrative practices to enable them to deliver more services to citizens more cheaply. But bureaucratic layoffs do nothing to silence the political voices of rulers' rivals, since many hold state offices and increasing administrative or economic efficiency will likely limit their influence and wealth. Further, officials who remain cannot be expected to police their own private use of state offices for personal profit.

Inefficient though the alternative may be, reducing state employment also undermines regime support among educated youth, previously a key constituency of many patronage-based regimes. Guinea's government, for example, has hired virtually no new employees since 1984 and has cut civil service rolls in half.[24] Frustrated graduates consequently seek opportunities in clandestine trades—sometimes in collaboration with regime opponents, which magnifies factional splits in national politics. Guinea's president confronts this challenge within his own paramilitary unit, which engages in clandestine commerce. I have observed that this unit plays a major role in petroleum commerce in Conakry, the national capital. Not surprisingly, a 1996 coup attempt occurred along these commercial-political fault lines.

Creditor interests thus become tied even more closely to the survival of rulers of weak states as a political counterbalance to the disruptive potential of rival factions and strongmen engaged in unregulated (and untaxed) commerce. Some rulers exploit this internal vulnerability, presenting themselves as very worthy of outside support against anti-reform rivals. Creditors then join the rulers in measuring reform policies against the rulers' ability to triumph over unruly local strongmen, and creditors' short-term interests shift from boosting state capacity to helping rulers vanquish internal enemies. Both parties tacitly agree on the need to insulate and buffer rulers while restraining the organized interests of others—including unruly state officials—in society. As the World Bank chief of the Africa region's Capacity Building Division put it, "It is becoming clear that the first order of business is to restore stability over an increasingly fragmented political and administrative environment."[25]

World Bank officials increasingly prescribe direct attacks on the Cold War patronage networks they hold responsible for policy failure. Radical privatization along with deep cuts in state employment, they argue, subjects state agents to the discipline of the market.[26] Pushed out of inefficient patronage networks, enterprising individuals should seek private gain in newly deregulated private economies. This strategy, which is modeled on reforms in Côte d'Ivoire, entails privatizing every possible state service. The hope is that transferring state services to private firms will eliminate the political influence of Cold War–era strongmen and their patrons. Ivoirian reformers have sold roads and electric, gas, and water utilities, helping to place those assets beyond the reach of local political cliques. Corrupt state officials now face bosses whose primary concern is with generating profits rather than placating threatening rivals and their followers with privileged access to state resources. Officials either become efficient or lose their jobs. Greater efficiency is expected to boost the quality and increase the availability of popular services and infrastructure, thereby generating goodwill toward continuing reforms. In principle, this practice insulates reform-minded rulers from disgruntled former clients and supports property holders whose interests rulers protect in return for revenues and political support.[27]

Meanwhile, the use of private firms to supply customary state services clears the way for reformers to slash civil service employment, which translates into massive layoffs of those who held jobs as rewards for political loyalty and eliminates huge salary costs that yielded little or nothing in the form of public services. Since 1986 in Ghana, about 50,000 persons, or one in thirty adults active in the formal economy, have been laid off.[28] World Bank officials pressed successfully for the elimination of a third, or 16,000 members, of Sierra Leone's civil service.[29] One-third of Uganda's civil service faced the same fate after 1989.[30] Congo's civil service is slated to shrink by 550,000 people, down to the 60,000 that World Bank officials consider essential.[31] In fact, those officials recommend that Congo's state budget be abolished and that an independent agency with private business representation manage budget operations with a focus on financing development projects and social services.[32]

But the way these reforms are implemented has much to do with the probability that rulers can make political appeals to a significant segment of the population to back reform as they attack the privileges of entrenched strongmen. According to one observer, Ghana's President Rawlings was able to recruit community leaders to support him, but he did so only by taking decentralization seriously and by sidelining his allies who were using state bureaucracies for private purposes.[33] In Uganda, the unpopularity of previous regimes and the conversion of a popular insurgency organization into an administrative apparatus allowed President Museveni to implement a more conventional state-building strategy. But Museveni's strategy has been significantly modified as he has experimented with unorthodox means of control in the face of continuing insurgencies.

And although building internal political support for reform may be much touted by creditors, it is not the only reason they prescribe policies. The cases in this book strongly suggest that creditors regard deregulation and trimming bureaucracies as giving them the best chance to collect payments for loans. Africa's debt burden has continued to climb, reaching $223 billion in 1995—double the amount owed a decade before.[34] Creditors' desperation to maintain a facade that all countries pay their debts can be seen in their treatment of states such as Somalia, which "performs" in a program that rewards the absence of "bad" policies while in fact no central government exists to make policy. Somalia, Sierra Leone, and Liberia are included in a World Bank Rights Accumulation Programme in which the absence of "antireform" policies allows debtors to cancel small amounts of principal. More important, the program supports the illusion that debts are being collected, thus preventing the discounting of bad loans against World Bank assets even if some principal is slowly written off.

Periodic payments by foreign firms that collect revenues on behalf of debtor states also help creditors claim those loans are performing effectively. Cooperative regimes benefit from kinder treatment under creditor-managed debt relief schemes. Sierra Leone, for example, had its foreign debt reduced by 20 percent in the 1994 and 1995 Paris Club negotiations.[35] Excused from acknowledging bad loans, creditors such as the World Bank and the African Development Bank can maintain their excellent credit ratings. Apparent good management of debt also helps creditors to convince officials in powerful member states to contribute new capital for loans to much bigger clients such as Russia.

Internally, creditors' interest in minimizing the international consequences of Africa's debt is compatible with the warlord strategy of simply evicting clients from the resource-starved bureaucracy (by destroying it) and asserting direct, private control over resources. As one junior official for a creditor averred, "Corrupt officials are our problem here. We have to kill off the bureaucracies to shake them out. Then we can talk about building bureaucratic capacity."[36] Foreign firms that stand in for corrupt state officials strengthen weak-state rulers' internal control without necessarily promoting a reciprocal political bargain with potential supporters. Without their own indigenous followers, foreign firms make good partners for rulers, allowing them to exploit new opportunities and force rivals out of old ones. Given these coinciding interests of creditors and rulers of weak states, we can see how a new kind of foreign firm has gained prominence in the reconfiguration of weak-state politics.

FOREIGN FIRMS AND THE PRIVATIZATION OF VIOLENCE

African sources of investment are changing. Fifty percent of British firms that invested in Africa have retreated since 1986, French investment is stagnant, and U.S. sources registered a 10 percent increase during the period.[37] Meanwhile, South African firms posted a fivefold increase in investments from 1991 to 1995—albeit from a low base—rising to 24 percent of total investment in 1995.[38]

More important are alliances formed between South African firms and other foreign investors that use the special skills, expertise, and political connections some South African firms enjoy. South African investors have received special advantages as a result of the end of the Cold War. The end of the apartheid regime removed economic sanctions against South African businesses, making those advantages accessible to other investors. Sanctions were completely lifted in 1994, and creditor-backed reform policies elsewhere in Africa suddenly opened new investment opportunities for South African firms. In Stephen Jay Gould's terms of "punctuated equilibrium," private capital and political elites in both South Africa and weak states faced dramatic changes and new opportunities in their relations with one another.

Specifically, practices opponents of apartheid condemned during the Cold War now gave some South African firms a competitive advantage in weak states, advantages found in apartheid-era ties established between some South African firms and African politicians. Some entrepreneurs had belonged to South Africa's security establishment and received direct government support to trade abroad. They developed clandestine ties to African politicians in efforts to conceal such commerce, which contravened then-existing economic sanctions against South Africa's apartheid regime. African politicians acted as intermediaries with other firms and governments in return for handsome rewards from South African businesses and state officials who were desperate to trade abroad.

Subsequent chapters show how weak-state rulers, including Sese Seko Mobutu in Congo and Joseph Saidu Momoh in Sierra Leone, permitted South African businesses to edge out threatening local politicians and control resources. The clandestine nature of these ties forced South African firms to accept barters, by-passing foreign exchange shortages that limited African contacts with other, aboveboard foreign firms. Vulnerable rulers mortgaged natural resources to the South African firms, allowing them to extract resources directly from territory often under the control of rival politicians. Some firms also provided political resources—weapons, for example—to cement relations with vulnerable regimes. Barter arrangements continue, which makes deals with South African firms more attractive to cash-strapped hosts.

These strategies unexpectedly became advantages for both sets of partners after the Cold War. Creditors' emphasis on bureaucratic cutbacks and privatization in weak-state economic reform programs reinforced and helped to rework ties between long-term partners. South African firms that had once helped vulnerable rulers with spare parts, cash, and weaponry showed the flexibility necessary to wrest enterprises and resources away from disgruntled clients at the behest of creditors. From weak-state rulers' perspective, it is better to have important state assets fall into the hands of reliable foreigners than to see them removed from rulers' control by less accommodating investors. Even more threatening to rulers of weak states, purchasers could appear from the ranks of political rivals, using ill-gotten gains from past corruption to buy their way into the reformed economy.

Barter arrangements, coupled with the previous military links of some South African firms, give cash-poor rulers easy access to global arms markets on more advantageous terms than with cash-and-carry trade. The same advantages extend to many recent Russian entrants into investment in Africa. This situation shows how some previously less significant global elements of the old patrimonial state politics in Africa have adapted to new conditions that demand commercial viability. Old networks are taking on unexpected new functions as the overall calculus of political survival undergoes major shifts.

Changes in sub-Saharan Africa are also giving new commercial advantages to smaller South African firms that are less able to compete with foreign rivals in more crowded markets, especially firms that enjoyed market protection from apartheid-era politicians or security forces in the interest of national security. As with Soviet Communist Party bureaucrats, these domestic security and political organizations lost their old functions but retained their political connections. In light of concerns that reforms in neighboring states might attract larger, more competitive firms from Japan, North America, and Europe, Southern Africa has become Johannesburg's "*Lebensraum*" (realm), explained a South African businessman. "South African firms want to conquer it before anyone else does and before they themselves move in to more competitive markets."[39] A South African mining executive has referred to South Africa's "near abroad," likening South African business relations with neighboring weak states to Russia's claims of special privilege in its relations with former Soviet republics.[40]

South Africa's special relationship with the rest of the continent puts South African firms in a good position to act as intermediaries for other private investors. Some South African businesspeople comment that "we know the Africans," meaning they recognize and deal with the informal political demands that win contracts or lead to successful bids for a privatized enterprise in a weak state. This harmony of interests with rulers of weak states facing early stages of reform enables politically astute and well-connected firms to profit from the weak-state political vulnerability that deters most other investors. They become integral to rulers' internal strategies to control commerce, a partnership that bestows monopoly control upon the lucky partner. Commercial partners are also well situated to profit from rulers' manipulation of the perquisites of sovereignty to protect the favored partnership at the expense of rivals.

Sectoral strengths of the smaller South African businesses that evaded sanctions, especially in mining and infrastructure, fit well with creditor and weak-state ruler interest in radical privatization. Mining firms that build enclave operations are better able to cope with poor infrastructure and low levels of state services than are other operations and are more adept at providing their own services, including security. The cases in this book show that the presence of these firms, and especially their propensity to take over vital state functions, accords well with policies designed to take bureaucratic tasks away from of hopelessly corrupt state officials.

Some South African politicians are also eagerly promoting the smaller mining firms. They, along with creditors, are concerned that the three large mining conglomerates that provide 80 percent of the Johannesburg stock market's capitalization are stifling competition.[41] Populist politicians point to the concentration of economic power in a few hands. Smaller firms, which creditors see as more enterprising and politicians regard as diluting the dominance of established firms, are more likely to have roots in clandestine Cold War networks, since their small size made them more adept at concealing operations. South Africa's new rulers have little choice but to support these firms to help boost South African exports and help raise South African employment and standards of living while limiting state spending. Voters were promised greater economic equality in 1994 at the same time that politicians professed respect for less regulated markets as a guarantee to attract creditors and foreign investors.[42]

COMMERCIALIZING SOUTH AFRICA'S REGIONAL SECURITY NETWORKS

Recent pressure from South Africa's creditors to privatize state-owned firms in utilities and manufacturing has also helped to promote the expansion of South African firms into neighboring African states. In South Africa, privatization ends direct government financial and political support of old state-owned firms, which in some cases forces them to build on old clandestine ties to weather the competitive pressure of the global economy. Sudden exposure to outside competition forces those firms to turn to smaller firms that had clandestine ties with weak-state rulers. The smaller firms give their more established partners privileged access to weak-state rulers who desperately need capital and are willing to make deals with less efficient firms, provided these firms are willing to help shift the local political balance in the weak-state ruler's favor. For example, Eskom, the state-run electrical utility, has been targeted for privatization. Meanwhile, its managers envision expansion into very difficult investment environments as far north as Congo as the key to reducing reliance on inefficient South African facilities that were justified as vital to national security during sanctions.[43]

State-owned utilities and infrastructure in South Africa have enjoyed a number of advantages over their state-run counterparts in weak states. A Total National Strategy of the apartheid government in the early 1980s required that state-run firms serve a national interest in defending the white minority from popular challenges and international sanctions while contributing to national wealth. In contrast, rulers of weak states built state-owned firms with Cold War patronage to provide payouts to political clients at state expense. Thus, privatized South African firms are adept at pursuing interests based on profit and long-term competitiveness to a degree unparalleled in Africa.[44]

Privatization in South Africa also takes place in a more informal setting. South Africa's new rulers must learn how to dismantle the old regime's security establishment now that the task of defending apartheid has ended. Elements of security networks supported front companies and directly performed tasks that now have commercial applications. This is especially true among engineering, arms, transportation, and military service (mercenary) firms that have roots in South Africa's military units and clandestine sanctions-busting efforts. Politicians once gave these state-associated enterprises independence of action, including tacit official permission to ally with criminal operations in the interest of greater strategic aims—which, in turn, gave politicians a cover with which to plausibly deny involvement in operations they authorized. The resulting commercial networks are adept at operating and profiting in difficult circumstances that deter competitors. Similar to the forays of the People's Liberation Army into profitable commercial ventures in China, South Africa's current rulers promote private efforts by units that formerly served state security to contribute to national wealth.[45]

For example, Armscor, once a state-run enterprise designed to procure weapons in violation of sanctions, has spun off numerous private firms to trade in global markets. Facing competition from abroad and under pressure from creditors to privatize at home, Armscor created Denel, a private firm, in 1992. Denel sold arms valued at $127.5 million abroad in 1992 and by 1995 had grossed $415 million from foreign arms sales.[46] The firm has supplied armored personnel carriers to UN forces in former Yugoslavia and elsewhere. Eager to sell merchandise, Denel used Armscor's apartheid-era ties to sell weapons to Lebanese armies and to the Rwandan government prior to the 1994 massacre.[47] Other apartheid-era connections have translated into commercial advantages for Denel. The firm's Rooivalk attack helicopter, for example, adapted the versatile and easily maintained Soviet Mi-8 design, incorporating it into an even more easily maintained, inexpensive craft. Recognizing the commercial advantage of this Cold War strategy, Armscor executive André Buys has said, "We can maintain and upgrade Soviet equipment, possibly in cooperation with Russia, and we are looking at this business."[48] As we will see in the Sierra Leone case in Chapter 4, South Africa's familiarity with Soviet weapons facilitated service and supply arrangements among former Soviet technicians, pilots, arms manufacturers, and South African firms.

Postapartheid South African firms are also benefiting from heavy regional dependence on South African–run utility and transportation infrastructure. Official policy during the Cold War stressed integrating regional telecommunications, electricity grids, and railroads into a South African–run system to promote economic dependence on South Africa by neighboring states. Despite hostile rhetoric, Zambia, Zimbabwe, Botswana, Congo, Malawi, and Mozambique routed over 80 percent of their foreign trade through South Africa's railroads and ports.[49] This translates today into what an analyst of South Africa called a "gateway to the continent. . . . Its transport and energy systems will play a crucial role in the development of sub-Saharan Africa" and will be valued as "knowledgeable intermediaries" by other foreign investors.[50]

Postapartheid rulers in South Africa have continued to support this dependence as a unique commercial advantage. Vice President Thabo Mbeki has urged South African energy conglomerates, including state-owned utilities in the process of privatization, to bid on African projects and privatizations to "support South Africa's position in the world."[51] Eskom, the electrical utility that is in the midst of privatization, for example, generates half of the electricity consumed in sub-Saharan Africa.[52] An improved global position for South African business also provides security at home. The Mandela government has acknowledged that stable neighbors with growing economies are less likely to send massive waves of refugees to South Africa, which had to deal with 300,000 illegal migrants in 1994 alone.[53]

Private enterprise—including firms that were part of the old security establishment—might provide work for some of the estimated 55 percent of all black South Africans not in the wage sector of the economy in 1992.[54] This additional employment would help South Africa's politicians address a key political demand of those who put them in power.[55] Meanwhile, massive cutbacks under the apartheid-era regime between 1990 and 1994 eliminated about 90,000 (about half of the total) defense-related jobs and cut military spending by 44 percent. Officials currently plan to integrate 20,000 African National Congress fighters and 10,000 Pan African Congress fighters into a reduced military.[56] South Africa's rulers still must be concerned about the capacity of armed unemployed men to challenge their authority, although that group poses nowhere near the threat strongmen represent to weak-state rulers. The current regime has called on commanders of the old 32 Buffalo Battalion, which waged anti-insurgency warfare in Angola and Namibia in the 1980s, to confront and disarm Self-Defense Units. These units are made up of youths in urban areas—the "comrades" of the townships—who have grown impatient with the pace of reform, the regime's support for the country's business establishment, and the lack of economic redistribution. Some of these informal paramilitary units grew powerful and autonomous enough to directly challenge local authorities.[57]

Consequently, politicians have weakly opposed redeploying military units as private mine clearance experts, military medical service units, riot control advisers, border patrols, surveillance and intelligence services, and disaster relief firms. All of these operations are ideally suited for taking over tasks from vulnerable regimes in weak states that are under pressure to privatize state services. The Denel consortium, for example, includes firms that haul cargo (TFM), build roads and bridges (OMC Engineering), and provide communications (Grinel). A Denel subsidiary (Mechchem Consultants) removes the mines another subsidiary (Naschem) manufactures. Most of these private firms provide management positions for retired military officers who can use personal connections both in South Africa and from Cold War operations abroad to aggressively seek new business opportunities. This arms industry, which provides 4 percent of South Africa's industrial jobs, hosted the country's first international military trade show in 1994, which featured private South African military service firms.[58] Denel subsidiaries such as Kentron (electronics), Lyttleton Ingenieurswerke (artillery), Asmera and Auitronic (cluster bombs), Routech Radar, Grinaker Avitronics (retrofitting attack helicopters), and Aerotek and Airconcor (avionics) were highlighted on the program.

This aggressive export policy gives South African firms an additional comparative advantage over foreign rivals. Few other firms with military experience in the region will invest in countries near South Africa that are plagued by pirates, smugglers, and warlords. Privatizing portions of South Africa's military creates firms designed for operations in such places. Firms with access to military expertise can also act as intermediaries and bring in associated firms to handle other tasks once security has been restored. Close ties between firms encouraged to trade abroad under the Total National Strategy and spin-offs from the security establishment enable South African investors to offer comprehensive services geared toward weak-state rulers' need to control rivals—by the use of violence, if necessary—while generating wealth and appeasing creditors.

Efforts to build commercial ties to strengthen and stabilize neighbors also serve South Africa's strategic interests. Defense Minister Joe Modise has commented that South Africa intends to create a "viable defense industry in the continent that would lower costs and decrease dependence on foreign suppliers, save foreign exchange and create jobs in our domestic economy."[59] Defense Secretary Pierre Steyn agreed that "as a tool of foreign policy, judiciously used arms sales can prove valuable economically and politically."[60] South Africa's pursuit of strategic aims thus becomes tied to an aggressive commercial offensive on the African continent that takes account of the interests and problems of weak states. Those who promote private enterprise as a solution to Africa's economic crisis interpret their proposal as integration of South African capital into global commerce. South African firms stake out markets and prosper, helping new rulers make peace with old regime elites and reassure other foreign investors. South African politicians also recognize constraints on their actions with regard to the country's export sector, even arms. "Politicians must realize," said former Armscor Chair Ron Haywood, "that they cannot make export too difficult. Our industrialists, engineers, and scientists are no longer locked into South Africa. They can go anywhere with their technology."[61]

Although it benefits old apartheid-era elites, the current government's strategy differs from efforts of weak states to build political authority through ties to private firms. In South Africa, an independent class of military-commercial operators controls sufficient resources to force governments to bargain with them to promote investment and generate revenue. The power agents of apartheid possess may ultimately force postapartheid regimes to include those groups in political bargains. Paradoxically, old agents of apartheid, although they constrain South Africa's rulers at home, may give those rulers the necessary tools to exercise commercial and strategic dominance in the region.

FIGHTING WAR AND THE GROWTH OF ANGOLA'S PRIVATE ECONOMY

Recent foreign investment in war-torn Angola has highlighted the commercial strategies and political alliances that give some South African firms a competitive advantage in weak states. In 1995, the Economist Intelligence Unit, for example, included Angola in the twenty-three African countries it felt were the world's thirty riskiest investment environments.[62] Firms that can address the political concerns of weak-state rulers, however, may regard such environments as virgin terrain that is filled with unexploited resources. High costs of production, collapsing infrastructure, civil disorder, and unruly and demanding local officials require a special kind of organization among firms willing to deal with such problems.

The South African firm Executive Outcomes and the companies that work with it illustrate the ease of conversion from apartheid state agents to private allies of weak-state rulers. The firm highlights the techniques and alliances that give some companies a competitive advantage in doing business in weak states. Executive Outcomes has supplied "security specialists," a euphemism for a private military force, for state officials and private-firm clients in Angola, Sierra Leone, and several other countries.[63] The approximately 2,000 men who work for Executive Outcomes come from demobilized South African military units such as 32 Buffalo Battalion, Koevoet, Recce squadrons, and the Civil Cooperation Bureau. Many conducted anti-insurgency, surveillance, and bush warfare both abroad and inside South Africa.

These men who are now a political liability for South Africa's elected government, are seeking their own fortunes as South Africa's military shrinks and is assigned new tasks. Some are selling their military, technical, and organizational expertise; others are translating personal connections to, or experience in, apartheid-era clandestine commercial operations into new businesses. Some anti-insurgency units, for example, illicitly sold ivory in the 1980s to help finance the arms purchases and operations of Uniõ Nacional para a Independencia Total do Angola (UNITA) rebels in Angola.[64] These political and commercial connections also help individuals start new commercial operations.

Business and personal concerns within South Africa are also creating new commercial opportunities. A postapartheid crime wave boosted the number of registered security firms in South Africa from 525 in 1991 to 3,500 in 1995; the firms employed 200,000 people and were growing at a rate of 30 percent annually.[65] This domestic private security sector serves as a reservoir for contract workers and also helps to maintain some continuity of organization among apartheid-era armed units. This is true not only of former government units but also of Inkatha units, some of which have joined the foreign and domestic private security industry.[66]

As a special operations expert, Executive Outcomes' head, Eeban Barlow, helped to organize long-range reconnaissance for 32 Buffalo Battalion, assisting South Africa's Cold War allies in UNITA in the rebellion in Angola. His job included contact with front companies used to hide supply routes to covert operations. Executive Outcomes now operates within a network of these and other companies spun off from previous operations; the firms specialize in oil drilling, arms sales, arms refurbishment, diamond mining, transportation, engineering, and land mine detection and clearance. Executive Outcomes associates have ties with many firms that share business contacts and financial resources (Box 2.1). The collapse of Soviet and Cuban support for the Angolan regime, the end of official South African support for UNITA—on whose behalf many Executive Outcomes employees once fought—and Barlow's exit from the military left Barlow free to sell his military

Figure 2.1   Executive Outcomes' Reported Associates

Executive Outcomes (Pretoria) has ties to numerous companies, re-
    ceives financial backing from British and Canadian companies as-
    sociated with *Branch Energy* (partially owned by *Diamond-
    works*), and is listed on the Vancouver stock exchange.
Branch Mining (Sierra Leone subsidiary of Branch Energy) holds
    mining licenses in Kono District. Press reports disclose that
    Branch Energy owns 60 percent, the Sierra Leone government
    holds 30 percent, and private investors own 10 percent of those li-
    censes. Branch energy also operates in Angola (the Luarica and
    Alta Kwanza concessions) and reportedly in northern Uganda
    (Kaabong). It holds shares in *Heritage Oil,* which has holdings in
    Uganda and Angola.
Saracen International (South Africa) is a security firm that has Execu-
    tive Outcomes and Portuguese investors. The firm reportedly
    guards mine sites in Angola and northern Uganda. Kaleb Akand-
    wanaho, the half brother of Ugandan president Museveni and
    commander of an army offensive against rebels, holds shares in
    Saracen Uganda.
Afro Mineiro (Angola) mines diamonds with Executive Outcomes pro-
    tection. Executive Outcomes and Angolan partners hold stakes.
Advance Systems Communications, Ltd. (UK) has Executive Out-
    comes as its company agent in Africa.
Aqua Nova drills for water in Zambia. Executive Outcomes holds a
    majority stake.
Double A Designs (South Africa) is an engineering firm with majority
    Executive Outcomes backing.
Life Guard (Sierra Leone), a security firm under Executive Outcomes
    management, guards Sierra Leone diamond mines.
Teleservices (Angola) is a mine security service with significant Execu-
    tive Outcomes links.
Mechchem (South Africa) is a Denel–Executive Outcomes mine re-
    moval service that bids on UN contracts to demine roads in Angola.
Ibis Air, Ltd. provides air services for Executive Outcomes operations
    in Sierra Leone and Angola. The firm operates out of a facility
    provided by *Simera,* an aviation affiliate of the South African
    arms firm *Denel.*
Falconer Systems provides logistical support and services to non-
    government organizations.
Westair leased planes to fly Executive Outcomes prisoners out of An-
    gola and flew Executive Outcomes personnel in to seize Angola's
    Sonongol oil fields.
Wrangal Medical (South Africa) provides military field hospitals to
    Mozambique's and Angola's governments.
Bridge International is an engineering firm with shared Executive Out-
    comes–Angola backing.
Stuart Mills is a mine removal service associated with Executive
    Outcomes.

Continues

Figure 2.1   Continued

Sources: Jim Hooper, "Sierra Leone—the War Continues," *Jane's Intelligence Review,* Jan. 1996; Al J. Venter, "Gunships for Hire," *Flight International,* 21 Aug. 1996; "Sierra Leone: No Soldier Saviors," *Africa Confidential,* 6 Oct. 1995; Human Rights Watch Arms Project, "Angola Between War and Peace," 8:1 Feb. 1996; Herb Howe, "South Africa's 9-1-1 Force," *Armed Forces Journal* 134:3 Nov. 1996, 38–39; "New Takeoff in Exploration," *Africa Energy and Mining,* 22 Jan. 1997; Talif Deen, "Mercenaries 'Capitalise' on Mineral Resources," *Jane's Defense Weekly,* 13 Nov. 1996, 5; Chris Gordon, "Mercenaries Grab Gems," *Business Mail,* 9 May 1997; and interviews with a London-based industry analyst, two South African–based journalists, and Sierra Leone and U.S. sources. For a denial of some of these associations, see "Branch Energy Bursts into Africa," *New African,* June 1997, 32–33.

expertise and connections to both Angola's government and firms that do business with it, which he did in February 1993.

Executive Outcomes also offers its Angolan clients insights into UNITA tactics and operations, since the rebel group was its Cold War ally. By 1993, UNITA controlled an estimated $1 billion in annual earnings from gemstone exports.[67] Angola's government needed those revenues to finance its effort to rearm and to fight UNITA, an effort that cost an estimated $1 billion in 1995.[68]

Executive Outcomes' first assignment was to seize and guard Soyo oil installations, which had been under attack since a 1992 UN-brokered peace agreement collapsed. The assignment later included conquering and defending diamond mining areas in Cafunfo province and elsewhere near the Congo border where UNITA diamond traders did business with Congolese. The struggle to control this trade showed that other clandestine Cold War commercial networks had survived. As one part of an old network attacked former allies, the targets of that offensive mobilized Cold War Congolese intermediaries, fake aid organizations, and several air cargo companies through which U.S. arms flowed to UNITA in the 1980s.[69]

Executive Outcomes' conquest of Soyo oil installations benefited its Pretoria-based associate, Strategic Resources, a shareholder in Heritage Oil, which later received drilling rights in the Soyo area.[70] Other companies associated with Executive Outcomes, such as Saracen International, provide security for Heritage Oil. Associated firms took over operations after UN and U.S. pressure led Executive Outcomes to formally withdraw from Angola in January 1996. Transport and construction firms associated with Strategic Resources continue to provide logistical services to the Angolan regime and help to refurbish enterprises for privatization.

Other South African Cold War military ties to Angola have translated into business opportunities. A South African commission of inquiry, for example, uncovered an extensive air cargo network operating in southern Africa that had its origins in clandestine military operations.[71] During the 1980s, Recce squadrons and other security units set up a front company, Frama Intertrading, to market ivory and rhino horn clandestinely to help finance UNITA's operations; South African military officers later moved into private ivory and rhino horn trading. These operators found they could use their military expertise to sell antipoaching services to World Wildlife Federation officials eager to police wildlife poaching in southern Angola and Namibia.[72] Other Frama associates, set up to transport arms and wildlife products for UNITA, appear among bidders to provide services to the Angolan regime. These firms have also benefited from ivory cartel connections to Portuguese, Greek, Italian, and Taiwanese mafias, along with ties to other South African military units.[73]

Angola's rulers recruit these commercial operations not only for specific services but also to keep international trade routes under Angolan control to help the country manage resources and strongmen. This task also involved increasing and controlling the distribution of revenues from Angola's natural resources. Angola is sub-Saharan Africa's second-largest oil producer, generating about $800 million in oil revenues annually since 1993. Control over these resources helps the precarious Angolan regime fight UNITA. Market control helps to finance arms purchases, such as the April 1996 delivery of Russian Mi-17 and Mi-24 attack helicopters and Su-22 and MiG-23 fighter jets, which cost $350 million.[74] Although Angola's President Dos Santos lost access to Soviet arms on concessional terms in return for diplomatic support, he now benefits from the post-Soviet republics' eagerness to sell cheap weapons for quick cash or to barter. Likewise, Executive Outcomes and other firms contract out weapons maintenance duties to Russian and Ukrainian technicians at low cost. South African arms producers' Cold War strategy of copying Soviet designs facilitates these post–Cold War partnerships.

Russian arms exporters face pressure to sell weapons abroad, which provides incentives to create those partnerships. Estimates of the number of defense industry employees in Russia vary from 4 million to 9 million.[75] Russian President Boris Yeltsin has protected the defense industry and military associates who supported him in his showdown with the Russian Parliament in 1993. This protective stance and creditor pressure on Russia to boost export income to service a $90 billion foreign debt helped to ensure that arms exports would receive special favor in the 1995 Russian budget.[76] Even the poorer, hard-pressed former Soviet republics face intense versions of this pressure and incentives to sell weapons abroad.

South African (and post-Soviet) security firms and their associates have also helped the Angolan president rein in members of his regime. UNITA's stake in the Angolan diamond industry—estimated at between $300 million and $1.5 billion in annual revenues—had attracted the interest of presidential associates, especially as Dos Santos's capacity to reward allies has declined.[77] In a pattern common to many weak states, Dos Santos is plagued with strongmen "*garimpeiro* [wildcat miner] generals" who take advantage of chaos in mining areas to make their own deals with UNITA miners or conquer turf for themselves.[78] This activity does not directly aid rebels, but it can threaten Dos Santos's hold on power. If left uncontested, Angolan military units and the officers that head them could build their own political power bases, using revenue from diamond sales as patronage. This would undermine the military's incentives to defend the regime against UNITA attacks. Instead, the military's reaction to UNITA activities would reflect the separate interests of military units to retain their independent access to diamonds. In fact, enterprising generals may see rebel attacks as a chance for them to take direct control over diamonds for personal gain, which can also be done in collusion with rebels. Foreign mercenaries and associated mining companies can help the president deny to potential rivals that these resources exist. The most attractive foreign firm partners for a ruler such as Dos Santos are those willing to use private, profitable violence (those who control it are wealthy) against rogue military units and not just rebels. South African firms such as Executive Outcomes, with roots in military networks, are ideally suited to perform such tasks.

This situation also helps smaller firms grab market shares over globally more competitive rivals. The large, well-established diamond mining firm De Beers, for example, sits on the sidelines in Angola and Congo, abjuring direct involvement in violent local conflicts and less able than smaller firms to cut informal deals with insurgents or provide security services to beleaguered regimes. De Beers executives, who hold major investments across the globe, are sensitive to the image problems that would arise if other host regimes saw the firm directly meddling in an internal conflict. De Beers instead tries to recruit smaller firms—giving financial backing to some—to sell directly to its diamond marketing cartel, the Central Selling Organisation (CSO). Smaller firms find they are adept at operating in this niche, helping weak-state rulers (or insurgents) manage creditors and deal with internal political threats and also acting as the agents of larger firms in marketing resources from especially difficult investment environments such as Angola. Aggressive investors can also grab market shares, thereby threatening CSO market control, then sell to their larger rivals at a large profit. Other small firms help weak states repay loans to anxious creditors. The cases in this book reveal how these South African firms have played direct intermediary roles between weak-state regimes and outsiders.

Increasing numbers of small firms from Canada and Australia are also appearing in ventures in weak African states. Smaller firms adapt to local circumstances more easily than large firms in their bids to claim a greater market share. They team up more willingly with enterprises such as Executive Outcomes to provide stability, security, and infrastructure development for investments with terms that still help creditors to promote radical privatization and foreign investment. Indeed, the reluctance of larger firms to commit resources in states where regimes are at war with their own people means creditors have few options. Ultimately, those firms insinuate themselves into the political networks of regimes in weak states, as they take advantage of (and promote) changes in the global mining (particularly the diamond mining) industry. The presence of these investment opportunities that only the flexible, politically well connected (or accommodating) firm can exploit in the context of weak-state politics is crucial to this development.

Flexible newcomers also pioneer novel business arrangements to help their weak-state partners while reworking old practices. For example, holders of mining concessions have long circumvented state bureaucracies entirely by charging the services they perform against tax and royalty payments. This arrangement permits regimes to mortgage future production by trading future revenue for services up front;[79] it also helps vulnerable regimes finance mercenary services and arms purchases without building an autonomous revenue collection capacity. One South African firm, for example, allegedly offered the Angolan government a $1 billion line of credit that was mortgaged by future production, which helped Angola's ruler to choose that firm as a partner over a rival Swiss-owned competitor.[80]

Other firms have tried to claim benefits from dismantled and reshaped Cold War security networks in Angola and elsewhere. Some South African businesspeople have complained that U.S. pressure on the Angolan regime to end a contract with Executive Outcomes was an attempt to edge out South Africans in favor of a U.S. military training firm.[81] As with their South African rivals, Military Professional Resources, Inc. (MPRI) boasts a wealth of Cold War connections transferable to private business in places such as Angola. MPRI's board of directors includes retired U.S. military officers, and the company presented its bid to the Angolan government through a private firm run by Herman Cohen, former assistant secretary of state for Africa under President Bush.[82] MPRI's directors include a former director of the U.S. Defense Intelligence Agency.[83] MPRI has benefited from U.S. government concern about the stability of UN peace agreements in Angola amid reluctance to commit direct U.S. military or large-scale economic aid. But ulti-mately, MPRI is a poor partner for the Angolan regime; it needs U.S. State Department approval to import arms. The State Department also regulates MPRI's relations with Angola's military, thereby denying it the capacity to easily limit training to politically reliable units. This factor probably explains why Executive Outcomes, a firm much more able to use former Cold War connections to operate freely, remains in the coun-try under new names.

Angola is not an isolated case. Executive Outcomes plays a major role in the politics of Sierra Leone. Regional elites in Congo contest for access to similar alliances. Nigeria's politicians vie for control over more clandestine versions of these operations. Sovereign and nonsovereign rulers outside of Africa mobilize former Cold War networks for political and commercial gain. Afghanistan's "Pasha" Rashid Dostum for exam-ple, is growing rich and financing an army and a personal air force with taxes from trade with former Soviet republics in Central Asia. Repubska Srebska's (Serbian Bosnia's) Zeljko "Arkan" Raznatovic, wanted for bank robberies in Western Europe that he committed in the 1970s and 1980s, supports his Tigers militia with trade in oil, currency, and arms. Thai generals trade with Cambodia's Khmer Rouge. Burma's Khun Sa operates his drug trade through ten joint-venture front companies and holds a government contract to privatize Rangoon city bus services, ac-cording to U.S. authorities.[84]

TRANSNATIONAL NETWORKS AND POLITICAL CHOICE

The proliferation of alternative means to accumulate resources holds a powerful attraction for strongmen and for rulers who face internal secu-rity woes. Thus, the presence of associated networks can significantly in-fluence the political choices of rulers in modestly successful but strug-gling states. In Uganda, for example, President Yoweri Museveni has presided over about 6 percent annual growth since 1987, following sub-stantial economic deregulation and massive civil service layoffs. Al-though it is heavily dependent on external loans and grants, his regime increased domestic revenue collection by 800 percent from 1986 to 1995, albeit from a low base.[85] This would appear to indicate a recovery of ad-ministrative capacity along the lines reformers had predicted.

At the same time, Museveni's regime faces intractable insurgencies in Uganda's northern and western reaches. Some supporters of former President Obote (1980–1986) have teamed up with the Lord's Resis-tance Army (LRA), which was formed in 1987. This group, which is most active close to the border with Sudan, is believed to receive aid from Sudan's government in return for support against the Sudan People's Liberation Army (SPLA) insurgents north of the border. The LRA has no administrative capacity or committed mass following, so rather than build an organizational alternative to the central government, it attacks and destroys local bases of production. Its primary objectives are to loot local resources for the benefit of its members and to deny the Ugandan government the capacity to organize the local population to either oppose the LRA or provide revenues to the government.[86] The LRA's reliance on external sources of support further insulates it from the need to cultivate local support in exchange for revenues. This warlord organization fits well with Sudanese goals to retaliate against perceived Ugandan regime support for the SPLA without the need to spend much money or undertake the political risks of building an effective bureaucratic organization that could develop an autonomous capacity and eventually threaten Sudanese regime interests.

Museveni's regime also faces challenges from the West Nile Bank Front (WNBF), launched in May 1995 by Colonel Juma Oris, a senior officer in Idi Amin's regime in the 1970s; the WNBF also receives support from Sudan. Additionally, the Alliance of Democratic Forces (ADF) plagues the regime in the north and west. Made up primarily of unemployed youth, this group draws aid from ethnic Rwandan Hutu organizations, which are retaliating against Museveni for his support for their Tutsi rivals who took power in Rwanda in 1994. The ADF and the WNBF also drew support from Congo's President Mobutu, who regarded Museveni's association with Rwandan Tutsis as part of an anti-Mobutu regional coalition.

Faced with this considerable threat, an orthodox strategy for Uganda would entail boosting military capability to provide security to threatened people and territory. But because half of Uganda's budget comes from grants and loans, such a plan would require the assent of donors and creditors. The less costly strategy the regime employs relies on denying resources to insurgents. Thus the army creates "protection centers" in Uganda's north that separate local producers from insurgents.[87] This context of austerity, coupled with fears that a truly effective army will take power for itself, is well suited to groups such as Executive Outcomes, which can deny resources to adversaries and pay for them through their own commercial ventures.

Private South African military experts have played increasingly important roles in Museveni's management of internal threats. The president's half brother Kaleb Akandwanaho (whose nom de guerre is Salim Saleh), has been charged with managing military operations against insurgents. Accordingly, he is also a partner in the local subsidiary of Saracen, a South Africa–based security firm. Meanwhile, firms such as Branch Energy and Heritage Oil operate concessions in Uganda's north and east; Saleh is a director in the Branch Mining operation. Although it has not been proven in this case, the Sierra Leone case (Chapter 4) shows how concessions such as these can also perform as conduits for organizing arms shipments and training local irregular units in anti-insurgency warfare, in exchange for either resources or preferred access to other business ventures in the country.[88] As we will see in Chapter 4, other firms associated with these companies have a record of involvement in such operations in Sierra Leone. Regardless of its organization, Uganda's regime has clearly managed to build up its anti-insurgency capabilities by tapping into reconfigured South African (and Chinese and other) arms trade networks.[89]

Trends in Uganda are significant because foreigners tolerate the privatization of warfare and Museveni's reluctance to liberalize politics out of fear that without a strong ruler anarchy might return. Also, instability in neighboring Rwanda, Congo, and Sudan raises fears that this disorder might spread to Uganda. In contrast, donors suspended aid to Kenya in 1991 to force President Daniel arap Moi to accept multiparty elections. The difference in external responses to nonorthodox methods of exercising political authority lies in the more recent convergence of ruler and outsider interests in stability and foreign investment.

PRIVATIZING RELATIONS WITH WEAK STATES

Executive Outcomes and MPRI are examples of how officials in strong states and global development agencies shift their strategies to influence events in weak states in ways compatible with the militarization of commerce. A UN official in Sierra Leone, which also hosts an Executive Outcomes detachment, has said: "The idea of private armies helping to settle some of Africa's problems does have an appeal. No particular country will have to pay for the services, which forces some kind of hard thinking on regimes not noted for their clarity of mission."[90]

Troubled UN interventions in Somalia and Bosnia have left rulers of strong states and their military commanders wary of entanglements in conflicts that generate more domestic criticism than strategic benefit. It is better to tacitly support foreigners (if not one's fellow citizens) who will resolve crises of weak-state instability quietly, cheaply, effectively, and at their own risk. Even better is a plan in which the weak state that receives the "aid" pays for it itself by mortgaging resources to foreign firm partners.

South African and U.S. interest in private solutions to the Angola regime's security and fiscal crises is not unique. MPRI is also involved in the Bosnian war, helping the Clinton administration and supporters in the U.S. Congress to quietly arm Bosnian Muslims and Croats in contravention of European allies' wishes. As with Angola, direct U.S. military commitments to either side in that war would attract domestic and international criticism. MPRI is training Bosnian soldiers to provide a quiet conduit through which to ship arms paid for by Saudis to the Bosnian government.[91]

These cases modify conventional realist notions that officials in strong states prefer that all states exercise a monopoly over violence in the international system. Strong states' relations with weak states have often taken the form of informal influence through intermediaries, thus by-passing formal diplomatic channels. The U.S. government's failure to prosecute private financiers of Mozambique National Resistance Movement (RENAMO) guerrillas in the 1980s and its encouragement of private aid to Afghan guerrillas in their fight against Soviet troops did more than lay the seeds for post–Cold War conduct of strong state–weak state relations.[92] Recent research has uncovered elaborate ties between Italian politicians and mafia organizations that collaborated to prevent a Communist victory in Italian elections during the Cold War.[93] Central Intelligence Agency (CIA) ties to the ill-fated Bank of Credit and Commerce International (BCCI) during the 1980s are well documented.[94] According to U.S. congressional investigations, CIA head William Casey used BCCI connections to create holding companies, shell entities, and secret loans to support and finance Afghan resistance to Soviet invaders. Casey likely realized that his partners were trading drugs and weapons.[95]

What has changed since the end of the Cold War is the extent to which these private firms are filling in for direct strong-state action and financial backing in places conventional diplomacy has written off as irrelevant or hopelessly corrupt. The alternative has become tacit support for a weak-state politics that increasingly resembles warlord politics rather than conventional strategies for state building. This support also reflects concerns of strong states that clandestine, illicit, and unconventional commercial networks would be very difficult to regulate in the context of a total collapse of centralized state authority. Strong states prefer to have disruptive or threatening activities remain within at least the nominal influence of their own officials through mechanisms of the state system such as international agreements and conventions. Strong-state use—or tolerance—of privatized foreign policy in the post–Cold War era acknowledges the problems of institutionalizing relations between dissimilar political units.

These actors are becoming more closely enmeshed in the exercise of political authority. Weak-state rulers who are no longer dependent on rigid alliances with strong states are showing considerable capacity to shape and benefit from these ties. Control over commerce rather than territory has become the key demarcator of political power. Partnerships with Executive Outcomes show how weak-state rulers have willingly relinquished direct control over coercion, abandoning attempts to impose a comprehensive internal order or directly mobilizing citizens and civil servants. Without this internal order no civil society exists unless groups can address state power by force. Further, a dialogue with society is unlikely to develop, since the purpose of governance is no longer to provide a foundation for order and security. Strong-state and creditor officials acquiesce in this new arrangement when a weak-state ruler's crisis management appears to avoid total state dissolution without direct financial or political costs for them.

For the rulers of weak states, continued global recognition of their regimes' sovereignty gives them a critical tool with which to prevail over domestic challengers. Sovereign rulers' advantage over rivals lies in their capacity to manipulate sovereignty to strengthen and regularize even clandestine ties to outsiders. Critical for them, the language of sovereignty remains absolute, even if it strays from reality. The viability of the weak-state rulers' strategy of manipulating commercial networks in lieu of state institutions rests on the sovereign's legal moorings and their capacity to exploit ambiguities between a legal and a more sociological meaning. These rulers benefit from the fact that no intermediate status for weak states exists in international law; no colonial or mandate status awaits the realm of a ruler who strays from globally recognized norms. In fact, in three of the four cases that follow, officials of strong states defer action, hoping that preserving existing regimes will avoid chaos and eventually produce reliable governments that have the will and the capacity to carry out international obligations.

These coinciding interests empower organizations such as Executive Outcomes. The consequence is variation among political units in global society. The words of Hedley Bull have come to pass:

> If modern states were to come to share their authority over citizens, and their ability to command their loyalties, on the one hand with regional and world authorities, and on the other hand with sub-state and sub-national authority, to such an extent that the concept of sovereignty ceased to be applicable, then a neo-medieval form of universal political authority might be said to have emerged.[96]

The new form of universal authority for contemporary rulers of weak states is not a medieval church or an emperor. Instead, it is a global market to whose imperatives they are exposed much more than their strong-state colleagues. The cases that follow strongly suggest that this global economic change may in fact more strongly influence the reconfiguration of weak-state politics than do the interests and policies of those who seek to force rulers to conform to a particular set of standards. For example, rulers in fairly bureaucratized states such as Côte d'Ivoire and in weaker ones such as Guinea, which borders Liberia, openly acknowledge that the main threat to their regimes comes from the influence of the Liberian syndicates and commerce they control into their own political networks.[97]

Sovereignty remains important, but its actual exercise is increasingly relative to the new strategies rulers of weak states devise to assert their political authority. The closer examination in Chapter 3 of the collapse of Liberia's Cold War patron-client politics and the rise of competing nonsovereign strongmen illustrates this point. That case also stands as a reference point from which to compare the workings of nonsovereign political units—which the casual observer is most likely to label warlords—with the strategies of sovereign rulers who face similar conditions.

NOTES

1. Marguerite Michaels, "Retreat from Africa," *Foreign Affairs* 72:1 (Jan.–Feb. 1993), 95.

2. Stephen Jay Gould, *The Panda's Thumb: More Reflections in Natural History* (New York: W. W. Norton, 1980), 179–185.

3. Joshua Epstein and Robert Axtell, *Growing Artificial Societies: Social Science from the Bottom Up* (Cambridge: MIT Press, 1996).

4. Stephen Krasner, "Approaches to the State: Alternative Conceptions and Historical Dynamics," *Comparative Politics,* 16:2 (Jan. 1984), 242.

5. Fernand Braudel, *On History,* trans. Sarah Matthews (Chicago: University of Chicago Press, 1980), 93–97.

6. Barrington Moore, *Social Origins of Dictatorship and Democracy* (Boston: Beacon Press, 1966).

7. Herman Schwartz, *States Versus Markets: History, Geography and the Development of the International Political Economy* (New York: St. Martin's Press, 1994).

8. For a demonstration of this approach, see Aristide Zolberg, "Strategic Interactions and the Formation of Modern States: France and England," *International Social Science Journal* 32 (1980), 687–716.

9. Gerard Prunier, "The Great Lakes Crisis," *Current History* 96 (May 1997), 193–199.

10. Bruno Lautier, Claude de Miras, and Alain Morice, *L'État et l'informel* (Paris: Harmattan, 1991), esp. 152–203.

11. Observatoire Géopolitique des Drogues, *The Geopolitics of Drugs* (Boston: Northeastern University Press, 1996), 21.

12. U.S. Department of State, Bureau of International Narcotics and Law Enforcement, *International Narcotics Control Strategy Report, 1997* (Washington, D.C.: BINLEA, 1997), xliii–xliv.

13. World Bank, *World Debt Tables, 1996* (Washington, D.C.: World Bank, 1996), 17.

14. Michael Barrett-Brown and Pauline Tiffen, *Short-Changed: Africa and World Trade* (Boulder: Pluto Press, 1992), statistical appendix.

15. World Bank, *World Debt Tables, 1996,* 24.

16. Interview by the author, Grand Popo, Benin, 31 July 1994.
17. Quoted in Peter Beinart, "Out of Africa," *New Republic* 26 (Dec. 1994), 18.
18. Lynda Loxton, "Africa Takes Its Place on the Mining Map," *Mail and Guardian*, 9 (Feb. 1996).
19. Indra Wahab, "Structural Adjustment and Government Consumption: Sub-Saharan and Industrialized Countries Compared," in David Simon et al., *Structurally Adjusted Africa* (Boulder: Pluto Press, 1995), 193–194.
20. Interview by the author with creditor official, Alexandria, Va., 6 April 1996; World Bank, "Mali Public Expenditure Review," Report No. 13086, 1 June 1995.
21. World Bank, *Adjustment in Africa* (New York: Oxford University Press, 1994), 112–113.
22. World Bank, *Bureaucrats in Business* (Washington, D.C.: World Bank, 1995).
23. Robert Armstrong, *Ghana Country Assistance Review* (Washington, D.C.: World Bank, 1996); World Bank, Africa Regional Office, *Ghana 2000 and Beyond* (Washington, D.C.: World Bank, 1993); Claude Ake, "The New World Order: A View from Africa," in Hans Henrick-Holm and Gregory Srensen, eds., *Whose World Order? Uneven Globalization and the End of the Cold War* (Boulder: Westview, 1995), 19–42.
24. Observatoire Géopolitique des Drogues, *Geopolitics*, 195.
25. Mamadou Dia, "Indigenous Management Practices: Lessons for Africa's Management in the '90s," in Ismail Serageldin and June Taboroff, eds., *Culture and Development in Africa* (Washington, D.C.: World Bank, 1994), 171.
26. Bonnie Campbell, "Débats actuels sur la reconceptualisation de l'État par les organismes de financement multilatéraux et l'USAID," *Politique Africaine* 61 (March 1996), 18–28.
27. The Côte d'Ivoire model is described in World Bank, *World Development Report, 1994* (New York: Oxford University Press, 1994), 44–47; World Bank, "Côte d'Ivoire Private Sector Assessment," Report No. 14112, 1995; Gregory Ingram and Christine Kessides, "Infrastructure for Development," *Finance and Development* 31:3 (Sept. 1994), 18.
28. Armstrong, *Ghana*, 30.
29. John Karimu, *Government Budget and Economic and Financial Policies for the Fiscal Year, 1995/96* (Freetown: Government Printer, 30 June 1995), 11.
30. Charles Harvey, "Constraints on Sustained Recovery from Economic Disaster in Africa," in Charles Harvey, ed., *Constraints on the Success of Structural Adjustment Programmes in Africa* (London: Macmillan, 1996), 137.
31. "Bemba haut de GAMM," *La Lettre du Continent*, 22 Dec. 1994.
32. "Zaire: World Bank's Guarded Optimism," *Africa Economic Digest*, 7 Dec. 1994.
33. Maxwell Owusu, "Tradition and Transformation: Democracy and the Politics of Popular Power in Ghana," *Journal of Modern African Studies* 34:2 (June 1996), 307–343.
34. World Bank, *World Debt Tables, 1996*, Vol. 1, 17.
35. Bank of Sierra Leone, *BSL Bulletin* (Freetown: BSL Printer, April 1995), 68–69.
36. Interview by the author, Washington, D.C., 8 June 1996.
37. "Is the UK Pulling Out of Africa?" *Africa Economic Digest*, 28 Aug. 1995, 10–11.

38. International Monetary Fund, *International Financial Statistics* (Washington, D.C.: International Monetary Fund, 1996); Loxton "Africa Takes Its Place on the Mining Map."

39. Quoted in "Investing in Africa: A New Scramble," *Economist,* 12 Aug. 1995, 17.

40. Interview by the author with Durban-based mining executive, Denver, 29 March 1996.

41. Gavin Maasdorp, *Can South and Southern Africa Become Globally Competitive Economies?* (Basingstoke: Macmillan, 1996).

42. Patrick Bond, "Neoliberalism Comes to South Africa," *Multinational Monitor* 17:5 (May 1996), 14.

43. "SNEL: Small Rubs, Big Plans," *Africa Energy and Mining,* 17 Jan. 1996; "RSA Funding for Sounda," *Africa Energy and Mining,* 29 Nov. 1995.

44. On the Total National Strategy and internal economic policy, see William Minter, *Apartheid's Contras* (Johannesburg: Witwatersrand University Press, 1994), 37–39; Robert Price, *The Apartheid State in Crisis* (New York: Oxford University Press, 1991), 85–97.

45. Barry Naughton, *Growing Out of the Plan* (New York: Cambridge University Press, 1995).

46. Stefaans Brummer, "SA Embarrassment at UN Security Council," *Mail and Guardian,* 16 Feb. 1996; "Weapons for Sale," *Economist,* 29 July 1995, 31–32.

47. Government of South Africa, *Commission of Inquiry into Alleged Arms Transactions Between One Eli Wazan and Other Related Matters* (Cameron Commission), 15 June 1995.

48. *Defense News,* April 1994.

49. Adebayo Adedeji, *South Africa and Africa: Within or Apart?* (Atlantic Highlands, N.J.: Zed, 1996).

50. Tony Hawkins, *The New South Africa: Business Prospects and Corporate Strategies* (London: Economist Intelligence Unit, 1994), v–vi.

51. "The Urge to Demerge," *Economist,* 12 Aug. 1995, 18.

52. Robert Tyerman and Bill Jamieson, "The Scramble for Africa," *Daily Telegraph,* 5 May 1996.

53. Jide Owoeye, "What Can Africa Expect from a Post-Apartheid South Africa?" *Africa Insight,* 24:1 (1994), 44–46; Xavier Carim, "Illegal Migration to South Africa," *Africa Insight* 25:4 (1995), 221–223.

54. Stephen Gelb, "South Africa's Post-Apartheid Political Economy," in Larry Swatuck and David Black, eds., *Bridging the Rift: The New South Africa in Africa* (Boulder: Westview, 1997), 46.

55. "Super-Charged Mbeki," *Africa Confidential,* 1 March 1996.

56. Ravinder Pal Singh and Pieter Wezeman, "South Africa's Arms Production and Exports," *SIPRI Yearbook, 1995* (New York: Oxford University Press, 1996), 576; Gary Kynoch, "The 'Transformation' of the South African Military," *Journal of Modern African Studies* 34:3 (Sept. 1996), 441–457.

57. Roger Matthews, "South Africa Calls Up Troops for War on Crime," *Financial Times,* 31 Aug. 1996.

58. Economist Intelligence Unit, *South Africa: Country Profile, 1995* (London: Economist Intelligence Unit, 1996), 30; Simon Segal, "The Double Edged Sword of Privatisation," *Mail and Guardian,* 23 Feb. 1996.

59. "Uniting Africa Through Defense," *Jane's Defense Weekly,* 29 April 1995, 40–41; see also *Jane's Defense Weekly,* 15 July 1995, 18.

60. "Uniting Africa," 40.

61. "Interview with Ron Haywood," *Jane's Defense Weekly,* 29 May 1996, 32.

62. Economist Intelligence Unit, *F and T Risk Advisor* (London: Economist Intelligence Unit, 1995).

63. Jeremy Harding, "The Mercenary Business: 'Executive Outcomes,'" *Review of African Political Economy,* 24:71 (March 1997), 87–97.

64. Ross Reeve and Stephen Ellis, "An Insider's Account of the South African Security Forces' Role in the Ivory Trade," *Journal of Contemporary African Studies* 13:2 (1995), 213–233; Government of South Africa, *Commission of Inquiry into the Alleged Trade in Ivory and Rhinoceros Horn in South Africa* (Kumleben Commission) (Pretoria: Government of South Africa, Jan. 1996). (Available at www.polity.org.za:70/00/govdocs.)

65. Sudarsan Raghaven, "Africa Puts Its Money Where Its Fear Is," *Business Weekly,* 15 July 1996, 52.

66. Interview with South African National Defense Force officer, Washington, D.C., 14 Sept. 1996.

67. Al J. Venter, "Mercenaries Fuel Next Round in Angolan Civil War," *International Defense Review* 29:3 (March 1996), 65; Al J. Venter, "Executive Outcomes' Mercs and MiGs Turn Tide in Angola," *Soldier of Fortune* (Jan. 1996), 31–76.

68. John J. Ingles le-Nobel, "Former Belligerents Ready for Renewed Conflict in Angola," *Jane's Defense Weekly,* 3 April 1996, 18.

69. François Misser and Olivier Vallée, *Les Gemmocraties: l'economie politique du Diamant Africain* (Paris: Desclée de Brouwer, 1997); Filip De Boeck, "Postcolonialism, Power and Identity: Local and Global Perspectives from Zaire," in Richard Werbner and Terence Ranger, eds., *Postcolonial Identities in Africa* (Atlantic Highlands, N.J.: Zed Books, 1996), 76–80.

70. Human Rights Watch Arms Project, "Angola."

71. Government of South Africa, Kumleben Commission.

72. Interview by the author with UNITA representative, Washington, D.C., 7 June 1996.

73. Reeve and Ellis, "An Insider's Account," 213–233.

74. Venter, "Mercenaries Fuel Next Round," 66.

75. On the high end, see Andrei Shoumikhin, "The Weapon Stockpiles," *Comparative Strategy* 14:2 (1995), 211. For the low end, see Igor Khripunov, "Conventional Weapons Transfers," *Comparative Strategy* 14:4 (1995), 455.

76. Khripunov, "Conventional Weapons Transfers," 453–466.

77. Low end: Suzanne Daley, "Foes in Angola Still at Odds over Diamonds," *New York Times,* 15 Sept. 1995; intermediate: "Angola: Congo Guns," *Africa Confidential,* 6 June 1997, 8; high estimate: Venter, "Mercenaries Fuel Next Round," 64.

78. "Angola: Diamond Buildup for SPE," *Africa Energy and Mining,* 27 March 1996.

79. "Angola: The Big Diamond Battle," *Africa Energy and Mining,* 4 Oct. 1995.

80. "Angola: Á la recherche de diamants et d'or," *Lettre du Continent,* 18 Jan. 1996.

81. Interview by the author, Durban businessman, 14 April 1996.

82. "Securite priveé," *Lettre du Continent,* 14 March 1996.

83. "Herman Cohen," *Lettre du Continent,* 28 March 1996.

84. Susan Woodward, *Balkan Tragedy: Chaos and Dissolution After the Cold War* (Washington, D.C.: Brookings Institute, 1995), 254; Global Witness,

Thai–Khmer Rouge Links and the Illegal Trade in Cambodia's Timber (London: Global Witness, 1996); F. Guilbert, "Les dangers de l'homo-economicus Khmer Rouge," *Défense Nationale* 50 (1993), 133–150.

85. Tarsis Kabwegyere, *The Politics of State Formation and Destruction in Uganda* (Kampala: Fountain, 1996).

86. Gerard Prunier, "Le Soudan au centre d'une guerre régionale," *Le Monde-Diplomatique,* Feb. 1997; "Uganda's Three-Sided War of Attrition," *Jane's Defense Weekly,* 25 Sept. 1996, 41–43.

87. "Uganda Raises Defense Spending to Take on Rebels," *Jane's Defense Weekly,* 14 Aug. 1996, 15; Wyger Wentholt, "Protected Villages, Don't Work," *New African,* April 1997, 26.

88. "Not Quite the Fifth Cavalry," *Indian Ocean Newsletter,* 8 Feb. 1997.

89. Crespo Sebunya, "South Africa Arms Uganda," *New African,* May 1997, 32.

90. "We're the Good Guys These Days," *Economist,* 29 July 1995, 32.

91. Eric Schmitt, "Retired American Troops to Aid Bosnian Army in Combat Skills," *New York Times,* 15 Jan. 1996; John Barham, "US and EU Split over Bosnian Recruitment," *Financial Times,* 15 March 1996; Daniel Nelson, "Arms Flow Threatens Balkan Peace," *Defense News,* 25 March 1996.

92. Kathi Austin, *Invisible Crimes: U.S. Private Intervention in the War in Mozambique* (Washington, D.C.: Africa Policy Information Center, 1994).

93. Alexander Stille, *Excellent Cadavers: The Mafia and the Death of the First Italian Republic* (New York: Pantheon, 1995).

94. Peter Truell and Larry Gurwin, *False Profits: The Inside Story of BCCI, the World's Most Corrupt Financial Empire* (New York: Houghton Mifflin, 1992); John Beatty, *The Outlaw Bank: A Wild Ride into the Secret Heart of BCCI* (New York: Random House, 1993).

95. John Kerry, "Trip to Thailand, Cambodia and Vietnam," report to the Committee on Foreign Relations, U.S. Senate, Washington, D.C., 30 Sept. 1992.

96. Hedley Bull, *The Anarchical Society: A Study of Order in World Politics* (New York: Columbia University Press, 1977), 254–255.

97. "L'unité nationale doit être plus forte," *Horoya,* 16 April 1996; "Charles Taylor acune frontière," *Le Jour,* 24 March 1996.

3

▼ ▼ ▼ ▼ ▼

THE ORGANIZATION
OF WARLORD POLITICS
IN LIBERIA

I want to make Liberia the Hong Kong of West Africa.
—Charles Taylor[1]

Chieftains should always aim high. Focus upon opportunities, rather
than on problems.
—Attila the Hun[2]

The way we think about Liberia is strongly influenced by images of
chaos and random violence. War broke out on Christmas Eve 1989 when
a former government administrator, Charles Taylor, led an invasion
force of 150 troops into Nimba County in the country's northeast region.
As many as 200,000 people, or about 8 percent of the population, died in
fighting or massacres, and more than half of the country's people became refugees.[3] Press reports featured disturbing images of AK-47-
toting child fighters "dressed gaudily in outlandish clothes and make-
up."[4] Some have called it "a war without purpose in a country without
identity" that was terrorized by "teenagers in NBA T-shirts."[5]

In fact, war in Liberia has followed a clear logic. Warlord pursuit of
commerce has been the critical variable in conflicts there. Strongmen
have used commerce to consolidate their political power within a coalition of interest among themselves, businesspeople, and local fighters.
Taylor, for example, has presided over commerce in gold and diamond
mining, timber, and rubber. Taylor's main rivals, who appeared after
1991, have based their authority on control of these and other markets.

The current warlord politics of Liberia demonstrates a new logic of
organization that has emerged against the background of shifting foreign investment and new commercial opportunities that appeared with
the end of the Cold War. As with the three cases discussed in Chapters 4,
5, and 6, strongmen rule through control of commerce rather than by

mobilizing a bureaucracy. They do not seek to infuse their political rule with universal claims to sponsor "development" or to defend any broad-based popular interest. Unlike the other three cases, Liberia's warlords assert their authority without the benefit of globally recognized sovereignty. This case demonstrates the similarities between warlordism and changing politics in weak states and also provides a reference point for measuring the impact of globally recognized sovereignty on rulers facing similar threats and opportunities.

Contrary to the common explanation, which traces warlord politics primarily to the collapse of state authority and capacity, I argue that warlord politics emerged as the result of a social coalition of enterprising strongmen, small-scale foreign commercial operators, and a small segment of the country's youth. Previous Liberian rulers influenced and changed elite social arrangements in ways that later, as external conditions changed, gave strongmen the political and financial autonomy to seek their own fortunes at the expense of a central authority. It is the choice of political alliances among elites that determines how Liberian politics makes the transition to warlordism within these constraints. Taken together, these variables help to explain why some governments continue to be structured on the principles of sovereignty and territoriality (even if they incorporate features of warlord politics), whereas in Liberia strongmen encounter relatively less difficulty in building their authority through more purely private means.

For analytical purposes, I separate the decline of old arrangements from the development of new ones. How did enterprising state officials in Liberia take advantage of new circumstances amid changing conditions in the 1980s in ways the sovereign ruler did not? Alternatively, why did the ruler's strategies to control those changes fail? By addressing these questions, I analyze some of the roots of the unorthodox social and political structures that have emerged in Liberia's warlord politics since 1990. I then proceed with the central question of the impact these arrangements have had on the nature and capabilities of the warlord political authorities and their effect on other weak states in Africa.

THE PATRIMONIAL BASIS
OF STRONGMAN INDEPENDENCE

On 12 April 1980, Master Sergeant Samuel K. Doe violently overthrew President William Tolbert (1971–1980). Doe's coup appeared to unseat an aristocracy dominated by Americo-Liberians, the descendants of about 300 families of American blacks who settled in Liberia in the nineteenth century. Doe decreed that thirteen top officials would be publicly executed on a Monrovian beach. The new president tapped public ire at elite privilege, and the executions entered popular culture as a cleansing "Liberian Beach Party."

Critics of the Doe regime noted that Doe appointed fellow Krahns, who made up less than 4 percent of Liberia's population, to key military and security units.[6] This favoritism weakened Doe's control over inherited civil servants and strongmen, who owed him no special loyalty but who staffed key positions in the state bureaucracy and controlled large portions of the country's economy. For that reason, Doe could not simply do away with America-Liberian influence. Doe especially needed to tap into the benefits of that group's commercial operations and convert that wealth into political resources. For its part, this elite group could not continue to profit without access to state power, and it used this mutual dependence to preserve its control over capital, overseas contacts, and local political standing and thus to take advantage of opportunities created by Doe's weak control of the state administration and the economy.

The public drama of the Liberian Beach Party was part of the twenty-eight-year-old Doe's effort to gain popular approval and was a desperate bid to eliminate powerful individuals from the old political establishment. But the strategy did not sweep away or bring to heel old political networks, which turned out to extend well beyond a small ethnic group. Doe tried hard to redirect the benefits of state power to new beneficiaries, but America-Liberians and other elites held onto their customary privilege, which included holding a stake in state power. In addition to the approximately 300 settler families, most of the elite came from assimilated "tribal" elites who had adopted America-Liberian culture over the years. Because of this diversity and the depth of local ties, this group was not the exclusive ethnic elite Doe claimed it was.

Doe's earlier career reflects this process of assimilation. Chosen for officer training, the young Doe, who was Krahn, was on a trajectory to join at least the margins of the country's elite alliance. Doe had other elite connections as well. His foster father was reported to be Gabriel Doe, who in 1978 married Carenia Pierre, the widow of former minister of finance and presidential relative Stephen Tolbert.[7]

The elite assimilation of new members reached beyond Liberia's borders. For example, Daisy Delafosse, the adopted daughter of Côte d'Ivoire's President Felix Houphouet-Boigny, had married President Tolbert's son Adolphus. Doe discovered too late the true power and reach of this elite family network after he had executed Tolbert's son at his 1980 Liberian Beach Party. Happy to avenge the death of their relative, Houphouet-Boigny and his son-in-law, President Blaise Compraore of Burkina Faso, gave Charles Taylor material aid for his 1989 invasion of Liberia.

Doe lacked an effective bureaucracy and faced an entrenched, self-interested political and economic elite that had global ties; he thus found he could not automatically acquire impressive wealth, fix Liberia's economic problems, build a popular following, or finance a military capable of defending his regime. His best short-term strategy was to limit the elite network's independence, foster its reliance on his control of economic opportunity, and recruit its members as surrogates to rule in lieu of an effective bureaucracy.

Driven by his vulnerabilities and in spite of the fact that he had executed their colleagues, Doe's first cabinet included four ministers from Tolbert's era, and others from that era were promoted into the top ranks of the civil service. Of twenty-two cabinet ministers listed in 1985, at least half had held bureaucratic positions in pre-Doe governments. Many were "pure" Americo-Liberian descendants of settler families, but a sizable portion had reached their positions through marriage or by adopting Americo-Liberian social behavior. Many used their connections to the capital to consolidate their deep roots in local politics.

Thus, whereas Doe had thought he could build an independent political base through populist appeals, he did gain temporary leverage by manipulating his sovereign powers as a state ruler to reward others for their cooperation and loyalty. This position allowed Doe to manipulate local factions and disputes while appearing to remain above the fray.

Doe made his political choices within the circumscribed context of Tolbert's earlier search for formulas that would increase his own power. When Tolbert's predecessor, William Tubman (1944–1971), died in office, he left a government apparatus and an aggressive business establishment dominated by a circle of relatives, other Americo-Liberian families, and more recent local assimilated tribal entrants into this "honorable" class.[8] These structures were the result of Tubman's efforts to expand economic activity and a political franchise in Liberia. As opportunities grew, he discovered that his small, underfunded bureaucracy—which had previously served a tiny, homogeneous community in coastal settlements—could no longer control the ambitions of regime allies. Tubman thus relied more heavily than his predecessors on the informal manipulation of state power to reward loyalty and punish disobedience and independence, which allowed loyal associates to take advantage of Tolbert's reforms that were designed to boost economic activity and further integrate Liberia into global markets.

For example, Tolbert and Tubman pressed to convert land tenure from communal to private holdings to boost agricultural exports and create new sources of government revenue.[9] The policy also disrupted local economies by throwing many farmers off their land, thus undermining the authority of the "traditional" rulers who customarily adjudicated land tenure issues. At the same time, the reforms created new, informal opportunities for already powerful elites to extend their economic and political reach, and a few powerful families gained control over large portions of Liberia. The twenty largest Liberian-owned logging concessions, for example, covered about 8,500 square miles, or 20 percent of the surface of Liberia, in 1977.[10] Amos Sawyer has estimated that by the time Doe rose to power, about 3,000 independent private rubber estates had been created, which turned local inhabitants into agricultural laborers dependent on those families for jobs; the estates covered about 15 percent of Liberia's territory.[11] In some cases, cooperative "traditional" authorities mobilized forced labor in return for payouts. This enhanced local role for enterprising elites translated into stronger local political authority vis-à-vis rivals and gave the elites a new opportunity to build ties to foreign purchasers of their products.

Such connections and resources gave the elite families the capacity to act against threats to their positions from both Tolbert and Doe. Further, neither leader could easily mobilize the economy to generate revenues to satisfy popular demands for services and opportunity beyond the reach of these elites. The fact that many privileged elites served as key state officials complicated efforts to redirect resources. Elites also maintained some commercial autonomy by tapping into a West Africa–wide network of ethnic Lebanese traders that gave those families independent access to foreign capital and markets independent of Doe's state. The decentralized, flexible, and transnational nature of the commercial organizations made them ideal partners to help elite families shift the basis of exploitation of economic opportunities. Commercial operations shifted away from heavy reliance on access to state power, and thus on presidential patronage, to establishing independent connections to global markets and regional nonstate actors. Although the elites still needed to maintain good relations with Monrovian authorities if they wanted to conduct business, they managed local production and overseas marketing themselves. This independence boosted their importance to Doe relative to his role in their enterprises, especially as global recession, economic mismanagement, and departing foreign investors led to a decline of formal (taxable) gross national product (GNP) from $461 million in 1979 to $321 million in 1983.[12]

Doe also inherited a population that expected more benefits from the national government. Migration to cities doubled Monrovia's population to 400,000 in the period 1963–1972,[13] in part as a consequence of relentless land grabs by beneficiaries of Tubman's and Tolbert's land reforms. Doe and his predecessors had difficulty drawing popular support, since strongmen regime favorites still maintained a tight grip over the resources needed to provide services and build effective bureaucracies to make economic development programs a success. Consequently, Doe saw less risk in appeasing incumbent elites than in launching any program that would increase the efficiency of state bureaucracies (and the autonomy of commercial strongmen) and thus endanger his political survival. Doe's creation of nine distinct security agencies—none effective enough to challenge him but all capable of interfering with rivals—was a response to the ever present threat of local strongmen to his regime.[14]

Doe also adapted his predecessor's short-term strategy of abjuring reliance on local business to raise the bulk of state revenues, relying instead on politically loyal foreign investors, multilateral creditors, and U.S. aid. Previous Liberian presidents had brought in foreign firms and aid organizations to collect revenues and provide social services that were distributed for political gain to fill in for missing bureaucratic capacity and a local revenue base. Firestone Tire and Rubber, a major investor in Liberia since 1926, had long assessed and collected taxes, provided housing for employees, managed local chiefs, and enforced local laws.[15] This arrangement allowed Doe's predecessors to finance elite privilege with foreign income while limiting political conflict.

Advertising an "open door" policy, Liberian governments invited foreign enclave investment on easy terms. In 1926, for example, Firestone leased a million acres for ninety-nine years at 6 cents an acre.[16] By 1970, Firestone and the Liberian Iron Mining Company (LIMCO) were providing 50 percent of government revenues. The year before Doe's 1980 coup, those two companies still supplied 52 percent of government revenues.[17] More important for the future of warlord politics in Liberia, this arrangement did not interfere with strongmen's independent sources of income from international trade, which they used to consolidate their political positions. Although conflict was avoided at that time, the situation allowed many of the strongmen to preserve their privilege at the expense of Doe's power at a later date.

In his quest for resources, Tolbert's only other immediate source of income lay in loans from multilateral creditors. But such loans came with conditions, one of which—the lifting of price subsidies on rice—clashed with popular expectations of a more responsive government. Continuing and highly visible corruption among top administrators and politicians further damaged Tolbert's popular credibility and led to riots over cuts in rice subsidies in 1979—in a context in which Daniel Tolbert, the president's cousin, owned the country's largest rice importing firm. Such reform undermined from below Tolbert's social control, which had already deteriorated because of elite land consolidations, alienation of peasants from the land, forced labor on plantations, and unmet popular expectations.

DOE'S STRATEGY OF INTERNATIONALIZATION

Under these circumstances of limited resources and weak social control, Doe took power in 1980. Without effective social control, Doe could not mobilize people or resources to develop significant autonomy for his regime or regulate inherited political arrangements, especially in the countryside. He needed to consolidate his own power and control existing political networks or at least limit the ambitions and autonomy of inherited strongmen.

Doe's public execution of high officials contributed to his short-term popular support. But he found that any viable long-term strategy for consolidating power included buying off his opposition, because Doe was surrounded not only by incumbent elites but by threatening associates as well. One example of the latter was his army commander and fellow coup plotter and "country man" (in contrast to the privileged Americo-Liberians), Thomas Quiwonkpa. Quiwonkpa hailed from Nimba County, as did many enlisted troops; Doe came from Grand Gedeh County, where Doe would later rally supporters to battle his Nimba County rivals. Quiwonkpa attracted a considerable following, commanding respect for his refusal to give up his Honda Civic for a luxury automobile or to move into a lavish home when many of his government colleagues had done so. Quiwonkpa fled in 1983 when Doe accused him of plotting a coup. Doe then largely disarmed the army and delegated security to several paramilitary units, a decision that would complicate his efforts to fend off warlord challenges in 1990.

Doe's lack of control (despite ridding himself of other rivals after half a dozen real and fabricated coup attempts) caused him to remark to U.S. Secretary of State George Schultz in 1987 that "corruption is everywhere. I don't know who to trust anymore."[18] Doe himself was at the center of much of that corruption. Nonetheless, his comment is important in underlining his incapacity to control the distribution of illicit resources. For example, a 1985 task force, set up to collect $150 million in arrears to government corporations, reported that most of the debtors were government officials—including two heads of Doe's security services.[19]

Doe responded to his political vulnerability and lack of control over resources by intensifying his manipulation of state power. Accordingly, he increased public service employment by 300 percent in a five-year period (1980–1985).[20] Personnel salaries accounted for 74 percent of budgeted spending in 1985, compared with 55 percent in 1979.[21] Beyond these additional budgeted expenses, Doe is thought to have diverted another $300 million for patronage payoffs and personal profit during the 1980s.[22] Doe's primary source of patronage funds was the state-owned corporations. Doe ran the Forestry Development Authority (FDA), which was responsible for collecting logging fees independent of the Ministry of Finance. (Doe's warlord successors would use the FDA in a similar fashion in the 1990s.) Doe used the Liberian Petroleum Refining Corporation (LPRC) to receive subsidized oil imports, which he sold for his own profit. About $100 million of Liberian Produce Marketing Corporation (LPMC) funds disappeared in the first half of the 1980s.[23] A U.S. government audit revealed that the LPMC diverted $16.5 million in U.S. food aid to Liberia for private profit.[24]

The significance of these arrangements goes beyond corruption alone. All of these essentially private arrangements had little to do with sustaining a Liberian state or serving some mission of development. Instead, they would prove to be well suited to warlord politics in the 1990s, as Doe's rivals incorporated clandestine commercial arrangements for their own purposes.

The results of this corruption were chaotic tax and investment policies and corresponding yearly negative growth of 3 percent during Doe's decade in power. Formal-sector export earnings declined as some larger firms pulled out of Liberia. Exports of rubber, iron ore, and timber fell from $484 million in 1980 to $362 million in 1983.[25] The Liberian American Mining Company (LAMCO) departed in 1989; the National Iron Ore Company joint venture left in 1985; and Bong Mining Company's German owners wound down operations in 1988. As it gutted iron ore exports, fiscal and administrative malfeasance tended to favor smaller, better-connected Americo-Liberian and ethnic Lebanese operations, which could use personal connections and capacity to conceal commerce in more portable and marketable resources such as timber, rubber, gold, and diamonds. Clandestine control over resources also became proportionally more important to Liberia's overall export economy. For example, one of Doe's security agencies reported that an Americo-Liberian senator from Maryland County in eastern Liberia used his connections to divert $500,000 from local government agencies to set up his own timber export business.[26]

Doe's own commercial dealings became increasingly clandestine and private to counter such activity. One such venture in 1987 with a U.S. firm that managed maritime registry fees involved setting up a credit scheme for small farmers; instead, the money was doled out to a select few.[27] In many of these transactions, Doe and his associates used Doe's position as head of state to manipulate differences between "official" and market exchange rates—effectively playing clandestine markets for personal gain—far better than could unruly strongmen in the provinces.

This clandestine commerce on all sides grew at the expense of more reliable and easily regulated larger foreign firms. It utilized personal connections to Lebanese and Ivorian operators to sell logs, for example, to small, fly-by-night buyers. This policy may have helped Doe weather short-term challenges, but in the long run it internationalized and decentralized trade in ways that made it difficult for any statelike authority to regulate in the future. Clandestine producers, who relied less on the ruler's permission and on his manipulation of state power to profit from international commerce, joined with regional traders who were less concerned with obtaining necessary documents, licenses, or tacit permission from a sovereign ruler to do business. Liberian logs, for example, attracted commercial intermediaries such as Thai generals who had experience marketing timber from Cambodia and firms attached to private armies in Lebanon.[28]

How was Doe to manage the urgent task of asserting his political authority over strongmen (not to mention satisfying his expensive personal tastes)? Doe discovered that the interest of officials in strong states could be translated into cash. Beyond his harsh anti-Soviet and anti-Libyan rhetoric during the 1980s, Doe learned U.S. officials would pay him $400 million for a vague commitment to multiparty elections, which helped him weather Liberia's declining value as a strategic asset as the Cold War wound down and U.S. interest in Liberia diminished. In 1984, Doe agreed to hold elections to choose a civilian regime. Doe's windfall aid came as the U.S. Congress and State Department were pressuring Philippine President Ferdinand Marcos to step aside and civilian regimes were taking power in Latin America. To Washington, Doe appeared to be a pliable candidate to lead an African state along a similar path toward multiparty democracy.

THE END OF DOE'S U.S. ALLIANCE

U.S. relations with Doe soured when he announced that he would stand in the October 1985 election. The indefatigable Doe found he could manipulate his "misbehavior" for profit. For example, he jailed Ellen Johnson-Sirleaf, a former finance minister and leading member of the opposition Liberian Action Party, after she declared that Liberia was ruled by "many idiots" in a speech she gave in the United States. Doe released her two weeks before the election and immediately collected $24 million in economic aid in return.[29] He could less easily justify his actions as a paragon of multiparty democracy to foreign backers after 1985, but he could still sell his anti-Libyan rhetoric. Influential Washington insiders such as North Carolina Senator Jesse Helms proved effective in blocking sanctions against Doe. Even after Doe's fraudulent claim of 51 percent of the vote in the 1985 election was widely known, Undersecretary of State for Africa Chester Crocker remarked that such a result was "virtually unheard of in the rest of Africa where incumbent rulers normally claim victories of 95 to 100 percent."[30]

Official U.S. support for Doe finally ended in 1988, with the failure of the Operating Expert (Opex) scheme. Doe's U.S. supporters had proposed that U.S. experts oversee Liberian government finances to reduce corruption and respond to congressional criticism of the misuse of U.S.

aid to Doe. The seventeen auditors identified many corrupt officials and practices among Doe's associates. But in the end, the state officials and other associates found numerous ways to get around new controls. The premature exit of Opex in late 1988 left Doe without his crucial foreign fiscal supporters, and he thus lost access to loans from the World Bank, the IMF, and the African Development Bank. U.S. aid ended with Doe's failure to pay $7 million in arrears on a military loan from Washington. Doe attempted to salvage something from the situation, calling for an "Operation Pay the United States" to coerce Liberian citizens to contribute pocket change to his regime's finances.

This cutoff of resources abruptly and fundamentally weakened Doe's regime. Doe's vulnerability lay in his incapacity to wield resources to counterbalance those controlled by Liberian strongmen or to finance patronage obligations to Liberia's state bureaucrats. The withdrawal of more established foreign corporate investors considerably weakened the customary Liberian fallback of contracting out state services and revenue collection to those firms to fill in for the country's weak-state capacity. One option for Doe was to consolidate his political authority and control strongmen by more directly interfering in their private commerce. Such a move, however, risked drawing a violent response from increasingly independent strongmen and would have required finding foreign backers who could fill in for the collapsing state bureaucracy, generate revenue from other sources, and help field a loyal military to discipline errant strongmen.

In spite of his problems, Doe was still useful to other outside partners. Timber operations under Doe's control through his FDA helped mobilize overseas aid for paramilitary forces. Israeli strategic interests in Liberia during the 1980s focused on concerns that illicit Liberian diamond traders were marketing stones through intermediaries that were serving warring factions in Lebanon's civil war. The Israeli government valued Doe's willingness to receive Israeli diplomats in exchange for military aid and commercial ties, thereby lessening Israel's diplomatic isolation.[31] The diplomatic ties were complemented by the establishment of a large private Israeli logging firm in Sinoe and Grand Gedeh Counties, areas that had hosted numerous small logging operations. This investment, which constituted West Africa's largest timber concession, helped Doe to survive collapsing state revenues, as it privately maintained local infrastructure of strategic concern to Doe such as communications facilities that could be used to coordinate paramilitary operations. The firm also reportedly provided financing and contractors to build a new Ministry of Defense building in Monrovia.[32]

More important, Doe allegedly received Israeli help to arm and train his paramilitary Executive Mansion Guard and Special Anti-Terrorist Unit soldiers at the concession site. This operation enabled Doe to turn over critical state functions such as military training and communications to a reliable foreign partner. Doe recruited other firms to help him manage internal security threats and funnel revenue directly to him. For example, a U.S. mining firm in northern Liberia allegedly provided training grounds and equipment for a loyal military commander charged with attacking critics of the regime during the 1985 multiparty election campaign. Charles Julue, a Doe loyalist who later played a role in Liberia's warlord politics, reportedly used mining company vehicles to transport troops and used company grounds and communications equipment to coordinate attacks on civilians.[33] The firm also helped to support the paramilitary group financially by hiring its members to act as mine security guards.

Doe's manner of mixing logging and mining endeavors with military operations attracted other firms that were interested in providing both. A critic in Britain's House of Commons claimed timber profits had encouraged a British arms producer to seek a logging concession in Liberia. This firm, which boasted ties to Margaret Thatcher's son, reportedly offered to take over a 330,000-acre concession to finance Doe's import of its automatic weapons and troop carriers in 1989.[34] At the same time, declining prices of weapons and the expansion of suppliers in the wake of the end of the Cold War not only made weapons more accessible to the cash-strapped Doe but also spawned new firms interested in trading surplus arms for natural resources.

Doe's flexible enforcement of laws attracted other businesses. Bankers discovered that Liberia's use of the U.S. dollar as its national currency offered opportunities for money laundering. Growth in this illicit business, even as the formal economy rapidly declined, may have been behind the increase in the number of Monrovia banks from six to fourteen during Doe's tenure.[35] This commercial setting, in turn, attracted speculative capital, loan sharks, and con artists who needed access to credit without the normal background checks and surveillance. Consequently, prewar Monrovia hosted flamboyant businesspeople, including a supposed Indian maharajah, Nigerian millionaires, and a Belgian count.

Doe attempted to disrupt economic activity in situations where he did not directly control the distribution of opportunities and to centralize those activities in which he could interest private foreign investors or overseas state intelligence services. Thus, Doe (like Mobutu) appeared to be equipping himself to weather the seemingly endless contraction of state bureaucracies, as most of those agencies were becoming less important to his exercise of power. Doe's political authority emanated from his capacity to manipulate the transnational commercial coalitions to balance and divide the power of strongmen who were doing the same thing but on a smaller and less coordinated scale. But as we will see,

Doe's critical vulnerability lay in his incapacity to control the regional trade networks in portable products such as logs and diamonds, even if he could temporarily deny those assets to rivals. Without market control, the opportunity always existed for enterprising, powerful, or physically distant strongmen to market goods for themselves and collect profits that were not contingent on loyalty to the president.

Nonetheless, the disintegration of Doe's state bureaucracies in Liberia was not a consequence of state collapse in the sense of incapacity and lack of organization in the face of overwhelming challenges. In fact, Doe proved surprisingly adept at seizing new internal and international opportunities to keep his regime afloat after the sudden cutoff of U.S. and multilateral creditor support. Doe's intentional destruction of his state bureaucracies questions conventional realist assertions that states are the *result* of responses to exogenous constraints. Doe avoided the constraints of his loss of strategic importance to the United States, his incapacity to fund or rely on the loyalty of bureaucracies, and outsiders' demands that he step aside for an elected regime. Instead, he shifted the basis of his political authority into new realms, translating global economic developments and foreign firms into political advantage. Doe faced virtually no criticism from abroad for his destruction of bureaucracies, since many creditor officials concerned with Liberia saw their decline as an opportunity to reduce deficits in Doe's formal state budget.[36] Doe's strategy also shifted Liberia's internal social and political arrangements in ways reformers, his commercial partners, and probably Doe himself had not intended but that became central to the imminent development of warlord politics.

First, Doe's strategy and the actions of his rivals created new, decentralized points of access to resources as Doe tried to manage a burdensome patron-client network on an empty treasury. Doe was likely convinced that if the strongmen were preoccupied and their trades sufficiently fragmented, they could not challenge his rule. The danger of this strategy of avoiding outright conflict with old regime clients and strongmen lay in its tendency to leave independent sources of wealth to those groups, which include Liberia's warlords. Paradoxically, these groups also represent the closest thing in Liberia's recent history to an autonomous business class, which is supposedly the foundation of a liberal notion of independent state capacity. But we find already that in Liberia, private economies are compatible with starkly different forms of political authority.

Second, many of those elites who collaborated in Doe's commercial rackets could still rely on old family ties and access to regional trade networks. This capacity gave even Doe's close associates the viable option of quickly withdrawing their support in times of crisis, a fact that explains why almost all of the major warlord figures in the 1990s have come from within Doe's political clique. Ultimately, the inability of Doe's bureaucracy to directly control economies and politics in the countryside undermined his otherwise successful efforts to control some—but not all—centers of accumulation with the help of foreigners.

Finally, the vast majority of Liberians who derived no profit from Doe's new arrangements had scant reason to support his regime. Most people, especially young men whom Doe could no longer patronize, were likely to look to local strongmen or even Doe's close associates, who employed them in their own rackets and clandestine operations. Strongmen-turned-warlords later recruited fighters from this group, enticing them with resources and opportunities they could procure without Doe's permission.

Charles Taylor's dramatic Christmas Eve 1989 appearance in Nimba County as head of the National Patriotic Front of Liberia heralded the unraveling of Doe's patron-client political organization. Taylor's arrival was the catalyst that toppled Doe's dual patronage system, as his capture of Doe's commercial networks encouraged strongmen to desert the president and seek security in cooperation with Taylor's organization. Other strongmen saw the collapse of Doe's control over patronage as an opportunity to expand their commercial reach and build their own political authority with new wealth. Taylor and other strongmen who have contested his authority have shown how the decentralized nature of Doe's inherited patronage network and his incapacity to control that network shaped the subsequent character of nonsovereign warlord politics. In doing do, Taylor and others demonstrated considerable innovation, departing from a predominantly territorial logic of organization to create a new kind of political authority based on the private control of resources. We now turn to the consolidation of Taylor's political power at the apex of this new arrangement.

THE POLITICAL ECONOMY
OF POWER IN TAYLORLAND

Stephen Ellis has observed that Taylor's violent 1989 arrival in Liberia unleashed ethnic conflicts there.[37] Early reports of the war highlighted the Krahn ethnic identity of many of Doe's paramilitary units and loyal elements of the Armed Forces of Liberia (AFL).[38] Mandingos, or Muslim traders with historical ties to the Niger River Basin, also became a specific target of rebels and civilians who accused them of collaborating with the Doe regime. This ethnic dimension of the conflict, although important in and of itself, also traces the fragmentation of Doe's patronage network. Mandingos, for example, provided Doe with a counterbalance to strongmen whose local power and commerce were out of his direct control. As "foreigners" who lacked an extensive Liberian power base of their own, the Mandingos accepted Doe's offer to protect them in exchange for a cut of their regional transit trade. But ultimately, one finds no cohesive ethnic bloc behind Doe. As with others in Liberia, the Mandingos deserted Doe once his powers as a head of state came into question, since many possessed family and commercial ties that extended well beyond Liberia's borders. Many families had significant informal ties to officials in neighboring Guinea, who could tide them over during the difficulties in Liberia.[39]

The attraction of the NPFL to most Liberians in 1989 lay in Taylor's rejection of Doe. Taylor led a group of fighters from at least a dozen ethnic groups and counted dissidents from Sierra Leone, Gambia, and Guinea among his supporters.[40] Taylor's chief strategist, Elmer Johnson—who died early in the war—hailed from Boston, Massachusetts, held a degree in political science from Boston University, and was a grandson of a Liberian vice president.[41] Paul Richards has observed that Taylor also recruited fighters from among Sierra Leone political dissidents and that commandos from Burkina Faso accompanied his forces, harkening back to the enmity between the Burkina Faso ruler's family and Doe.[42] The successful strategy of the multiethnic and multinational NPFL brought it to the suburbs of Monrovia in June 1990. At times since then, as much as 90 percent of Liberia (and occasionally parts of neighboring states) has been under NPFL control and has been popularly dubbed "Taylorland."

Taylor's background shows how the character of Doe's patronage network shaped its collapse. Taylor was born in Monrovia in 1948 to an Americo-Liberian father and a Gola mother. Taylor lived in Boston during much of the 1970s and received his undergraduate degree in economics from Bentley College. Although he was a son of the Americo-Liberian privilege Doe claimed to overthrow, Taylor returned to Liberia in 1980 and served in a cabinet position under Doe as head of the General Services Administration (GSA). Responsible for purchasing equipment in the United States for the Liberian government, Taylor allegedly used his GSA position to embezzle $922,382 in 1981–1982.[43] The ruse was discovered, and Taylor was arrested in May 1984 and was held in a Massachusetts prison to await extradition to Liberia.[44] Taylor's personal connections to Quiwonkpa, who also ran afoul of Doe at that time, may have accounted for the timing of Doe's complaint more than his concern about the missing money. After escaping from prison in 1985, Taylor visited Doe's opponents in Libya, Burkina Faso, Côte d'Ivoire, Ghana, and Sierra Leone.[45]

Taylor's original goal was to capture the executive mansion for himself. Had Taylor done so, he, too, would likely have tried to assemble his own patronage network with resources from his position as the head of a sovereign state. But in late August 1990 a multilateral 12,000-person intervention force known as the Economic Community of West African States Monitoring Group (ECOMOG) prevented Taylor from entering Monrovia.[46] The intervention, for which Nigeria provided the bulk of the soldiers, effectively partitioned the county into two zones. ECOMOG, surviving remnants of Doe's AFL, and security forces under Hezekiah Bowen's command held the capital and its port and, most important, denied Taylor international recognition of juridical sovereignty. In another blow to his claims, Prince Yormi Johnson, a former Taylor adviser, and his breakaway Independent National Patriotic Front of Liberia (INPFL) captured and killed Doe in September 1990. Johnson videotaped the murder to show the populace that he rather than Taylor had eliminated Doe.[47] Regional leaders and ECOMOG participants agreed to seat Amos Sawyer, an opposition politician since the 1970s, as head of an Interim Government of National Unity (IGNU) in September 1990. Meanwhile, Taylor's forces controlled most of Liberia but without formal international recognition.

ECOMOG's intervention and its denial of sovereign authority to Taylor were decisive in shaping political authority in Taylorland. Taylor, who was not the head of a state, could not sell diplomatic support in exchange for aid or politically motivated foreign investment as Doe had done. He could not convincingly attract aid in return for promises to hold elections until he captured Monrovia, and his organization could not receive large-scale relief aid from overseas. Unlike Doe, Taylor's only option was to acquire resources by controlling local accumulation and regional markets to finance his own military rather than using foreign aid to counterbalance local strongmen. In other words, Taylor had to control or eliminate strongmen himself rather than manipulate the prerogatives of state sovereignty. Taylor would thus ideally incorporate as many commercial networks as possible into his warlord league, regardless of the ethnicity of participants, even though ethnic claims were used to motivate fighters to target uncooperative groups or individuals.

As with the Medellin cartel, Taylor's political authority could tolerate multiple allegiances. The target of his claims was control of the more universal realm of commercial transactions rather than of a specific territory. Thus, collaborators could owe allegiance to overlapping authorities. For example, a Lebanese trader could hold Lebanese citizenship, manage clandestine cross-border trade with Ivorian customs officials who were an integral part of Taylor's commercial network, and still play a role in Taylor's NPFL provided the trader's actions helped to finance Taylor's warfare and deny resources to rivals. Taylor and his NPFL did not promulgate a political ideology as much as a political theology, an all-encompassing commitment to a political authority across a wide range of realms.

In such a case, the warlord authority focuses its pretensions to reign on the universal realm of the market, which leaves open the possibility for individuals to profess allegiance to alternate authorities in other affairs that are normally affairs of interest to conventional states. Without a state, Taylor and other warlords who are not rulers of sovereign states cannot attempt to subordinate regional commerce to a state framework but instead build authority directly through commerce. Acceptance of this strategy obviates the need to build bureaucracies, since warlord political authority that fails to replace the Liberian state would make no pretention of carrying out statelike functions. Accordingly, Taylor's control of commerce did not recognize formal borders and it was not spread evenly over a territory but was localized in places of intense commerce at the same time it was transnational and far-flung. Taylorland did not have citizens. Commercial operators were automatically political agents by virtue of their central positions in the realm of warlord authority. These individuals could call themselves Liberian or not.

Authority based almost solely on control of commerce can tolerate this ambiguity of legal allegiance to states—weak or strong, overlapping or distant from the warlord's realm. Development as commonly understood is not a priority of an authority that lacks a bureaucracy. The breakdown of Doe's state and the rise of Taylor's warlord political authority was not strictly a consequence of Liberia's economic marginalization; on the contrary, the organization of Taylor's authority moved it closer to global economic networks and privatization of markets. In contrast, Doe attempted to use what little state capacity he commanded to block or manipulate individuals' access to markets and foreign exchange. Without a state that defined legality, distinctions between clandestine markets and others faded as Taylor recruited everyone to his task of building political authority.

The failure of Doe's regime shows not so much the weakness of state institutions as the inadequacy of his response to the possibilities of global markets. Taylor's success in building political authority on control over markets, to which I return next, shows the further development of the threat that Doe failed to manage and that faces the rulers of weak states everywhere.

TAYLOR'S COMMERCIAL ALLIANCES

Taylor recognized at the start of his conquest of Liberia that he would have to quickly find money to buy guns. He could not rely on remaining bureaucratic structures outside of Monrovia, since most of Doe's appointees to state offices had fled prior to the NPFL advance. Taylor also lacked access to Doe's external state and private sources of support. The fastest way to generate hard currency lay in selling abandoned assets in areas under NPFL control. Taylor appointed his brother Gbatu Taylor to head an "official" Bong Bank and act as an intermediary with foreign arms dealers.[48] Early revenue for the purchases came from sales of abandoned equipment from the German-owned Bong Mining Company's mine site, which helped to recruit notable individuals who had regional connections. The company's local general service manager was Doe's former foreign minister, who had been fired in a cabinet reshuffle in 1986. The man, who was from a prominent Americo-Liberian family, had fallen into NPFL hands when the mine was captured in June 1990. In addition to providing a connection to Bong Mines, he also knew many Ivorian politicians, because he had managed Doe's difficult relations with Côte d'Ivoire's leader after the Liberian Beach Party in 1980.[49] He resurfaced several months later as the NPFL's "foreign minister," allegedly using his prior regional connections to tap into official Burkina Faso and Ivorian dislike of Doe and recruiting officials in those countries to help organize private arms imports into NPFL-held Liberia.

Taylor soon found he could tap more sustainable logging operations to fund military operations. As Doe's strategy had showed, logging firms had already played an important role in linking Doe's regime, his security apparatus, arms dealers, and income from timber exports. Taylor continued this pattern of organization, holding that "government is willing to give maximum protection to expatriate logging companies."[50] Taylor appointed a relative of Doe's minister of state for presidential affairs to take control of both Doe's FDA and a "Ministry of Internal Affairs" to work out arrangements with logging firms. He had earlier been a liaison between Italian financier Giancarlo Parretti, who had been accused of links to organized crime in Italy, and Doe while he served as Doe's minister of lands and mines. He found overseas investments for Doe while offering Parretti Liberian investment opportunities.[51] According to NPFL documents, this man helped to reorganize logging concessions in Liberia in 1990.[52]

Taylor was not locked into a system in which he would have to build his political-commercial network among preexisting families and firms. Even more than under Doe, firms that remained in Liberia were made to understand that they would serve Taylor's military. At least in southeastern Liberia, agencies such as Doe's FDA were integrated into the NPFL's Special Forces Commandos, who oversaw commercial operations. Larger firms could directly assist NPFL military operations with communications equipment and supplies. Some firms left Liberia, especially those that feared earlier collaboration with Doe on security matters would draw attacks from the NPFL. But Taylor still tried to entice those firms to return to Liberia.[53]

The firms that remained in or returned to Liberia took on additional tasks to support Taylor's war-fighting capabilities. One association of loggers, based across the international border in San Pedro, Côte d'Ivoire, served as a logistic and financial intermediary between NPFL-held Liberia and the outside world. For example, some NPFL organizations that demanded levies from the loggers were paid through Ivorian and Swiss banks.[54] Greenville port levies paid in this manner or in U.S. dollars amounted to about $500,000 in the first half of 1991.[55]

Taylor also made logistic requests of logging and mining firms for fuel, oil, spare parts, and vehicles.[56] Some requests came directly from Taylor's base at Gbarnga, but loggers also complained of irregular local requests for (or appropriations of) equipment.[57] The challenging business environment prompted loggers to explore avenues for mutual benefit to ameliorate their situation, including proposals to undertake management of ports and to import fuel for Taylor's organization. In fact, Taylor was already contracting these tasks out to local syndicates of Liberians and ethnic Lebanese entrepreneurs.[58] This arrangement gave Taylor another cross-border commercial connection, as both groups boasted Ivorian ties, and permitted him to manipulate those firms' monopoly control (about which loggers had complained) for his and his associates' profit. Logging companies were pressed, however, to make direct salary payments to port managers. In addition, Taylor's associates demanded money from firms to pay Taylor's National Security Agency expenses, and NPFL agents directed loggers and miners to generate electricity for eastern Liberia—again to be coordinated through an NPFL-appointed intermediary firm located in Côte d'Ivoire.[59]

Taylor gained additional access to foreign exchange by requiring that foreigners pay workers and fees in U.S. dollars.[60] This arrangement also gave Taylor the capacity to manipulate his associates' access to the different exchange rates between Liberian and U.S. dollars by fixing a variety of rates.[61] Whereas this technique of manipulating exchange rates to extract from producers and reward allies or profit personally has been used extensively in many African states, it is transferable to warlord organizations that do not issue currency. Taylor accomplished this feat by permitting the establishment of internal borders—mostly roadblocks set up by young fighters—to disrupt commerce. Even this plan required no specific organizational control beyond simply allowing fighters to collect their "pay" for themselves rather than providing for them from a (nonexistent) state treasury.[62] Taylor supplemented this indirect control with decrees concerning the use of U.S. dollars, pre-1990 Liberian currency, and "Liberty dollars" issued in Monrovia in January 1992. Differential rates and prohibitions on currency use gave Taylor a tool with which to manipulate the flow of resources among himself, his partners, and outsiders.

Despite these burdens on foreign partners, cooperative firms took part in removing up to 200,000 cubic meters of logs on concessions, worth about $20 million, during 1992.[63] Money from sales of the timber is believed to have been deposited in Burkinabe bank accounts, which some suspect were a source of funds for arms purchases.[64] Figures published in a French trade journal show French imports of raw logs from Liberia in 1991—when nearly all logging areas were under NPFL control—at 94.4 million cubic meters, which ranks Taylorland as France's third-largest African supplier of logs.[65] Taylor also promoted other exports. Although the dates are inexact, IMF figure for overall exports in 1991 is $557 million, compared with $410 million in 1989.[66]

Other NPFL incorporation of existing commercial networks occurred in Lofa County in northwestern Liberia. Mandingo traders had long dominated cross-border informal market trade with Sierra Leone and Guinea that supplied goods for export through the Monrovia Freeport. Diamond smuggling into Liberia in the 1980s was estimated at about $50 million a year, although not all of this market was in Mandingo hands.[67] In exchange for consumer goods, the Mandingos bought diamonds, gold, and agricultural products from their customers in the interior. As noted before, Taylor depicted Mandingos as collaborators with Doe's Krahn-dominated security network. Vulnerable Mandingo traders thus made easy targets for fighters eager to grab their share of profits from Liberia's informal market transit trade. By late 1990, trade in Lofa County towns such as Voinjama and Bella Yella was directly controlled by NPFL fighters organized in Special Commando Units, who took direct control over trade to buy more weapons and expand their commercial reach.

Like Doe, Taylor placed himself at the center of markets, but he did so through almost purely private, nonbureaucratic arrangements to grant selective privilege or impose punishment on traders operating outside formal legal boundaries. Although the shift from bureaucracies to private personal syndicates (in the sense of abjuring articulation or provision of a public interest) is one of degree, the effect was qualitatively different. NPFL associates now dealt directly with individual Sierra Leone and Guinea state officials, military officers, and traders who engaged in informal trade on their side of the border. This arrangement more thoroughly merged regional clandestine trade networks with Taylor's organization at the expense of neighboring states' remaining administrative and territorial control over trade and hierarchical control over officials; it also expanded the scope of conflict over this commerce. For example, fighting broke out in March 1991 when a deal to smuggle cars into Sierra Leone went bad in Koindu, a border town in Sierra Leone. In response, commanders of Sierra Leone's army proclaimed that they had sent soldiers to occupy a "buffer zone" in Liberia's Lofa

County.[68] Taylor recruited dissident Sierra Leoneans—some of whom were junior army personnel who did not share in the profits of their superiors—and NPFL fighters to grab Sierra Leone's diamond mining fields, which were less than 100 miles from the border.

To the extent that Taylor's rule was tied to the destiny of commerce, he could not confine his power to rigid territorial limits. As one Liberian fighter noted, the invasion of Sierra Leone in part followed the NPFL's "sharp business practices" and efforts to add to Taylor's profits from regional trade in diamonds, timber, and cash crops beyond Liberia.[69] In some cases dissident army personnel and harassed illicit diamond miners welcomed the NPFL invaders, discovering as had their counterparts in southeastern Liberia that they could accommodate themselves to a rebel group interested more in ruling through commerce than in ruling over them through a bureaucracy. Taylor's decision to appoint a Sierra Leone army dissident as "governor of Sierra Leone"[70] indicated the extent to which his rule had deviated from norms of territorial authority demarcated by conventional borders and was governed instead by commerce in certain commodities.

The same policy was pursued along Taylor's eastern marches and in Monrovia. Complaining about Ivorian participation in Taylor's warlord commerce, a Monrovia daily wrote that "for over five years, Ivorian politicians and businessmen have rejoiced at Liberia's nightmare, and benefitted from the flames of death and destruction which they decided to fan."[71] Some Ivorian politicians recognized the threat of undermining state authority this participation posed. "The consequence of all this for Côte d'Ivoire," wrote one Abidjan daily, "is the rise of crime rates thanks to the weapons we are supplying to Liberian rebels, and which are in turn sold on the Ivorian black market by these very same Liberians."[72]

Taylor incorporated commercial networks as a quick, cheap, and efficient means of extending his authority precisely because they are so integrally connected to the exercise of violence. He received the support of existing strongmen and more marginal foreign entrepreneurs who wanted to keep a foothold in Liberia's natural resources market. Both groups understood that they could continue to profit while they followed Taylor's directives. Areas under Taylor's control were (and are) a domain organized through selective access to rights to profit rather than by rule over a specific territory. NPFL attacks on Liberian Mandingos and then on Sierra Leone constituted a more ambitious attempt to replace a vulnerable minority group and foreign traders as intermediaries and directly conduct commerce for the benefit of NPFL fighters.

NPFL control over commercial networks represented an attractive source of revenue. Although exact calculations of the value of trade in Liberia during Taylor's first two years at war are difficult to obtain, through estimates of the trade described earlier one can deduce that the total yields of Taylor's warlord economy approached $200–$250 million a year (Table 3.1). To this amount was added the trade in looted goods, mostly stolen autos, stockpiled iron ore, building materials, office equipment, and even street light poles and zinc roofing.[73] But decentralized trade such as looting and readily available guns and the attraction of a quick route to riches, the Khalashnikov lifestyle, complicated Taylor's efforts to organize and dominate long-distance commerce without clear hierarchical authority within formal territorial borders.

Taylor's failure to command the sovereignty of a globally recognized state was a more formidable obstacle to building a commercial empire and defending himself against enemies. The sovereign IGNU regime in Monrovia could (and did) exercise its right to bring suits in foreign courts against firms that did business with Taylor.[74] Starting in 1991, the NPFL increasingly came into conflict with other strongmen who opposed Taylor and sought to control commerce for themselves. Both ECOMOG forces and sovereign state rulers, including the Monrovia regime, regularly used the material and diplomatic advantages of sovereignty to aid rival militias and entice NPFL members away from their support of Taylor. Yet amid these challenges, Taylor has survived more than seven years at the time of this writing and has continued his quest to become the sovereign ruler of Liberia.

Table 3.1   Value of Warlord Trade in Liberia, 1990–1994 (in $ millions)

	1990	1991	1992	1993	1994
Diamonds	$100 to $150 million throughout the period				
Timber	ca. $15.0	$21.3	$30.3	ca. $30.0	ca. $25.0
Rubber	ca. $27.0	ca. $27.0	ca. $27.0	—	—
Iron ore	$40.0	$30.0	$25.0	—	—

Sources: William Twaddell, Assistant Secretary of State for African Affairs, "Foreign Support for Liberian Factions," testimony before the International Relations Committee, U.S. House of Representatives, Washington, D.C., 26 June 1996; Reeves and Moulard, *Postwar Strategy;* Economist Intelligence Unit, *Liberia* (numerous issues); Mohammed Lawal Garba, "Le bois tropical africain," *Marchés Tropicaux,* 12 Feb. 1993, 436–440; Bills of Lading, Buchanan and Greenville, 1992; Michel De Montclos, "Liberia: des predateurs aux ramasseurs de miettes," in Françoise Jean and Jean-Christophe Rufin, eds., *Economie des guerres civiles* (Paris: Hachette, 1996) 137–159. Philippa Atkinson, *The War Economy in Liberia: A Political Analysis.* London: Overseas Development Institute Relief and Rehabilitation Network Paper No. 22, 1997; S. Byron Tarr, "The ECOMOG Initiative in Liberia: A Liberian Perspective," *Issues,* 21:1–2 (1993), 74–83.

FIXED FOREIGN INVESTMENTS
AND WARLORD ORGANIZATIONS

Despite the lack of predictable organizational control, some larger firms from the Doe period were able to do business with Taylor. Their presence belies notions that the global economy or a universal standard forces rulers to conform to a particular pattern of behavior. It is thus appropriate to ask how Taylor could have bargained his way to a greater capacity to wage war with more foreign firm support.

Taylor quickly discovered that he could work with Firestone Tire and Rubber Company, which had been a major corporate presence in Liberia since 1926. Taylor reached an accommodation with the firm, using his security force to control workers on the plantation and using Firestone marketing connections to sell rubber abroad.[75] In return for NPFL protection, the IGNU regime charged that Firestone provided communications facilities—including satellite linkups for cellular phones—and a supply base that helped Taylor to launch Operation Octopus, the NPFL's October 1992 attack on ECOMOG positions in the Monrovia enclave.[76] Skeptics may conclude that Firestone was merely trying to protect fixed assets during the war and that collaboration was minimal. Operation Octopus did not involve active Firestone investment, but it did involve reinstituting production and payment of levies to the NPFL, which helped Taylor in numerous other ways.

Another collaboration was centered on a joint iron ore mining venture planned for the Guinea-Liberia border at Nimba County. A consortium of European Community, U.S., and Japanese steel producers planned to open a new mine astride the Liberia-Guinea border (the Mifergui project) that would be linked by a short rail line to existing facilities at Nimba County's Liberian Iron Mining Company. By late 1990, the entire Liberian portion of the project was in NPFL hands, yet the consortium took concrete steps to do business with Taylor. In particular, it shipped stockpiled ore from the old LAMCO site. In return for the ore and NPFL cooperation, the consortium paid Taylor $10 million a month.[77] The operating railroad also provided the NPFL with the means to ship timber and other commodities to Buchanan. According to a French newsletter, Taylor actually gained a financial stake in the operation that represented a 5–10 percent partnership in 1994.[78]

Why would large, established firms do business with a man who could not claim juridical sovereignty over Liberia or guarantee long-term support for property rights? A closer look at the Nimba County Iron Ore Mining Company (NIMCO) participants reveals more than commercial interests. Beginning in March 1991, a French state-owned firm, Sollac, bought 70,000 tons of ore from the NPFL on a contract basis, paying Taylor $80,000 per shipment. A French daily accused the

French government of using this arrangement as a means of indirectly funding Taylor.[79] At least in the early 1990s, Taylor could depict himself to French officials as a foe of Nigerian regional influence through ECO-MOG and show solidarity with his anti-Doe francophone backers in Côte d'Ivoire and Burkina Faso. As we saw with Uganda in Chapter 2, outside interest in regional conflicts could still translate into some aid even after the Cold War. Unlike the past, however, this outside interest tends to work on behalf of firms' access to resources, either to act as surrogates to finance another state's clandestine influence or to promote the private interests of powerful business groups. Whichever the case, the growth in the relative strength of this vector of outside influence and interest meshes well with the focus of warlord politics.

Taylor tapped concerns of French government officials that the Nigerian ECOMOG intervention in Liberia signaled an intrusion into a region of Africa that historically had been dominated by French commercial interests. French failure to back UN and World Bank criticism of the environmental consequences of the NIMCO project demonstrated the strength of French interest in resisting criticism of Taylor's commercial deals.[80]

Meanwhile, Taylor used consortium members as surrogates to conduct diplomacy with states. He engaged a Washington, D.C., firm that also represented a consortium member. With the firm's help, Taylor could publicize his plausible argument that the Nigerian intervention represented a threat to Liberian sovereignty. Taylor used other U.S. ties—including to former U.S. Attorney General Ramsey Clark, who was his attorney for his extradition case, and to Jimmy Carter—to advertise his position that he represented the interests of Liberian people. Taylor advertised his 1991 meeting with former U.S. president Carter on T-shirts, on his radio station, and in the press as evidence to Liberians that he was globally recognized and would remain a force to be dealt with.

Taylor could use those ties, along with his knowledge that no non-African state was likely to intervene in Liberia, to further isolate the IGNU Monrovia enclave. Commercial rivalries coincided with political battles among ECOMOG, its IGNU host, and Taylor's NPFL. In this case, the regional state system treated the sovereign IGNU enclave and Taylorland roughly the same when mediating in peace negotiations. Even though negotiators were careful to distinguish between Taylor and representatives of sovereign states, they did have to deal with the fact that Taylor's troops had guns, controlled resources, and threatened the stability of Liberia's neighbors. Warlord groups became parties to interim governments starting in 1994, thereby legitimating their pretensions to represent an alternative to the IGNU regime. Regional negotiations included warlord organizations that were not states but tended to exclude Liberian civil society groups that represented those who were not directly connected to resources or to networks incorporated into the conflict.[81]

But ultimately, Taylor's ties to larger, more bureaucratized firms were predicated on those firm's assumption that he would win the war and become ruler of a sovereign state. IGNU showed some of the benefits of that sovereignty when it sued to defend its interpretation of concession agreements. Larger firms also paid greater attention to other weak-state rulers' perceptions that those firms may be politically disloyal. Individual entrepreneurs could more easily shed corporate labels, recombine with partners, and reappear elsewhere with less notice.

The IGNU enclave also suffered from burdens of sovereignty. In 1991, IGNU faced an external debt of $3.5 billion, lawsuits in Britain and the United States over unpaid private debts, and threatened suspension from the IMF.[82] The heavy obligations of juridical sovereignty and the loss of revenue sources limited IGNU's capacity to attract foreign firms or even to pay civil servants. Politicians in Monrovia, who lacked Taylor's military capacity, were highly dependent on support from other states in the ECOMOG coalition to press their claims against opponents.

Taylor continued to seek the office of president of a sovereign Liberia. His inability to attract large new firms to Taylorland left him with diminishing returns from firms seeking to protect assets or that had bet earlier that Taylor would take Monrovia. He soon found that others like him—former Doe colleagues with their own regional connections—could control commerce and build warlord organizations. Taylor's accommodations with various commercial and political networks showed remarkable innovation. But the limits of his alliances with various existing political and commercial networks showed in their lack of strong incentive to remain loyal to Taylor or to support his centralization of power.

THE LIMITS OF WARLORD POLITICS WITHOUT A STATE

Taylor's rivals have deep roots in Liberia's state politics and international commercial networks. For example, the first serious armed opposition to the NPFL occurred in Lofa County in mid-1992, led by a group called the United Liberation Movement for Democracy (ULIMO). Headed by Mandingo intellectual and former Doe deputy minister for information Alhaji Kromah, ULIMO moved to protect the Mandingo community from NPFL predations. ULIMO, which had no large base of support elsewhere in Liberia, centered its activities on northwest Liberia, expelling Taylor's forces there in 1993.

The conditions surrounding ULIMO's rise echo many of those of Taylor's takeover of Doe's connections to regional and global economies. Again we find deep roots that old state institutions obscured. For example, Kromah organized the Malinké-speaking people south of the Guinea-Liberia border not only to fight NPFL forces but also to seek commercial and military alliances north of the border. Kromah has maintained a residence in Conakry, the Guinea capital, overseeing clandestine trading and political networks that support his associates in Liberia. He has also allegedly used his ethnic and commercial ties to recruit Casamance (Senegal) separatists to the ULIMO cause of their ethnic kinsfolk.[83]

Kromah's efforts to acquire resources to finance his own fighters have centered on reasserting Mandingo control over transit trade. This plan has not only denied resources to Taylor but has also drawn resources away from Guinea's formal economy, as ULIMO supporters have mined diamonds on both sides of the border. In 1995, Guinea's formal diamond exports dropped 40 percent in value from 1994, a drop attributable in part to ULIMO mining at the expense of state-run and recently privatized firms.[84]

Kromah's supporters have also built alliances with Malinké-speaking people (like themselves) associated with Sékou Touré's regime in Guinea (1958–1984). During that time, state officials were allied with entrepreneurs, providing state assets and exemptions from regulations in exchange for personal profit.[85]

ULIMO's collaboration with old networks widened factional splits in Guinea. In particular, Kromah's associates gave their partners new opportunities to tap into trades without approval from President Lansana Conté, a Soussou who ruled precariously over inherited political alliances. Kromah's ULIMO also illustrated how the presence of militarized commerce in a region widens factional splits in neighboring states, since a warlord recruits across borders and taps into existing networks. State rulers who control alliances within fixed territories have difficulty permitting associates to split their allegiance with a rival patron outside the state's territory. Underscoring this vulnerability, Conté faced a February 1996 coup attempt. The coup leader, General Gbagbo Zoumanigui, appeared to recruit support from among frustrated Malinké officers and entrepreneurs with Casamance and ULIMO links.[86] Thus, Conté has been forced to confront this threat in the commercial and informal political milieu in which it operates.

ULIMO also found backing from among surviving elements of Doe's security forces, especially the paramilitary First Infantry Battalion. These former Doe confederates met in Freetown, Sierra Leone, in mid-1992 to hammer out a joint strategy to oppose Taylor.[87] Freetown was also a rear base for the primarily Nigerian ECOMOG troops who were protecting the Monrovia enclave. Out of the meeting came a primarily Krahn group that was attached to Kromah's ULIMO, later led by General Roosevelt Johnson, a former AFL officer. A partner to the agreement was George Boley, a Krahn who had once served as Doe's education minister and presidential secretary. The coalition fit well with ECOMOG's low-cost strategy of trying to manage the Liberian conflict. Bereft of financial means, ECOMOG's West African members were especially sensitive to the cost of the operation and opted to use warlord organizations as surrogates in the attempt to weaken Taylor. Other elements of the AFL centered around Charles Julue and operated their own foreign relations through New Horizons, based in Providence, Rhode Island. In 1994, the group allegedly raised $2 million, some of which financed Julue's September 1994 coup attempt in Monrovia.[88]

The ECOMOG strategy paid off after Taylor launched his October 1992 Operation Octopus invasion of Monrovia. ECOMOG's 10,000 troops held the city and then used their AFL-ULIMO contacts to pursue retreating NPFL forces. But it was difficult for ECOMOG to coordinate these contacts and to control associates who lacked a bureaucracy. For example, it was difficult to regulate looting, checkpoints, protection rackets, sale of travel "permits," and the like by freelance fighters who owed allegiance in exchange for opportunities to loot and extort. An eyewitness to the NPFL operations reported, for example, that "left to the commandos the roads out of NPFL territory would remain closed for an indefinite period. . . . For them to talk of opening the roads only remained an illusion because their business was at stake if that happened."[89] As we will see in Chapter 4, status as head of a sovereign state gives a ruler the tools to craft alternate strategies for dealing with this problem.

More coordination problems appeared with a de facto split within ULIMO in March 1993. The Johnson faction (ULIMO-J) became involved in mining operations in mineral-rich Bomi County, the site of most of Liberia's diamond production. As with Taylor's NPFL, local commanders distributed opportunities to mine alluvial diamonds and gold to maintain control over fighters. Johnson had access to these opportunities by virtue of his position as minister of rural development under a 1995 peace agreement, which gave him access to earth-moving machinery. ULIMO-J fighters and commanders also profited from a transit trade in diamonds from illicit operations in Sierra Leone. By the end of the first half of 1995, Liberian exports of gem-quality diamonds had reached 1.4 million carats, about equal to the total of the entire previous year. The stones were sold for just $217 million, compared with $391 million the previous year.[90] The lower price may have signalled the desperation of individual fighters to cash in their gems to buy weapons and ammunition rather than lower-quality gems.

As with the NPFL, ULIMO-J appeared to be establishing a new political arrangement on the base of an old illicit diamond mining network. Johnson acted as a local purchasing agent, providing fighters with ammunition and immediate payment for stones.[91] Ammunition and guns, which ULIMO-J sold to fighters, established the young fighters' right to engage in this commerce, set up roadblocks to collect tolls, or loot local farms. This independent activity eventually conflicted with the interests of allies and ULIMO individuals. Both Johnson and ECOMOG's local Nigerian commanders were in a position to offer protection to miners. Both vied for the opportunity to do so, in return for which they received a portion of mining profits.

Fighting became endemic after 1993, as these different factions struggled to control western Liberia's diamond market and its connections to overseas markets.[92] For example, an ECOMOG commander backed ULIMO-J fighters in disputes against their boss. This strategy weakened Johnson until late 1995, when the thirteenth and longest-lived peace agreement went into effect and ECOMOG's commander replaced the local ECOMOG officer. The new officer refused to collaborate with ULIMO-J fighters (and with his own troops) in mining operations. ULIMO-J fighters attacked ECOMOG forces, killing as many as sixty troops. The arrival of an officer who bargained with no one further undermined Johnson's control over his fighters and led to his suspension from ULIMO-J in March 1996. This commercial conflict helped fuel violence in Monrovia in March and April 1996, as other faction leaders struggled among themselves—in part to eliminate the weakened Johnson and grab his assets.

The ULIMO-J case also shows how ECOMOG and the AFL manipulated factional and commercial networks to redirect the benefits of accumulation. This anti-NPFL strategy fought Taylor on the same ground on which the NPFL built its political arrangements. But the anti-NPFL struggle produced its own factional battles to win or conserve commercial power. This factionalism appears in another spinoff of the original ULIMO coalition, the Liberian Peace Council (LPC), which under George Boley's direction, battled NPFL forces in eastern Liberia. The LPC cooperated with ECOMOG and reportedly received weapons from the multinational force.[93] Boley's fighters also displaced NPFL fighters, co-opted others, and built its commercial operations in the same networks the NPFL used. In 1993, Boley's fighters captured the Liberian Agriculture Company's rubber plantation outside the ECOMOG-held port of Buchanan. As had the NPFL and ULIMO-J, Boley's LPC used access to a means of accumulation, in this case a rubber plantation, to cultivate the support of fighters.[94]

Factional divisions also appeared within the NPFL. Portions of Taylor's NPFL under the command of Samuel Doki, Lavalli Supuwood, and

Tom Woewiyu split off as the NPFL–Central Revolutionary Committee (NPFL-CRC) in collaboration with Boley's LPC. As long as outside mediators reward control over resources with inclusion in peace negotiations and Monrovia coalition governments, these three men have an incentive to seek an independent role in Liberia's conflict. They have tapped into networks of Ivorian border officials, families familiar from Doe's time and before, ECOMOG officers, and young fighters to build their own power bases.

GLOBAL RECOGNITION OF WARLORDS?

As the continuation of factional struggle in 1997 shows, peace agreements have not dismantled the warlord politics of Liberia's post-Doe period. Agreements have established coalition governments led by the country's main factions in what outside mediators suppose are formulas for restoring the shattered institutions of the Liberian state. What is important is the way actors have organized in factions to win or conserve power acquired in the field or in battles for market share. Observers have condemned this state of affairs in which representatives of different factions sit on a Council of State in Monrovia set up by the terms of the peace agreements and conduct business outside the city. Faction leaders have used outside recognition to weaken colleagues, as when Roosevelt Johnson lost his position as "minister of rural development" when he was under attack by his own fighters and diamond miners. ECOMOG and NPFL leaders then vied for the privilege of occupying ULIMO-J positions and absorbing ULIMO-J fighters.

What is significant about post-1989 Liberian warlord politics is the extent to which that politics has grown out of the conjunction of long-running Liberian factional struggles and the international economy. The defining feature of this case is the extent to which these factions were given the means to operate independent of a state by both Doe's patrimonial but revenue-starved strategy of rule and changing opportunities in the global economy. Enterprising political and military leaders in Liberia have tapped into overseas commercial networks without presidential assent. Note, for example, the increased role of foreigners in warlord operations in which foreign firms make deals with warlords and not just state leaders.

Factional ties to overseas networks are hardly new in Africa. President Omar Bongo of Gabon has long maintained ties to French political parties.[95] Former president Mathieu Kérékou of Benin relied heavily on Mohamed Cissé, a Malian religious scholar, presidential adviser, financier, and go-between with U.S. and European banks.[96] The difference in Liberia is that the sovereign state has been challenged as the primary reservoir of rewards. It will thus be difficult for a future ruler to command obedience by reassembling old networks that have now built independent connections to the outside commercial world. The tremendous debt burden of the Liberian state ($4 billion in 1995), cutbacks in U.S. direct aid, and a paucity of other overseas resources reduce prospects that a Liberian state could have sufficient resources to attract entrepreneurs. In fact, aid could become yet another resource for warlord organizations that are able to manipulate disarmament programs and influence the distribution of aid in areas under their control. Meanwhile, each warlord sees his group controlling commerce in particular commodities; consequently, each is likely to come into conflict with rivals. As the search for new tactics in this struggle continues, warlord groups will also come into conflict with the dictates of neighboring sovereign states that cannot brook interference in internal matters.

The deregulation of factional politics in Liberia brings a political shift that reduces the common people's position in elite networks. Liberia has not lacked citizen groups protesting the war, often at considerable risk. Whereas competition for commercial networks has brought war for all, it has brought benefits for few. Factional leaders and assorted foreign partners have profited, as have perhaps 60,000 armed young men, or about one in forty Liberians.[97] Warlords, having privatized coercion for the sake of a faction, are under less compulsion to compete for supporters outside of commercial circles or to cultivate mass political bases. The gap between those on top and those at the bottom is growing wider, which parallels colonial state monopolies over sources of accumulation when rulers could safely divide territories into an *Afrique utile* that deserved official attention and an ignored *Afrique inutile* that had little commercial value.

Could a single faction capture all of Liberia, perhaps with the aid of ECOMOG troops or foreign mercenaries? Some Liberians believe they need a strong leader who can impose discipline on all Liberians. If one group were to triumph, it would not necessarily relinquish its warlord style of politics, however. More likely, it would recruit large foreign firm partners, especially those that have armed troops to impose discipline on the economic activities of fighters and local strongmen. Foreign creditors and other outsiders will tolerate this strategy, since it appears to put into place a market economy more closely connected to global markets. The result would be the transformation of a warlord politics into a warlord politics with globally recognized sovereignty. This added political tool would enable a ruler to end postcolonial patrimonial politics and replace it with a *mise en valeur* (putting the natives to work) based on discipline and completing the task of jettisoning obligations to followers that warlord politics began.

NOTES

1. "Interview with Charles Taylor," *West Africa,* 6 Aug. 1990, 2231.

2. Wess Roberts, *Leadership Secrets of Attila the Hun* (New York: Warner, 1989), 33.

3. Janet Fleischman, "U.S. Policy on Liberia," testimony before the Africa Subcommittee, Foreign Relations Committee, United States Senate, Washington, D.C., 21 Sept. 1995; U.S. Department of State, "Liberia Country Report on Human Rights Practices for 1996" (Washington, D.C.: Department of State, 1997).

4. "Liberian Warriors," *Financial Times,* 19 July 1990, 2.

5. Jeffrey Goldberg, "A War Without Purpose in a Country Without Identity," *New York Times Magazine,* 22 Jan. 1995, 36.

6. Christopher Clapham, "Liberia," in Donal Cruise O'Brien, John Dunn, and Richard Rathbone, eds., *Contemporary West African States* (New York: Cambridge University Press, 1989), 103.

7. F. P. M. van der Kraaij, *The Open Door Policy of Liberia* (Bremen: Bremer Afrika Archiv, 1983), 620.

8. J. Gus Liebenow, *Liberia: The Quest for Democracy* (Bloomington: Indiana University Press, 1987), 107–110.

9. Government of Liberia, Land Reform Commission, *Guidelines for Drafting of Land Tenure Decree* (Monrovia: Government Printer, 1981).

10. Van der Kraaij, *Open Door,* 606–623.

11. Amos Sawyer, *The Emergence of Autocracy in Liberia* (San Francisco: Institute for Contemporary Studies, 1992), 252.

12. Clapham, "Liberia," 108.

13. Government of Liberia, *National Housing and Population Census* (Monrovia: Ministry of Planning and Economic Affairs, 1974).

14. Bill Berkeley, *Liberia: A Promise Betrayed* (New York: Lawyers Committee for Human Rights, 1986), 31–39.

15. Arthur J. Knoll, "Firestone's Labor Policy, 1924–1939," *Liberian Studies Journal* 16:2 (1991), 61.

16. Robert W. Clower, *Growth Without Development* (Evanston, Ill.: Northwestern University Press, 1966), 173–174.

17. National Bank of Liberia, *Annual Report of Operations* (Monrovia: Government of Liberia, 1989), 14.

18. "Living with Americans," *West Africa,* 14 Dec. 1987, 2427.

19. "Liberia: Towards Collapse," *Africa Confidential,* 10 April 1985.

20. D. Elwood Dunn and S. Byron Tarr, *Liberia: A National Polity in Transition* (Metuchen, N.J.: Scarecrow Press, 1988), 17.

21. Economist Intelligence Unit Country Report, *Ghana, Sierra Leone, Liberia* (London: Economist Intelligence Unit, 1986), 29.

22. Blaine Hardin, "Liberia, in Grip of Graft, Puts Americans at Treasury's Helm," *Washington Post,* 29 May 1988; Bill Berkeley, "Liberia's Warring Currencies," *Institutional Investor* (Sept. 1992), 224.

23. "Liberia: What to Do with Doe?" *Africa Confidential,* 21 Oct. 1988.

24. James Butty, "The Indictment Stands," *West Africa,* 27 July 1987, 1430–1431.

25. Peter Blackburn, "Dollar Drain Fuels Liquidity Crisis," *Financial Times,* 30 Oct. 1985, 3.

26. PRC-III/NS/MB-5681, "Security Brief," 20 May 1982 (Monrovia).

27. "What to Do with Doe?"

28. "Report of Forest Operations," from a British timber company operating in Grand Gedeh County, 18 April 1989.

29. Blaine Hardin, *Africa: Dispatches from a Fragile Continent* (New York: Norton, 1990), 245; "Liberia: Last Rites," *Africa Confidential*, 18 Sept. 1985.

30. Chester Crocker, "Recent Developments in Liberia," Testimony before the Subcommittee on Africa, Washington, D.C., Foreign Relations Committee, United States Senate (10 Dec. 1985).

31. George Kieh, "An Analysis of Israeli Re-penetration of Liberia," *Liberian Studies Journal* 14:2 (1989), 117–129; Yekutiel Gershoni, "Liberia and Israel," *Liberian Studies Journal* 14:1 (1989), 34–50.

32. "Liberia: Presidential Security," *Africa Confidential*, 9 April 1986.

33. Berkeley, *Liberia*, 62–70.

34. Ruby Ofori, "Ecological Terrorism," *West Africa*, 19 Nov. 1990, 2864–2865.

35. Government of Liberia, Ministry of Commerce and Industry, *Liberian Trade Directory, 1989–1990* (Monrovia: Unity Printing Press, 1989).

36. Interview by the author with Western diplomatic official, Freetown, 19 April 1990.

37. Stephen Ellis, "Liberia 1989–1994: A Study of Ethnic and Spiritual Violence," *African Affairs* 94:375 (April 1995), 165–197.

38. Africa Watch, *Liberia: Flight from Terror. Testimony of Abuse in Nimba County* (New York: Africa Watch, 1990).

39. Alain Morice, "Guinée 1985: État, corruption et traffics," *Les Temps Modernes* 487 (Feb. 1987), 97–135.

40. On Guinea connections to Alpha Conde, see "Taylor, le candidat francophone," *Lettre du Continent*, 12 Jan. 1995; to Gambians, see Barki Gbanaboma, "Enfant Terrible," *West Africa*, 4 May 1992, 756, "Campaign Against Charles Taylor Launched," *We Yone*, 8 Feb. 1992, 5. Interview by the author with Monrovia informant, 22 June 1995.

41. Linda Matchan, "For Liberian Coup Leaders, Mass. Connections," *Boston Globe*, 8 June 1990.

42. Paul Richards, "Rebellion in Liberia and Sierra Leone: A Crisis of Youth?" in Oliver Furley, ed., *Conflict in Africa* (London: I.B. Tauris, 1995), 138.

43. Matthew Brelis, "Rebel's Saga: Mass. Jail to Showdown for Power," *Boston Globe*, 31 July 1990. For an insider's allegations, see Edward Wonkeryor, *Liberia Military Dictatorship: A Fiasco "Revolution"* (Chicago: Strugglers' Community Press, 1985), 166–168.

44. For details of the charges against Taylor, see "Charges Against Charles A. Taylor," U.S. District Court, District of Massachusetts, Magistrate's Docket No. 84-1251-R, 1984.

45. "Portrait of a Rebel," *African Concord*, 24 Feb. 1992; "Charles Taylor—the True Story," *New African*, July 1991, 22–23; "Sierra Leoneans Remember," *We Yone*, 22 Feb. 1992, 3.

46. E. John Inegbedion, "ECOMOG in Comparative Perspective," in Timothy Shaw and Julius Emeka Okolo, eds., *The Political Economy of Foreign Policy in ECOWAS* (London: Macmillan, 1994), 218–244; Robert Mortimer, "ECOMOG, Liberia, and Regional Security in West Africa," in Edmond Keller and Donald Rothchild, eds., *Africa in the New International Order* (Boulder: Lynne Rienner, 1996), 149–164.

47. "INPFL Forever," video, Monrovia, September 1990.

48. "Taylor to ECOMOG—Go to Hell," *Newswatch*, 2 Nov. 1992, 38.

49. Libby Jukes, "Liberian Rebels Suffer a Setback," *Times* (London), 9 June 1990.

50. Peter Cooper, "FDA Chides Loggers," *Patriot* (Gbarnga—Taylor's "official" newspaper), 19 Feb. 1992.

51. Michael Cieply and Alan Citron, "Parretti Lost Ally in Liberian Strongman," *Los Angeles Times,* 13 Sept. 1990, sect D.1.

52. Correspondence from the Office of the Minister of Internal Affairs, National Patriotic Reconstruction Assembly, 1990.

53. Correspondence from the Office of the Chairman, Special Economic Committee, Greenville, and "Official Business Permit," Buchanan, 1990.

54. Learned from inspection of payment records of logging firms.

55. Ministry of Finance and Development Planning (NPFL), "Tax Payment Bills (files)," 1991.

56. For example, J. M. Gbehyanue, FDA/NPRAG/MD/048/'91 (NPFL), 21 Nov. 1991.

57. Complaint to J. M. Gbehyanue dated 5 June 1991.

58. Correspondence of Sinoe Port Management Corporation (San Pedro, Côte d'Ivoire) to H. E. Charles Taylor, 15 July 1991; Liberian Port Management Authority, "Circular No. 1," 1 Nov. 1991; "Takeover Attempt at Buchanan Port?" *Patriot,* 20 April 1992.

59. FDA/MD/314/'91, correspondence from J. M. Gbehyanue, 15 Aug. 1991; correspondence from National Hydro-Carbon Corporation, 5 Feb. 1992; FDA Management, "Request for Payment," 18 July 1991.

60. Cabinet Committees on the Economy (NPFL), "Circular Notice," Gbarnga City, 30 March 1992.

61. MOF/CCE/WED/014/'92, "Circular Notice No. 2," Gbarnga City, 16 April 1992, CCE/CC/022/'92, "Circular Notice Number 2A," Gbarnga City, 24 April 1992.

62. Roadblocks described by eyewitness in Bayo Ogunleye, *Behind Rebel Line: Anatomy of Charles Taylor's Hostage Camps* (Enugu: Delta, 1995).

63. Mollai Reeves and Michel Moulard, *Postwar Strategy for Forestry Development and Environmental Management in Liberia* (Monrovia: Ministry of Planning and Economic Affairs, 1993).

64. Robert Block, "EC's Timber Imports Fuel Liberia's Civil War," *Independent,* 22 Nov. 1992; "Confusion in Gbarnga," *West Africa,* 16 Dec. 1991.

65. *Marchés Tropicaux,* cited in Economist Intelligence Unit, 3, 1992, 33.

66. Economist Intelligence Unit, *Liberia,* 4, 1992, 33.

67. Economist Intelligence Unit, *Country Survey: Guinea, Sierra Leone, Liberia, 1993–94,* 69.

68. Sierra Leone newspapers; "Border Bother," *Economist,* 6 April 1991, 43.

69. Interview by author with NPFL fighter, Cotonou, Benin, 4 July 1994.

70. "Checking the Advance," *West Africa,* 27 May 1991, 863; "Charles Taylor to Annex Part of Sierra Leone?" *We Yone,* 30 March 1992; "Fighting for Diamonds," *West Africa,* 24 June 1991, 1034.

71. "Attacking Defenseless Liberians, *New Democrat,* 15 June 1995.

72. "Charles Taylor acune frontière," *La Voie,* 24 March 1995.

73. "NPFL Men Still Looting," *Inquirer,* 24 Nov. 1995; "More Looted Goods on the Market, *Inquirer,* 27 Oct. 1995; "Looting in S/western Liberia," *Monrovia Daily News,* 7 Nov. 1995.

74. Bureau of Concessions, "Memorandum GOL-Firestone—Historical and Future Relationship," Monrovia, 31 March 1993.

75. Economist Intelligence Unit, *Ghana, Sierra Leone, Liberia,* 3rd quarter, 1992, 38; "Charles Taylor fait des affaires," *Jeune Afrique,* 23 April 1992, 12; National Patriotic Reconstruction Assembly Government, "Memorandum of

Understanding," Gbarnga City, 17 Jan. 1992, and "Firestone Restart Timetable," 16 Jan. 1992.

76. "La compagnie américaine Firestone accusée d'aider le NPFL," *Marchés Tropicaux,* 19 March 1993, 763; "The Firestone Factor," *West Africa,* 5 April 1993, 550–551; Bureau of Concessions (IGNU), "Memorandum GOL-Firestone—Historical and Future Relationship," 31 March 1993.

77. Economist Intelligence Unit, *Ghana, Sierra Leone, Liberia,* 4th quarter, 1992, 32. See also "Liberia," *Mining Annual Review,* June 1992, 133.

78. "Guinee: Le projet du Nimba s'ebranle," *Lettre du Continent,* 14 April 1994.

79. *Figaro,* 8 Jan. 1992; Johnathan Browne, "LIMCO Reacts," *Patriot,* 4 March 1992.

80. United Nations General Assembly, "18.51 Protection of Mount Nimba, Guinea," *New Resolutions* (New York: United Nations General Assembly, 1990), 47. See also, "Liberia Iron Mining Corporation Warmly Salutes His Excellency Charles Ghankay Taylor," *Patriot,* 27 July 1992.

81. See Max Sesay, Charles Alao, and Samuel Kofi Woods, eds., *The Liberian Peace Process 1990–1996* (London: Conciliation Resources, 1996).

82. John Momoh, "The Debt Scourge," *West Africa,* 20 May 1991, 798.

83. "L'écheveau casamançais," *Lettre Du Continent,* 14 Dec. 1995.

84. "Antwerp's Brilliant 1st Half," *Africa Energy and Mining,* 28 Feb. 1996.

85. I. Baba Kaké, *Sékou Touré: Le héros et le tyran* (Paris: Jeune Afrique, 1987), 168–172.

86. "Que sont devenues ces officiers?" *L'Independant,* 15 Feb. 1996.

87. James Butty, "What Does ULIMO Want?" *West Africa,* 7 Sept. 1992, 1519.

88. Daniel Volman, "Arming Liberia's Factional Gangs," *African Policy Report,* no. 5, 15 Aug. 1996.

89. Ogunleye, *Behind Rebel Line,* 137–138.

90. "Shifts in Africa-Antwerp Sales Patterns," *Africa Energy and Mining,* 5 July 1995.

91. "Youlo Expresses Concern," *Inquirer,* 25 July 1995.

92. For example, Sidiki Trawally, "Diamond Linked to ULIMO Men Attack," *Inquirer,* 1 Aug. 1995.

93. Human Rights Watch—Africa, *Liberia: Human Rights Abuses by the Liberian Peace Council and the Need for International Oversight,"* (New York: Human Rights Watch, 1994); Janet Fleischman, "An Uncivil War," *Africa Report* (May–June 1993), 56–59.

94. "Extortion Racket!" *Monrovia Daily,* 7 Feb. 1995; "Les warlords se caoutchoutent," *Lettre du Continent,* 16 Nov. 1995.

95. Stephen Smith and Antoine Glasser, *Ces Messieurs Afrique: Le Paris-Village du continent noire* (Paris: Calmann-Levy, 1992).

96. Maurice Chabi, *Banqueroute: Mode d'emploi* (Porto Novo: Éditions Gazette Livres, 1994).

97. United Nations High Commission for Refugees, "PI Fact Sheets: Liberia," in *Inquirer,* 28 Feb. 1995.

4

▼ ▼ ▼ ▼

SIERRA LEONE'S TRANSITION TO WARLORD POLITICS

It is strange to say, but I believe without diamonds this country couldn't have been in this state of exploitation and degradation.
                    —*Desmond Luke, Sierra Leone politician*[1]

Our company's goal in Sierra Leone—as it was in Angola—is to give support to a country moving towards democracy. No one can dispute that we have been a stabilizing factor in Africa.
                    —*Eeban Barlow, managing director, Executive Outcomes*[2]

This chapter addresses changes in the nature of political authority in Sierra Leone since the end of the Cold War. Rulers of the bureaucratically weak state faced warlord rulers in neighboring Liberia who based their political authority on a different logic of organization. Sierra Leone's rulers discovered that warlord politicians within their eastern neighbors are difficult to accommodate in a state system, particularly one such as Africa's in which most members' capacity to act is feeble. This incapacity became pronounced in 1991 when Revolutionary Unity Front (RUF) rebels, backed by Taylor's NPFL, invaded Sierra Leone. By 1996, the war had left at least 25,000 Sierra Leoneans dead.[3] The intrusion of warlord politics from Liberia was also the catalyst that transformed Sierra Leone's economy and led its rulers to experiment with innovative new political arrangements, which prompted the transformation of a weak state into a political authority that has borrowed from a warlord model of politics.

We saw in Chapter 3 how Charles Taylor and his local rivals based their exercise of political power on control over production and exchange rather than on mobilizing populations through state institutions. This expansive exercise of authority does not conform to formally recognized boundaries. Consequently, these strongmen have managed the frontiers of their control not as boundaries but as temporary points at which potentially unlimited organizational expansion has come to a brief halt. Taylor's backing of the RUF invasion of Sierra Leone shows his willingness to extend his political control across international boundaries by co-opting and further politicizing cross-border networks. The invasion diverged significantly from previous African regional norms, which respected formal demarcations of political authority and defined the political authority of weak states on territorial grounds. But the present practice is consistent with the warlord's need to control accumulation and exchange.

For Sierra Leone's rulers, the end of the Cold War–era respect for formal boundaries forced changes in the logic of how they ran their weak state, and they built new political coalitions without recourse to bureaucracies as they responded to those changes. Rulers shed old clients and formed new partnerships with foreign firms based on mutual material interests and a shared new conception of politics. Their choices have also addressed the constraints warlord neighbors impose. First, rulers have been forced increasingly to rationalize Sierra Leone's economy and to mobilize resources—taking care not to mobilize a dangerous society—in ways creditors and foreign firm partners prescribe. Second, and in contrast to warlords in Liberia, Sierra Leone's rulers have used their international recognition of sovereignty over a territorial state to exploit and manipulate creditors and diplomatic partners. Third, they have applied these tools to pursue internal strategies that select, delegitimate, and economically marginalize rival politicians and deny them their own local power bases.

This effort to manage crisis has moved the behavior of Sierra Leone's rulers even farther from conventional norms of sovereign statehood. The appearance of an external foe amid rising internal security threats has ruled out old strategies. This situation occurred as Sierra Leone's rulers discovered that at first, global recognition of their authority over a sovereign state weakened their capacity to respond to threats, both from Liberia and at home. They later learned they could manipulate sovereignty to their benefit. But initially the advantages of sovereignty seemed to be more minor than was the case in Liberia in the 1980s. Presidents Siaka Stevens (1968–1985) and Joseph Momoh (1985–1992) did not enjoy lavish subsidies from a single Cold War ally, which left them without the political leverage to manipulate a single wealthy patron such as Samuel Doe had enjoyed. Instead, they received resources from many patrons by virtue of their poverty rather than the country's strategic importance (Table 4.1). This broader-based dependence made them less vulnerable to a sudden cutoff of resources.

Fortunately for Sierra Leone's rulers, strongmen in the country have also proven less able to grab economic opportunities as efficiently as

Table 4.1   Development Aid as Percentage of Internal Revenue, 1985–1993

	Liberia		Sierra Leone	
1985	46.3	($94.2m)	—	—
1986	58.0	($101.3m)	—	—
1987	44.0	($81.4m)	—	—
1988	34.7	($69.7m)	123.3	($90.0m)
1989	35.6	($57.8m)	141.2	($100.8m)
1990	61.2	($112.1m)	60.9	($62.8m)
1991	98.0	($158.0m)	174.5	($104.9m)
1992	94.0	($118.9m)	140.2	($95.7m)
1993	96.0	($125.8m)	178.2	($204.0m)

Source: National Bank of Liberia, *Statistical Bulletin* (various issues) (Monrovia: National Bank of Liberia); Bank of Sierra Leone, *Statistical Report* (various issues) (Freetown: Government Printer).

their Liberian counterparts, in part because of the failure of previous Sierra Leone presidents to build a large, well-financed political network to absorb lesser networks capable of surviving when the center weakened. Thus, when post–Cold War austerity loomed, individual clients inherited fewer paramilitary fighters, weapons, viable state enterprises, and contacts with foreign traders than did their counterparts in Liberia.

The nature of this weak capacity has given regimes in Sierra Leone some leeway to make mistakes and survive to learn from them. Beginning with Momoh, the absence of dependence on a dominant external patron gave Sierra Leone's rulers greater room than Doe enjoyed to experiment with new arrangements to rein in threatening strongmen. This "benefit" is pursued in desperation, however; it conforms to Stephen Jay Gould's and Stephen Krasner's point that sudden change promotes innovation by an existing authority but only if that authority is not fatally dependent upon rapidly disappearing circumstances (discussed in Chapter 3). A second paradox appeared as conditions in Sierra Leone that many had taken as indications of the weak institutionalization of political authority (especially as measured against Liberia) became unexpected advantages in the battle to preserve a central authority after the Cold War ended.

THE FAILURE OF CONVENTIONAL STATE STRATEGIES

In 1985, retiring dictator Siaka Stevens picked Joseph Momoh as his successor. Stevens chose Momoh because the latter enjoyed some authority within the military, virtually the only state institution that retained any significant organizational identity. But Momoh was politically weak, which was another virtue to the retiring president who explained that he wanted to enjoy his wealth in Sierra Leone. Stevens's strategy of limiting army recruitment to about 2,000 troops and relying instead on loyal paramilitaries left Momoh in a materially weak position vis-à-vis the former dictator and his associates.[4] Momoh was thus incapable of ending the private control many of Stevens's associates enjoyed over the country's resources.

Stevens and his associates continued to dominate informal and clandestine commerce in Sierra Leone after 1985 at the expense of Momoh's efforts to claim resources for himself and his supporters. This situation left intact the commercial dealings of the extensive patronage network Stevens had built since the 1970s and through which he had personally distributed the proceeds of the country's mineral wealth to his allies.[5] Before Stevens's rule, diamonds had generated about $200 million in profits in Sierra Leone's formal economy, or about 30 percent of national output, and had provided 70 percent of foreign exchange reserves.[6] By 1987, the diamonds that passed through formal, taxable channels were valued at only $100,000.[7] Stevens and several associates—foremost among them Jamil Said Mohamed, a trader of Lebanese extraction who had been born in Sierra Leone—had appropriated much of the rest. They also diverted profits and assets from other state enterprises, most notably from oil and rice marketing. In doing so, they destroyed the effectiveness of most state institutions, starving them of formal sources of revenue and turning them into extensions of their private patronage networks. They also manipulated state regulation of the economy to sabotage rival private ventures that claimed a portion of the profits from trade.[8]

The bulk of state revenues that were still collected went into the pockets of politicians and their associates.[9] This wealth underwrote patronage networks that each succeeding president tried to elevate over his predecessor's. Meanwhile, state spending on health and education fell by 60 percent from 1980 to 1987.[10] Some of this diversion reflected personal greed. For example, Stevens hosted an Organization of African Unity conference that consumed the equivalent of a year's government spending, and he eventually built a personal fortune estimated at about $500 million.[11] Corruption, especially later under Momoh, also likely reflected not just greed but also presidential concern with building a personal power base against the freewheeling strongmen who increasingly diverted the state's traditional sources of revenue under the patronage of previous rulers. The independent capabilities of strongmen rendered dangerous any attempt either to reform bureaucracies (in which many strongmen held offices) or to threaten them with private security forces as Doe had done.

These clients and their private interests virtually overruled state agencies. For example, one of Stevens's business associates hosted a visit by Yasser Arafat to Sierra Leone in 1986. Arafat reportedly offered Momoh $8 million to use an offshore island to train Palestine Liberation Organization (PLO) fighters, a deal Momoh refused.[12] Stevens developed independent commercial ties with Iranian oil suppliers using a nominally state-run company in an operation some suspect was a sanctions-busting effort by South African businesspeople who used Stevens as an intermediary.[13] Other ties existed between Sierra Leone's Lebanese community and the Middle East. Nabih Beri, head of Lebanon's Amal militia and speaker of the country's postwar parliament, was from Jamil's Sierra Leone hometown and allegedly played a role in Jamil's financial dealings, which Stevens exempted from official scrutiny.[14]

Momoh faced the dilemma of finding a strategy to control the diverse activities of clients of the former ruler without provoking a coup. To do nothing would leave him without internal financing to pay for public services or even for the salaries of the soldiers and police charged with defending his regime against internal enemies. He also lacked opportunities from which his loyal associates could profit. Momoh's loss of control over state functions hampered his efforts to reach an accommodation with foreign creditors who demanded fiscal discipline before dispensing the loans Momoh needed to pay off his supporters and run what remained of formal state bureaucracies. For example, Momoh had to rely upon a Lebanese associate of Stevens's to supply personal loans to pay foreign printers of the national currency. Bereft of official sources of foreign exchange, Momoh allowed the businessman to keep a portion of currency shipments as payment.[15] That decision undermined Central Bank attempts to rein in money supplies as creditors demanded. This compromise was typical of those Momoh had to make with unruly strongmen in which he traded diminished overall control of the country's resources for short-term crisis management.

Momoh was incapable of undertaking even cosmetic actions that would have attracted creditors to bolster his political network against the growing power of rivals inherited from his predecessor. Meanwhile, many politicians and military officers were staking out mining operations.[16] Unlike Doe, Momoh could not prevent enterprising strongmen from establishing arrangements with market intermediaries, and rogue strongmen built diamond trades with ethnic Lebanese traders who had access to overseas buyers and foreign exchange. Those independent strongmen provided opportunities for up to 50,000 illicit miners, mostly young men, to work under their patronage.[17] This relative power of strongmen was greater in Sierra Leone than in Liberia in the 1980s, since the decline of State House patronage, the absence of basic services, and overall poverty left young men few options but to seek patronage from one of the strongmen.

The strongmen's independent power rendered dangerous any move by Momoh to reclaim state or private resources, either for state-led development or to finance his own loyal patronage network. Such a move would have provoked those whose control over wealth gave them the power to defy Momoh's authority. At the same time Liberia's President Doe was using half a billion dollars in U.S. patronage to attract internal allies and battle internal foes, Momoh lacked the central control over the distribution of external resources to graft his predecessor's patronage network with his own political power base.

Not surprisingly, several of Stevens's associates launched a coup attempt in 1987, which alerted the president to the dangers of directly challenging the authority and resources of strongmen. Many observers predicted Momoh's imminent demise at the hands of strongmen from Stevens's clique.[18] Momoh remained wary of provoking coups yet exercised little power to stave them off, as his downfall at the hands of junior officers in 1992 attests. But the chronic internal political crisis of weak-state power in Sierra Leone prompted Momoh to experiment with alternatives to bureaucratic state institutions to exercise authority, as did the absence of a dominant external patron and the failure to arrive at an agreement with creditors until 1990 (and receiving no significant resources until 1992). The lack of reliance on a single strategy or outside patron minimized the damage from the failure of a particular arrangement, since it forced Momoh to pursue a diversity of strategies to attract external help in his struggle to survive.

INNOVATION BORN OF CRISIS MANAGEMENT

Momoh pinned his hopes for political survival on regaining control of the country's considerable diamond resources, which were held mostly by his rivals. Creditors agreed with this approach, noting that the country's main obstacle to rooting out corruption and servicing its foreign debt was the hold over diamond mining exercised by rogue state officials and clandestine businesspeople inherited from the Stevens era.[19] Creditors recommended inviting foreign firms to "regularize," or impose control over, diamond mining.[20] This plan would displace strongmen and their illicit diamond mining operations without relying on state officials to police attacks on their own private operations. Momoh and the creditors agreed that foreign firms were the key to providing the capability to intervene in this internal crisis. Creditors needed foreign firms to generate state revenues so they could receive loan repayments; Momoh needed foreign firms as allies in his struggle to cut off wayward strongmen from their independent sources of wealth and political authority.

If one looks at formal bureaucratic institutions, Sierra Leone's extremely poor economy and lack of predictable government control have complicated efforts to implement reform policies or recruit a wide range of foreign investors.[21] But the country's high degree of chaos and weak central control did attract some businesspeople. Momoh found that a few foreign firms were attracted by his capacity to offer them selective exemption from local regulations and to protect their operations from external scrutiny. Thus, Momoh used his state office to provide patronage to private business partners as Stevens had done, but Momoh focused on finding foreign allies who had no independent contacts in Sierra Leone that could serve rivals' interests against his own. Shady operators were hardly what creditors envisioned for reform programs, but their frustration and anxiety over Momoh's financial straits caused them to ignore the fact that clandestine commercial opportunities were attracting firms to Sierra Leone.

LIAT Finance and Construction, an Israeli firm, appeared in 1987 with promises to underwrite and build expansive development projects. Of more immediate interest to Momoh was the promise by Shaptai Kalmanowitch, LIAT's chief, to mine and market diamonds through taxable official channels in exchange for a concession to control the bulk of the country's mining region. This was the "regularization" creditors and Momoh were looking for; both hoped LIAT could expel unruly strongmen from mining areas and boost the revenues under the president's control. The LIAT arrangement highlights the extent to which Momoh (and probably his creditors) saw the replacement of competing clandestine operators with a private monopoly answerable to the president as the key to "reform." Creditors likely acquiesced because they felt the arrangement was preferable to the continuing collapse of a debtor state. Momoh grew more ambitious, however. He launched an army campaign to pacify mining areas and shut down illicit operations for LIAT's benefit, a move that probably sparked the 1987 coup attempt.

The appearance of new clandestine global economic opportunities also influenced the way efforts to attract foreign firms to Sierra Leone played out. Israeli firms had previously facilitated clandestine arms deals with apartheid-era South Africa.[22] Operations such as LIAT could use partnerships with desperate weak-state rulers to recruit them as intermediaries in South Africa's Total Strategy, which included giving Kalmanowitch a Sierra Leonean diplomatic passport—he was a cultural attaché—so he could travel abroad while conducting business. LIAT allegedly shipped South African gems to Europe as Sierra Leonean products and imported machinery and supplies to South Africa with manifests listing Sierra Leone as their destination.[23] LIAT gave Momoh some payoffs, including, for example, rice he distributed at the State House to supplicants and to civil servants in lieu of salaries and new buses for his wife's transportation company. To Momoh's disappointment, LIAT did not molest rogue miners in the diamond fields, since the company was more interested in passing off other gems as Sierra Leonean than in actual mining. The company's clandestine operations fell afoul of the law abroad. Kalmanowitch was arrested in North Carolina on charges of fraud in 1987 and was extradited to Israel to face additional charges, which promptly ended LIAT's Sierra Leone operations.[24]

Official diamond exports hit bottom in 1988, yielding only $22,000. Momoh's rivals were exporting diamonds estimated to be worth $250 million from an economy that, with its accelerating economic decline, was generating less than a billion dollars a year.[25] That same year was the low point in Momoh's relations with creditors, as debt arrears went unpaid. Triple-digit inflation, spotty electricity, shortages of basic supplies, and the loss of television, radio, and most health and education services convinced many that Momoh had lost all formal capacity to manage the economy and all informal capacity to manage his rivals, who benefited from his weakness.

Bereft of access to local resources, Momoh's highest priority was to regain access to creditors' loans. A deal discussed in 1989 eventually offered prospects of loans totaling about $300 million, crucial for a government that was wringing only $50–$60 million from the local economy.[26] Regularized relations with creditors also held out hopes that debt payments would be reduced through Paris Club negotiations, which excluded Sierra Leone from the failure to service debts.

SCIPA Finance, a second Israeli firm, arrived in 1989 with an offer to manage and expand Sierra Leone's diamond mines. SCIPA's head, Nir Guaz, manipulated Momoh's fears about internal security, cultivating his favor by paying overdue civil servant salaries. Guaz also allegedly paid a portion of Sierra Leone's arrears to creditors, helping to put debt negotiations with the IMF back on track in late 1989.[27] But as with LIAT, SCIPA did not actually mine diamonds. Even worse for Momoh's political situation, Guaz appeared to cultivate a following among illicit mining operators. SCIPA evidently purchased diamonds mined in Sierra Leone for export elsewhere as a money laundering operation. To dominate local diamond markets for his and his overseas clients' interests, Guaz sought local influence by giving gifts to Momoh's allies and rivals alike. So although Guaz had helped Momoh out of extremely difficult financial straits in mid-1989, Momoh had Guaz arrested for "economic sabotage" on Christmas Eve 1989, thus ending SCIPA's operation.

Momoh's struggle to control diamond mining continued, and the difficulty of attracting foreign investors to a state dominated by rogue politicians and illicit private miners remained. Nonetheless, a partnership between Sunshine of Dallas, Texas, and Jean-Raymond Boulle, a former De Beers manager in Sierra Leone, was attracted to what it saw as new opportunities in Sierra Leone's hitherto inaccessible mines—an advantage a small, flexible operation could use to boost its market share against better financed and more experienced competitors. The project never materialized, in part because the partnership collapsed in the United States.

The firm's impact on Sierra Leone was significant, however, in unintended ways. Contract terms stipulated that Sierra Leone's government would provide greater security in mining areas.[28] To accomplish this, Momoh presided over two military campaigns (Operation Clear All and Operation Clean Sweep). This assertive strategy, which seemed appropriate to centralize state control over resources, instead widened the gap between the state's authority in the capital and its capacity to control the minefields. Illicit miners fled from the mining areas, thereby losing their source of income. Many had become miners out of desperation to find an income as job opportunities in the civil service and the formal economy disappeared. "These operations were the best recruiting tool the rebels had," said an army officer, referring to the insurgency that broke out months after the campaigns had disrupted the livelihoods of 25,000 unskilled workers.[29]

The military also disrupted the commercial networks of Momoh's rivals, as it was designed to do. Although this disruption may have provided some short-term relief for Momoh and his anxious creditors, it further alienated rival strongmen, some of whom later tried to cut deals with rebels. Finally, the behavior of the poorly paid army, which lost some soldiers to their own mining operations, increasingly blurred the distinction between an action to defend the state and one to find personal profit in warlord-type operations.

Boulle's brief flirtation with the Sierra Leone regime highlights additional lessons about the nature of foreign firm involvement in very weak states. Ironically, the clandestine, mostly transit-trade activities of Momoh's Israeli partners left him in a somewhat stronger position as head of a bureaucracy, since the partners funneled him some resources he could use to operate a state and pay off his followers while leaving rival strongmen preoccupied with their private businesses in the mining areas. The weakness of the state became apparent when firms, or the government on behalf of firms, actually moved to push the strongmen out of business, since it was then that rivals began to make their final break with the state bureaucracy. In the face of hostility from the capital, state offices and affiliation with a centralized patronage network no longer offered opportunities or protection, which forced strongmen to experiment with new ways of controlling local resources and people without the benefit of affiliation with a state. Paradoxically, the very actions that had seemed necessary to strengthen the state were decisive in further weakening it.

The experience may have been instructive for Boulle as well. He later headed American Mineral Fields (AMF), which hired its own army in its concession in Angola.[30] In that case, the foreign investor participated in an essentially warlordlike strategy, in which military power is a consequence of a profitable commercial operation, rather than a statelike strategy that relies on the autonomous interest and organization of a national military that seeks to impose a ruler's authority over a territory.

But in Sierra Leone, both creditors and Momoh turned their attention to reviving other sources of state revenue. World Bank field coordinators used Momoh's difficult situation to experiment with their own approaches to dealing with weak states. Sierra Leone was well suited for radical privatization to help boost debt payments. Frustrated with the nearly total loss of customs and fishery royalty collections to corrupt officials, Bank officials proposed privatizing those operations to foreign firms and trimming state employment rather than trying to reform those bureaucracies. West African Fisheries, a subsidiary of a British firm, bid to manage the collection of fishery royalties. The firm understood that its offer of a $10 million "donation" to help clear arrears to creditors would guarantee a sympathetic hearing in the president's office. Creditor officials discouraged awarding the firm the bid, however, when it was discovered that several of Momoh's close associates were among its board.[31] Instead, the contract went to Marine Protection Services of Sierra Leone, a British firm that was later revealed to have made payoffs to Momoh's associates in 1991, although it also added $500,000 to formal state revenues.[32]

A customs collection and port management contract was awarded to Specialist Services International, a subsidiary of a German security firm. The firm, along with Marine Protection Services, helped to halt the slide in official state revenues that could be tapped for debt servicing, although the two companies left the president's rivals in control of the diamond fields. Sierra Leone's return to the good graces of creditors in 1991 opened the possibility for new loans that could help greatly to at least replace the potential revenues—for both official and informal political uses—rivals monopolized in the diamond fields. But the country's fiscal affairs would improve at the expense of the president's remaining bureaucratic means of control and would strip away more of his patronage network. Further, the loans would give already unruly strongmen more incentive to carve out their own authority independent of the ruler.

Unfortunately for Momoh, his success in attracting creditor support coincided with the rebel invasion of Sierra Leone in late March 1991 discussed in Chapter 3 as part of Taylor's widening search for resources. The rebel invasion and the initial cooperation of some Sierra Leoneans opened opportunities for strongmen to grab more resources and squeeze out rivals. The "loss" of the diamond fields was not a heavy blow to the president, since he had never controlled or greatly benefited from them. Momoh faced aggressive and expansive foes, however, whether Liberians, disgruntled illicit miners, enterprising strongmen, or a combination. This tense position forced Momoh to deploy a stronger military—precisely the kind of growing but ineffectively controlled bureaucracy that would prove to be prone to disintegration as individuals cast their lots with more powerful strongmen or used their weapons to stake their own claims on resources. Within a year, Momoh had lost his office—not to a former Stevens client but to Valentine Strasser, a twenty-six-year-old poorly paid but armed junior officer recruited to fight rebels. Strasser reportedly made his move after a rebel attack had disrupted his unit's illicit mining operation.[33]

POST–COLD WAR RUPTURE IN THE NEIGHBORHOOD

As we saw earlier, the end of the Cold War did not immediately threaten Momoh's hold on power, since he had no dominant patron to lose. Instead, a rupture appeared with the sudden collapse of the regime of neighboring Liberian ruler Samuel Doe. Faced with the need to control as many resources as possible as quickly as possible, Charles Taylor's NPFL organization had moved to the international border with Sierra Leone by late 1990 as we saw in Chapter 3. Although they were concentrating on efforts to seize Monrovia, Taylor's troops moved to seize the cross-border commerce with Liberia, Sierra Leone, and Guinea that was controlled by Mandingo traders. For a time, NPFL fighters and Sierra Leoneans collaborated in this clandestine trade, which deprived the Sierra Leone government of revenue and helped to arm the NPFL.[34] But the involvement of officials in the trade blocked NPFL designs to gain direct access to Sierra Leone's wealth.

Fighting broke out in March 1991 along Sierra Leone's eastern border. Taylor used the conflict to draft RUF and other dissident Sierra Leoneans to conquer the economically valuable areas of Sierra Leone and use foreign exchange earned from the country's trade to support his NPFL, which entailed either removing or co-opting Sierra Leonean strongmen who controlled mining operations. Taylor promptly named former Sierra Leone army corporal, photographer, and RUF leader Foday Sankoh "governor of Sierra Leone."[35] RUF, which was organizationally distinct from Taylor's group, made use of NPFL backing. "The APC [All People's Congress, Momoh's government]," said Sankoh, "believes in force and we are going to use the same force against them to get them down."[36] In practical terms, this meant that, as Doe's rivals had, Sankoh would violently attack the resource base of Sierra Leone's patronage networks rather than fight Momoh through nonviolent political means. Sankoh differed from Momoh's internal rivals who defended personal fiefdoms from greedy neighbors and presidential control but were too weak to mobilize resources for an expansionary push beyond the realms of local rivals or across international borders.

The rebel invasion posed an even greater threat in its capacity to mobilize economically active segments of Sierra Leone's population. Some young men who sought their fortunes in the diamond fields found the disruption caused by RUF gave them more freedom to take control of their own operations and to collaborate directly with either RUF or Liberians. Gangs of miners had little reason to fight to defend a government that defined their activities as illicit, launched periodic military campaigns against them, and provided virtually no social services.[37] Further, they had no material incentive to remain loyal to Stevens-era strongmen who were losing their control over resources and could no longer act as attractive patrons. Paul Richards has documented that RUF forces initially saw themselves as fighting for the interests of young men, giving them the opportunity to avenge their and their families' treatment by politicians, which resulted from the abandonment of those men from either the slimmed-down state patronage networks or the patronage of local strongmen who now looked more toward personal profit.[38] According to eyewitnesses, Taylor helped to recruit Sierra Leoneans in Liberia to his and Sankoh's cause and gave RUF fighters a rear base in Liberia.[39]

RUF also grafted an assortment of dissidents from Sierra Leone and abroad onto this new alliance. Early in the conflict, Sankoh reportedly received financial backing from a business associate of President Stevens who had been involved in the diamond industry and was a target of Momoh's efforts to rein in strongmen.[40] Early reports of fighting in Sierra Leone note the presence of troops from Burkina Faso, where Taylor had visited President Blaise Compaore.[41] Evidence also shows that RUF shared Taylor's ties to Ivorian merchants and had developed its own ties to impoverished Guinean soldiers and even ULIMO fighters—nominal foes of their Liberian backer—who sold weapons to RUF in exchange for loot and local products.[42] Sankoh broadened his own ties through commercial and family links in Liberia and Gambia.[43] Later, RUF moved to establish an office in Brussels. Claiming it wanted to work in "the capital of Europe," the group rejected allegations that the choice of location was related to its proximity to Antwerp's major diamond markets.[44]

Momoh also took advantage of the cross-border nature of warlord insurgency in the region. Reports indicated that Liberian irregulars, many from Doe's paramilitaries, joined Sierra Leonean troops in fighting NPFL and RUF forces.[45] Momoh eventually hosted a cross-border anti-NPFL force that was able to advance 100 kilometers into Liberia by late 1991. But even with this help, the rebel invasion forced Momoh to rely heavily on the disorganized military to protect his regime. He expanded enlistment from 3,000 to about 14,000 troops,[46] but he lacked the capacity to finance the expanded military. Sierra Leonean army commanders tended to "lead" campaigns from the rear, leaving young, non-commissioned officers in charge of actual battle operations. Valentine Strasser was one such commander, leading troops who received pay late, if at all, and who were backed with field hospitals short of supplies and stocked with defective equipment. Strasser and his armed supporters marched to Freetown to complain, which resulted in a coup against the Momoh regime on 29 April 1992.[47]

A more persistent threat to Momoh and then to his successor, Strasser, appeared with "sobels," or soldier-rebels. Underpaid soldiers, mostly young men who shared the same limited prospects as workers in the diamond mines, found they could exploit the chaos caused by rebels to extort or loot from local inhabitants. Many Sierra Leoneans suspect rogue military units, organized much like mining gangs, were behind a large number of "rebel" attacks. The disruption of diamond mining operations caused by the attacks also created opportunities for diamond diggers to find new patrons and marketing opportunities. Thus, politicians, miners, rebels, and sobels competed to shape the redistribution of resources to their own advantage.

Consequently, significant military advances against rebels in 1992 and 1993 soon dissolved into banditry, which came from within the army but resembled rebel attacks. Battles among miners, patrons, and newcomers threatened to exacerbate factional divisions within the Sierra Leone military, as officers rushed to take advantage of disruptions to translate their command of troops into control of private mining operations. Warlord politics was proving to be contagious, not only territorially but also in further fracturing old patronage networks and widening existing factional splits. Conflict and the disruption of old political hierarchies also brought into play the material interests of army officers who used the continuing conflict as a cover for their own commercial operations and as a pretext for attacking local rivals.

Strasser was even more menaced than his predecessor had become. His main threat came from within his own military and from among rogue mining operations, whose independence also undermined the power of other, more established strongmen. Strasser attempted to use his youth and military origins to appeal to young Sierra Leoneans and cultivate legitimacy. The regime had modest success mobilizing volunteers in Freetown, which was well away from fighting until 1995, to perform municipal cleanup tasks the government could not afford and lacked the capability to perform. Strasser billed himself as "the redeemer" and encouraged expression of grassroots national pride by sponsoring wall murals in the capital.[48]

But the burdens of war taxed what little was left of Sierra Leone's formal state structure. The army consumed 75 percent of state spending by early 1995.[49] Even so, Strasser could not finance an effective army, much less provide social services to the population from which soldiers were recruited who now expected that the "redeemer" might actually solve some of Sierra Leone's pressing economic problems. Strasser backed his authority with strategies that did not depend on effective bureaucracies or state spending, such as executing prisoners in Freetown's Pademba Road Prison for allegedly plotting a coup and investigating corruption among civil servants. Tellingly, anticorruption tribunals focused on low-level or exiled officials with no mention of incumbent strongmen, even though many of the latter posed a threat to the regime.[50]

Under the strains of war, the collapse of state revenues, which had begun under Stevens, was almost complete by early 1995. The RUF invasion and military units engaged in diamond mining diverted significant foreign exchange earning away from Strasser's control. In January 1995, attempts to bring new mining operations under a legal framework promised freer private access to mining opportunities. But government pronouncements that also portended taxation without enforcement were ignored by those who profited from clandestine operations.[51] In any case, government officials appeared unaware of new policies or judged that those policies were meant to manipulate creditors.[52] Additionally, successful RUF attacks on foreign firms that mined other minerals destroyed the government's last reliable sources of revenue.

Sierra Rutile, a U.S.-Australian firm, exploited titanium oxide (Sierra Leone was the world's third-largest producer in 1993) in an enclave operation throughout the war. In late 1994, RUF fighters kidnapped foreign employees of the firm and workers at Sierra Leone Ore and Metal Company (SIEROMCO), a Swiss-owned bauxite mine. Both firms closed their operations, which ended SIEROMCO's annual $5 million tax payment and Sierra Rutile's annual $7 million payment.[53] Together, the two companies had generated 15 percent of Sierra Leone's gross national product.[54] Sierra Rutile alone grossed $61 million in 1993, accounting for 57 percent of the country's total export earnings; it was also country's largest private employer.[55]

The shift in relative economic power looked grim for Freetown. A combination of RUF fighters and rogue military officers and units controlled an estimated $250 million annual trade in diamonds and controlled (or at least denied Freetown the benefits from) agricultural exports valued at $60 million in the eastern province in 1990.[56] Meanwhile, government domestic revenues totaled only $60 million in 1994–1995.[57]

Exports and the revenues of a government heavily dependent upon taxes from foreign trade had fallen so low that by 1995 even the most extreme economic austerity program could not balance the budget or generate debt service payments (Table 4.2). Economic gains from reforms, such as the recovery of official diamond exports from negligible amounts in 1988 to over $20 million annually in the early 1990s, had been wiped out. Nonetheless, creditors promised loans in return for strict adherence to reform plans, thus offering the president one of his few apparent hopes for external help in managing the crisis. Thus, it is not surprising that the Sierra Leone regime closely followed its creditor-mandated reform plan, laying off a third of its civil servants and cutting budgets even as war threatened the regime's existence.

Rebel attacks on Freetown suburbs in March and April 1995 were as much a result of the implosion of Sierra Leone's state institutions and the factionalization of its army as of shrewd rebel strategies. The slower pace of collapse reflected the fragmentation of Sierra Leone's decaying patronage network. First, the appearance of an armed group from Liberia undermined the capacity of local strongmen to organize broad challenges to the central government. The absence of a concerted attack by strongmen on Momoh's and then Strasser's authority also reflected the failures of these rulers to build centralized patronage networks that later would be capable of dominating a whole region's resources for themselves. This fragmentation can be traced back to Stevens's use in the 1970s of single-party elections with multiple candidates to localize competition for patronage, reserving control over marketing natural resources for himself and Lebanese partners.[58] Thus local strongmen of relatively equal strength dominated Sierra Leone's political scene when

Table 4.2   Sierra Leone Exports, 1991 and 1995 (in $ millions)

	1991	1995
Agricultural products	$10.4	$2.7
Palm kernels	$0.05	0
Cocoa	$2.3	$0.006
Coffee	$2.4	$1.3
Minerals	$134.0	$0.9
Diamonds	$20.6	$0.8
Gold	$0.5	$0.013
Bauxite	$26.0	0
Rutile	$69.1	0

Sources: Bank of Sierra Leone, *BSL Bulletin* (Freetown: Rogers TPI, Jan. 1996), 20, 33, 34, 36.

RUF appeared. In contrast to Sierra Leone, Doe's delegation of influence over particular sectors of the formal and clandestine economies to ethnic or regional components of his inherited patronage network in the 1980s put Liberian strongmen in positions from which they could appropriate particular trade routes and resources as Doe's authority waned.

Sierra Leone's social configuration of warlord politics also differed from Liberia's with respect to the low levels of coordination between armed bands. The success of anti-Taylor factions in Liberia cut Sankoh and his RUF off from Taylor's NPFL. Forced to strike out on their own, many RUF fighters forsook Sankoh's direction and made private deals with local army units, commanders, and local strongmen who wanted to make new accommodations with armed rebel units.

RUF attacks on diamond traders of Lebanese ethnicity also differed from the situation in the Liberian conflict. Lebanese traders had overseen many mining operations on behalf of politician patrons, providing access to commercial networks in return for a cut of the profits. RUF targeted the traders to mobilize popular support against a class of commercial outsiders and to extort protection payments. Emigration reduced the number of traders to 8,000 in 1995 from a prewar figure of 35,000.[59] Nonetheless, some were able to shift their operations and collaborate with rebels. "In effect," reported one observer, "the Lebanese merchants are commandos themselves as they can be seen in mufti similar to the camouflage worn by the Burkinabe army."[60] This commercial disruption left control of mining up for grabs more so than had been the case in Liberia and attracted a wide array of new commercial contacts—Armenians, Americans, Bulgarians, Russians, and eventually South African mercenaries—who had no previous affiliation with a particular group.

Thus, central authority in Sierra Leone could now collapse more completely, leaving a vacuum of competing groups that, apart from RUF, were too disorganized to dominate a particular area or resource. Among the many ironies of this case is that the extreme incapacity of the state gave Strasser's regime and its foreign backers more room to experiment with radical solutions with a broader array of outsiders. The near total collapse of state institutions also cleared the old accommodations with strongmen that had hobbled post-Stevens rulers. Paradoxically, Sierra Leone's more gradual collapse of old patronage networks resulted in more radical change than had occurred in Liberia. In contrast, the speed of political collapse in Liberia had left old branches of the patronage network capable of protecting and in some cases expanding their hold on resources. Thus, Strasser had more room to engage in radical innovations to support his authority, a subject to which I turn next.

THE WARLORDIZATION OF SIERRA LEONE

Before they withdrew in January 1995, Sierra Rutile's managers explored the possibility of hiring their own defense force to guard the company's mine site. Through a British firm, J & S Franklin, Sierra Rutile contacted Gurkha Security Guards (GSG). SIEROMCO had explored hiring British-based Special Project Services, but the loss of the company's mine site to rebels and the expense of a military operation cooled its interest.[61] Refashioning old Cold War arrangements, GSG recruited soldiers who had lost their jobs in cutbacks of British Special Forces, which had used Nepalese Gurkha fighters during the Cold War.[62] Now, some Gurkhas were working for this private firm, which was registered on the island of Jersey. GSG also drew upon old Cold War intelligence and covert operations networks. Robert MacKenzie, an American, served as GSG's Sierra Leone commander. MacKenzie's qualifications included having worked for Rhodesia's security service in the 1970s after seeing action in Vietnam. After the demise of Rhodesia in 1980, he spent time in South Africa before returning to the United States to work with private organizations seeking funding for Mozambique's REN-AMO rebels.[63] As with many future Sierra Leone regime partners, MacKenzie, a son-in-law of former CIA Deputy Director Ray Cline, had deep roots in Cold War security circles.

For all of MacKenzie's experience with special operations and anti-insurgency, the task of fighting insurgents in a country that lacked effective bureaucratic organizations proved his undoing. Unlike the cases of Rhodesia and South Africa, he found his employer's enemies were not confined to the battlefield. GSG erred in attempting to train Sierra Leonean soldiers and relying on the army's command hierarchy. Effective action threatened vested interests among sobel mining gangs and the commanders who backed them. MacKenzie was murdered in February 1995 in an ambush in which someone appeared to have had inside information regarding his schedule.[64] Other dire warnings of increasing rivalries within the army followed the death of a Ukrainian combat helicopter pilot who had been contracted to fly recently purchased surplus Soviet helicopters and was murdered at the army's headquarters in Murraytown, just outside Freetown. An anxious regime spokesperson dismissed the event as a suicide following a love affair that had gone bad. But the incident underlined the extent to which factions in Sierra Leone's military were struggling to profit from the economic opportunities the war had created.[65]

Strasser and foreign investors desperately sought a replacement for GSG as RUF fighters moved just outside Freetown. The danger to the regime and to citizens lay in the likelihood that soldiers would join RUF in looting the city if the government and military command collapsed further. Rumors surfaced that another British firm employing a dozen former British Special Air Services personnel had been hired after MacKenzie's death.

But a more effective fighting force was found in Executive Outcomes, the South African firm examined in Chapter 2.[66] Executive Outcomes could also tap into Cold War military expertise and resources. The firm's Sierra Leone operations used Russian Mi-17 and Mi-24 attack helicopters and hired Russian and Belarussian firms to provide maintenance. The man who trained Sierra Leonean government forces was once a senior officer in South Africa's parachute battalion. Under South Africa's apartheid-era Total National Strategy, that unit recruited black fighters from southern Africa, some of whom were co-opted into anti-insurgency units. Many of these fighters, who had once committed what their communities regarded as atrocities, found they could not return home after the political settlement in South Africa. Executive Outcomes made efforts to win local support for anti-insurgency operations, stressing to local people that the organization alone was capable of providing communities with security amidst low-intensity warfare. The company drafted local initiation and hunting societies that were armed for self-defense (later known as Kamajors), which had appeared as early as the 1991 RUF-NPFL invasion.[67] Provided with better weapons and training, the societies were powerful allies for cultivating local acceptance of a foreign, private military. In terms of Sierra Leone's factional politics, this arrangement created an armed force of irregulars, and Executive Outcomes expected the members to be reliable allies of both the firm and its government client. This change in political balance, as much as Executive Outcomes' immediate military assistance, made the firm valuable to Strasser.

Executive Outcomes also wisely abjured using the army's officer corps as intermediaries with its employer. Instead, the company retrained Sierra Leonean units that collaborated in Executive Outcomes operations under the command of (supposedly) reliable regime insiders such as Brigadier Julius Maada Bio, Strasser's second in command. The security Executive Outcomes provided enabled the retrained units and Kamajors to strike against rebels with dramatically improved results. The collaborative effort also strengthened a hard line under Bio's leadership that sought to beat rebels and wayward politicians on the battlefield. Together, the collaborators cleared the capital area of rebels in one week in April and reconquered diamond mining areas in July–August 1995.[68]

Reconquered areas were cleared of rogue military units along with rebels. This arrangement served multiple interests. Creditors could expect increasing formal state revenues at low expense. The country appeared increasingly stable to outsiders concerned about the political ramifications of yet another collapsed state. Differentiation between reliable irregulars and army units on the one side and rogue units and rebels on the other also permitted Strasser to discuss with nongovernment organizations (NGOs) and foreign aid donors the option of trimming army enlistment. In reality, this meant marginalizing and attacking, if necessary, units that were essentially unpaid and that operated more like brigands than like a military hierarchy.

Unfortunately for Strasser, he was unable to avoid the security threats of improving the efficiency of even a small segment of the army. Bio used his liaison position with Executive Outcomes to depose Strasser in February 1996. With little fanfare, he bundled Strasser onto a plane and sent him into exile. The change in rulers reaffirmed the new alliance between the Freetown regime and its new foreign firm partners. Policies toward external actors and war-fighting strategies were virtually unchanged.

One of the more useful innovations of the presence of Executive Outcomes involved strategies to pay for military services for a regime that had almost no cash. At first, with about 200 employees, Executive Outcomes' services cost several million dollars a month. Strasser's regime did not have such money, but it could exercise its sovereign right to mortgage natural resources to a foreign firm. Arrangements reportedly promised that Executive Outcomes could claim favored commercial arrangements in conquered territory if it organized the exploitation and marketing of resources.[69] The firm did so through its association with Branch Energy, a British diamond mining firm that was part of a group of companies owned partly by Strategic Resources of Pretoria, South Africa—Executive Outcomes' holding company. Branch also had ties to Heritage Oil and Gas, a firm active in Angola where Executive Outcomes employees worked for associated firms.[70]

Branch Energy and the Sierra Leone government entered into an $80 million joint venture project that allowed Branch Mining, the Sierra Leone subsidiary, to dig for diamonds in areas conquered and patrolled by Executive Outcomes. Presumably, Branch Mining helped pay for Executive Outcomes' services or at least made it possible for Strasser's government to do so. In any event, Executive Outcomes had an extensive presence at Branch Mining's Kono District mine site in 1996. Reports also surfaced that other companies guarded by men associated with Executive Outcomes had signed agreements with the Sierra Leone government to mine in other locations.[71] As in Angola, the arrival of a network of firms associated with Executive Outcomes enabled the firm to contract out tasks to smaller firms that trained and equipped reliable local fighters. In Sierra Leone, new firms appeared such as Life Guard, which used Executive Outcomes trainers but recruited Sierra Leonean employees. This change paved the way for a formal Executive Outcomes exit in early 1997.

On the economic front, the security Executive Outcomes and its associates have provided has helped to attract other foreign investors. Diamond Corporation, a De Beers subsidiary, signed a concession agreement to mine offshore diamond deposits, although it did not begin operations. Cassierra Development Fund, a Canadian firm, and Golden Prospects of Britain also acquired licenses to do business in Sierra Leone. Other, less established foreign entrepreneurs have set up operations in Sierra Leone. A former associate of the U.S. partner in the 1990–1991 Sunshine Boulle concession negotiations returned to manage a privatized Freetown resort hotel that catered to the growing numbers of foreigners exploring business possibilities in the country.[72]

More difficult to trace but politically important in the regime's attempts to control resources has been the growth of small mining operations in areas that are now secure. In some cases, these operations consisted of agreements between foreign entrepreneurs who acquired a position to mine diamonds in exchange for arming local irregulars to guard mine sites. Local politicians who were loyal to the president appeared alongside the foreigners to receive their cut of the business.[73]

Branch's operations and signs of foreign investor interest also addressed creditor aims to increase state revenues and to remove corrupt officials and illicit marketeers from access to Sierra Leone's sources of wealth. Subsequent Paris Club debt reduction talks have treated Sierra Leone well; the country's foreign debt in June 1995 stood at $969 million, or 20.1 percent less than a year earlier.[74] Good relations with multilateral creditors have led to more bilateral aid projects and budget support, which totaled $204 million in 1995 compared with $62 million three years earlier.[75] This support has increased the Sierra Leone government's overall reliance on outsiders to finance its formal operations.

Executive Outcomes also played a critical military role. According to eyewitnesses, the firm was decisive in clearing rebels from the Freetown area in 1995. Firm employees went on the offensive in June 1995, attacking rebels in the minefields.[76] Executive Outcomes employees later engaged in combat against rebels concentrated close to the Liberian border.[77]

Protection from internal threat and some amelioration of fiscal hardship gave Bio more leeway to execute creditor-mandated reform policies. Outside protection also allowed him to pare surviving patronage networks, an integral part of creditor prescriptions. He continued Strasser's policies that had led to the layoff of a third of the country's civil service.[78] Bio's regime also continued radical privatization along the lines of the Côte d'Ivoire model. This program was extended to the effective privatization of security operations when Strasser and Bio presided over the profitable partnership among mining firms, foreign soldiers, and a sovereign state—creating new private opportunities for those close to the regime. For example, Stephen Bio, cousin of the president, acquired a 30 percent share of Sorus, a Russian air cargo firm that flies between Russia and Sierra Leone.[79]

The two rulers made significant progress toward resolving the fundamental dilemma of African patron-client regimes: How can rulers assure their own security when the potential power of strongmen and the costs of patronage render bureaucracies either dangerous tools in the hands of rivals or impossible to finance? Further privatization dismantled more of the state by jettisoning local partners when feasible and replacing them with foreigners who could improve regime security. The Public Enterprise Reform and Divestiture Committee (PERDIC) presided over the privatization of six of the country's twenty-four state-owned firms. Interestingly, the country's oil refinery was sold to the Nigerian National Petroleum Corporation, a firm that has played an important role in the Nigerian ruler's effort to manage his own political network. Although they did not play a major role in fighting against RUF, Nigerian troops and supplies arrived in Sierra Leone soon after the initial 1991 incursion from Liberia.

The radical model of privatization has extended to finding private foreign management firms to run the Central Bank and the state-owned National Development Bank, as has already occurred with the state lottery.[80] The port has been effectively privatized to Iranian firms, which have been contracted to build a new $45 million complex and then to manage it to recoup construction costs.[81]

Privatization has extended to coercion in a manner that has reduced threats to rulers but not increased the state's bureaucratic capacity. Executive Outcomes' local commander highlighted the extent to which foreigners had become surrogates for state institutions when he noted upon his arrival that "there was no intelligence service. I had to create one. The problems of elementary supply, communications and transport had to be solved."[82] Sierra Leone's rulers have become terribly dependent upon shared interests with foreign businesses. In this regard, the Sierra Leone government has appeared to take on the guise of what marxist scholar Walter Rodney described as a comprador, or an agent of foreign economic interests.[83] A more meaningful analogy, however, is found in Michael Doyle's concept of "imperialism by invitation" in which he views the arrival of foreign groups as the outcome of efforts by local elite factions to recruit outside help to deal with local rivalries they cannot handle alone.[84]

CONSOLIDATING A NEW
WARLORD POLITICAL ALLIANCE

Executive Outcomes' presence established enough security to hold elections in March 1996. The proposition of electing a civilian president still did not appeal to everyone in Strasser's entourage. But outside support for a poll and, most critically, Executive Outcomes' interest in being seen as a facilitator of elections strengthened the hands of those rhetorically committed to the idea. In his January 1996 palace coup against Strasser, Bio promised not only elections (which gained him Executive Outcomes and outside support) but also to form strong ties with Kamajors and reliable anti-insurgency units in the army.

Voters elected Tejan Kabbah, a politician from the southern part of the country. On the surface, it seemed the return to electoral politics and a hotly contested election marked a decisive turn in the country's political life. But in reality, the election helped to consolidate a reconfigured political alliance rooted in Executive Outcomes' presence—the firm's alliance with a new group of politicians and the destruction of Sierra Leone's old bureaucracies, including much of the military. All of this left the political alliance heavily dependent on the presence of foreigners.

Executive Outcomes and its successors have been critical links in tying Sierra Leone to global markets. Generating revenues from diamond mining was not simply a matter of liberalizing mining regulations and unleashing the energies of small operators who might support political opponents and build their own private armies. Instead, Executive Outcomes cleared mining areas of politicians and military strongmen who had accumulated wealth without the approval of the president.

Paradoxically, the arrival of Executive Outcomes and its partners signaled the opposite of liberalization, even though it was consistent with creditor policies and aims. Presidents and creditors had concluded that when conventional state institutions are weak, effective control over commerce and revenues can be exercised by foreign firms that dominate supplies of resources and fight off competitors. In this manner, the Sierra Leonean arrangement with foreign firm partners resembled Liberian warlords' use of foreign firms as revenue sources and tools with which to wrest resources from rivals. In return for high profits, foreign firm partners that survived the end of the Cold War with the comparative advantage of intact commercial-security networks have served as intermediaries to recruit other foreign investors and perform functions previously reserved for states.

Meanwhile, Sierra Leone's rulers discovered that continuing global recognition of their sovereignty brought significant additional benefits. As Taylorland showed, sovereignty is not an absolute requirement for attracting foreign firms to do business in troubled places, but it is the key to including multilateral creditors in the new political alliance. The presence of Branch Mining in Sierra Leone helped to routinize minimal payments on debts and enabled creditors to engage in face-saving write-offs of debts. Executive Outcomes used elections in Sierra Leone as a powerful marketing tool to appeal to both future clients and international organizations that still play a major role in the financial affairs of very weak states. Internally, the political detaching of resources from the old Cold War political network allowed the president to proceed with harsh economic reform policies and to do so with more security. This, in turn, assured that rival strongmen were unable to mobilize resources and people to threaten the ruler.

Creditor representatives, diplomats, and members of major NGOs in Freetown found that the presence of Executive Outcomes and other foreign firms in Sierra Leone made their jobs easier. Foreign officials concerned about disorder in Africa appreciated the fact that Strasser, Bio, and Kabbah remained in place as globally recognized interlocutors with foreigners interested in Sierra Leonean affairs, whatever they thought about Executive Outcomes or private military services in general. This preference on the part of officials in other states reflects their difficulty in carrying out diplomacy with people who may exercise real power but who do not fit within current regimes for determining concessionary credit arrangements, protecting foreign investments, receiving overseas aid, and other global relations that are usually negotiated between sovereign states.

This reconfiguration is much less disruptive for outsiders as long as firms such as Executive Outcomes prop up rulers who can address mutual interests without forcing diplomats to acknowledge the true nature of political authority. Officers of foreign organizations involved in Sierra Leone prefer to avoid Liberia- and Somalia-type situations in which personal insecurity makes their jobs impossible to perform. As long as foreigners can move freely about the country, food aid and development projects can be administered, donors can see positive results, and more money can be collected from satisfied contributors. As Executive Outcomes commander Lafras Luitingh pointed out "Had we not gone in when we did and pushed the rebels out of the suburbs of Freetown, you would have the same situation here that you have in Liberia. Does anyone really want that? Do the people need such anarchy?"[85] A Western embassy official and a UN worker echoed each other, saying of Executive Outcomes that "the stability is appreciated."[86]

The security foreign mercenaries provide and the local operations of foreign aid organizations help to further marginalize most people from the centers of power. Inhabitants of marginal areas may benefit from some of those activities, but benefits appear to be coincidental to their proximity to essentially private commercial operations.

With help from outsiders to protect him from the demands of his own citizens, Kabbah found greater flexibility to construct a new political network. Unlike Stevens but like Momoh, Kabbah could not use state assets or manipulate economic policies as the major incentives to attract supporters, since corruption, creditor prescriptions, and military offensives against rivals had drastically pared down or eliminated those options. Instead, as with warlords in Liberia, Kabbah used his privileged ties to foreigners to facilitate favored private business operations or at least to deny them to disfavored groups or individuals. His reliance on Executive Outcomes and related private firms such as Branch Mining gave him a measure of autonomy vis-à-vis local rivals and the global economy. Foreign participation was much more integral to local political networks than had been the case in the recent postcolonial past. These partners were more easily watched from the State House as they exploited resources, squeezed out rivals, and generated profits according to the rules of global markets.

For example, Kabbah used concessions to small foreign mining firms to attract political supporters. Private security forces kept these mining areas relatively free of interlopers, so smaller, more marginal foreign operations found Sierra Leone an attractive place to do business. The presence of foreign security forces and local anti-insurgency irregulars recruited by small firms allowed the president to award mining licenses with less concern about cooperation from local strongmen who had previously exercised authority in their own right. Small firms learned that they could milk outsiders for themselves if they created and financed closely associated "NGOs" to attract money and political support from overseas donors. In joint venture arrangements with favored local politicians, "social service" spending by firms through "NGO" fronts encouraged local people to associate benefits with the firm's and the politicians' presence.

A small U.S. gold mining firm provides an example of such an arrangement. The firm was attracted to Sierra Leone once Executive Outcomes had pacified the mining areas, and it created a charitable organization when it arrived. This "NGO" had the same initials as a much better known organization. Heads of the organization—Congolese originally involved in charitable agencies that bid on food supply contracts to Mozambique—raised funds in the United States. The leaders, who did not conceal their association with the mining operation (which was also active in Congo), advertised their partnership in Sierra Leone as an attempt to create "self-sustaining local capacity" to help finance more relief operations with contributions from the mining firm. A politician from the area in which the mine is located helped to sponsor a "women's movement" that shares offices with and receives goods from the "NGO." Once in operation, the "NGO" applied for grants from aid agencies and creditors eager to demonstrate their commitment to grassroots civil society organizations as part of their efforts to display support for marginal groups.[87]

One worker for a more established NGO cynically observed that local politicians have discovered that it is profitable to include words such as *women's movement, peace, or micro* in organization titles to attract external funding.[88] Members of truly independent grassroots organizations in Sierra Leone have complained that foreign-sponsored conferences to identify and advise those groups hamper their efforts to do real work, but they must attend as a precondition to receive grants. Meanwhile, the conferences also educate enterprising heads of front NGOs about the current trends in development administration that win grants. This addition to the new warlord political network incorporated even more foreigners into Sierra Leonean politics who identified stability and security as pressing imperatives.

Could this novel, transformed global network of private and official organizations provide Sierra Leoneans with security and revive economic opportunities? Economic opportunity has remained in privileged hands, although new members have been added to that group, some have been removed, and others have either ascended or descended in the hierarchy of privilege. Some disengaged citizens not included in the group found protection in the *Afrique utile* that attracted foreigners and their arms. But the dominance of a favored economic network, as with the patrimonialism that preceded it, forced enterprising Sierra Leoneans to work with select foreign firms and a clique of politicians. More important, massive civil service cuts and the necessity of running conventional state operations on a for-profit basis eliminated politicians' long-term option to build popular legitimacy through state provision of services. When alternative front NGOs provided local services, their operation was subordinate to the interests of foreign shareholders and investors rather than accountable to local people who received benefits.

THE FUTURE FOR MERCENARIES

The centrality of foreign private soldiers to the weak-state coalition in Sierra Leone became especially apparent after Kabbah's election. He faced at least three coup attempts in his first ten months in power, mostly from officers concerned about what they saw as the president's growing alliance with Kamajors and Executive Outcomes at the expense of the unreliable army. Those alternative military forces also allowed Kabbah to take seriously the demands of outside mediators in the conflict who argued that marauding soldiers undermined government legitimacy, diverted scarce resources, and justified radical cuts in army enlistment. All of these factors warned these soldiers that Kabbah would not allow them easy access to their customary rewards.

This disaffection made Executive Outcomes' presence very important to Kabbah. Reportedly, the firm's intelligence efforts uncovered the coup plots, and the firm moved directly to defuse them.[89] Executive Outcomes was also essential in the successful military campaign against RUF. Counterinsurgency efforts continued in 1996, pinpointing rebel strongholds. This success forced Sankoh to leave Sierra Leone for Abidjan and was likely decisive in forcing him to sign a cease-fire agreement in November 1996. The firm also mediated between Kamajors and the regular army, separating clashing fighters in an October 1996 skirmish in which 100 troops were killed.[90]

Although all of this activity sustained the outward image of a Sierra Leone state and permitted mining to continue, it did virtually nothing to address the needs of the people in Sierra Leone who had gone to the polls expecting a civilian government would mark a decisive change in the way the country was governed. Instead, a locally conducted opinion poll six months after the election showed that

> The majority of the people interviewed expressed disappointment about the performance of the Kabbah government, citing indicators like the deteriorating economic situation, growing hardships and poverty, galloping inflation, irritating blackouts, mass unemployment, [and] growing insecurity in the country evident in increasing rebel ambushes upcountry and armed robbery in the cities. Allegations of corruption in high places, [and] undue exploitation of our mineral resources with little or no benefit to the people, also feature prominently in the various responses.[91]

The essentially private nature of the new political accommodation combined with the exigencies of economic austerity programs meant the benefits of even civilian rule were primarily private and were limited to members of the accommodation.

This makes Kabbah's refusal to renew Executive Outcomes' contract beyond January 1997 all the more curious. IMF concerns about the diversion of state revenues to mercenaries appear to have been responsible in part for Kabbah's action.[92] Kabbah also likely perceived that the political benefits of loyal Kamajor units were separable from Executive Outcomes. But the integral role played by foreign, private soldiers became apparent as soon as they departed in February 1997 when the country's security immediately worsened. Johnny Koroma, a junior officer, led a combined sobel force of army troops and rebels in a successful coup against Kabbah on 25 May 1997.[93] In April 1995, undisciplined soldiers joined with RUF fighters to loot Freetown.

Unlike Taylor's organization, those fighters lacked large-scale connections with foreigners who could help them negotiate with outsiders or organize commerce. Thus, their control of Freetown left them conspicuously unable either to assume the role of an interlocutor with global organizations or states or to assuage the anxiety of foreigners who had to confront the fact that the capital was occupied by unorganized brigands. This weakness made the sobel "government" an easy target for foreign sanctions designed to restore Kabbah's regime. The difficulty lay in how to negotiate (or force) the departure of an unorganized group of armed fighters. This crisis shows the extent to which, when pressed, outsiders define "stateness" much less in terms of an administrative capacity to do something than in terms of sustaining a suitable interlocutor who acknowledges obligations and can organize profitable commerce with outsiders.

At the time of this writing, the most stability in Sierra Leone is found within the archipelago of mineral resources scattered across the country. Firms such as ArmSec International and Lifeguard continue to guard mine sites at which some Kabbah government officials seek protection.[94] The restoration of a political authority recognizable as a government of Sierra Leone will probably have to rely on the resumption of a partnership with private militaries and foreign firms, even if the internal configuration of that authority substantially resembles warlordism. This assessment recognizes that other states and international organizations are unlikely to bear the considerable financial expense and political risks of state building and that the restoration of a central authority in Sierra Leone will have to be compatible with the private pursuit of profit in a very bad neighborhood.

VIOLENCE AND STATE FORMATION

Ultimately, foreigners who take on military tasks will likely remain a crucial part of the new political configuration of some very weak states—whether as large, visible firms such as Executive Outcomes; as smaller-scale operations that rely on foreign firm contacts for financing, training, and supplies; or as specially trained paramilitary units firms leave behind. This scenario is likely because minimal formal state revenues and ruler fears of renewed security threats preclude reviving large armies to combat rebels or building effective state agencies to address the problems that generate rebel groups. Foreigners who correctly regard African armies and corrupt bureaucracies as threats to new electoral politics such as Sierra Leone's also help to preclude a more conventional state-building strategy. The lack of widespread development through state agencies also means young people will continue to be drawn to gangs that loot for a living, even if, as in Sierra Leone, formal agreements are reached with rebel leaders.[95]

Sierra Leone turns on its head the Weberian notion that a state's viability is proportional to its capacity to monopolize the exercise of violence. This monopoly became a liability to Doe when he ran out of external funds to maintain it and his associates turned this state "strength" into a weapon against him. Sierra Leone's rulers avoided a similar fate for a time by privatizing violence, contracting out the task of disciplining wayward politicians and social groups. The subsequent failure of that strategy will likely make at least some outsiders more tolerant of ruler alliances with mercenaries in the future.

The dog that does not bark in Weber's analysis of the character of individual states is the expansion both of military services by nonstate actors and of global economic opportunities that favor those actors. Both forms of expansion have consequences that bear heavily on the reconstitution of political authority in places such as Sierra Leone. As Charles Tilly has argued, warfare creates expanding demands for revenue, which allows the lower strata to demand a voice in decisionmaking. Tilly wrote, "No taxation without representation" is a universal slogan.[96] But the option of incorporating foreign financiers and fighters into a new political alliance offered Sierra Leone's rulers (as was true with warlords in Liberia) an alternative arrangement. In those cases, warfare does not force militaries to enmesh themselves in civilian oversight of budget procedures.

Furthermore, outsiders' preferences helped to discourage Sierra Leone's rulers from building political authority in the image of conventional states. Recognized statehood by itself, however, provides validation by outside authorities. Strasser, Bio, and Kabbah had the advantage of associating themselves with the historical memory and prestige of the polity that preceded them. This external standing gave them the illusion that the suppression of rebel activity and economic "reform" constituted state restoration as far as outsiders were concerned. Rulers' effective use of this resource in Sierra Leone contrasted starkly with Charles Taylor's frantic search for external legitimacy. His idiom of mystical powers, of traditional war leader, or having been bilked out of rightful possession of the Executive Mansion evoked no response from outsiders. Hence follows his and his foreign lobbyist's efforts to style himself as a statesman—a friend of former U.S. president Jimmy Carter—and his efforts to stage a successful (if violent) electoral campaign to become the president of the Republic of Liberia.

But lip service to and exploitation of statehood, even in Sierra Leone, remain at odds with standard definitions of sovereignty. Sierra Leone, as with Taylorland, shows that the privatization of violence in the interest of new political alliances means size and uniform control over territory matter less. Control of resources has greater weight than uniform administrative control over one's entire corner of the world, especially in places such as Sierra Leone where valuable resources are concentrated and portable.

Congo, the next case, demonstrates the even wider applicability of the notion of a global coalition of warlord politics in Africa. It also highlights the crucial role foreigners play in reconfiguring patronage politics when they conclude that pared-down, commercially viable political networks are superior to liberal democracy. This is particularly the case in politically tumultuous states that otherwise risk joining the ranks of "failed" states such as Liberia, Somalia, Afghanistan, and Bosnia—states that haunt the foreign ministers of powerful states.

NOTES

1. Interpress news agency dispatch, 11 March 1996.
2. Quoted in Jim Hooper, "Sierra Leone—the War Continues," *Jane's Intelligence Review*, 8:1 (Jan. 1996), 43.
3. Stephen Riley, *Liberia and Sierra Leone: Anarchy or Peace in West Africa?* (London: Research Institute for the Study of Conflict and Terrorism, 1996); U.S. Department of State, *Sierra Leone Country Report on Human Rights Practices for 1996* (Washington, D.C.: Department of State, 1997), 3.
4. "Sierra Leone: End of the Road," *Africa Confidential*, 13 Feb. 1985.
5. David Luke and Stephen Riley, "The Politics of Economic Decline in Sierra Leone," *Journal of Modern African Studies* 27:1 (March 1989), 133–142.
6. Bank of Sierra Leone, *Economic Review*, nos. 1–16 (Freetown: Bank of Sierra Leone, 1965–1969).
7. Sierra Leone Government, Government Gold and Diamond Office, *1988: Annual Report* (Freetown: Government Gold and Diamond Office, 1989). On state recession, see Fred Hayward, "State Consolidation, Fragmentation and Decay," in Donal Cruise O'Brien, John Dunn, Richard Rathbone, eds., *Contemporary West African States*, 2d ed. (New York: Cambridge University Press, 1989), 165–180.
8. Robert Bates, *Markets and States in Tropical Africa* (Berkeley: University of California Press, 1981).
9. Sahr John Kpundeh, *Politics and Corruption in Africa: A Case Study of Sierra Leone* (Lanham, Md.: University Press of America, 1994); Sahr John Kpundeh, "Limiting Administrative Corruption in Sierra Leone," *Journal of Modern African Studies* 32:1 (March 1994), 139–157.
10. C. Magbaily Fyle, ed., *The State and Provision of Social Services in Sierra Leone Since Independence, 1961–91* (Dakar: Codesira, 1993).
11. "Sierra Leone's Currency Conflicts," *Africa Confidential*, 25 April 1979.
12. "Sierra Leone: The South Africa Connection," *Africa Confidential*, 17 Sept. 1986. On other PLO links to Sierra Leone through the Lebanese community, see "Sierra Leone: In Trouble," *Africa Confidential*, 17 March 1982.
13. Stephen Ellis, "Les prolongements du conflit israélo-arabe en Afrique noire: le cas du Sierra Leone," *Politique Africaine* 30 (June 1988), 69–75.
14. "Sierra Leone: Lebanon's Shadow," *Africa Confidential*, 20 Aug. 1986.
15. Personal sources in Momoh's government, Freetown, Dec. 1989.
16. Author's visits to Kono District mining operations, 1989–1990; "Review and Revitalisation of the Mining Economy" (mimeo) (Freetown: Ministry of Finance, March 1990).
17. A. B. Zack-Williams, *Tributors, Supporters and Merchant Capital: Mining and Underdevelopment in Sierra Leone* (Aldershot: Avebury Press, 1995).

18. "Sierra Leone: Momoh Strengthens His Hand," *Africa Confidential,* 21 Oct. 1987; Eban Davies, "Sierra Leone: Momoh's Woes," *Third World Week,* 2 Dec. 1988, 3–7.

19. International Monetary Fund, "1988 Article XIV Consultations" (mimeo) (Nov. 1988).

20. International Monetary Fund, EBS/89/233, "Sierra Leone: Staff Report for the 1989 Article IV Consultation," 27 March 1990.

21. Max Sesay, "State Capacity and the Politics of Economic Reform in Sierra Leone," *Journal of Contemporary African Studies* 13:2 (June 1995), 165–191.

22. Yo'av Karny, "Byzantine Bedfellows: What Israel Does for Itself— and for Us," *New Republic,* 2 Feb. 1987, 23–28.

23. On LIAT, see "Sierra Leone/South Africa: The Strange Story of LIAT," *Africa Confidential,* 24 June 1987; "Sierra Leone: More South African Connections," *Africa Confidential,* 7 Jan. 1987; "LIAT to Task!" *For Di People,* 18 March 1988.

24. "A Dose Too Much," *West Africa,* 6 July 1987; "Africa/Israel: In One Bound, Kalmanowitch Is Free," *Africa Confidential,* 2 April 1993.

25. Sierra Leone Government, Ministry of Mines, "Report of the Inspector of Mines" (mimeo) (Freetown: Ministry of Mines, July 1989).

26. International Monetary Fund, "Sierra Leone."

27. "Sierra Leone: Middle Eastern Affairs," *Africa Confidential,* 8 Sept. 1989; "Don't Confuse Issues Guaz!" *For Di People,* 23 Nov. 1989; "SCIPA to Shape Up or Ship Out," *New Nation,* 20 Jan. 1990.

28. National Diamond Mining Company, correspondence, "Kimberlite Project Negotiations with Sunshine Boulle of Texas, USA," 6 Feb. 1990.

29. Sierra Leone military source, Freetown, June 1994. See also, "Fighting for Diamonds," *West Africa,* 24 June 1991, 1034.

30. "Voisey's Bay Man Aims to Repeat Success," *Financial Times,* 26 Sept. 1996.

31. Sierra Leone Government, Ministry of Agriculture, Natural Resources and Forestry file, "Proposed Joint Venture Agreement for Management and Control of Fishing Rights in Sierra Leone's Territorial Waters" (Freetown: Ministry of Agriculture, 1990).

32. "MPSSL Deal to Scrap!" *We Yone,* 11 Dec. 1991; Bank of Sierra Leone, *Economic Trends* (Freetown: Bank of Sierra Leone, July–Sept. 1992), 8.

33. Eddie Momoh, "Revolution in Crisis?" *West Africa,* 7 Dec. 1992.

34. "Taylor's War in Sierra Leone," *New African,* July 1991, 17–18; Bernadette Cole, "Taylor's Hand," *West Africa,* 22 April 1991, 591.

35. "Charles Taylor to Annex Part of Sierra Leone?" *We Yone,* 30 March 1992; "Politics of Rebellion," *West Africa,* 21 Sept. 1992, 1608; "Checking the Advance," *West Africa,* 27 May 1991, 863.

36. "Interview with Foday Sankoh," *National,* 21 March 1991 (transcript of BBC program of 6 March 1991).

37. Fyle, *The State and Provision of Social Services,* 51–59.

38. Paul Richards, "Video and Violence in the Periphery: Rambo and War in the Forests of Sierra Leone–Liberia," *IDS Bulletin* 25:2 (April 1994), 88–93; Paul Richards, *Fighting for the Rainforest: War, Youth and Resources in Sierra Leone* (Portsmouth, N.H.: Heinemann, 1996). The same young men appear in the formal military ("the militariat"), wrote Jimmy Kandeh in "What Does the 'Militariat' Do When It Rules? Military Regimes in The Gambia, Sierra Leone and Liberia," *Review of African Political Economy* 69 (1996), 387–404.

39. Scott Stearns, "In Rebel-Held Country," *West Africa*, 15 April 1991, 560.

40. "Help from Guinea and Nigeria," *West Africa*, 22 April 1991, 625.

41. Paul Richards, "Rebellion in Liberia and Sierra Leone: A Crisis of Youth?" in Oliver Furley, ed., *Conflict in Africa* (London: I.B. Tauris, 1995), 150; S. Byron Tarr, "The ECOMOG Initiative in Liberia: A Liberian Perspective," *Issues* 21:1–2 (1993), 74–83.

42. On Guinea ties, see Steve Riley and Max Sesay, "Sierra Leone: The Coming Anarchy?" *Review of African Political Economy* 63 (March 1995), 123.

43. "RUF from All Sides," *Concord Times*, 23 Nov. 1995.

44. "Sieromco-EO Contract," *Africa Energy and Mining*, 11 Sept. 1996; for allegations that this was a diamonds-for-arms operation, see K-Roy Stevens, "Is the Honeymoon Over?" *West Africa*, 21 Oct. 1996, 1630.

45. "Checking the Advances," *West Africa*, 27 May 1991, 863.

46. U.S. Arms Control and Disarmament Agency, *World Military Expenditures and Arms Transfers*, 1993–1994 (Washington, D.C.: U.S. Government Printing Office, 1995), 81.

47. Siaka Massaquoi, *Sierra Leone: The April 29 Revolution* (mimeo) (Freetown: 1992); Comi Toulabor, "Le capitaine Strasser croque le pouvoir au pays des diamants," *Politique Africaine* 57 (March 1995), 149–154; C. Magbaily Fyle, "The Military and Civil Society in Sierra Leone: The 1992 Coup d'État," *Africa Development*, 18:2 (1994), 17–30.

48. Joseph Opala, "Ecstatic Renovation: Street Art Celebrating Sierra Leone's 1992 Revolution," *African Affairs* 93:371 (1994), 195–218.

49. John Karimu, *Government Budget and Economic and Financial Policies for the Fiscal Year, 1995/96,* (Freetown: Government Printer, 1995); Economist Intelligence Unit, *Sierra Leone*, 1st quarter, (London: Economist Intelligence Unit, 1995), 26.

50. Sierra Leone Government, *White Paper on the Report of the Mrs. Justice Laura Marcus-Jones Commission of Inquiry* (Freetown: Government Printer, Jan. 1993); Sierra Leone Government, *White Paper on the Report of the Justice Beccles-Davies Commission of Inquiry*, 2 vols. (Freetown: Government Printer, Aug.–Oct. 1993).

51. "New Mining Policy Measures Relating to Artisanal Mining and Marketing of Precious Metals," *Sierra Leone Gazette*, 11 Jan. 1996.

52. Personal source, Ministry of Finance, Freetown, 14 Feb. 1996.

53. Sheku Saccoh, "Capital Flight in Sierra Leone," *Africa Economic Digest*, 13 Feb. 1995; "Sierra Leone's Mines Evacuated," *Mining Journal*, 27 Jan. 1995, 57.

54. Economist Intelligence Unit, *Guinea, Sierra Leone, Liberia*, 2nd quarter (London: Economist Intelligence Unit, 1995), 26.

55. "Sierra Leone Nears Collapse," *Africa Economic Digest*, 13 March 1995, 17.

56. Mike Butscher, "Counting the Costs," *West Africa*, 22 July 1991, 1203.

57. Karimu, *Government Budget*, 17.

58. Fred Hayward and Jimmy Kandeh, "Perspectives on Twenty-Five Years of Elections in Sierra Leone," in Fred Hayward, ed., *Elections in Independent Africa* (Boulder: Westview, 1987), 25–59.

59. A. K. Kamara, *Sierra Leone: The Agony of Independence* (Freetown: Tarus Communications, 1996), 41.

60. John Momoh, "Life Under Taylor," *West Africa*, 22 July 1991, 1205.

61. Jim Hooper, "Sierra Leone," 41–43.

62. Sibyl MacKenzie, "Rent-a-Gurkha," *Soldier of Fortune* 19:3 (March 1994), 30–31.

63. Sibyl MacKenzie, "Death of a Warrior," *Soldier of Fortune*, 20:7 (July 1995), 36–41; William Minter, *Apartheid's Contras* (Johannesburg: Witwatersrand University, 1994), 156–158.

64. Personal source, Freetown, 27 Jan. 1996.

65. Interview by the author with informant, Freetown, 29 April 1995.

66. François Picard, "L'etrange mission des mercenaires sud-africains en Sierra Leone," *Le Monde*, 2 Oct. 1995; Hooper, "Sierra Leone," 41–46.

67. Interview by the author with West African military official, 29 January 1996. See also James Butty, "Recourse to Arms?" *West Africa*, 24 June 1991, 1035.

68. Al J. Venter, "Sierra Leone's Mercenary War Battle for the Diamond Fields," *International Defense Review* 28:11 (Nov. 1995), 61–66; Al J. Venter, "Not RUF Enough," *Soldier of Fortune* 20:12 (Dec. 1995), 32–37.

69. "Soldiers for Sale," *Africa Confidential*, 19 July 1996; "Valentine Strasser," *Lettre du Continent*, 21 Sept. 1995; "Angola: The Big Diamond Battle," *Africa Energy and Mining*, 4 Oct. 1995.

70. Alec Russell, "Africa's Soldiers of Fortune Discover That Peace Can Pay," *Daily Telegraph*, 26 Feb. 1996; "Angola: The Big Diamond Battle," *Africa Energy and Mining;* "Tony Buckingham," *Intelligence Newsletter*, 29 Sept. 1995; Herb Howe, "South Africa's 9-1-1 Force," *Armed Forces Journal* 134:3 (Nov. 1996), 38–39.

71. "Sierra Rutile Reopening Depends on Funding," *Mining Journal*, 11 Oct. 1996, 283.

72. Interview with journalist, Freetown, 28 June 1996.

73. Discussions with a Miami-based businessman with mining interests in Sierra Leone, January–March 1996. See also holiday greeting advertisements in *Expo Times*.

74. John Swaray, Governor of the Bank of Sierra Leone, "Debt Reduction Programme" (mimeo), 4 April 1995; "Paris Club Debt Relief Negotiation," *BSL Bulletin* 2:2 (April 1996), 42.

75. Economist Intelligence Unit, *Sierra Leone: Country Survey, 1994–95* (London: Economist Intelligence Unit, 1995).

76. Hooper, "Sierra Leone."

77. Jim Hooper, "Peace in Sierra Leone: A Temporary Outcome?" *Jane's Intelligence Review*, 9:2 (Jan. 1997), 91–93; Venter, "Not RUF Enough."

78. Economist Intelligence Unit, *Guinea*, 4th quarter, 1995, 21.

79. "Liberian Connection Back," *Africa Energy and Mining*, 10 April 1996.

80. "Sierra Leone: Privatisation Goes All Gears," *Africa Economic Digest*, 27 May 1995, 24.

81. Economist Intelligence Unit, *Sierra Leone*, 2nd quarter, 1996, 29.

82. Venter, "Not RUF Enough," 74.

83. Walter Rodney, *How Europe Underdeveloped Africa* (Washington, D.C.: Howard University Press, 1982).

84. Michael Doyle, *Empires* (Ithaca: Cornell University Press, 1986).

85. Venter, "Not RUF Enough," 76.

86. Telephone interview, Miami to Freetown, 4 April 1996; Washington, D.C., 7 June 1996.

87. See, for example, Mariama Coker, "[———] Donates," *Expo Times*, 21 Feb. 1996.

88. Interview with a representative of a religious charitable organization, Washington, D.C., 7 June 1996.

89. Hooper, "Peace in Sierra Leone," 91.

90. Ibid., 91–93.

91. "Opinion Poll Report," *Gazette Times,* 30 Sept. 1996, 3.

92. "Sierra Leone Accord Ends Five-Year Civil War," *Jane's Defense Weekly,* 11 Dec. 1996, 15.

93. See "Sierra Leone: Koroma's Coup," *Africa Confidential,* 6 June 1997; Stephen Riley, "Sierra Leone: The Militariat Strikes Again," *Review of African Political Economy* 72 (June 1997), 287–292.

94. Interview with an official of an international organization, Washington, D.C., 17 June 1997.

95. "Sierra Leone: Not in Charge Yet," *Africa Confidential,* 21 June 1996, 5.

96. Charles Tilly, *Coercion, Capital and European States, 990–1990 A.D.* (New York: Blackwell, 1992).

5

▼ ▼ ▼ ▼ ▼

SOVEREIGNTY AND THE FRAGMENTATION OF THE DEMOCRATIC REPUBLIC OF CONGO

Look again at the glorious empire of the French, Seek there the price of sad Zaire's ransom.
                                                                    —*Voltaire*[1]

France remains an enemy, by nature, of anarchy and its outcomes in the immense territory of Zaire.
          —*Business journal commentary on French support for Mobutu*[2]

Zaire's[3] true political system operates outside the conventions of formal state sovereignty. Military and political associates of Zaire's president Mobutu Sese Seko (1965–1997) contended for power with Kengo wa Dondo, head of a legislative opposition, after 1994. Ethnically based regional cliques have used extensive ties to outsiders and the familiar medium of control over markets to manipulate access to wealth and enhance personal or factional power. As in previous cases of warlord politics, Zaire's contending strongmen have benefited from the concentration of portable, valuable natural resources—which have also attracted foreign-run enclave operations—and have regarded formal state institutions as threatening because they fear bureaucracies acquire their own interests and power.

This fragmentation of Zaire's political system represents a stark contrast to what Thomas Callaghy called a "Zairian absolutism" of effective patrimonial control in the 1970s and 1980s.[4] This shift strongly resembles the disintegration of Samuel Doe's patronage networks in Liberia. As with Doe, Mobutu's remarkable success at co-opting and balancing different political factions, once financed with reliable outside sources of income, encouraged him to persist in past practices even when resources suddenly declined. Mobutu's first response to crisis was to intensify old strategies. As with Doe, Mobutu's apparent monopoly over the distribution of resources to a single patronage network discouraged him from innovating even as the pace of change quickened in the late 1980s. And as in Liberia, strongmen quickly discovered that changing conditions brought them new opportunities to profit on their own, and enterprising politicians used old positions of privilege to take advantage of new opportunities and resources offered by defection from the president's network.

How did Mobutu weather for so long the collapse not only of Zaire's state institutions but also of his presidential network of strongmen and aspiring politicians who actually ran Zaire before the 1990s? And in the months since Laurent Kabila finally removed Mobutu from power in May 1997, how has the nature of state collapse under Mobutu influenced Kabila's own construction of authority?

THE POLITICS OF RESOURCES IN ZAIRE

Mobutu realized that he needed global recognition of the sovereignty of a Zairian state to attract diplomatic support and foreign aid. Unquestioned formal sovereignty also simplified deals with some foreign firms and creditors. This analysis follows the observations of those who have concluded that the exercise of political power in Zaire has owed more to the syncretic amalgamation of colonial and precolonial political networks based on economic control than to formal notions of proper state behavior. They have stressed, however, that this exercise of political power has clashed with economic efficiency.[5] Yet starting at least in 1990, Mobutu discovered that this incompatibility, which post–Cold War shifts aggravated, suddenly and rapidly decreased his capacity to reward associates for their loyalty. He had to find a way to fragment the power of increasingly unruly strongmen while tapping new sources of wealth.

As with Doe in Liberia, Mobutu's success as a patrimonial ruler saddled him with an extensive network of clients who were powerful in their own right. Mobutu proved more able at managing this problem by using Charles Taylor's innovative nonbureaucratic strategies of rule through control by manipulating market opportunities, even when actual sources of accumulation were not under his direct control. As with Taylor, Mobutu left individual military units and commercial syndicates to forage on their own. Different factions jealously guarded useful territory and opportunity from rival entrepreneurs. Competition among these groups reduced the chances of mutiny or coordinated attacks on Mobutu. Individual strongmen appealed to Mobutu for protection against local rivals even as they consolidated virtually autonomous fiefdoms organized around commerce in diamonds, gold, coffee, timber, cobalt, and arms.[6]

The center of politics shifted, however. As Mobutu's role as a patron declined, questions such as who was an "original inhabitant" acquired new importance as local strongmen and their followers jockeyed to control local resources. For example, debates in eastern Zaire over who was an "authentic Zairian" provoked ethnically based attacks on descendants of eighteenth-century migrants from Rwanda. Local strongmen incited communal rivalries to drive critics away. The victims of that strategy usually abandoned their assets and fell prey to extortion by their tormentors who demanded goods or money in return for safe passage. Local strongmen then distributed those goods to local followers or exported them for personal profit.[7] As with RUF, shocking acts of violence against civilians were used to encourage populations to abandon property and flee from fighters. This policy benefited Mobutu insofar as it forestalled resistance and contained challenges after the collapse of patron-client networks. Whereas Doe relied on his well-armed and trained paramilitaries to help him fend off rivals, Mobutu realized that his best chance for survival lay in also using opposition among factions of his patronage network to neutralize the network's threat to him.

Mobutu used this method for the same reasons warlords use it—because it does not require a command hierarchy that can acquire interests of its own, and it obstructs rivals' attempts to build their own organizations. But Mobutu also worked to retain control rather than to overwhelm another's control over a sovereign state. Mobutu's strategy showed some parallels to the anti-insurgency doctrine of his foreign supporters by disrupting opponents' attempts to organize rather than trying to control them directly. Eeban Barlow's former associates in South Africa's Civil Co-operation Bureau, for example, had recruited members of opposition communities to sow suspicion, create confusion through assassinations, and use torture to shock others into passivity.[8] This tactic of strong states in the past proved to be within the grasp even of rulers of very weak states who also appreciated its low cost and indirect nature.

The existence of multiple centers of accumulation in Zaire promotes this radical decentralization of politics. As with Sierra Leone and Liberia, Zaire's resources are concentrated and portable. But the formal state territory is thirty-two times larger than Sierra Leone's with ten times as many people. Deposits of copper, cobalt, gold, and diamonds are scattered about the country, thereby avoiding a scramble for a single piece of territory as is the case in Sierra Leone's diamond fields. The country's vastness and its archipelago of resources leave broad stretches of *Afrique inutile* that physically separate some political groups. Because of the breakdown of rail and road networks, mineral-rich provinces such as Shaba and Kasai do much more business with their southern neighbors than with Zaire's domestic market. Kivu in the east has closer contact with Rwanda, Burundi, and Uganda than with most of Zaire. Collapsing infrastructure also encouraged Mobutu's associates to exploit local opportunities, thus making life difficult for rivals, rather than collaborating with others to mutiny against Mobutu. In this context, the ownership of air cargo firms highlights contours of political competition or alliances better than do formal agreements or individuals' titles.

Competition within these centers of accumulation for control over trade left a political space for Mobutu to manage crises in old ways. In contrast, Doe's former clients quickly overwhelmed him as they shifted allegiance to Taylor as the likely future president and patron or fought among themselves for control of resources. Even foreign firms initially scrambled to Taylor's side. More akin to Zaire, Sierra Leone's rulers found foreign friends just in time to help them weather the loss of their relatively limited indigenous sources of wealth. But sovereignty is even more important to Zaire's state rulers in attracting allies, since rivals there are less quickly or handily defeated with foreign private military and private firm help.

The Kengo government's pretense to implement reform and impose austerity showed how the benefits of sovereignty were actually shared while factions struggled to control resources. Some outsiders have treated Kengo, as head of the "democratic opposition" Union pour la démocratie et le progrès social (UDPS), as a "responsible" alternative to Mobutu. Creditors saw Kengo as an interlocutor who acknowledged debts and agreed to implement reforms. His status as a reformer positioned Kengo to reap the benefits of manipulating liberalization to favor his faction's power and attract foreigners interested in Zaire's resources. But Mobutu, the target of Kengo's manipulations, also benefited from Kengo's reputation as a reformer when renewed creditor and foreign firm interest in Zaire provided Mobutu with assets and relationships that he could use as political resources.

Political struggle focused on resources and trade—as opposed to formal declarations of political authority—or on state institutions has created a special role for some South African firms and other mining companies that have an unusual capacity to do business in the contentious political environment in Zaire. Their arrival has reinforced the decentralization of Zairian factional politics, since many of these firms have become insinuated into local strongmen's political strategies and have shared in the commercial benefits of Zairian state sovereignty under Mobutu and then Kabila. Here, too, firms have found that they can manipulate liberalization to attract creditor support for their operations—some have even tried to convince creditors to subsidize their joint ventures with local strongmen. For outsiders, the cloak of Zaire's sovereignty helps to conceal the extent to which their deals are integral to strengthening one group vis-à-vis another.

The specific features of decline after the end of the Cold War and of Mobutu's response to that crisis highlight the innovative strategies Mobutu and his rivals used to reshape politics within the conventions and formal boundaries of Zaire in ways familiar to global society. Those actions then imposed constraints and introduced opportunities that have influenced Kabila's efforts to rule the country. First, I examine how Mobutu's rejection of conventional state-building options and specific features of his patrimonial politics reshaped Zaire and promoted the rise of warlord politics.

Mobutu's Elimination of State-Building Alternatives

Zaire has many commercial and diplomatic opportunities that can be translated into political resources. If we take 1986 as a baseline before mineral exports began to fall precipitously, the copper, cobalt, zinc, and diamond exports of state-run firms generated $1.15 billion in the formal economy that year. Coffee, the country's main agricultural export, added an additional $80 million.[9] This left uncounted the profits from money laundering, illicit exports, and drug trade, which Mobutu translated into patronage when he exercised direct control over the clandestine trade of those goods. Giving up a staunch anti-Communist stance in exchange for aid from superpower patrons netted him $448 million in 1986.[10] Total visible nontax resources at Mobutu's disposal thus stood at almost $1.7 billion that year. Added to that amount was U.S. diplomatic support for loans from multilateral creditors in return for aiding UNITA rebels in Angola and permission to use a Zairian air base at Kamina to resupply UNITA.[11]

During the 1980s, Mobutu was more successful than Doe at incorporating creditors into his political alliance. Callaghy observed that Mobutu masterfully manipulated relations with creditors, alternating promises with brinksmanship to keep loans coming.[12] The International Monetary Fund returned to Zaire in 1983 after a five-year absence and disbursed $1.3 billion to Mobutu's government over the next five years. A senior IMF official in Washington resigned in protest of what he claimed was improper U.S. pressure on the IMF to treat Zaire leniently in Paris Club debt negotiations that granted Zaire a six-year grace period on bilateral debt payments. Creditor patience with Mobutu seemed almost limitless during the Cold War. From 1976 to 1990, IMF officials devised fourteen stabilization programs for Zaire. Between 1975 and 1985, continual gentle treatment at Paris Club debt renegotiations led to the rescheduling of $3.5 billion of Zaire's 1985 $7.5 billion external debt. Mobutu also boasted personal ties to World Bank officials. In one instance, he actually hired as his personal assistant a World Bank official who had access to confidential information about granting aid to Zaire.[13] These examples show the extent to which Mobutu exercised autonomy in relations rather than simply acting as a French or U.S. Cold War client.[14]

These resources underwrote Mobutu's patron-client network, giving him control over the distribution of resources to loyal associates. The prevalence of large, politically motivated projects in the 1970s and 1980s underscored the importance of outside finance in sustaining Mobutu's patronage network. The Inga-Shaba project, which cost $1.5 billion in 1983 alone, typified the reliance on external resources. The project included a hydroelectric dam to supply electricity to mining areas in Shaba province, 1,100 miles away. Although electricity could have been generated more cheaply closer to the mine sites, the project provided construction contracts for foreign firms in exchange for U.S. and French support of Mobutu during revolts in Shaba—which supplied about half of Zaire's mineral exports—in 1977 and 1978.[15] Shaba's massive and inefficient Tenke-Fungurume copper mine, designed to tie in to the Inga project, typified Mobutu's increasing reliance on outside help to exploit natural resources and thus accumulate wealth.

Mobutu's November 1973 nationalization of large local firms played a major role in foreclosing a political strategy based on collecting revenues from entrepreneurs who would be supported by pro-growth economic policies. Mobutu instead expropriated agricultural and commercial enterprises from primarily foreign owners (what he called Zairianization) and converted them to political resources he could distribute to loyal associates. Most of the beneficiaries had no managerial experience.[16] The economically destructive policy drove down the proportion of agricultural exports in Zaire's foreign trade from 28 percent of total earnings when Mobutu took power in 1965 to about 6 percent in 1990.[17] Although it provided commercial and agricultural properties for political clients, the policy gutted tax revenues from agricultural trade, which declined from 61 percent of state revenues in 1973 to 28 percent in 1978.[18]

This internal shrinkage of productive capacity, along with the availability of external wealth, reinforced Mobutu's reliance on arrangements with foreigners to run state-owned mines, the most promising remaining indigenous source of wealth. This reliance on outsiders ended Mobutu's need to underwrite expensive state bureaucracies, some of which had tended to become vehicles of secessionist movements (discussed later). Mobutu, who exercised private control over many of Zaire's resources with foreign help, safely abandoned expensive health care facilities, schools, and public works—all of which served citizens but contributed little to his stock of political resources. Rural areas that no longer provided much state revenue could be abandoned as an *Afrique inutile* as Mobutu faced growing pressure to choose which clients would be patronized and which would be jettisoned.

Mobutu's decision to allocate 2.1 percent of state spending to health and education in 1990, compared with 17.5 percent in 1972, reflected a rational choice from the perspective of a weak-state ruler.[19] The dramatic decline of formal-sector agricultural production for export also followed Mobutu's disinterest in cultivating support among small agricultural producers and entrepreneurs in exchange for revenue and legitimacy. Those who produced crops for export in the 1980s thus faced extremely low official prices for their goods. For example, the Zairian state marketing board that bought and sold coffee, Office Zairois de Café, paid farmers seven cents per kilogram of coffee in 1985, whereas smugglers paid forty-two cents.[20] Most marketing boards had disappeared by the early 1990s, as farmers smuggled their produce or grew only subsistence crops.

Meanwhile, Zaire's state resources had become thoroughly concentrated in Mobutu's hands, even exceeding the personalization of state resources in Sierra Leone in the 1990s. The long-term shift of government expenditures to the president's office reflected Mobutu's personal control of state resources (Table 5.1). World Bank statistics consistently reported lower percentages of state spending under direct presidential control. For example, in 1992 the World Bank reported that 64.7 percent of Zaire's budget was reserved for Mobutu's discretionary spending compared with an official Zairian report of about 95 percent.[21] A former Zairian official suggested that this discrepancy reflected creditor efforts to portray Mobutu's corruption in the best possible light to convince observers that perhaps Mobutu would support reform after all and that debts could be collected.[22]

The rapid increase in the privatization of the state budget in 1990 coincided with creditors' post–Cold War impatience with Mobutu's unkept promises of economic reform. In 1991, the IMF announced that Zaire was behind on $81.7 million in payments to the organization and would receive no new loans. Three years later, the IMF expelled Zaire. This event helped to start a rapid increase in outside pressure on Mobutu, along with rising popular demands for reform—all of which led Mobutu to even more radically privatize the state. At first, he did not completely abandon his strongmen associates. Instead, he allocated virtually no state expenditures to social services or physical infrastructure after 1992, using the money to replace resources lost elsewhere.

This state retreat from citizens reflected the extent to which Mobutu relied on his extensive personal networks rather than effective institutions

Table 5.1   Privatization of Government Expenditures 1972–1992 (percent)

Year	President	Agriculture	Social Services
1972	28.0	29.3	17.5
1974	26.0	32.1	12.4
1976	29.0	30.9	13.2
1978	29.0	41.0	11.0
1980	33.0	42.0	11.0
1982	35.0	32.0	10.0
1984	39.0	30.0	9.0
1986	39.0	29.0	7.0
1988	49.0	18.0	4.0
1990	80.0	11.0	2.0
1992	95.0	4.0	0.0

Source: Banque du Zaire, *Rapport annuel,* various issues.

for regime survival. This philosophy differs from Sierra Leone under Momoh's rule in that Mobutu actually controlled the distribution of the bulk of state resources through those networks. The extremely negative effects of Mobutu's rule on most Zairians, however, likely foreclosed a reversal, since any official accountability to popular needs would have generated organized calls for him to leave office.

Most Zairians faced the harsh consequences of an economy that had shrunk 40 percent between 1988 and 1995 and of inflation that had risen to 23,000 percent in 1995.[23] Twenty-five years after independence, only 15 percent of the roads inherited from Belgian colonial rule remained passable.[24] Guidebooks for foreign travelers reserved lurid language for Kinshasa, warning that rampant daytime banditry and rogue police exceeded the fabled dangers of Lagos. Infrastructure collapse provided publishers abroad with tales of arduous travel up the Zaire River. Authors evoked Joseph Conrad's description of the gigantic, anonymous forests and the lassitude from which state structures were absent.[25]

As private control over state resources destroyed the productive capacity of state agencies, Mobutu's ability to extract resources from the informal sector assumed ever greater importance. Abjuring "development" in any conventionally understood sense, Mobutu used state power exclusively to help associates profit from clandestine trade, avoid taxation, and explore new rackets in activities that made use of state regulatory power such as passport sales, money laundering, and drug trafficking. Those activities generated considerable wealth. Estimates of exports of gold and diamonds from Zaire in 1992, for example, suggest a trade worth over half a billion dollars annually.[26] Mobutu's control of radical privatization required reining in enterprising associates, since he had to control external commercial networks to consolidate his position as the exclusive regulator of access to even clandestine foreign exchange as formal economic opportunities disappeared and state institutions collapsed.

Mobutu's intensified strategy of building political authority through market control increasingly impinged upon local authorities who used access to illicit trade to help themselves and their neighbors weather the collapse of state institutions.[27] Janet MacGaffey and Mukohya Vwakyanakazi have shown how community trade networks that developed in the 1970s and 1980s contravened predations of Mobutu's political network. Many of those entrepreneurs still had to deal with local strongmen who used state offices and ties to Mobutu for extortion. But MacGaffey and others found some entrepreneurs operated independent of political interference,[28] which would have threatened Mobutu's authority.

The financial and political stakes for Mobutu of controlling a greater proportion of trade were high. If we take 1990 as a base, Mobutu controlled over $3 billion. His control of the output of state-run mining firms alone contributed $1 billion to his political resources. These and other state revenues devoted to the president's office totaled $1.5 billion annually, a figure that rose in the late 1980s to compensate for the decline in multilateral creditor lending. Overseas development assistance in 1990 brought in $822 million, despite Mobutu's otherwise deteriorating relations with creditors and donor governments.[29] Together, these same sources of income generated only $1.121 billion in 1993 (Table 5.2). Mobutu no doubt also benefited from Zaire's half a billion dollar diamond trade and possibly from another half a billion dollars from diamond and arms traded between Zairian and Angolan UNITA rebels in the 1980s.[30] Thus, even if Mobutu had controlled all of Zaire's trade and production, formal and clandestine, he would have faced declining overall accumulation of wealth. As creditors and more foreign firms left Zaire, declining investment in mining equipment cut production in the formal sector even further.

Mobutu's dilemma was that he could intrude more deeply into clandestine economies, but to do so would generate the ire of strongmen and local authorities who tapped those economies for their own benefit. In any event, he could not have replaced all of the lost political resources. Mobutu's strategy of milking state assets had reached its limits. Mobutu had weathered the collapse of a bureaucratic state, which many had thought would be his downfall, with greater finesse than his Liberian colleague, President Doe; Mobutu, however, now faced a true crisis: the serious recession of his patronage system.

THE ILLUSION OF LIBERALIZATION

By 1990, Mobutu faced serious challenges to his ability to rule through patronage. Foreign state officials not only ended their support of Mobutu,

Table 5.2 Recorded Trade Originating from Congo (Zaire), 1989–1995 (in $ millions)

	1989	1990	1991	1992	1993	1994	1995
Oil	$167.0	$148.0	$165.0	$40.0	$130.0	$156.0	$160.0
Tin	$16.4	$14.2	$8.2	$5.3	$3.9	$5.0	$5.5
Diamonds	$400.0	$320.0	$220.0	$200.0	$289.0	$296.0	$376.0
Coffee	$692.0	$548.0	$483.0	$487.0	$330.0	$432.0	$450.0
Copper	$813.0	$892.0	$525.0	$302.0	$136.0	$120.0	$150.0
Cobalt	$404.0	$418.0	$218.0	$125.0	$54.0	$120.0	$160.0
Zinc	$82.0	$79.0	$59.0	$28.0	$0.0	$0.0	$12.0
Overseas development assistance	$634.0	$823.0	$494.0	$262.0	$178.0	$235.0	—
Total	$3,208.4	$3,242.2	$2,172.2	$1,449.3	$1,121.9	$1,364.0	ca. $1,313.5

Sources: Figures refer to the origin of trade and thus include known clandestine transactions. International Monetary Fund, *International Financial Statistics Yearbook* (Washington, D.C.: International Monetary Fund, 1990); Knight-Ridder Financial/Commodity Research Bureau, *The CRB Commodity Yearbook* (New York: John Wiley); United Nations Conference on Trade and Development, *Commodity Yearbook* (New York: United Nations); United Nations, *International Trade Statistics Yearbook* (New York: United Nations); various issues of *Mining Journal* and *Marchés Tropicaux.*

but many now openly backed his rivals. A Troika of former backers—Belgium, France, and the United States—pressured Mobutu to begin political and economic reforms. A key Belgian Socialist Party leader, Ronald van den Bogaerd, openly supported Etienne Tshisekedi, a longtime Mobutu rival, as an alternative to the president.[31] Formerly supportive French officials condemned Mobutu's regime, cutting aid in 1991 to about $100 million—one-third the level of aid two years earlier—and distancing themselves from Mobutu. French President Mitterrand promised that "French aid will be conditional towards authoritarian regimes and more enthusiastic for those beginning a democratic transition."[32]

Impatience among U.S. officials posed even greater problems for Mobutu. U.S. Undersecretary of State for Africa Herman Cohen criticized Mobutu in testimony before the U.S. Congress in 1991. Zairian reformers cited those statements and others by Melissa Wells, U.S. ambassador to Zaire, as evidence that U.S. officials expected a democratic transition in Zaire.[33] More than on democratization, however, U.S. official ire toward Mobutu focused on Mobutu's inability to service his debts to the U.S. government, which under provisions of the Brooke Amendment required that the U.S. Congress cut off aid.

Soon thereafter, the World Bank broke its ties with Mobutu. The immediate cause was Mobutu's appropriation of $400 million from Gécamines, the state-run copper mining conglomerate, and his refusal to allow an audit of the firm's books. The break with the United States and the end of South African and U.S. backing for his alliance with UNITA rebels in Angola, who were heavily involved in diamond mining, deprived Mobutu of a key clandestine patronage resource. Mobutu's diminished importance to UNITA reduced his capacity to manage his associates' clandestine diamond mining and arms transfer businesses with Angola.[34]

Mobutu appeared to bend to domestic and outside pressure to reform in April 1990 when he announced the legalization of independent opposition parties. The convening of a national conference in Congo across the river from Kinshasa appeared to provide a model for reform. The conference opened in Kinshasa in August 1991 under the leadership of Archbishop Laurent Monswengwo Pasinya, known for his neutrality and apparent lack of political ambition. Television and radio carried live debates. The conference culminated in the formation of a Haut conseil de la Republique (HCR), which was expected to negotiate a handing over of power from Mobutu to Tshisekedi, the conference's choice as interim leader. Student protests in 1990, along with foreign condemnation of Mobutu's repression of those protests, generated even higher popular expectations of change.

The rise of Tshisekedi as an opposition figure appeared at first as a formal legal challenge to Mobutu's authoritarian rule. More serious for

Mobutu, the new visibility of Tshisekedi, a Luba-Kasai from diamond-rich Kasai Oriental, revived memories of old struggles to control resources. Tshisekedi had achieved fame as a dissident parliamentarian in 1980 when he and twelve others charged the army with the massacre of over 300 diamond miners in Kasai Oriental. As with Stevens's associates in Sierra Leone, Mobutu's military strongmen and his business associate Bemba Saolona had long exploited diamonds in the region by controlling trade routes from UNITA-held diamond fields.[35] As an additional threat, Tshisekedi tried to use technocrats to run Zaire's Central Bank, which would have deprived Mobutu of the last of Zaire's state resources. Mobutu dismissed Tshisekedi, although he lacked the legal authority to do so. Critics responded with a Union sacrée (Sacred Union) to unify opposition parties.

As with sovereignty, formal political opposition needs to be understood in the broader context of disintegrating patron-client politics and extreme de-bureaucratization. Multiparty politics did not merely signal the surfacing of factions. Instead, factions marked the end of the more centralized patronage network, which Michael Schatzberg termed a "State as Bandit" in which rivals position themselves for the scramble to parcel out resources.[36] Closer observation reveals that de-bureaucratized patrimonialism instilled an individualistic, acquisitive "capitalist lifestyle" in the Weberian sense explored in Chapter 1. For example, a booklet from Mobutu's era entitled *Devenez Riche Rapidement* (Get Rich Quickly) advised, with apparent official sanction, "liberating the mind of all doubts as to the legitimacy of material wealth. . . . A man is more of a man when he has more wealth."[37] This philosophy was a "reinvention of [a previously unsustainable] capitalism" akin to Taylor's Kalashnikov lifestyle or even to aggressive acquisitiveness in industrial economies such as Japan's bubble economy of the 1980s. The philosophy was politically explosive in the Zairian context, since officially sanctioned private accumulation among strongmen is easily compatible with autonomy from a ruler and with freedom to make their own arrangements with outsiders.

Mobutu faced a serious contradiction. He could use his security forces to disorganize his rivals, but that risked bolstering military units that could remove him in his weakened state. Yet to do nothing would be to encourage his opponents. He chose the former strategy. Student protests and the HCR conference were met with army looting and attacks on opponents in 1990 and 1991. Mobutu could do little more than incite rather than command troops, since most soldiers were unpaid.

The violence had costs for Mobutu, too. Looting and the destruction of remaining infrastructure prompted Chevron Oil and many other foreign firms to leave Zaire, along with 20,000 foreign managers who were evacuated after rioting in September 1991.[38] Copper and cobalt production began radical declines. Without maintenance crews, machinery and production stopped. Banking services collapsed, making formal economic activity almost impossible. The recession of Mobutu's patronage resources was in full swing. Equally significant were shifts in those who controlled exports, a matter examined in detail later.

By 1992, the president had entered maximum vulnerability. Crawford Young has called this stage the "shattered illusion of the Integral State," akin to the authoritarian pretensions of Leopold's Congo. Recognizing the unsustainability of Mobutu's course, Young wrote that "surely a reinvented Zaire, whatever name it will bear, will be grounded in a relationship between state and civil society profoundly different from that imported by the integral state."[39] Centralized power in the hands of a state ruler had ended in Zaire. Nonetheless, Mobutu still had recourse to alternative strategies that would weigh heavily in the reconfiguration of Zaire's sovereignty and political economy.

MOBUTU'S CRISIS MANAGEMENT STRATEGY

Mobutu resorted to short-term measures to reverse the decline of his control over resources and, hence, of his political authority. In 1992 he purchased banknotes from a German company to pay troops, thus bypassing the Tshisekedi-controlled legislative council's legal responsibility for fiscal matters. This action led to hyperinflation, with the national currency—the zaire—declining to 110 million to the dollar in 1993. In Kinshasa, Tshisekedi's HCR, competing to control the benefits of economic activity, responded with its own currency. As in Liberia, one's use or refusal of a particular version of the country's currency became an indicator of which rival authority one obeyed. The ploy was also a desperate attempt by Mobutu to hold on to instruments of patrimonial control even though he was not in a position to accumulate wealth.

Mobutu's long-run problem lay in reasserting his political authority amid declining resources. His patronage network fragmented as he lost his capacity to match his old rate of payouts. Much of the (unpaid) army had disappeared by the early 1990s, for example, declining from a peak of 70,000 troops in the mid-1980s to close to 20,000.[40] Mobutu's first step was to give new roles to specialized security forces. He gave six distinct military units substantial new latitude of action to profit from clandestine trade. By decentralizing the military, Mobutu bent to the reality of radically declining patronage resources. In a vast country with many centers of accumulation, he could more easily tolerate private mining or trade rackets. Each unit jealously watched the others while struggling to control its own wealth. This situation turned organizations that had once served the ruler's, if not the state's, interests into a more exclusively self-interested commercial syndicate.

The Guarde Civile, for example, had 10,000 troops under the command of General Kpama Baramoto, a close associate of Mobutu. The general expanded his role in clandestine trade after 1992, especially in Kivu where he ran gold and diamond mining operations.[41] Here, factions were exploiting ties with outsiders on their own, a feature central to the breakdown of state-centered patronage systems. By 1996, Baramoto was involved in a joint venture with the U.S.-based Barrick Gold Corporation to mine in Bunia. Barrick also provided funds to refurbish a local airport, which helped Baramoto to compensate for his unwillingness and incapacity to spend money on local infrastructure.[42] A local airport likely attracted Baramoto, who needed transportation to keep close track of his diamond mining operations in Kasai and his stakes in air cargo companies. The Bunia airport also helped to cement Mobutu's ties with outside allies when Sudan's regime, for example, used it to ship weapons to Ugandan insurgents.[43]

But rather than threatening Mobutu's control, this situation gave Mobutu the capacity to interfere with the diamond trade in Tshisekedi's home base in Kasai and helped to move clandestine trade from UNITA-held areas in Angola into Baramoto's hands. Joint military-UNITA mining operations allegedly spread to Angola itself. In Kasai, Baramoto's soldiers protected LIZA, a diamond mining venture owned by Mobutu's son Manda. This syndicate operated several other mining ventures in which soldiers guarded alluvial miners who clandestinely gathered diamonds within Miniére de Bakangwa (MIBA) mine sites.[44] Since Mobutu's Kasai-based opposition now controlled MIBA, those operations deprived that political faction of resources.

Other units went into business. Mobutu's Division Spéciale Présidentielle (DSP), under General Nzimbi Ngbale Kongo, organized cobalt shipments from Shaba province to Zambia in coordination with Kyungu wa Kumwanza, Mobutu's governor of the province.[45] Mobutu benefited indirectly from ties between Kyungu and another old crony from Shaba, Nguza Karl-I-Bond. Mobutu could not block the faction's separatist tendencies under its Union des Federalistes et Republicains Independants (UFERI). Although he could not control the group's actions directly, he could use UFERI to deny his rivals in Kinshasa and elsewhere access to Shaba's resources. Kyungu reportedly enlisted South African militias, including Inkatha units, to help protect and run mining operations on his own.[46] Again, apartheid-era security organizations reappeared as commercial partners. Kyungu and his allies also targeted immigrants who shared Tshisekedi's Luba-Kasai origins, seizing their property, distributing it to local supporters, and sending perhaps a million immigrants back to Kasai.[47] This action ended the possibility of a united opposition or an alliance of separatists against Mobutu. Similar attacks by "local" people against immigrants of Rwandan origin took place in north Kivu, with the support of Mobutu and his associates.[48]

This divide-and-rule strategy gave military organizations considerable leeway to act as private armies. Although he was unable to reward allies directly, Mobutu encouraged units to commit acts of violence against opposition groups and thus create a climate of distrust and instigate local conflict. Even the Kinshasa government joined the looting in 1996, supporting a decree that stripped Zairian citizenship from people of Rwandan-Tutsi ancestry and directed them to give up their property.[49] As with private armies in former Yugoslavia, loosely organized militaries used terror to remove unwanted people; mutilated captives, for example, were sent back to their communities to display their injuries, create fear of the troops, and promote flight.

This minimalist strategy fragmented political authority by "inviting" the exit from the polity of those no longer useful to warlord politics after stripping them of their assets. The strategy was cheap and easy to employ, and it created its own stability based on balancing contending forces without the need for a bureaucratic military organization. It also showed that disorder in Zaire was not the result of anarchy but rather of a deliberate strategy. The strategy also harkens to aspects of Rhodesian and South African military doctrine that disrupt enemy societies and create confusion. This strategy of using military experts in strong states against insurgents proved adaptable to Mobutu's interest in minimizing cost, providing plausible denial, and managing his associates and rivals. The strategy was especially suitable because it was not designed to seize territory or control institutions. In the context of Mobutu's warlord politics, control could not be sought in this expensive and politically unmanageable way. Instead he aimed to preoccupy, destroy, and disorganize any rival—especially multiethnic—authority.

Mobutu remained in power and thus prevented Tshisekedi from establishing political authority capable of moving against the president, despite Tshisekedi's more populist character and his location in the capital. Meanwhile, Mobutu used his remaining resources to buy off critics, pay off his supporters and defectors from the Union sacrée, and entice some notable people to serve as ministers in his government. By June 1994, the HCR had compromised with Mobutu's old parliament, and the two merged under Kengo wa Dondo, a former Mobutu ally and a technocrat who attracted backing from creditors and the Troika. This consolidation of Mobutu's position came just in time to allow him to exploit opportunities to further buttress his powers as a result of the Rwanda crisis in 1994 and the sudden expansion of South African and foreign mining firms in Africa. The new alliance made Mobutu's presence more palatable to those among his old clique who now opposed him, since

Kengo appeared much less hostile toward Mobutu than had Tshisekedi and thus seemed less likely to hold the old guard's former association with Mobutu (and its ill-gotten wealth) against its members.

The division of his internal opposition did not restore the control over wealth Mobutu had enjoyed in the 1970s and 1980s. For that to occur, outsiders would need to provide patronage or serve as partners to help to exploit Zaire's natural resources, a prospect that looked slim by 1994. Among the Troika, the French government backed away from the now isolated Tshisekedi in early 1994. The 1992 election of President Bill Clinton in the United States brought no new initiatives to punish Mobutu but left him without a supporter in the White House. Meanwhile, Belgian officials still refused to deal directly with Mobutu.[50] This external political rejection cut off most aid and loans to Mobutu. Mobutu's divide-and-rule strategy may have become less relevant in Zaire as his control over resources diminished further, but sudden developments in the region gave him more access to new, cross-border sources of wealth and new alliances that buttressed warlord politics among Mobutu's associates and rivals alike.

MOBUTU'S NEW DIPLOMATIC RESOURCES

Mobutu's global isolation eased rapidly as the Revolutionary Patriotic Front (RPF), an army composed of Rwandan exiles, advanced deep into Rwanda from Ugandan territory in October 1993. French military forces flew 150 troops stationed in the Central African Republic to Kigali, Rwanda's capital, to defend the incumbent regime, and Belgian forces contributed 400 paratroopers to the intervention. Recognizing an opportunity to emphasize coinciding interests with his former patrons, Mobutu immediately sent several hundred troops from his DSP, which had remained loyal to him during Zairian army mutinies in 1991 and 1992. Unlike the European troops, the DSP troops actually battled the RPF.[51]

Without concerns about domestic popular opinion opposing the intervention, Mobutu could offer political and military services to French politicians who would otherwise have faced political criticism at home for taking such direct action. For example, Mobutu provided French officials with a rear base for their troops who arrived to protect Rwandans when President Habyarimana's regime crumbled against the RPF onslaught. This support helped to reintegrate Mobutu into Central African and global diplomatic circles. His support of the French goals also pleased French officials concerned about RPF links to outsiders who were hostile to French clients in Africa. Some RPF leaders had fought with Ugandan president Museveni's guerrilla forces a decade earlier, thus helping him to come to power. From the perspective of some members of the French government, Museveni appeared to be an "Anglo-Saxon force of instability." Minister for Cooperation (a bureau distinct from the French Foreign Ministry) Jacques Pelletier seemed especially attached to the view that "Uganda is only a pawn of Anglo-Saxon imperialism and the RPF is simply a marionette of Kampala."[52]

French officials broke with Belgian rejection of and U.S. coolness toward Mobutu and met him at his home in Gbadolité in April 1994 at the height of the Rwanda crisis. The meeting opened new diplomatic channels for Mobutu. Herman Cohen, U.S. undersecretary for African affairs under President Bush, attended the meeting. As president of the private Global Coalition for Africa, Cohen received World Bank financing to help mediate political conflicts on the continent. Michel Aurillac, former minister of cooperation and later an adviser on Africa to President Chirac, also attended, as did Jacques Foccart, a former adviser on Africa to DeGaulle and éminence grise of France's Africa policy.[53]

Some have suggested motives for the French officials–Mobutu meeting. Michel Lambinet, editor of *Lettre d'Afrique,* reported that Robert Bourgi, Mobutu's personal adviser (and brother of Albert Bourgi, editor of the influential weekly *Jeune Afrique*),[54] was eager to make amends with Mobutu to sustain his role in a "Franco-Lebanese part of the Foccart clan that takes advantage of the diamond trade abroad to finance Jacques Chirac's campaign."[55] Lambinet landed in court, accused of defamation. Nonetheless, Foccart took credit for having organized contributions from African rulers to finance neo-Gaulist party election campaigns in France.[56] French foreign policy experts also allegedly lobbied Mobutu to allow Sudanese troops to cross Zaire on their way to fight rebel forces in the country's south. France rewarded Mobutu by lifting visa restrictions on him and his associates after the Foccart visit.[57]

Some journalists reported that the French-Mobutu collaboration also brought Mobutu aid from Egyptian military trainers for the DSP intervention in Rwanda. Mobutu's foreign contacts expanded when he met with South Africa's secret service chief, and he also attracted the interest of private U.S. political advisers. Barbara Hayward, a former Reagan and Bush adviser, and Cohen's business partner James Woods, former secretary of state for defense for Africa, met with Mobutu in December 1994 after he had engaged Woods and Cohen's public relations firm to represent him in the United States.[58]

Cohen's influence came from his former position as undersecretary of state for African affairs; his partner's influence came from his former position as chief of African affairs in the Department of Defense. Cohen is also director of the Global Coalition for Africa, which mediates conflicts and introduces business leaders to African rulers. Both Cohen and

Woods have good relations with officials in Angola and South Africa, since they mediated agreements with U.S. officials that led to Namibian independence and the withdrawal of Cuban troops from Angola.[59]

Mobutu received considerable local political benefits from his reconciliation with French foreign policy officials. Eastern Zaire, especially the Kivu area, is culturally and economically tied to East Africa. With the large number of people of Rwandan ancestry in the east who had ethnic ties to the RPF, the RPF victory in Rwanda posed a threat of weakening the hold of Mobutu and his associates over Kivu. Mobutu thus instigated violence among refugees, the local population, and potential separatist politicians in Kivu, as he had done earlier.[60] Mobutu also shared the French suspicion of President Museveni of Uganda who backed English-speaking Rwandan forces.

Mobutu's reconciliation with foreign backers encouraged some of his domestic opponents to agree to a conclave to merge the rival legislatures and replace Tshisekedi with Kengo. The choice of Kengo as prime minister gave Mobutu more control over affairs in Kinshasa. Kengo, who had a Polish father and a mother who was part Rwandan, lacked ethnic connections that had given Tshisekedi an autonomous power base. Kengo's isolation increased further with the violence in Kivu, since his mother came from the disfavored "outsider" Rwandan-Tutsi group.

Mobutu's reconciliation with France paved the way for France's Opération Turquoise, an armed intervention into Rwanda in late June 1994 as the RPF captured the Rwandan capital. French politicians pronounced the intervention, which was managed from Goma in Kivu province, a mission to stop remnants of the old government—still entrenched in western Rwanda—from continuing to massacre Tutsis. The operation helped Mobutu to rapidly find a place in the diplomatic world as a principal player in Central Africa, which garnered him an invitation to the Franco-African summit in Biarritz in November 1994 (from which the new Rwandan regime was excluded). This recognition ended Mobutu's diplomatic isolation with the French. Mobutu even hosted his own "summit meeting" on the Rwanda issue in Gbadolité in late 1994. France gave Mobutu leeway to play a domestic game without having institutions or material patronage. He could allow anti-Tutsi ethnic extremists exiled from Rwanda to organize on Zairian territory. His willingness to allow humanitarian organizations to supply refugee camps in Zaire gave extremist groups access to resources they could use to feed their fighters and distribute to their supporters in those camps. This relationship prolonged the refugee crisis to Mobutu's benefit, since extremists joined original inhabitants to attack outsider groups.[61]

In August 1995, Kengo's government moved to expel Rwandan refugees, some of whom had armed themselves to fight the Rwandan regime and to intimidate local refugees and Zairians. At first, this move appeared to challenge Mobutu's political balancing act. Reports alleged that the wife and brother-in-law of the president of the defeated Rwandan regime who now supported the extremists had accompanied Mobutu to China in November 1994 to buy arms.[62] Such ties reflected DSP links to Rwandan militias in exile in Zaire that had solidified during the earlier DSP intervention into Rwanda. Even though expelling refugees would have helped to defuse Mobutu's game of aggravating ethnic tensions, outsiders decided that changes in Mobutu's behavior rather than Kengo's would encourage Rwandan refugees from Zaire to return home. Kengo's and the HCR's hostility toward the refugees was condemned by aid agencies, which feared another unorganized exodus. This concern translated into new promises of aid, which could be used as a resource to destabilize political groups in Kivu. At the same time, those anxious to protect the Rwandan government had to deal with Mobutu to block destabilizing expulsions of refugees from Zaire.

Mobutu halted expulsions four days after Kengo's order. As with Taylor, his centrality to a crisis attracted the attention of former U.S. president Jimmy Carter, who met with Mobutu in Portugal in September 1995 to convince him to attend a conference on Central African security later that year.[63] Carter sought to play a mediating role and to enlist Mobutu in an effort to resolve the refugee crisis. In fact, Mobutu used the opposition to expulsions as a diplomatic weapon against the Rwandan government, using it to serve French patrons and to reinforce his position as the sovereign of Zaire in global eyes.

By 1996, Mobutu had completed his diplomatic rehabilitation, at least in the French view. In April he met French president Jacques Chirac on French soil—a meeting arranged through the Cellule Africaine, a bureau in Chirac's office that manages relations with francophone African leaders.[64] The head of the Cellule, Michel Dupuch, was a protégé of Foccart, who was one of Mobutu's strongest supporters in the French foreign policy establishment—a situation that eased Mobutu's diplomatic return. The meeting dealt with Zairian arms sales to rebels in Burundi, the president of which had personal ties to some of Mobutu's Gbadolité entourage.[65] Mobutu used those ties and foreign concern about Hutu exiles from Burundi as he had used Hutu refugees from Rwanda to manipulate internal and external actors for his personal benefit. The normalization of Mobutu's global status (despite his having armed Hutu militias) attracted bilateral aid. German officials visited Gbadolité after Mobutu's French tour, offering an ECU 84 million aid package.[66]

MOBUTU, RELIGION, AND PROFITS

Mobutu used his ties to foreign governments to exploit their concerns about the possible state collapse in Zaire and instability in Central Africa. At the same time, Mobutu used his status as the globally recognized ruler of Zaire to attract foreigners who had little interest in maintaining global norms or advancing official policy. They used Mobutu's status as ruler of a sovereign state to pursue activities that had more to do with personal profit. Foreign public relations firms collected fees to bolster Mobutu's image as ruler of a sovereign state and used their connections to introduce business associates to Mobutu. More significant, ties with foreign religious organizations that were attracted to profitable opportunities in Zaire gave Mobutu a new means with which to regulate domestic rivals in the spiritual, as well as the commercial, world. Mobutu used these and other firms to help him secure acceptance by members of the increasingly fractious Troika.

Mobutu vainly sought to attend the UN's fiftieth anniversary celebration in New York in late 1995. He engaged another lobbying firm, that of conservative activist Paul Erickson, to procure a U.S. visa, expanding his lobbying efforts beyond the firm of Cohen and Woods, discussed earlier.[67] As former political director of Pat Buchanan's 1992 presidential campaign, Erickson had high visibility in Washington. Jack Abramoff joined Erickson in this venture. Abramoff provided contacts from his previous position as executive director of the conservative lobbying group Citizens for America and as national president of College Republicans.[68] Abramoff's contacts may have been even broader. A South African Truth Commission report in 1996 alleged that (unknown to Abramoff) some of Abramoff's political activities in the 1980s had been financed by South African intelligence networks to promote right-wing U.S. political activists' claims that the African National Congress was a Communist front organization.[69]

Mobutu's allies also included Henri Damas Ombga, a Cameroonian businessman accused of illegal drug and arms dealing.[70] Other contacts, including a delegation of French businesspeople who visited Gbadolité in 1996, advanced Mobutu's cause among commercial networks recruited to undermine diplomatic pressure on his regime.[71]

Mobutu's relationship with 1988 U.S. presidential candidate and evangelist Pat Robertson revealed a more innovative private diplomacy that reached beyond conventional public relations firm or lobbyist efforts. Mobutu recruited Robertson in his quest to secure a U.S. visa. More important, Robertson brought his African Development Company (ADC), which was active in diamond, timber, gold, and power-generation businesses to Zaire. This commercial venture operated alongside Robertson's Operation Blessing, an enterprise billed as a humanitarian relief effort for Rwandan refugees in eastern Zaire. Operation Blessing included commercial ventures, too, including a 50,000-acre farm near Kinshasa. Robertson justified the profit-seeking nature of what was otherwise a religious venture as part of his efforts to generate cash for his relief work.[72]

As with the charity-mining operation in Sierra Leone, Robertson's operation used the rhetoric of "sustainable development" to attract contributions from foreigners and to depict its business as a nongovernmental organization that was providing social services. Mobutu collaborated in this commercialization of charity by appointing Tonga Boki, the head of Mobutu's old state-run labor union, to run an "NGO union" to coordinate "private" activity and solicit overseas support.[73] Foreign religious charities were also used to undermine homegrown religious-based political opposition groups in Zaire, some of which were inspired by the leadership of Catholic Archbishop Monsengwo, who had gained popular respect for his intransigent anti-Mobutu stance. To counter Monsengwo's popularity as a religious critic of Mobutu, Mobutu used 1990 measures that liberalized the media to attract U.S. ministries that would not question Mobutu's authority. Pat Robertson's fiery preaching appeared alongside that of fellow U.S. evangelist Jimmy Swaggart, who suggested that the downtrodden should accept their lot in this life and expect relief in the next.

The evangelizing-commercial spirit spread to Mobutu's entourage. Honore "the Terminator" Ngbanda, once Mobutu's intelligence service head and now "Brother Ngbanda," ran a Christian café and appeared on television giving Bible sermons.[74] Mobutu's visitors included the Reverend Moon, Jehovah's Witnesses, and various U.S. Baptist and Pentecostal groups.[75] Moon's interest extended to mass conversions in the military and in Frente de Liberação do Enclave do Cabinda (FLEC), a separatist movement in Angola's Cabinda enclave under Mobutu's patronage. Moon's organization also appears to have run a logging company, as it had done in Taylorland during the Doe period.[76]

FOREIGN FIRMS AND "REFORM"

Although Mobutu's regime fell seriously into arrears on debts, he managed to maintain contacts with creditors who looked favorably on Kengo's austerity efforts. The HCR remained committed to layoffs in the country's civil service and anticipated reducing state employment from 600,000 to 50,000 employees and trimming the size of the army.[77] Kengo thus took political responsibility for unpopular and harsh austerity measures, whereas Mobutu benefited from tentative contacts with creditors that were anxious to receive payments and to avoid Zaire's disintegration.

Meanwhile, Mobutu manipulated the creditor prescriptions needed to reach a comprehensive agreement with the IMF to profit his political network. IMF officials made clear that future loans depended on establishing a free market in Zairian currency. Accordingly, several ethnic Lebanese diamond dealers associated with Mobutu's entourage proposed that their Qualitoles Company would set up exchange bureaus in cooperation with the Central Bank of Zaire. Qualitoles would sell dollars below informal market rates, and the bank would pay the difference between the two rates. The plan was promoted as a way to lower unofficial exchange rates as private traders competed with Qualitoles to sell dollars.

Instead, Qualitoles transferred "cheap" dollars to Promodiam, a mining company made up of ethnic Lebanese Zairian diamond dealers and an Israeli military trainer in Mobutu's DSP with close ties to DSP head, General Nzimbi. Promodiam's directors used those dollars to expand their activities in Zaire's diamond mining industry and to buy imports to supply to local traders.[78] Together with Guarde Civile head Baramoto's LIZA, Promodiam controlled 35 percent of recorded diamond sales in 1996.[79] The Israeli trainer was also reportedly involved in Sozabanque, a bank operated on behalf of Bemba Saolona, a close Mobutu associate. This arrangement turned "reform" into a state subsidy of Promodiam's and Sozabanque's private trading and diamond mining businesses and helped to finance greater control by Mobutu's clique of Zaire's illicit diamond business, which accounted for 70 to 80 percent of the country's diamond industry.[80]

Pointing to broader business dealings, U.S. Drug Enforcement Agency officials detected the circulation of dollars in Zaire suspected to have come from the Colombian drug trade.[81] Such illicit wealth could be recycled through Qualitoles and the Central Bank as dollars and later leave the country as diamonds for sale abroad. For Mobutu, money laundering helped to promote control over the illicit diamond trade to allow him to support loyal traders, generate income to buy and trade arms, and attract illicit diamond trading from neighboring states. Zairian and French reports pointed to the success Mobutu associates had in redirecting the diamond trade from Angola's UNITA rebel group into Zaire during the 1990s.[82]

Illicit diamond dealing formed a cornerstone of Zaire's warlord political economy. It helped Mobutu to finance the arming of extremists among the Rwandan refugees, to influence both rival and loyal commercial networks, and to consolidate ties to associated foreign commercial networks. Interlocking air cargo routes and the companies that fly them traced these transactions and were thus a more accurate indicator of the business of politics in Zaire than were formal reform programs or pronouncements from Kinshasa or Gbadolité.[83] These and other natural resource trade networks became a focus of struggle when rebels challenged Mobutu in 1996–1997.

Greater payoffs from foreign investment and normalized relations with creditors required a new, innovative strategy. As in Sierra Leone, creditors demanded radical privatization along with promotion of foreign investment to boost production and generate revenues to pay debts. This demand coincided with Mobutu's need to establish alliances with larger, better financed foreign firms that had a greater capacity to negotiate with outsiders on behalf of the ruler's failing state bureaucracy and, eventually, to seize resources directly as organizations such as the state-run mining conglomerate, Gécamines, collapsed. Creditors targeted Gécamines for privatization, arguing that privatization would remove mineral resources from Mobutu's political control and harness the country's main source of foreign exchange for economic reform. But as had occurred in Sierra Leone, Mobutu used his commercial ties to new foreign investors to monopolize resources and exploited the firms' presence to marginalize rivals.

Mobutu's chance to both satisfy creditors and advance his political control over his rivals came with the Swiss Procurement Company's (SWIPCO) proposal to privatize Gécamines (copper and cobalt), Miba (diamonds), Kilomoto (gold), and telecommunications to a consortium of South African, French, Canadian, and U.S. firms in mid-1995. The unprecedented offer to privatize all of Zaire's large-scale mining ventures held the promise that foreign investors would revitalize production (with Mobutu and his associates as business partners). The SWIPCO proposal also revealed the extent to which Kengo's associates appeared in deals alongside Mobutu's allies. Earlier, for example, SWIPCO's director had provided Kengo with a private jet. SWIPCO also had ties to SICPA, a company that had been involved with Mobutu's associates in the Qualitoles deal and had printed currency Mobutu commissioned privately when Tshisekedi threatened to eliminate presidential control over Central Bank operations.[84]

SWIPCO proposed to pay Zaire's $475 million in arrears to the African Development Bank (ADB) to facilitate the release of $600 million in pending credits to upgrade enterprises targeted for privatization. The deal was designed to recruit ADB support (Zaire held half of all unrecovered ADB arrears in 1995). The SWIPCO consortium would take over state assets, which it would refurbish with capital provided by state-guaranteed loans. SWIPCO and Zairian officials would receive a commission for procuring the new loans.[85] IMF officials disapproved of the deal, since it treated the ADB as a privileged creditor. The IMF wants its own loans to be paid off before it approves new credits or reform policies needed to attract other creditors and investors. In spite of this, the IMF sent a consultation mission to Kinshasa in December 1995, which reported "very encouraging" findings and received a token $3 million debt payment from the Kengo government.[86]

The SWIPCO deal throws light on ties among Mobutu's associates. Bossekota Watshia, a member of the Central Bank's board and Mobutu's personal adviser, helped to negotiate the deal. He was also involved in a 1992 deal as an intermediary between ADB's Pierre Moussa and Pay Pay wa Kasige, Zaire's former finance minister and a Mobutu associate. Press reports indicated that an Israeli military trainer close to the DSP and Bemba Saolona (who worked together in the diamond business), also appeared in the SWIPCO deal.[87]

After SWIPCO, privatization of state-run enterprises occurred in a piecemeal fashion. A U.S. mining firm, for example, bid to take over the state-run diamond mining firm's (OKIMO) operations. It promised to rebuild a local airport in Kasai, thus currying favor with officials there. The foreign firm also negotiated a longer-term deal with Mobutu associates.[88] Meanwhile, a Polish firm used Kengo associates to negotiate with Kasai officials to refurbish an OKIMO power station. The local attraction came from the firm's offer to rebuild the power plant in exchange for payment in coffee.[89]

The state-run Gécamines copper mines attracted the greatest foreign attention. Once the source of $900 million annually and 10 percent of the world's annual copper production, Gécamines' operations had fallen into decrepitude, as had the formal state institutions. The Kipushi mines, located in Shaba, became a useful tool for Mobutu to use to influence local political struggles. The Kipushi project, intended to make Zaire into a major zinc producer, involved American Mineral Fields, in which Jean-Raymond Boulle was a principal investor. Boulle's firm also owned part of Sierra Rutile in Sierra Leone. Mobutu associate Pay Pay wa Kasige brokered the deal between Boulle and South African and U.S. investors who acquired Kipushi project rights as part of a larger consortium.[90]

Boulle, through the AMF, also participated in a joint venture with South Africans to mine diamonds in Angola's Cuango River area.[91] If Boulle's Sierra Leone and Angola operations had set the pattern for his business in Zaire, his firm's association with the security firm International Defense and Security (IDAS) would have mirrored the relationship between Branch Energy and Executive Outcomes. That is, the profitable mineral venture would have provided corporate alliances and financing for its own private protection. In this deal, AMF was able to edge out the more established Anglo-American Corporation. Ironically, Boulle and other senior AMF officers had started their careers with Anglo-American and the associated De Beers Corporation in Sierra Leone and elsewhere.[92]

Beneficiaries of the proposed venture included separatist-minded strongmen who behaved more loyally toward their president now that he was negotiating deals with foreigners. This loyalty allowed Mobutu to reach an accommodation with politicians such as Kyungu in Shaba who found that an association with a ruler of a sovereign state still translated into personal gain.

Shaba's Tenke-Fungurume mine also attracted foreign investors. Here, too, we see the intersection of factional struggle with foreign mining firms. A Canadian firm met with Kengo to discuss its interest in the site. It faced a formidable alliance of Australian and South African firms that proposed to invest up to $1.5 billion to bring copper production to over 100,000 tons per year.[93] The Canadian firm signed an agreement that proposed a 55 percent joint venture with Gécamines, thereby positioning itself to take control of a part of Gécamines Mobutu could no longer control personally.

MINING COMPANIES AND MOBUTU'S SECURITY

In the realm of security, this situation left Mobutu free to divide and rule his enemies and his rivals. In Zaire, battles between forces organized by Mobutu's (and Kengo's) allies in Kivu mobilized people to attack Zairians of Rwandan Tutsi origin, which eased Mobutu's task of recruiting local supporters and Hutu refugees who fled Rwanda in 1994. Mobutu even proposed allowing these pro-Mobutu "insider" outsiders to vote in elections scheduled for May 1997.[94] A recent parallel to Mobutu's strategy appeared within private Bosnian Serb armies. As with Mobutu, Bosnian Serb strongman Radovan Karadzic harnessed the aspirations of local strongmen as central authority collapsed. Looting operations that targeted victims on the basis of ethnicity received weapons and tacit support. Instigators of conflicts operated with little formal organization and could plausibly deny responsibility. Inhabitants evacuated communities, leaving behind assets and becoming easy targets for extortion as they fled.[95]

Yet with international support, rulers of these recognized states retained the benefits of sovereignty even as some used tacit alliances with strongmen and their private armies to keep rivals at bay and attract outsiders. Yugoslavia and Zaire also show how local struggles over resources reinforced ethnic divisions and broke down multiethnic alliances, thereby undercutting moderates who challenged the rulers as people sought protection in revived or newly discovered communal ties. Those who threatened the rulers directly were more easily isolated, co-opted, or eliminated.[96]

As in Yugoslavia, in Zaire this method of control was compatible with the rise of enterprising ethnic strongmen who pioneered a de facto stealth secession as a consequence of their newfound autonomy. Like Bosnia's ethnic politicians, the strongmen promoted an informal, low-key separation that makes no demand for global recognition of the extinction or the birth of a sovereign entity. Zaire's sovereignty thereby remained a political asset for Mobutu, despite the nearly total collapse of bureaucratic capacity and later of patrimonial control.

A New Name, Same Politics

Global recognition of Congo's (former Zaire's) sovereignty still creates incentives for Congolese rivals to acknowledge a state within the old colonial boundaries. Arguably, warlord authorities in Congo (and in Bosnia) possess the capability to create separate states by virtue of their de facto control. Yet, the current attraction of existing sovereignty as a political resource gives warlords in both places strong incentives not to challenge the sovereignty of recognized states, even if the reality on the ground is somewhat different. Uncontested sovereignty adds to their local capacity by leaving in place a framework that gives those associated with it the capability to enter into a full range of international agreements. Nonstate actors, including foreign firms, hide partnerships with strongmen behind the shield of recognized state sovereignty. Sovereignty also simplifies questions concerning the legitimacy of contracts and insurance and adherence to laws in the firm's home country. In Congo, this has meant access to deals that firms negotiated with Mobutu's regime. Unchallenged formal state sovereignty also leaves in place an interlocutor who acknowledges debts and provides a point of contact between foreign state officials and strongmen without raising politically disturbing questions of recognition.

One sees this dynamic in the stealth secession of Congo's provincial authorities. Ethnic Rwandan rebels in Kivu, along Congo's border with Rwanda, have voiced no irredentist or secessionist desire except for the occasional utterances of field commanders as they reflected on their de facto control on the field of battle. Shaba's and Kasai's de facto authorities refrained from declarations of independence despite extensive cross-border alliances and hostility toward authorities in Kinshasa.

Sovereignty sustained through the coincidence of those mutual interests shared with regional strongmen, foreigners, and the globally recognized ruler is one of the few resources left to a very weak Kinshasa regime. None has the incentive to disrupt tacit agreements between provincial warlords and the ruler in the capital that permit both to control resources. This extensive decentralization of authority effectively reduced the Mobutu clique (and now Kabila) to warlord status, since they also had to scramble to control rivals through primarily commercial and almost entirely nonbureaucratic means, bolstered with whatever resources and alliances their status as rulers of a sovereign state gave them. This balance based on the foundation of state sovereignty also permits fluidity in local alliances. Regional strongmen did business with Mobutu's associates, for example, as they fought other members of his clique on a different front. Officials of foreign states were relieved to still encounter a recognizable state in which rulers might one day have the will and the capacity to fulfill all of their international obligations. With Mobutu's replacement by Kabila, those officials remain eager to continue to use the regime in Kinshasa as an interlocutor.

Paradoxically, Congo's effective dissolution and subsequent warlord politics show that that state formation is still very much a matter of law and not just of de facto capacity. Sovereignty in even a very weak state proves not only important but also unexpectedly divisible internally. The key to this innovation lies in Congo's absolute status in international law—short of total dissolution or some new configuration that would have to be arranged against the short-term interests of many outsiders who prefer the postindependence framework of Africa's sovereign states, weak though those states may be. Congo's continuing sovereign status contributes to the simultaneous fulfillment of the material and the political interests of different groups. The structure and nature of Congo's warlord politics also bely expectations of anarchy or a major reordering of states as a consequence of bureaucratic and patrimonial collapse.

Jeffrey Herbst has predicted that weak-state rulers in Africa will refrain from interstate war as a solution to perpetual weakness, thus portending prolonged stagnation.[97] He correctly pointed out that barriers to changing frontiers remain (a situtuation he decries). But his view glosses over the considerable cross-border connections and informal regionalization that exist within the current context of formal sovereignty. Furthermore, these connections take place under the umbrella of, and with resources derived from, sovereign status, which many thought would forestall major change. This reality reinforces themes developed earlier in this book, which held that sovereignty is contextual and that this condition promotes (as it masks) a wider range of differently constituted units in the global state system. It shows that changing uses of sovereignty—and not Mobutu—saved Congo from dissolution.[98]

RESOURCES AND INSURGENCY

Despite Mobutu's status as head of a sovereign state, some foreign investors found his informal demands and incapacity to control his associates to be fundamental obstacles to doing business with him.[99] The frustration of some investors coincided with that of rulers in neighboring states who, like Momoh and Strasser in Sierra Leone, faced the cross-border effects of Mobutu's alliances with clandestine networks. For example, Mobutu's partnership with extremist Hutu exiles starting in 1994 posed a security threat to that Rwandan regime. His associates' diamond dealing with UNITA rebels helped to finance UNITA's war against the Angolan government. Ugandan rebels received supplies from Sudan through the Bunia airport, which serviced gold mining there.[100]

These alliances created a conjunction of interests such that when Kabila emerged as head of his Alliance des Forces Démocratique pour la Libération (AFDL), he had little trouble finding anti-Mobutu allies. Kabila received help from Angolan and Rwandan troops and was given Ugandan weapons.[101] Kabila's presence provided some personal payoffs. For example, Salim Saleh, the Ugandan anti-insurgent leader and brother of the president, expanded his business reach to include a gold mine in Kisangani after the AFDL had captured the area.[102] These arrangements also showed the reluctance of neighboring rulers and internal insurgents to dissolve Zaire, resorting instead to regional networks to achieve their aims.

Once he appeared successful, Kabila became an attractive alternative commercial partner to Mobutu, much as Taylor had done in Liberia in the period 1990–1992. The increasingly competitive nature of the mining business in Africa, with many new firms adapted to doing business in challenging places, generated a broad range of potential partners for the rebel war leader. Kabila recognized the centrality of resource exploitation to his war effort and welcomed foreign firms, provided they paid a "war tax" of 15 percent of projected investment.[103] As had Taylor, Kabila appointed his brother, Florent Kambale Kabila, "mining minister" to collect fees. He appointed another brother, Gaetanka Kakudji, governor of the mineral-rich Shaba province.

Kabila had developed some commercial expertise during his time as a rebel leader, beginning in the 1960s. Well before his successful 1996 campaign, he had presided over the Compagnie Mixte d'Import-Export (COMIEX), a venture with private merchants and Kabila's pre-AFDL Parti de la Revolution Populaire. The firm tapped into cross-border trade in coffee and gold with Uganda and other neighbors to the east before the rebel war began.[104]

Larger cash injections to Kabila's war effort came from outsiders. AMF signed a new billion-dollar deal with Kabila in April 1997, providing cash and a jet to transport the rebel leader's associates.[105] This was a calculated risk on the AMF's part. The renegotiated deal did not include the more established former partner Anglo-American, which could not risk dealing with rebels for fear of unsettling rulers of other weak states in which it had investments. AMF garnered additional benefits in the form of rights to buy diamonds in Kisangani, a trade that totaled $100,000 daily after rebels captured the city.[106] The state-run MIBA reportedly gave Kabila an additional $3.5 million in April 1997 when rebels took the head of the firm to the eastern part of the country after capturing him in Mbuji-Maye.[107]

These and other deals were critical in encouraging other investors to do business with Kabila and in establishing his credibility with outsiders. The deals helped Kabila to develop into a person who could engage in commerce and assume the sovereign state's fiscal responsibilities. The apparent stability that followed from the acknowledgment of the state's external obligations and Kabila's willingness to participate in global markets encouraged creditors and officials in other states to view him as an alternative to anarchy. As in Liberia, those relations continue to focus on the outward aspects of the state rather than on the changes in politics within it. Specifically, anti-Mobutu social action within the state is ignored, and aspects of warlord politics are accepted as long as they accord with external interests.

Other areas in Congo, however, present alternatives to the strategy of finding weak-state stability in a reworking of the warlord politics of Mobutu's successor. Kasai Oriental, especially the city of Mbuji-Maye, is a center of autonomous development efforts and separatist tendencies. The city has its own university, established in 1990 with funds from local operations of MIBA, the state-run mining company. The city government and the Catholic Church run the university, which set up a geology faculty with help from the Belgian firm Sibeka—which owns 20 percent of MIBA. The city plans to expand the capacity of the nearby Lubilanji hydro station to generate the electricity central government authorities fail to provide. Local officials and businesses have taken steps to institutionalize autonomous development by creating the Conference for the Development of Kasai Oriental (CODEKOR).[108]

Closer examination of Mbuji-Maye's economy reveals considerable ties to commercial networks that linked Mobutu's and Kengo's political associates, as well as a local struggle to keep those networks at arm's length. MIBA head Mukamba Kadiata Nzemba billed himself as a "friend" of Mobutu's even though MIBA helped to underwrite the local university. Local MIBA operations included joint ventures with foreign firms that operated in areas under more solid Mobutu control but also exclusive ventures with foreign firms to increase local autonomy to exploit resources. For example, Swanepoel, a South African engineering firm, demonstrated the political-private commercial nature of Kasai separatism, with its infrastructure projects benefiting Kasai. In return, Swanepoel appointed a member of its firm to the board of CODEKOR. This more purely autonomous infrastructure development threatened the Mobutu faction's hold on illicit diamond mining, since local miners and Angolan dealers gained easier access to Mbuji-Maye.

Kasai's autonomy has also changed regional strategic calculations. Kasai authorities, for example, were more interested in peace in Angola to protect independent access to the country's ports and railways than in Mobutu's interest in strengthening UNITA's diamond trade.

But ominously, Kabila's selective moves against firms have appeared to target and rein in this regional autonomy. In May 1997 Kabila, who has otherwise been fairly open to deals with foreign firms, moved to disrupt the South African railroad deal, as he had with the locally run diamond mining business mentioned earlier. Those actions have not interfered with Kabila's overall "free market" (actually a controlled but private and profitable market) approach as a whole, but they do not bode well for Congolese expecting more local autonomy. Instead, Kabila's actions represent the classic warlord politics of control by manipulating access to accumulation with the help of private foreign firms in lieu of a state bureaucracy.

In the process, Kabila has squeezed Kasai strongmen who tried to stand as popularly accountable actors insofar as they competed to control commerce but seemingly for broader popular benefit. Since local strongmen identified popular legitimacy and provision of social services as valued goals, they have been forced to build their authority in more conventional ways, such as striving to create efficient internal revenue and development bureaucracies. Why this is so bears a closer examination of internal Kasai politics, which is beyond the scope of this chapter.

Prospects for the survival of this experiment do not look promising as outsiders help Kabila establish control over the territory of Congo. The problem for Kasai is not the existence of a larger country of which it is a part; it is instead that the reassertion of central control and its manner of application are not decided by those who live under that control. Kabila deserves some blame for having made political choices that limit the possibilities of the people in his country. But outsiders—foreign firms, creditors, officials in other states—share responsibility when they act to preserve the outer form of a sovereign state. The result is warlord politics in a sovereign state.

Congo and Sierra Leone show that warlord politics is an option for state rulers who preside over almost total bureaucratic state collapse and, in the case of the latter, who face invasion. Nigeria, the next case, shows the conversion to warlord politics within the context of a fairly viable bureaucracy where there is less of an internal push (although it is still significant). Instead, the case highlights the pull or attraction of new, externalized political networks.

NOTES

1. Voltaire, *Zaire* (1732).
2. Editorial, *Marchés Tropicaux,* 14 July 1995.
3. I refer to the country as Zaire when discussing the Mobutu era in this chapter. I refer to the country as Congo for events from May 1997 to reflect the renaming of the country as Democratic Republic of Congo (not to be confused with Congo-Brazzaville which borders Congo on the northeast).
4. Thomas Callaghy, *The State-Society Struggle: Zaire in Comparative Perspective* (New York: Columbia University Press, 1984), 141–232.
5. Ibid., 3–137; Jean-Claude Willame, *Governance et Pouvoir: Essai sur trois trajectoires africaines* (Paris: Harmattan, 1994), 46–91.
6. Sennen Andriamirado, "Les nabobs," *Jeune Afrique,* 7 Feb. 1996, 25–27.
7. "The Great Lakes: The Poison Spreads," *Africa Confidential,* 26 April 1996.
8. See Alex de Waal, "Contemporary Warfare in Africa," *IDS Bulletin* 27:3 (July 1996), 6–16; Human Rights Watch—Africa, *Zaire: Forced to Flee: Violence Against the Tutsis in Zaire* (New York: Human Rights Watch—Africa, 1996); Human Rights Watch—Africa, *Zaire: Attacked by All Sides: Civilians and the War in Eastern Zaire* (New York: Human Rights Watch—Africa, 1997).
9. International Monetary Fund (IMF), *International Financial Statistical Yearbook* (Washington, D.C.: IMF, 1990). My discussion of Mobutu's strategies in this section benefited from my reading of Crawford Young and Thomas Turner, *The Rise and Decline of the Zairian State* (Madison: University of Wisconsin Press, 1985).
10. World Bank, *1992 World Development Report* (New York: Oxford University Press, 1992), 256.
11. Colette Braeckman, *Le dinosaure: Le Zaire de Mobutu* (Paris: Fayard, 1992), 73.
12. Thomas Callaghy, "Africa's Debt Crisis," *Journal of International Affairs* 38:1 (Summer 1984), 61–79; Callaghy, *State-Society Struggle,* 196–201.
13. Edward Pound, "IMF, World Bank Aide Has Dealings Hinting at Conflict of Interest," *Wall Street Journal,* 28 Dec. 1990. See also Erwin Blumenthal, "Zaire: rapport sur sa credibilité financière internationale," *La Revue Nouvelle* 77:11 (Nov. 1982), 360–378.
14. Braeckman, *Le dinosaure,* 145–147.
15. Jean-Claude Willame, *L'épopée d'Inga* (Paris: Harmattan, 1986); Pierre Péan, *L'argent noir* (Paris: Fayard, 1988), 161–166, Braeckman, *Le dinosaure,* 222–230.
16. On Zairianization, see David Gould, *Bureaucratic Corruption and Underdevelopment in the Third World: The Case of Zaire* (New York: Pergamon, 1980); Young and Turner, *The Rise and Decline of the Zairian State,* 326–362.
17. Banque du Zaire, *Bulletin Trimestriel* (Kinshasa: Banque du Zaire, March 1991), 9.
18. Banque du Zaire, *Rapport annuel* (Kinshasa: Banque du Zaire, various issues).
19. World Bank, *1992 World Development Report,* 238.
20. Kisangani Emizet, "Zaire After Mobutu: A Potential Case of Humanitarian Emergency," paper for the World Institute for Development Economics Research Seminar, Helsinki, 6–8 Oct. 1996, 21.

21. Compare World Bank, *1992 World Development Report,* 238, with Banque du Zaire, *Rapport annuel* (1992), 19.

22. Interview with former Zairian official, Helsinki, Finland, 7 Oct. 1996.

23. Economist Intelligence Unit, *Zaire* (London: Economist Intelligence Unit, 1st quarter, 1996), 19.

24. John Ayoade, "States Without Citizens," in Donald Rothchild and Naomi Chazan, eds., *The Precarious Balance: State and Society in Africa* (Boulder: Westview, 1988), 106.

25. Blaine Hardin, *Africa: Dispatches from a Fragile Continent,* (New York: Norton, 1990), 25–60; Helen Winternitz, *East Along the Equator: A Journey up the Congo and into Zaire* (New York: Atlantic Monthly Press, 1987); Paul Hyland, *The Black Heart: A Voyage into Central Africa* (New York: Paragon House, 1990).

26. "Zaire," *Mining Journal,* 26 Jan. 1996, 23.

27. Janet MacGaffey, ed., *The Real Economy of Zaire,* (Philadelphia: University of Pennsylvania Press, 1991).

28. Janet MacGaffey, *Entrepreneurs and Parasites: The Struggle for Indigenous Capitalism in Zaire* (New York: Cambridge University Press, 1987); Mukohya Vwakyanakazi, *African Traders in Butembo, Eastern Zaire (1960–1980),* Ph.D. dissertation (Madison: Department of Anthropology, University of Wisconsin, 1982).

29. World Bank, *1992 World Development Report,* 214.

30. Interviews with members of the Angolan Chamber of Commerce and a World Bank official, Washington, D.C., June–July 1996.

31. "Quelles sanctions contre Mobutu?" *La Cité,* 11 Feb. 1993, Braeckman, *Le dinosaure,* 279–315.

32. Christian Casteran and Hugo Sada, "Sommet de la Baule," *Jeune Afrique,* 27 June 1990, 15. See also Jean-Claude Willame, "Zaire: Années 90," *Cahiers du CEDAF* 1:4–5 (1991); Jean-François Bayart, "France-Afrique: La fin du pacte colonial," *Politique Africaine,* 39 (1990), 47–53.

33. "Accréditation du nouvel ambassadeur des États-Unis au Zaire," *Elima,* 13 June 1991.

34. Emmanuel Dungia, *Mobutu et l'argent du Zaire* (Paris: Harmattan, 1992).

35. Joseph Ngalula Mpandajila, "Lettre ouverte au Citoyen Président Fondateur du Movement Populaire de la Révolution," *Politique Africaine* 3 (Sept. 1981), 94–140; "Angola/Zaire: End of the Diamond Connection," *Africa Energy and Mines,* 5 April 1995.

36. Michael Schatzberg, *The Dialectics of Oppression in Zaire,* (Bloomington: Indiana University Press, 1988), 53.

37. Quoted in Basil Davidson, *The Black Man's Burden* (New York: Times Books, 1992), 259.

38. Economist Intelligence Unit, *Zaire,* 4th quarter, 1991, 13.

39. Crawford Young, "Zaire: The Shattered Illusion of the Integral State," *Journal of Modern African Studies* 32:2 (June 1994), 263.

40. Emizet, "Zaire After Mobutu," 16.

41. "Zaire: Military Operation," *Africa Confidential,* 20 Sept. 1996.

42. "Barrick-Okimo in Firm Deal," *Africa Energy and Mining,* 28 Aug. 1996.

43. "Zaire: Digging In," *Africa Confidential,* 3 Jan. 1997.

44. Interview with UNITA representative, Washington, D.C., 20 June 1996; "De Beers Exports as Much as MIBA," *Africa Energy and Mining,* 8 Jan. 1997.

45. Jacques Follorou, "D'anciens militaires français en cadrerainet des mercenaires au service du pouvior zairois," *Le Monde,* 8 Jan. 1997.

46. "Zaire I: Dual Control," *Africa Confidential,* 16 April 1993; "Zaire: The Long Goodbye," *Africa Confidential,* 6 March 1992; Interview by the author, Washington, D.C., 6 June 1996.

47. Fall Jean Karim, "La province zairoise de l'ex-Katanga continue de rever d'autonomie," *Le Monde,* 30 Dec. 1995; Braeckman, *Le dinosaure,* 184–186.

48. Colette Braeckman, "Le Zaire de Mobutu, 'parrin' des Grands Lacs," in André Guichaoua, ed., *Les crises politiques au Burundi et au Rwanda (1993–1994)* (Paris: Karthala, 1995), 387–394.

49. Anzuluni Bembe Isilonyonyi, "Le Haut Consiel de la Republique Parlement de Transition, Resolution sur la Nationalité" (mimeo) (Kinshasa, 28 April 1996).

50. "Zaire: Deserting a Sinking Tshisekedi," *Africa Confidential,* 29 July 1994.

51. Gerard Prunier, *The Rwanda Crisis* (New York: Columbia University Press, 1995), 100–101.

52. "Ouganda: Paris voit rouge," *Lettre de l'Ocean Indien,* 14 May 1994, 1. Also see Gerard Prunier, "The Great Lakes Crisis," *Current History* (May 1997), 193–199.

53. "Zaire/Ouganda: la guerre secrête," *Lettre du Continent,* 28 April 1994.

54. "Les Mobutu traqués par un ami français de la famille," *Le Soft,* 13 Oct. 1995.

55. "Zaire: Michel Lambinet, Robert Bourgi et Mobutu," *Lettre du Continent,* 8 June 1995.

56. Jacques Foccart, *Foccart parle: entretiens avec Philippe Gaillard* (Paris: Fayard, 1995); Stephen Smith and Antoine Glaser, *Ces Messieurs Afrique: Le Paris-Village du continent noir* (Paris: Calmann-Levy, 1992).

57. "Zaire: En direct de l'Elysée," *Lettre du Continent,* 21 Sept. 1995; "Zaire: la resurrection?" *Lettre du Continent,* 21 Sept. 1995.

58. "Zaire: Opération 'Leopard,'" *Lettre du Continent,* 19 April 1994; Prunier, *The Rwanda Crisis,* 317–318.

59. "Cohen, Woods, and Others," *Indian Ocean Newsletter,* 19 Oct. 1996.

60. Jean-Pierre Pabanel, "Conflits locaux et stratégie de tension Nord-Kivu," *Politique Africaine* 52 (Dec. 1993), 132–134.

61. Steven Metz, *Disaster and Intervention in Sub-Saharan Africa: Learning from Rwanda* (Carlisle Barracks, Pa.: U.S. Army War College, 1994); African Rights, "Humanitarianism Unbound? Current Dilemmas Facing Multi-Mandate Relief Operations in Political Emergencies" (London: African Rights discussion paper, 1995).

62. Human Rights Watch—Arms Project, *Rwanda/Zaire: Rearming with Impunity* (Washington, D.C.: Human Rights Watch, 1995); "Bears Guard Honey," *Africa Confidential,* 17 Feb. 1995.

63. *Africa Confidential,* 20 Oct. 1995; "Mobutu-Clinton: nouveaux et graves ennuis," *Le Soft,* 11 Oct. 1995.

64. "Mobutu Chez Chirac," *Le Soft,* 25 April 1996; "Mobutu à L'Elysée," *Jeune Afrique,* 1 May 1996, 4–5.

65. "Great Lakes 2: The Balance of Forces," *Africa Confidential,* 1 Nov. 1996.

66. "Bonn normalise déjà avec le Zaire," *Le Soft,* 7 Oct. 1996.

67. Thomas Lippman, "Seeking U.S. Visa, Mobutu Enlists Friends," *International Herald Tribune,* 7 Aug. 1995.

68. Kin Key Mulumba, "Mobutu-Clinton: contact normalisé," *Le Soft,* 19 Aug. 1995.

69. "Seeking U.S. Visa, Mobutu Enlists Friends," *Washington Post,* 6 Aug. 1995; Government of South Africa, *Interim Truth Commission Report* (Pretoria: Government of South Africa, June 1996).

70. DDK, "Mobutu: chronique d'une réhabilitation," *Le Soft,* 11 Oct. 1995; George Moffet, "U.S. Taps African Despot for Help in Rwanda," *Christian Science Monitor,* 23 Aug. 1995.

71. "Bye bye la Troika, bonjour la France," *Le Soft,* 25 July 1996.

72. Carole Collins, "Zaire Remains Africa's Heart of Darkness," *National Catholic Reporter* 32:15 (Feb. 1996), 9–14. See also, Jeffrey Marishane, "Prayer, Profit and Power: U.S. Religious Right and Foreign Policy," *Review of African Political Economy* 52 (Nov. 1991), 73–117; James Adams, "Mobutu Champion Enrages Washington," *New York Times,* 20 Aug. 1995.

73. "Zaire: Les Grosses Légumes," *Africa Confidential,* 15 Dec. 1995.

74. Chris McGreal, "Zaire's Miracle Man Runs Out of Luck," *Guardian* (Manchester), 7 May 1996.

75. Kilolo Ngwalumuna, "La secte Moon reçoit la visite de son gourou," *Le Soft,* 16 Nov. 1995.

76. Personal communication, Amsterdam, 7 Nov. 1996; and from a Liberian logger, London, 5 March 1997.

77. "Bemba haut de GAMM," *Lettre du Continent,* 22 Dec. 1994.

78. "Zaire: Jump in Diamond Exports," *Africa Energy and Mining,* 6 Sept. 1995; Katupa Nkole, "SCIPA-Mines et le scandal de l'UZB," *Le Soft,* 7 Aug. 1995.

79. "New Diamond Export Regulations," *Africa Energy and Mines,* 29 May 1996.

80. "Zaire: Baisse de la production de diamant," *Lettre du Continent,* 10 Nov. 1994.

81. Economist Intelligence Unit, *Zaire,* 4th quarter, 1995, 24.

82. "Le saviez-vous," *Jeune Afrique,* 20 March 1996, 18; "Un Israélien de Kinshasa poursuivi par la police congolaise?" *Le Soft,* 25 March 1996.

83. Sennen Andriamirado, "Les nabobs," *Jeune Afrique,* 7 Feb. 1996, 25–27.

84. Kin-Kiey Mulumba, "Rebondissement dans l'affaire des privatisations," *Le Soft,* 28 July 1995; "Reprise de SWIPCO," *Lettre du Continent,* 25 July 1996; Thomas Turner, "Zaire: Flying High Above the Toads: Mobutu and Stalemated Democracy," in John Clark and David Gardinier, eds., *Political Reform in Francophone Africa* (Boulder: Westview, 1997), 259.

85. "Zaire: AAC to Call the Shots," *African Energy and Mining,* 24 May 1995.

86. Interview by the author, Washington, D.C., official, 16 Oct. 1996.

87. "Castel Balimaka s'apprête à saiser les avions Scibe," *Le Soft,* 21 Aug. 1995.

88. "Barrack-Okimo in Firm Deal," *Africa Energy and Mining,* 28 Aug. 1996.

89. "Polish Equipment for Zaire Coffee," *Africa Energy and Mining,* 10 May 1995.

90. "Heart of Anglo," *Africa Confidential,* 7 June 1996.

91. Kenneth Gooding, "Voisey's Bay Man Aims to Repeat Successes," *Financial Times,* 26 Sept. 1996; "Lundin Widens Its Interest," *Africa Energy and Mining,* 24 July 1996.

92. Chris McGreal and Stefaans Brummer, "De Beers in Secret Deal with Rebels," *Mail and Guardian,* 18 April 1997.

93. "Major Companies Court GCM," *Africa Energy and Mining,* 17 Jan. 1996; "Conclusive Decision on Tenke-Fungurume," *Africa Energy and Mining,* 4 Dec. 1996.

94. See Colette Braeckman, "Zaire at the End of a Reign," *New Left Review* 222 (June 1997), 129–138.

95. Peter Maass, *Love Thy Neighbor: A Story of War* (New York: Knopf, 1996), 21.

96. V. P. Gagnon Jr., "Ethnic Nationalism and International Conflict: The Case of Serbia," *International Security,* 19:3 (Winter 1994–1995), 130–166.

97. Jeffrey Herbst, "War and the State in Africa," *International Security* 14:4 (Spring 1990), 117–139.

98. Contra official U.S. policy outlined in Michael Schatzberg, *Mobutu or Chaos: The United States and Zaire* (Lanham, Md.: University Press of America, 1991).

99. Michael Ledeen, "African Scenarios: The Future of Zambia, Zimbabwe and Zaire," paper presented at Cobalt 94: Opportunities, Problems and Survival Strategies, Vienna, Va., 2–4 Nov. 1994; Interviews with mining executives, Denver, Colo., March 1996.

100. "Zaire: Digging In," *Africa Confidential,* 3 Jan. 1997.

101. Jean Boyne, "The White Legion: Mercenaries in Zaire," *Jane's Intelligence Review* 9:6 (June 1997), 278–281.

102. "Africa: New Fingers on Zaire's Trigger," *Africa Confidential,* 9 May 1997.

103. Alliance des Forces Democratiques pour la Libération, "Le Commissariat general a l'Economie et aux Finances aux Compagnies 'amies'" (photocopy, no date).

104. "MIBA and Its 'War Effort,'" *Africa Energy and Mining,* 16 July 1997; "New Underground Trade Routes," *Indian Ocean Newsletter,* 22 March 1997; "Zaire: Kabila Yaka!" *Africa Confidential,* 11 April 1997.

105. Stefaans Brummer, "Business at War for Zaire's Wealth," *Mail and Guardian,* 25 April 1997; Chris Gordon, "Kabila Dumps De Beers," *Business Mail,* 2 May 1997.

106. "Diamond Miners Seethe," *Africa Energy and Mining,* 16 July 1997.

107. "MIBA and Its 'War Effort.'"

108. "Kasai Takes Off," *Africa Confidential,* 19 Jan. 1996; "Zaire: SA Companies Grab Opportunities in Eastern Kasai," *Southscan,* 12 Jan. 1996, 15.

6

▼ ▼ ▼ ▼ ▼

"REFORM" AND THE REJECTION OF LIBERALISM IN NIGERIA

> We all know what it takes to build a house in Nigeria today, yet the men at the top are building houses all over the place.
> —*Ayo Obe, president of Civil Liberties Organisation*[1]

> Abacha has no *idea* of Nigeria. Beyond the reality of a fiefdom that has dutifully nursed his insatiable greed and transformed him into a creature of enormous wealth, and now of power, Abacha has no *notion* of Nigeria.
> —*Wole Soyinka*[2]

ABACHA'S DILEMMA

Nigeria's military ruler Ibrahim Babangida (1985–1993), annulled the 12 June 1993 presidential election, thus aborting a transition to Nigeria's third civilian regime. Defense Minister General Sani Abacha jettisoned this goal and staged his own rise to power on 27 November 1993. Some analysts have seen the events of 1993 as decisive, observing that the annulment provoked a protest of unprecedented vigor from a "civil society."[3]

On the other hand, these events marked an intensification and reshaping of personal rule in Nigeria in directions familiar from the cases of warlord politics in Chapters 3, 4, and 5. This is not to say that Nigeria's politics is of the warlord variety—yet. Nigeria has possessed a civil service that has considerable relative capability and expertise, which places the country further along the scale of state strength than Monrovia, Freetown, or Kinshasa. For example, the traveler arriving in Nigeria from Sierra Leone notices a far greater government presence outside the capital city. Although it is no model of efficiency, visitors encounter a functioning constabulary, rudimentary public health measures, and

183

telecommunications. Even provincial centers had sporadic electricity in the early 1990s, whereas Monrovia and Freetown had virtually none. A motorist can cover the 700-mile distance from Kano to Lagos in a day, compared with the two arduous days required to traverse Sierra Leone's 300-mile breadth by road. Historically, the government has simply been able to do more in Nigeria, even if it has done so with unwarranted expense and inefficiency.

This is not to overstate Nigerian state capacity. Richard Joseph observed that in 1983, "the boundary between the state and civil society seemed to have dissolved; public institutions had become as much a party to the struggle for gaining particular advantage as were the registered party organizations."[4] The dominance of oil in Nigeria's export earnings—90 percent in 1977 and as high as 97.1 percent in 1985—repeats the pattern of control of concentrations of valuable resources for personal gain.[5] But Nigerian politics has shown a greater range of choices that has allowed for building state authority through bureaucratic institutions and providing state services to citizens to mobilize legitimacy and revenue. This was President Babangida's announced strategy when he initiated a program of economic and political liberalization in 1986. Although reforms (discussed later) were selectively applied, they did raise popular expectations, which later made a warlord-type state disengagement from society more dangerous and difficult for Abacha.

But the selective nature of Babangida's reforms also permitted specific elements of the old patronage network to consolidate their positions. This chapter's examination of the manipulation of privatization and financial-sector reforms maps some of the changes. Specifically, financial "reform" gave local strongmen new means for autonomous accumulation through fraud and by building clandestine commercial networks in alliance with select state officials. This more decentralized political network localized the collection of wealth, helping Babangida and then Abacha to limit their need for bureaucrats to manage clients and to rely instead on exploiting "private" commercial opportunities. For Abacha, this situation has also created a dilemma: How is he to control access to benefits in this private economy of clients he inherited, especially if bureaucratic structures harbor potential rivals, allies of the deposed ruler, partisans of true reform, or simply professionals committed to the rule of law?

Abacha thus faces challenges not only from state institutions (patrimonialized or otherwise) but also from civic groups that grew up around Babangida's partial reforms.[6] This distrust and fear of bureaucracies extend to the military, within which a bombing campaign (examined later) indicates the presence of uncontrolled divisions and rivals. Like Mobutu, Abacha has partially resolved his dilemma of control by steadily replacing conventional bureaucratic state capacity with manipulation of factions, focusing on pitting narrow, usually ethnically based groups against one another to assert his authority as arbiter. As with Mobutu and his associates' manipulation of ethnic divisions in Kivu and Shaba or Taylor's use of rivalries with Krahns and Mandingos, this strategy does not require the direct assertion of control. Instead, it uses alliances with enterprising local strongmen to crowd out or defeat their local rivals and encourages the losers to then appeal to the ruler as arbiter.

This situation creates local ethnic strongmen who could become warlords as they gain the latitude to settle their own scores and accumulate wealth through alliances with a regime that represses other broadbased groups, whether nationwide bureaucratic institutions or opposition political organizations. Recently, some prominent groups have demonstrated this narrower associational focus. In the east, Mkpoko Igbo and Oha'Eze have asserted an ethnic identity. In the West, Yorubabased groups such as Oodu'a Youth Movement, Afenifere and Egbe Omo Yoruba have pressed for ethnic recognition, as has the Hausabased Northern Elements Coalition in the north.

More locally based conflicts have arisen in struggles over the creation of new states and local governments. Official "resolution" of bank fraud investigations (discussed later) has also placed Abacha's regime in a position to manipulate ethnic rivalries. Thus, the seeming national disunity that accompanies conflicts between Ijaws and Itsekiris in the oil city of Warri, Ugeps and Adims in Cross Rivers, Tiv and Idoma in Benue, and Ogonis and Andonis generally prevent the formation of a united front against Abacha and keep any single group (such as the Ogoni) from gaining access to a significant share of the regime's source of revenue. Soyinka has pointed to regime provocation in these conflicts as a conscious policy of "ethnic cleansing,"[7] a tactic we have found previously to be compatible with warlord politics. This tactic marks a further shift from the centralized patronage politics that used state bureaucracies to distribute goods and services to clients.

The regime and its apologists portray this fragmentation of the old patronage network as a threat to the unity of Nigeria and justify Abacha's authoritarian methods as a counter to this threat. Even though formal state institutions dissolve in conflicts between local strongmen or between citizens and the regime, apologists have cited strong state role models such as Chile's General Pinochet, General Chun of South Korea, Flight Lieutenant Rawlings of Ghana, and other military-turned-civilian rulers who have presided over economic "miracles."[8] These putative models have also tapped into foreigners' anxieties about the possible breakup of Nigeria. Abacha has attracted foreign support as a "reformer" with his "Vision 2010" and has promised an October 1998 political transition, with the civilianized Abacha poised to succeed his own military regime. Groups of regime supporters such as the National Patriotic Democratic Association and the shadowy Committee of Friends have articulated a probusiness, law-and-order image for Abacha abroad and at home.

The crucial difference between this image and the warlordization of Nigeria's patronage politics lies in the absence of a strongly institutionalized military. Abacha possesses no equivalent of Pinochet's reliable base of support in Chile's air force, for example. This structural absence of a bureaucratic constituency for strong-arm rule lies in part in the outcome of Babangida's partial reforms, to which I turn next. Babangida's actions enabled some regime clients to more intensively exploit a "private" economy while he repressed societal critics of that development. But Abacha's subsequent path was not inevitable. The seriousness with which many Nigerians—including military officers and other state officials—took Babangida's reforms, especially the 1993 election, has demonstrated that many have in mind a much more conventional state-building path for Nigeria.

BABANGIDA'S PRIVATIZATION OF PATRONAGE

Babangida, who occupied the office of president after leading a coup in 1985, appeared to have little choice but to promote market-based reforms. Nigeria owed over $30 billion to creditors, with most of the principle contracted over the previous decade as civilian and military rulers used the money to attract the loyalty of far-flung political networks with patronage. Above all, the new military ruler recognized that the use of state-run companies as conduits for payoffs could not be sustained. From 1980 to 1985, Nigeria's federal government spent $23 billion on state-run enterprises that added production valued at $1 billion to the economy. In 1986, industrial production fell below 40 percent of capacity.[9] The crisis coincided with a sharp decline in the price of oil, by far the largest component of patronage financing. Meanwhile, creditors made clear to the new president that privatization measures were indispensable if Nigeria was to receive future loans and favorable treatment in debt rescheduling negotiations.[10]

In conventional state-building fashion, Babangida planned to limit elite access to patronage opportunities, forcing elites to seek personal gain by developing the country's economy. He specifically aimed to privatize state assets and official support for export-led growth "to encourage citizens toward individual self-reliance and realization of ambitions outside of holding government office."[11] If successful, this plan would have ended the use of state office to promote private business interests—or consumption-based, nonproductive "pirate capitalism" as Sayre

Schatz termed it.[12] As Thomas Forrest pointed out, much of this activity involved using state assets to reward political allies and build political party control, especially during the 1979–1983 civilian interlude. Earlier, huge increases in revenue from oil exports had funded much of this spending spree. State spending of oil revenues rose 2,000 percent from 1970 to 1980, but in 1980 fell to one quarter of the peak in 1980.[13]

Official policy timed economic liberalization to coincide with a managed transition to civilian rule. The political transition, finally set for 1993, was designed to mobilize popular demands for economic growth and an end to corruption and elite privilege.[14] Supporters of the transition paid close attention to the problem of suppressing rivalries between political cliques, which they blamed for the extreme corruption, violence, and eventual failure of the 1979–1983 elected Second Republic.[15] Other commentators blamed the failure of the Second Republic on factional competition, a "Poli-Thug state" in Soyinka's words.[16] Still others called for a system in which the military would compel political parties to organize around broader issues that cut across religion, ethnicity, regionalism, and the interests of specific cliques.[17] Babangida agreed with the latter, decreeing that political competition must be channelled through two parties, each required to organize across regional and communal divides. He also excluded from participation in the new political institutions politicians from the failed Second Republic, the "old brigades" and "moneybags" of the corrupt past.[18]

In fact, these would-be former clients struggled to find exceptions, to find ways to undermine or gain preferential access to state offices from which reforms could be manipulated. Babangida found their entreaties for special treatment difficult to resist. Babangida's own forcible rise to power was in part the result of support from a military faction. This support left him vulnerable to elements within the military, a weakness that became apparent in a December 1985 coup attempt. The coup's supposed ringleader, Major General Mamman Vatsa, had played a visible role in the previous regime's security establishment. It became apparent that Babangida could not afford to alienate powerful political networks he inherited from his predecessor.

Following the coup attempt, Babangida began to deemphasize his origins (an ethnic minority in Niger State) and moved to bring Nigeria into the Organisation of Islamic Conference (OIC), a global organization of Muslim states. This move was intended to curry favor with Muslim elites who held key roles in state bureaucracies and the military command (the people against whom reforms were supposedly targeted) and to attract patronage from OIC member states. Babangida's appointments to the Armed Forces Ruling Council, his ruling body, increasingly included powerful strongmen inherited from previous regimes. But that favoritism further incited violence among some Christians and ethnic groups who felt the military was no longer protecting their interests. This communal violence increased throughout Babangida's tenure.[19]

If Babangida had sacrificed everything to economic efficiency in an attempt to undermine strongmen, his power base would have dwindled and his political survival would have been menaced. Babangida faced the contradiction of having to rely on the military and key civilian strongmen to implement reform and discipline other elites while also cultivating their support. But the military was a poor tool for carrying out reform, since many officers had been major beneficiaries of past corruption and favoritism. Babangida's predecessor, General Mohammed Buhari, for example, had been minister of petroleum under President Obasanjo (1976–1979) during a time when $2.8 billion in oil revenues had allegedly disappeared.[20] Thus, many officials in the bureaucracy that controlled the country's main source of revenues had benefited from corruption. Constrained in the bureaucratic realm, Babangida's banning professional politicians from holding future office did little to increase his autonomy to act, since those people still ran most of Nigeria's state institutions and economy. In stark contrast to World Bank visions of market reforms playing to a strong, autonomous business class that would demand continued reform, Nigeria's ruler faced commercial elites who were also key figures in the country's patronage politics.[21]

Babangida's inability to manage reform through bureaucratic means became apparent in his use of the existing Industrial Development Coordination Committee (IDCC), which assigned tariff remissions for targeted export industries, to privatize state-run firms. Bamanga Mahmud Tukur occupied a key IDCC board position. The choice of Tukur to head the agency illustrated the continuity of old political networks in the Babangida regime. Tukur had managed the Nigerian Ports Authority from 1975 to 1982, a position that gave him lucrative opportunities to award import licenses to his allies. Tukur later became governor of Gongola State in the last months of the civilian regime and reappeared as minister of trade after Buhari's coup.

More important to Babangida, Tukur was a major patron of powerful strongmen in northern Nigeria. He was involved with numerous northern state-run companies that distributed patronage to strongmen whose loyalty Babangida needed to cultivate. Private commerce, the intended beneficiary of reform, was also not free of patronage. Tukur sat on the board of the Nigerian subsidiary of the Bank of Credit and Commerce International (BCCI), as did Ibrahim Dasuki (who Babangida had elevated to the office of sultan of Sokoto ahead of the deceased Sultan's son), a prominent northern Nigerian businessman and key Babangida supporter. Some analysts have speculated that Dasuki, the head of many northern Nigerian state-run companies, financed Babangida's coup.[22] Earlier, the BCCI had given the Nigerian government a private loan of $1 billion after the government had lost access to other private credit and faced World Bank criticism in the early 1980s; the BCCI accepted crude oil as payment.[23] The board memberships and banking connections put Tukur, Dasuki, their associates, and even Babangida in good positions to personally profit from privatization.[24] Tukur, for example, served on the boards of four firms after he had helped to engineer their "privatizations."[25]

In response to creditor concerns and popular criticism of the obvious undermining of the IDCC's capacity to act independently of vested interests, a parallel bureaucracy—the Technical Committee for Privatisation and Commercialisation (TCPC)—took over reform of the state sector of the economy in 1989. By early 1991, the TCPC had privatized at least fifty-four firms.[26] Meanwhile, the head of the TCPC, Alhaji Hamza Rafindadi, had powerful connections of his own. Rafindadi also served on the board of the BCCI from 1983 until the bank's collapse in 1991. Dasuki, his colleague on the BCCI board, grabbed the most lucrative state assets—taking control, for example, of Agence Promotion et Financement Immobiliers (APROFIM) rice mills in partnership with an Israeli company. In 1990 Dasuki acquired the National Insurance Company of Nigeria (NICON), which had invested heavily in lucrative real estate holdings in Abuja, Nigeria's new capital.[27] Rafindadi also fared well, joining ventures with foreign firms such as United Trading Company, Tate and Lyle, and GTE. Tukur's, Dasuki's, and Rafindadi's positions in many state-run finance and development corporations also gave them access to state finances to underwrite privatizations to themselves.

Lists of the directors of other foreign banks willing to deal with Nigeria's elite illuminate other powerful political factions. For example, Major General Shehu Yar'Adua was chair of the Nigerian subsidiary of Pakistan's Habib Bank; Yar'Adua also acquired African Ocean Lines (with Bamanga Tukur), Sambo Farms, and Spring Waters (Nigeria). Yar'Adua was also reported to be Babangida's business partner in many ventures.[28] Yar'Adua shared his Habib Bank connection with Moshood Abiola, head of ITT's Nigerian subsidiary, a founder of the Second Republic's ruling National Party of Nigeria, and president-elect in the aborted 1993 presidential vote.

Privatization of this sort was more a recognition of de facto personal control of state assets than a redistribution of assets to a business class. But could even this manipulation of reform produce a business elite that could eventually develop its own distinct interests? The rapid growth in Indonesia, for example, has taken place in the context of a "crony capitalism" that concentrates assets in the hands of key politicians.[29] But privilege exists alongside an authoritarian regime with sufficient bureaucratic capacity to support a cadre of efficient technocratic managers who assert an independent definition of state interest in economic efficiency.

Also missing in the Nigerian case is the experience of the 1960s when Indonesia's military eliminated political rivals and disrupted their local bases of support, which considerably strengthened the ruler's dominant position vis-à-vis strongmen.

Despite flaws in Nigeria's reforms, economic indicators showed some improvement in the late 1980s. Nonpetroleum exports from Nigeria rose $400 million over a three-year period to reach $710 million in 1989. Foreign investment in Nigeria rose from $166 million in 1986 to $2.1 billion in 1989, reflecting not just foreign interest in Nigeria's oil fields but also a rise in joint ventures in privatized firms.[30]

Nonetheless, more significant problems related to the nature of Nigeria's elite politics appeared. By 1991, Nigeria's government was running a budget deficit equal to 45 percent of its revenue, compared with 20 percent when Babangida launched his coup and reforms.[31] Problems appeared in the financial sector as well. The Nigerian Deposit Insurance Corporation acknowledged that in 1990 nine state-run commercial banks were insolvent, with uncollected loans standing at fifty-five times shareholders' funds. Reports showed that twenty-eight private and private-state joint venture banks were "distressed" in April 1991.[32] Much of the banking industry's problem lay in politician–board members' use of banks to provide themselves with unsecured loans to, among other things, buy state assets. This distribution of wealth made nonsense of regime efforts to exclude old politicians from elections in a planned transition to a civilian regime. Control of these assets and access to credit continued the process of "teleguiding," or financing officially approved "new breed" candidates, through which formally banned backers fielded their own clients for elected office.[33] In this context, elections remained battlegrounds between local factions, with each struggling to gain elected office from which to manipulate future reforms and over which Babangida's formal screening process exercised little control.[34]

Babangida lifted the ban on former politicians in December 1991, thereby bringing the competition into the open. But as long as economic reforms saved the private interests of the elite, electoral democracy only continued the scramble for new sources of patronage, since the acquisition of state office was seen as the key to ensure that future "reforms" served one's personal interest. In this context, elections seemed little different from those conducted under Babangida's predecessors.

DEREGULATION AND
THE RISE OF BANKING FRAUD

Babangida found it difficult to back away from liberalization of foreign exchange transactions, a key part of the IMF's economic orthodoxy. But what is a bank in a patronage political system? Our brief glimpse of Nigeria's privatization exercise suggests that under conditions in which the logic of a political network overrides considerations of efficiency, a bank is a source of loans that do not have to be repaid. Banks can provide bogus documents, access to correspondent banks and other foreign businesspeople (who may be complicit in fraud), opportunities to launder money for others, illicit manipulation of state funds, and chances to rip off unwary depositors.[35] In some cases, bank fraud offers an opportunity to falsify government accounts so as to attract IMF and World Bank support, a ruse the Central Bank of Nigeria has assisted by publishing incomplete accounts that are up to two years out of date. Reflecting the gap between the formal and informal functions of banks in Nigeria, bank examiners complained (after several were killed) that "this job has a lot of professional risks! It is hazardous. We just pray that God [will] protect us!"[36]

Nigeria's banking industry also shows that creditor-sponsored reform policies applied to patronage politics helped to promote political fragmentation and increased corruption. Devaluation of the naira, Nigeria's currency, was a major component of Babangida's efforts to attract creditor support. Creditors argued that the move would promote Nigerian exports and limit the country's large import bill. Along with the commitment to privatize state-run firms, the relaxation of exchange controls would eliminate import licensing and the inefficient rationing of foreign exchange in the private sector, a major enticement to administrative corruption. In September 1986 Babangida backed the creation of the Second Tier Foreign Exchange Market (SFEM). The SFEM deregulated interbank exchanges, allowing banks to buy foreign exchange on an open market. This move was designed to force buyers of foreign exchange to pay a realistic but higher market price, thereby creating an incentive to reduce imports and buy locally produced products instead. The government retained a fixed exchange rate for critical official imports and collection of the country's oil revenues from foreign oil companies.[37]

In fact, when SFEM went into effect in 1987, a 50 to 60 percent spread developed between the fixed and market rates for the naira. Thomas Callaghy noted that this situation instantly created opportunities for arbitrage, merely replacing the import licensing scams reform meant to abolish.[38] For example, a person who had access to both foreign exchange markets could buy a dollar at the official rate of four naira, sell the dollar for nine naira in the open market, buy more dollars at four naira each, and so on. Complicity between Central Bank officials and private financiers preserved the spread.

Another critical element of the scheme lay in the massive expansion of opportunities through deregulation of the financial sector. Changes in bank licensing procedures in 1987 accelerated the process, shifting patronage opportunities from administrative corruption in matters such as import licensing to favoritism in an ostensibly private market. Two cases of bank deregulation show the different political implications of reform; both pioneered new opportunities for clandestine profit for a diverse group of associates in ways that gave local factional groups more autonomy to accumulate wealth. It is also important to see how this "privatization" of patronage (as in Liberia under Doe and in Mobutu's Zaire) exacerbated local ethnic rivalries. The reconfiguration of patronage politics from a relatively broad alliance regulated from the center to a more decentralized (and ethnicized) arrangement is important for understanding the nature of Abacha's patronage politics.

In the first example, the large Savannah Bank, previously Bank of America (Nigeria) until it was nationalized in 1976, shows how "reform" of the banking sector complemented the manipulation of privatization policies. The bank became a major player in the changing economic policies. In 1992 the Nigerian government reduced its stake in the firm, selling a portion to the Lebanese African Finance and Trading Company (LAFTRACO).[39] LAFTRACO, which could now show the role of foreign intermediaries in "privatized" patronage in the Nigerian context, used its access to foreign exchange, which it exchanged at its new bank at the open market rate. The bank used the naira to buy more dollars at the cheaper official rate, producing documents to certify that those dollars would be used for approved purposes.[40] Savannah had acquired the documents by including some state and local government officials in its operations. The bank gained further access to "cheap" dollars when it was designated to privatize state budget and expenditure procedures. Ironically, this "reform," designed to replace weak bureaucratic capacity with a private company, simply removed corrupt practices from the purview of (admittedly weak) administrative oversight. In 1994, LAFTRACO was accused of buying $7.06 million from Savannah at 4 nairas to the dollar against a prevailing market rate that grew to 22 nairas to the dollar.[41]

Meanwhile, the directors of LAFTRACO—while serving as officials of Savannah Bank—directed the bank to pay out unsecured loans to four other companies they owned. The business partners also moved some money into the lucrative rice importing business, which borrowed $500,000 from the bank but never paid back. Savannah Bank managers later testified that they had "lost track" of LAFTRACO when the Central Bank of Nigeria directed them to collect their loans, yet LAFTRACO officials continued to attend Savannah board meetings. LAFTRACO extended its reach to Lion's Bank of Nigeria, 30 percent of which was owned by the Plateau State government. Partial ownership of Lion's Bank gave LAFTRACO preferential access to Plateau State officials and opportunities for fraud in payments to Plateau State contractors.[42]

These partnerships between state governments and banks raised political tensions among local ethnic groups. For example, the public-private grip on state contracts and cheap dollars caused some members of the Idoma ethnic group in Kogi State to suspect that local Tivs were using their political dominance to move into the private banking business. Such complaints contributed to Idoma politicians' requests to Abacha for a new state in 1996, claiming Kogi had become a "Tiv state."[43] The conflict benefited Babangida and later Abacha, because local clients collected their patronage rewards from the local economy (with help from federal government financing of fraudulent state contracts) and then turned to the president when that activity widened local ethnic and factional conflicts.

Meanwhile, Savannah Bank staff members developed their own scams. A branch manager in Nnewi simply failed to note a loan of $2.2 million to firms in which he had personal stakes. The Kano branch manager granted several unsecured personal loans totaling $500,000. Bank examiners identified over 337 million nairas (about $20 million) in bad loans in 1994. They also discovered that Savannah staff members had written Savannah checks on their own accounts to open accounts at other banks. In connivance with officials at other banks, the checks were destroyed after the accounts were opened and before the issuers' Savannah accounts were debited. In one such transaction, bank staff declared that two $2 million checks from Equator Trust Bank and Pacific Merchant Bank to Savannah were "lost." Some bank officials even illegally withdrew funds from unwary depositors' accounts.

Hardly an isolated case, Savannah's story of personal favoritism and widening factional conflicts was repeated, with variations, at Progress Bank. The brother of the Imo State finance commissioner bought a stake in Progress as it was being partially privatized. The Imo State government retained a 58 percent share of the bank. Subsequently, thirty local state-run companies made unsecured loans from the bank. Most of the loans went to government agencies in territory inhabited by Messi Oweri people—the group from which the finance commissioner and his brother originated. The access gave the group a big advantage as backers of local candidates in the elections that led to the aborted 1993 handover to a civilian regime. Local activists complained that easy access to money had given the "Progress faction" resources to hire armed gangs to disrupt their rivals' attempts to organize.[44]

Overall, the increase in the number of banks from 41 in 1985 to over 120 in 1993 highlights the dimensions of fraud, as segments of Nigeria's political network built their own private sources of wealth. A 1992 Central Bank clampdown on financial institutions revealed that banks with combined state and private ownership registered the highest number of bad loans, at 66.3 percent of total loans in 1991 compared with 32 percent for completely private banks.[45] This finding is not surprising, since the new group of financiers could collude with local officials to use the powers of state office for mutual personal gain. Government efforts to limit new bank licensing after 1990 caused smaller, less tightly regulated community bank registrations to increase from about 100 in 1990 to 900 in 1993.[46] Nonbank financial institutions such as mortgage vendors, bureaux de change, and stockbrokerages proliferated for the same reason.

This shift in the distribution of patronage under Babangida's rule revealed a blurring of distinctions between state and private in commercial operations. But an association with a sovereign state was still important in the development of the new strategies, since it indicated an ability to manipulate laws behind the screen of global recognition, as well as the preferred access to officials that makes those operations so attractive. The actual outcome of privatization and financial-sector reform also showed that Babangida's political strategy ultimately continued the patron-client politics of his successors, although in new channels.

Business directories and association handbooks revealed that people from all of Nigeria's major regions still benefited from selective privatization in the early 1990s. But as Table 6.1 shows, this accommodation occurred along a continuum of types of firms. Private firms are firms that were originally privately owned and that presumably represent the pinnacle of meritocracy and the greatest insulation from political influence in Nigerian commerce. Next are private joint ventures with foreign firms, which are more reliant on politicians for licenses and other documents. Private-state joint ventures present greater opportunities for use as patronage. State-run firms and new banks clearly serve patronage networks.

These figures point to the problem Abacha faced after he launched his palace coup in November 1993. Even somewhat successful reforms would have seriously threatened vested interests as particular geographic or ethnic groups, mostly from the east and west, took advantage of market reforms. Still more threatening would have been the immediate reaction of the numerous political networks—the Owerri clique associated with Progress Bank, for example, or groups from Nigeria's north, a region not known for its business prowess—if their access to patronage had suddenly ended. Yet, the decline of Nigeria's economy and poor relations with creditors forced Abacha to do something, since continuing on the same unsustainable course would have further wrecked the economy and exhausted Nigeria's patronage politics.

ABACHA'S PATRONAGE CRISIS

Acting as head of the military, Abacha seized power from Chief Ernest Shonekan on 27 November 1993. Babangida had appointed Shonekan

Table 6.1 Regional Origin of Nigerian Firms, 1994 (percent)

Region	Total Population	Private Firms	Private Joint Ventures with Foreign Firms	Private-State Joint Ventures	State-Run Firms	New Banks
North	53	21	39	43	61	45
West	25	41	37	37	23	32
East	22	38	24	19	16	23

Sources: Osso, *Who's Who;* Segun Ilori, ed., *Nigeria: Who's Who in Business* (Lagos: Mednet, 1995); press reports.

when he found that his cancellation of the June 1993 elections did not enable him to rule on his own. Far from powerless, Shonekan put his own distinctive mark on his brief administration, but his actions highlighted the difficulties of breaking out of a patron-client mold of politics and economic decline. In 1994, Shonekan moved quickly to raise the consumer price of fuel, which met one of the World Bank's key demands for reform. Prior to the price increase, fuel had sold for about three cents a litre at the pumps, costing Nigeria's government about $2 billion a year in subsidies.[47] Heavily subsidized fuel created incentives for border guards, other state officials, and informal market traders to smuggle fuel to much higher priced markets in surrounding states. Shonekan's decree proved highly unpopular, because it boosted fuel prices by 700 percent. Organized labor opposed this basic element of reform, pointing to the problem of carrying out harsh economic reform amid a resurgent civil society. This opposition, which did not pose a dire threat to Shonekan, helped Abacha justify his takeover in November.

More threatening to Nigeria's elite were Shonekan's signals that he was prepared to root out corruption in the Nigerian National Petroleum Corporation (NNPC), a prime source of patronage. The NNPC had already been weakened by sales of several of its subsidiaries to politicians at bargain prices. Earlier, many military officers (including Babangida) had been complicit in the loss of state revenues—in particular the disappearance of $12 billion in windfall oil profits during the Gulf War surge in prices—which had helped to drain the company of operating capital and had rendered the company unable to contribute its portion of spending to joint-venture production arrangements with foreign firms. Arrears to those firms stood at $500 million when Abacha took power.[48] The danger to Shonekan (and to any other ruler) was that if foreign firms cut back their operations in Nigeria, the central source of state revenues would diminish—a situation that would have dire political consequences as strongmen clients concluded that their loyalty no longer translated into patronage from a ruler.

An effective investigation of corruption in the state-run NNPC risked implicating the military officers who were responsible for administering it, along with numerous beneficiaries of largesse. Any attack on corruption in the military threatened to widen conflicts within that institution. Enlisted personnel collected salaries of about $75 a month at the noncommissioned officer rank, with common soldiers receiving only about $35 a month. Living conditions were poor, with crowded housing and inadequate services at military bases.[49] In stark contrast, high-ranking officers lived well, an obvious consequence of their close ties to powerful politicians and state officials. Many had taken advantage of administrative assignments during the period of military rule under Babangida to enrich themselves. Any attack on the private benefits those officers received from patronage would carry the risk that another general would oust Abacha.

As with all of his predecessors, Abacha's first cabinet appointments emphasized co-optation of old regime supporters. They included appointments of prominent Abiola supporters such as Olu Onagoruwa, a leader of the prodemocracy Movement for National Reform, as attorney general. Abiola's running mate, Babagana Kingibe, became secretary for external affairs. Kalu I Kalu, Babangida's finance minister during the 1980s, brought his technocratic reputation back to his former job. Babangida supporters such as former Senate president Iyorchia Ayu became education secretary, Ebenezer Babatope became transport secretary (and later a bombing target after he renounced his position), and Lateef Jakande took over Public Works.[50] Umaru Dikko, who had been in charge of distributing lucrative import licenses during the Second Republic and thus virtually personified corruption, made frequent visits to Abacha's headquarters at Aso Rock.[51] The continuity reflected Abacha's roots in this elite network. Abacha had played a role in the three successful army coups since 1976, serving as chief of army staff, and then, before his own coup, as chief of defense and defense minister.

Abacha tried to attend to the personal interests of his associates and loyalists in both government and the military. The NNPC remained a source of patronage for distribution to allies. During 1994, for example, short-term contracts covered about 40 percent of the NNPC's production. Favored firms received contracts to "lift," or remove, oil from well sites in which the NNPC had joint venture operations to market. The oil was sold to the firms at an official price below market price and gave the firms' proprietors handsome rewards. A total of thirty-one companies received contracts to lift oil in 1994. Almost none fulfilled the official criteria of owning refining capacity, exporting petroleum products, or holding sufficient assets. Most politician-proprietors lacked the organizational or technical expertise to transport crude oil; therefore, Abacha used the private services of a local Lebanese family and a Swiss firm to actually handle the oil.

Owners of another such firm, the Chagouri family, had large real estate holdings in Lagos—including Lagoon Casino—and worked in the Abuja construction industry. Thus, Chagouri activities in the oil industry enhanced opportunities for elite partnerships with the family's other businesses in Nigeria. Other contracts went to Germany's Ferrostahl, which had not previously been involved in the oil industry. The firm worked on construction of Nigeria's $1.5 billion state-run aluminum smelter, an economically inefficient project but one with numerous opportunities for fraudulent contracts. Even Abiola's Summit Oil Company received a contract to lift 20,000 barrels a day, or just over 1 percent of Nigeria's production.[52]

But oil money could not finance a new expansive patronage network for Abacha. The NNPC's leakage of earnings to serve Abacha's patronage needs further undermined the firm's capacity to pay its share of oil production costs in joint ventures with foreign firms. By February 1994, arrears on joint venture operations stood at $700 million; later that year arrears approached a billion dollars. Foreign firms began to cut production in late 1994, as they became reluctant to invest in new operations in which their Nigerian partners were unable to provide their portion of the financing. Abacha permitted some divestiture of joint ventures with foreign firm partners (to creditor acclaim) to settle some of the financial demands of Shell and Elf Aquataine. But the move limited Abacha's future opportunities to use oil-lifting contracts as patronage.[53]

Direct regulation of exchange rates, a component of past patronage politics, reappeared in Abacha's 1994 budget. Most apparent was a retreat back to controls over foreign exchange. The budget revalued the naira to an official rate of four to the dollar, against an informal rate of 22 to the dollar. Far from resolving the banking crisis, this revaluation worsened it by providing a new opportunity for arbitrage in currency markets. Firms were required to deposit hard currency earnings in the Central Bank of Nigeria to supply the insatiable demand by politicians for cheap foreign exchange. Import licenses returned. The consequence of these changes was the breakdown of talks with the IMF over debt rescheduling. World Bank researchers declared that Nigeria had "abandoned ownership" of the hard-won benefits of even limited reform under Babangida.[54]

In 1997, Nigeria's Finance Ministry was still clinging to dual rates. Despite the damage this policy has done to relations with creditors and to the economy, its abandonment would cut many clients—including military officers—from lucrative deals.[55]

As in the crises of patronage politics described in previous chapters, Abacha abandoned efforts to provide social services to compensate for shortfalls in revenue while still distributing patronage. Most Nigerians faced harsh austerity without the benefits of economic reform. Prices doubled in 1994 by conservative estimates.[56] Lost revenue and unrestrained spending boosted the budget deficit to two-thirds of total revenue, or 15 percent of gross domestic product. The collapse of fiscal planning also derailed efforts to settle arrears to the World Bank and gain access to new credit. By the end of the year, arrears stood at $6 billion on the country's $33 billion debt.[57]

Amid this economic decline and popular hardship, Abiola declared himself president, a move for which he was arrested. This situation sparked a six-week strike by oil workers that threatened to choke off the regime's only reliable source of wealth and brought the country's woes to global attention. Despite regime claims that fuel production was not disrupted, the crisis was severe enough to clog the streets of Cotonou in neighboring Benin (where I was living) with Nigerian motorists seeking fuel.

Concerns from abroad about Nigeria's political situation and fiscal condition also interfered with Abacha's efforts to legitimate his coup to outsiders. The regime's U.S. representatives, the Washington, D.C., firm of Washington and Christian, were losing the public relations battle against, for example, the pro-Abiola Campaign for Democracy's Beko Ransome-Kuti and Femi Falana and criticism from Nobel Laureate Wole Soyinka. Abiola's arrest was condemned by the Nigerian secretary-general of the commonwealth, Chief Emeka Anyaoku.

The abrogation of the 1993 election raised some military officers' concerns that they might be excluded from future patronage. This was especially true for those associated with Babangida and would-be civilian President Abiola. More important, however, was the perception that the election's reversal was a strike against Yoruba influence in Nigeria's government (Abiola is Yoruba). To the extent that many of Abacha's critics were Yorubas, Abacha's own faction would come to share that view.[58] Widespread protests organized by the opposition National Democratic Coalition (NADECO) reinforced those impressions.

A more significant danger to Abacha, however, lay in the prospect that an enterprising senior officer might mobilize support among prodemocracy organizations in support of a coup. Rear Admiral Olu Omotehinwa, Air Commodore Dan Sulieman, former Chief of Defense Staff Lieutenant General Alani Akinrinade, former President General Olusegun Obasanjo, and Major General Shehu Yar'Adua aligned themselves with the civilian opposition to Abacha. This manner of military factionalization does not constitute warlord politics, since it plays to broad-based popular support. But it does contain the possible fracturing of a national patronage network in other ways compatible with warlord politics.

The seriousness of the military split was seen in a bombing campaign. Attacks on regime targets were not simply indications of a NADECO offensive (the group claimed to prefer dialogue). Instead, some bombings appeared to have originated within the military. Targets included a major cantonment and a stadium at which military leaders were present; additionally, an airplane bomb killed Abacha's son, and homes of pro-Abacha officers were bombed—often with sophisticated weapons. A response in kind was leveled against "opposition" targets within the military; for example, Akinrinade's house was bombed.[59]

Smaller groups within the military appear to have taken advantage of the broader disorder to serve their own interests, as enterprising freelancers and those pursuing personal vendettas took up arms. For example, young men in Lagos, locally known as "area boys," were alleged to have engaged in illicit trade in collaboration with military officers.[60] The group, which was well armed, even fended off an offensive of the State Security Service (SSS).[61]

These are the raw materials of warlord politics—the fracturing of a national patronage network within the context of repressing alternative popular political groups, and the growing brigandage among young men. Political and criminal violence transmutes relatively easily within this context. Officers become mafia-style bosses as military units shift into protection rackets and engage in smuggling, either for themselves or for the cause of some local faction.

The next significant step would be for leaders of factions to try to operate independent sources of accumulation. Except for freelance operations in illicit drugs and trading, little sign of this has surfaced as yet.[62] But the very possibility raises the stakes for Abacha, who must now co-opt, repress, or otherwise prevent independent action by rival officers. To do so, he must continue to manage factional politics at the local level (as in the banking sector) and above all, preserve his control over oil and gas. As in other cases, in this situation old bureaucratic instruments of control such as the army become less reliable as tools of regime security, which encourages rulers to experiment with more nonbureaucratic means of control.

Domestically, Abacha first resorted to another past tactic. His War Against Indiscipline and Corruption (WAIC), styled after Buhari's populist effort in 1984, promised to fight corruption by disciplining civil servants. Abacha's feeble version of Buhari's program led to purges of the Lagos telephone exchange, accusations of fraud at the post office, and desultory prosecutions of a few customs officials unfortunate enough to have been picked out of crowds of smugglers. The effort offered much less populist mileage than Buhari's, especially at its start in early 1994, since it targeted only Abacha's obvious political enemies. Visibly corrupt individuals close to the president were immune to prosecution. More significant, Abacha convened a Constitutional Convention to consider an eventual transition to civilian rule. Under pressure from Abacha and his allies, the convention pondered a 1995 handover, which became 1996 and then 1998.

Low oil prices, limits to production, economic collapse in the nonoil sector, creditor condemnation, and poor relations with other states limited Abacha's political resources. Yet, declining control over the military and the need to placate at least some of Abiola's supporters and others who expected to benefit from the aborted transition program meant that a patron-client strategy required even greater resources than before.

Thus, Abacha faced severe internal and external pressure to innovate as old bases of patronage politics crumbled. His innovations have had four broad components. First, coercion against challengers has been intensified, both within Nigeria's old elite networks and against those who support democratic rule. Second, conflict between local factions has been manipulated in ways that have led to increased violence. Third, Abacha has retained absolute control over income from oil. Fourth, and true to the form of the other cases, outsiders' recognition of Abacha's status as head of a sovereign state has given him decisive advantages in the reworking of patronage politics.

The fact that starting in 1995 economic indicators have shown some improvement has bolstered Abacha's appeal to outsiders. In one of Africa's most stunning fiscal reversals, the 1995 budget showed a surplus (so it was claimed).[63] World Bank officials exclaimed approvingly that "if reforms of 1995–96 are sustained and others are put in place, Nigeria can grow the non-oil economy at 7.5 percent per year, reduce poverty, and protect the environment."[64] Interestingly the innovations examined later bear little resemblance to World Bank prescriptions. To illustrate Abacha's changes of strategy, I return to the problem of failed banks to show how Abacha's tactics shifted from Babangida's strategy.

MANIPULATING REFORM
TO DISCIPLINE ASSOCIATES

Sam Aluko, head of Abacha's Economic Intelligence Monitoring Unit, is a trained economist. But instead of favoring free markets and supporting entrepreneurs as a solution to the crisis in the financial sector, he backed the use of tribunals to prosecute banking executives. In contrast, we saw earlier that unfettered markets permitted individuals from Nigeria's unwieldy patronage network to accumulate wealth on their own at the expense of central control over clients and against the continued viability of the country's financial and commercial sectors.

The 1995 Failed Bank (Recovery of Debts) Decree No. 18 curbed that independence. The decree provided a legal framework with which to prosecute the managers and directors of the nearly fifty failed and troubled banks in Nigeria. Abacha's spokespersons advertised the decree as a measure to restore stability and business confidence in Nigeria's banks. The decree also allowed Abacha to selectively target bank officials—picking off his enemies, removing threatening individuals, and playing bank officials and local political networks against one another. He thus avoided the pitfalls of Babangida's 1987 effort to bar politicians from future electoral competition while allowing them new access to wealth that allowed them to "teleguide" their own clients and manipulate presidential policy.

The nature of the decree and its effect on its targets provide a contrast to Babangida's strategies, especially in the decree's intensity of attacks on significant portions of Babangida's political network. For example, Ibrahim Dasuki—former BCCI head for Nigeria, the beneficiary of privatizations, and Babangida's business partner—became the subject of a probe of over $7 million in bad loans from the Alpha Merchant Bank. Dasuki was not only central to the former president's patronage network; his position as sultan of Sokoto gave him the status of spiritual leader of Nigeria's Muslims. Dasuki was targeted additionally for openly criticizing Abacha's failure to recognize Abiola's election.[65] Furthermore, Dasuki's son, a commissioned officer, organized and advised Abacha opponents from Benin, Nigeria's western neighbor.[66]

The decree was also significant for striking at a prominent member of northern Nigeria's traditional elite, a "Kaduna mafia," long considered a core of support for successive regimes and key beneficiaries of patronage. For example, banking tribunals listed Alhaji Ado Bayero, emir of Kano, as a target of investigation and cited his alleged involvement with the anti-Abacha NADECO.[67]

Banks such as Progress that were associated with state governments also came under scrutiny. Here, too, we find a paring down of old political networks, with some members relegated to prison as examples to those who remained dependent on favor from the president to protect them from prosecution. The prosecution of Progress Bank's managers was very selective, which highlighted regime efforts to side with one local faction against another and weakened any chance for unified opposition to the regime. The prosecutions were directed at individuals from the same area and clan as a crooked loan officer and his brother—the corrupt state finance commissioner—and partisans of this local political faction within the bank's organization were sent to prison.[68] Their rivals were not left to resume their old activities, however. Instead, the regime declared that Progress Bank was one of the six Nigerian banks targeted in a privatization move in which foreign investors, along with favored bank officers, would take over management.[69]

Privatization did not extend to all banks. At the same time the regime was touting the virtues of private ownership for Progress, Finance Minister Ani was defending an official proposal for the Nigerian government to take majority control of the country's four largest (and in the context of recent bank fraud relatively well run) privately owned merchant banks.[70] What first appears to be a policy contradiction instead reveals the variable political significance of private ownership depending on one's position within Nigeria's shifting patronage networks. For the banks, the fact that their managers hailed disproportionately from the Yoruba ethnic group—president-elect Abiola's strongest base of support—had political import. Street rumors questioned whether some of the businesspeople were helping to bankroll Abiola and other opposition figures. The managers of Union Bank, incorporated in 1917, were from the most entrepreneurial segment of western Nigeria's Yoruba business elite. Hakeem Bello-Osagie had recently emerged as the bank's head after a proxy battle that focused on the need to assert technocratic management rather than curry political favor to deal with the crisis in the banking sector. Similar debates took place among corporate officers at the United Bank for Africa, another regime target.[71]

Ultimately, Abacha canceled the planned bank takeovers. The World Bank's chief economist in Nigeria had warned that this policy "would do immense damage to the government's credibility at home and abroad."[72] The regime backtracked, valuing relations with its creditors more than the immediate disruption of an independent commercial network within the ethnic group that had showed the most sustained opposition to Abacha's cancellation of the 1993 election. Yet, the threat of takeovers had the intended effect of making the bankers more attentive to the political concerns of the regime. Management and boards at all four banks brought forward individuals who had close ties to the regime. The Nigerian government sold some shares in Africbank, once targeted for takeover. But of the four, Africbank had the closest ties to a foreign partner and helped to finance privatizations of state-run firms to regime favorites; thus, it was unlikely to act in coordination with any independent Nigerian group.

In 1996 inquires spread to the insurance industry. Minister of Finance Ani advertised the inquiry in terms familiar to readers of World Bank reports as a measure to "increase government capacity to introduce transparency" to the insurance industry. Former managers of state-run firms found themselves under official scrutiny in late 1996. Abacha claimed that Nigeria had spent $25 billion on state-run firms after the 1973 oil boom and that privatizations of the bulk of those firms had netted a mere $20 million.[73] Abacha's finance minister suggested that an investigation of customs officials would begin in 1997. An investigation into the conduct of former military officers who had become administrators under Babangida's rule began in early 1996, with occasional hints that the source of Babangida's own fortune might receive official attention. Investigator General Ibrahim Coomassie began to investigate the police. Documents revealing the fate of $12 billion in windfall revenues from the sale of crude oil during the Gulf War appeared in the press, directly implicating Babangida and his wife.[74]

These measures had populist appeal insofar as they targeted visible and obviously corrupt officials. One journalist wrote that "the masses are happy with the failed banks tribunal and the idea that there is no sacred cow in society."[75] Creditors expressed grudging approval. Unregulated Nigerian commerce had critics in the U.S. Drug Enforcement

Agency, where some officials have lauded what appeared to be a more concerted Nigerian effort to control commercial channels that may have played a role in financing drug transactions or laundering the proceeds.[76] Abacha has played his moves against errant Nigerian traders and financiers as helping U.S. officials in their efforts to control clandestine drug trading, which holds out to officials in strong states the possibility that the Nigerian ruler should be supported against wrongdoers in his own regime and raises hopes that he will one day have greater will and capacity to discipline those errant strongmen.

Greater discipline in Nigeria's political economy has supporters elsewhere, too. For example, Thai police have complained that the number of Nigerians arrested for smuggling heroin increased from 4 in 1988 to 700 in 1995.[77] Once again, a global coalition has arisen to support a weak-state ruler's moves against rivals, which he has presented to outsiders as measures to ensure internal stability.

These "reforms" indicate further fragmentation of the ruler's political network into tighter circles of ethnic and personal loyalties. The problem with this partisan use of state power, however, lies in its further destruction of an institutional framework of authority that can autonomously constrain or modify conflicts and factions if Abacha's power should weaken. As with Doe and Mobutu, the strategy leaves Abacha more intensely dependent on direct, personal control over the resources that are the major source of wealth in the society, as well as obsessed with controlling factions and groups whose commercial connections or local support might challenge his power. If Abacha weakens, those factions and local strongmen could exercise authority in their own right, struggling with each other to do so. Abacha's repression of political alternatives, both within the military and in the broad-based civilian opposition that developed around his abrogation of the 1993 election, would leave the political field more open to ethnic entrepreneurs and faction leaders who once collaborated with him.

New Matters for the Police

Heroin trafficking is much like illicit banking in that it is a new, decentralized source of wealth outside the old structure of patronage in Nigeria. Whereas fraudulent banks undoubtedly played a role in organizing the trade, allegations that military officers and civilian officials have been directly involved pose a considerably greater threat to Abacha. Suspicions have pointed to military officer involvement in criminal syndicates, just as bank fraud financed some politicians.[78] Within the context of intramilitary factional splits and the ongoing bombing campaign, criminality is easily merged with political struggle. Unlike bankers, drug syndicates are likely to be armed, bringing coercive and not just financial resources to politicians whose protection they seek—much as RUF allied with armed gangs of illicit diamond miners and some army officers during Sierra Leone's civil war. Because of its volume, the drug trade's capacity to undermine Abacha's control over his associates should unsettle him, especially when one considers the extent to which drug traffickers rival the power of state officials in much stronger states such as Colombia and Mexico (and occasionally even the United States).

The fastest way to gain domestic and outside support for using violence against errant elites was to label counterattacks on such people as a war against drug trafficking. For outsiders, this ploy appeared to be an effort by the Nigerian government to impose order and fulfill interstate obligations to control clandestine trade. Many Nigerians approved of law-and-order measures that promised relief from crime, especially in urban areas. Major General Musa Bamaiyi, the head of the Nigerian Drug Law Enforcement Agency (NDLEA), has played on public cynicism toward politicians, promising to "prevent drug barons from hijacking the politics of the Fourth Republic" and to ward off "narco-democracy."[79]

Bamaiyi's "task forces" have also found a broader range of targets. Tax evasion has long sapped the budgets of Nigeria's states. A paramilitary effort (along with a broad-ranging Tribunal for Miscellaneous Offenses) has pursued individual tax evaders, often in ways that have played to local factional battles. In Kaduna State, for example, an alleged evader was opposition figure Sunday Danladi-Okogwu, Babangida's brother-in-law. In Imo State, task forces targeted the Progress Bank faction that had fallen out of favor with the Failed Bank Tribunals. Members of the faction "protested to the government, criticizing the use of armed military personnel to enforce revenue collection."[80] Meanwhile, the fiscal results of coercive tax collecting efforts have played to a key World Bank demand to boost internal tax revenues. In Ondo State, for example, private armed "tax consultants" helped to increase the state's contribution to federal operating funds by 50 percent from mid-1995 to mid-1996. During the same time period Kaduna State's armed task forces doubled revenue collection. Efforts in Kaduna included publicly threatening prominent individuals and painting some key opposition figures as corrupt.[81]

More politically significant, police matters extended to local organizations that threatened Abacha's plan to pare down broad-based patronage networks. Playwright and former government administrator Ken Saro-Wiwa's Movement for the Salvation of Ogoni People (MOSOP) stood directly in the path of that effort. Saro-Wiwa's organization called for compensation from Shell Oil Company for environmental damage to the Ogoni home region in southeastern Nigeria and also for a percentage of oil revenues. Ogoni claims reflected a widespread regional dissatisfaction with the near total diversion of oil money from the areas in which it was produced into the political elite's pockets. Diamond estimated that Abacha and his associates skim about 25 percent of the revenues to distribute as political resources.[82] Only in 1992 did Babangida set up an Oil Mineral Producing Areas Development Commission (OMPADEC), which was mandated to spend just 1.5 percent of total revenues on areas affected by oil drilling.[83] Abacha and his allies depended on the $8 billion to $10 billion in annual oil revenues.

Abacha's security forces moved against Saro-Wiwa in May 1994. During a MOSOP rally, several Ogonis attacked and killed four Ogoni traditional leaders. Abacha's regime held Saro-Wiwa responsible for the attack, charging him with inciting the murders, even though he was not present at the crime. He and eight codefendants were sentenced to death in September 1995 and were hanged two months later. Critics have suggested that armed men close to the regime killed the four chiefs. Other events such as the machine-gunning murders of as many as a hundred Ogoni ferry passengers pointed to extensive outside involvement. Officials portrayed the event as a consequence of intra-Ogoni rivalries. But no recent history exists of bloody factional clashes in the area before 1992, when Adonis allegedly attacked Ogonis and killed as many as a thousand (indicating that the policy of instigation of local conflict actually began under Babangida rather than Abacha).[84] Other attacks such as the machine-gun attack on the offices of Gani Fawehinmi, Saro-Wiwa's attorney, allegedly had regime backing.[85]

Other recent instances of ethnic conflict in oil-producing areas point to a systematic regime instigation of violence. In 1994 sixty Okirka people were killed in what was supposedly a conflict over the possession of ancestral lands. In fact, local witnesses reported that the perpetrators of the attack were armed with automatic weapons. Elsewhere, after an attack left fourteen Nembe people dead, local officials claimed it was part of a Kalabari plot to take Nembe land. Here, too, witnesses reported seeing men in army uniforms with automatic weapons.[86] Of the latter conflict, a Kalabari politician urging reconciliation stated

> We have consistently refused to be drawn into a war with our Nembe brothers. But there are certain elements from without this state who are ready to do anything to foster disunity and mistrust among us. Some of us believe that certain elements within government are being used by the multinational oil companies to destroy the state.[87]

Here again we find a political authority asserting its influence by creating insecurity. That authority already appropriates resources in collaboration with foreign firms. But the firms need only the crudest sort of order to carry out their business. Thus, the militarization of local factions is an effective way to ensure that communities in oil-producing areas cannot unify to challenge the regime. This tactic effectively destroys civil society, replacing it with sets of rival ethnic organizations geared toward currying favor with the regime. Among Ogonis, rival organizations such as the Peacekeeping Movement in Ogoniland and the Patriotic Ogoni Youth both appear to receive official support.[88]

Significantly for a possible future warlord politics, these agents of political violence transmute into networks of criminal violence and agents of enterprising local strongmen. The administrator of Rivers State (which includes Ogoniland), for example, used a "private security company" linked to some of the armed groups to extract "tax" payments from businesses allegedly in arrears on payment of state taxes. The affected businesspeople were reportedly associated with opposition factions, and in several instances gangs took over neighborhoods and businesses.[89] This situation points to the creation of the raw materials of warlord politics in which enterprising local strongmen can exploit organized banditry for their own benefit.

This strategy incorporates tactics of patronage politics, but it relies more heavily on outright conflict between groups to control challenges to the regime. It is thus exclusionary rather than integrative. Tasks of discipline are de-bureaucratized and contracted out to regime allies, often groups headed by ethnic entrepreneurs who use their association with the ruler to pursue an ethnic agenda or a personal vendetta. This is the raw material of warlord politics. And in lieu of efforts to mobilize citizens and use the alliances to exercise authority, Abacha's regime has abandoned pretenses of promoting development as commonly understood or of providing any public benefit, most notably security.

But as we saw in Liberia, Sierra Leone, and Congo, even this crude type of order can sustain foreign investment in resource extraction. Royal Dutch Shell, for example, remains in Nigeria's oil fields and pumps 40 percent of the country's oil.[90] The company also appears to have intervened materially on behalf of the Abacha regime. Officials from the firm allegedly asked the Rivers State governor to suppress Ogoni protestors who they feared could disrupt production. Shell paid the transportation costs and salary bonuses for some troops—labeled oil field guards—to attack Ogoni protestors and later imported sophisticated weapons.[91]

World Bank urging that Nigeria's government increase production and privatize the oil industry has given Abacha foreign support in the domestic trend toward forming alliances with external partners to finance internal strategies. As Thomas Forrest pointed out in his study of Nigeria's postcolonial political economy, government control of oil has been the key to centralization and patrimonial control.[92] But in

Abacha's situation—where institutions are weak, the ruler is battling a vigorous group of societal critics and military factions all demanding a share of resources, and he does not trust his own state institutions and officials—Abacha has bargained that privatization will give him more reliable partners than his unreliable fellow Nigerians.

VISION 2010—LEGITIMATING THE REGIME TO OUTSIDERS

Abacha has sought long-term outside support for, or at least acceptance of, his regime that violates conventional notions of economic and political liberalization. Outside support from oil companies and states, which could disrupt Abacha's oil revenues, is pivotal if he is to forego autonomous bureaucracies and continue to manage enterprising strongmen through informal means. Liberal reform led to unregulated bank fraud and the fragmentation of civilian and military elite factions into rivalries for access to scarce resources. Control has thus come through decidedly illiberal limits on commercial enterprise and political criticism. As in the previous cases, the weak-state ruler's solution to his crisis of patrimonial control lies in a reconfigured, extroverted alliance based on the regime's promise to provide order in a fractious Nigeria. Ironically, the regime has presented itself as best suited to shield outsiders from the consequences of the state collapse its own internal tactics have promoted.

Abacha's regime has hired a wide array of public relations firms to help bridge the gap between outsiders' calls for reform and the actual crackdown on those the regime holds responsible for fragmentation.[93] Prominent Abacha critic Randall Robinson, head of the Transafrica Coalition, reported that he was offered $1 million by a Nigerian businessman to stop his attacks on the regime.[94] Abacha's regime has also sponsored its own version of fake NGOs to support interpretations that it is serious about domestic reform and that elite discipline and a strong ruler are needed if Nigeria is to overcome its economic crisis. Groups such as the Lagos-based Africa 2020 include agents of foreign firms and Nigerian businesspeople and officials who are friendly to the regime. Their proceedings advertise a need for stability, highlight errors of careless transitions to civilian rule, and praise the methods of rulers such as Chile's Pinochet.

Managed political "reform" has appeased internal and foreign public critics of the regime or at least made it easier for Abacha's outside supporters to ignore the critics. Abacha's announced October 1998 transition to a civilian regime has generated a new array of opportunities to screen elites. Offices and processes such as the Transition Implementa-

tion Committee (which will design the process), the National Reconciliation Committee (which will certify individual politicians), political
party registration (for screening organizations), and voter registration
lists (which will screen voters) will use customary patronage incentives
for enterprising individuals to demonstrate loyalty to the regime. "Not
participating in any local government elections," warned an aspiring
politician, "is a sure way of sealing off one's political career in the coming republic."[95]

The transition process will also guard against cooperation among
civilian politicians who are critical of the regime. The creation of six new
states and numerous new local government authorities in 1996 continued to stir local rivalries. Politicians bid against one another to consolidate their local power within new jurisdictions. Key personalities from
the Babangida era and earlier have scrambled to protect their privilege
by participating in the process. The leaders of one of the five approved
parties include two former ministers of petroleum resources, a former
inspector general, and one of Nigeria's most prominent businessmen
and publishers. Each approved party has rosters of luminaries from past
regimes, including figures such as Tukur, who appeared at the head of
Babangida's privatization program. Ten parties were disqualified, including some led by Nigeria's richest men—a few of whom were from
Abacha's home area. Meanwhile, the appearance of groups such as the
Council of Elders has publicized calls for Abacha to stay in power beyond 1998.

This use of patronage continues features of past politics in Nigeria,
but it combines patronage with greater institutional weakness and a rejection of popular mobilization amid violent factional politics. This
brings us back to Abacha's dilemma: The appearance of factions and the
challenge factions in state bureaucracies (such as the military) pose
make broad-based patronage difficult for Abacha to sustain. The record
of reform under Babangida shows the difficulty of controlling patronage
within the setting of a relatively bureaucratized Nigeria. Without conventional bureaucratic means of imposing his authority, Abacha has
turned to innovation born of crisis management. When challenges to the
regime strike close to centers of accumulation (the Ogoni threat) or
come from those with access to weapons (the military threat), those innovations have followed a decidedly warlord-type course.

Meanwhile, other aspects of the political reform process have been
paced to appeal to or appease outsiders. The slow, selective release of
political prisoners has muted harsh criticism overseas and convinced
some Nigerians that the regime may moderate its policies in the future.
In 1996, for example, Abacha approved the release of prominent human
rights campaigner and Civil Liberties Organisation head Abdul Oroh.
The head of African Human Rights Watch, Tunji Abayomi, was also

freed in 1996. This modulated release of prisoners has been yet another screening process. Under Abacha's 1994 Decree 2, which suspended habeas corpus, the president is free from judicial oversight to pick and choose prisoners for release.

Favored private groups have taken a more assertive stance in support of the regime's policies. Some officials, spearheaded by Minister of Finance Anthony Ani, have organized a policy group called Vision 2010. Like Africa 2020, Vision 2010 includes businesspeople (executives of foreign oil-producing firms) and calls for a role for Abacha as a civilianized strongman ruler beyond 1998. Unlike the case with Africa 2020, Abacha has officially recognized the group, announcing that "it will look at everything, the educational system, crime, agriculture . . . everything." Stressing the coercive element of his policies, Abacha has noted that "Vision 2010 will continue far-reaching measures to sanitize the system and instill some discipline in the operation of the economy and public management.[96] The group is also charged with playing a role in the privatization of banks and Nigeria's oil industry, key World Bank demands.

Nigeria has a long way to go before it becomes a haven for foreign investment. But initiatives such as Vision 2010 emphasize the quest for a more favorable business environment, which coincides with Abacha's domestic agenda of "rooting out obstructionist elements in our society.[97]

Some analysts have presented Vision 2010 as a more viable route to growth than complicated, failed transitions to disorderly elections and a corrupt civilian regime. For example, London's *Economist* has noted that "the economy is turning around."[98] Some French business leaders have confessed that military regimes might be more able at managing reform "where discipline is such a problem," allowing that adjustment with much more controlled liberalization might be a solution to West Africa's poor economic performance and corruption.[99] This philosophy is compatible with academics who have suggested "a need to insulate key economic management functions from direct political pressures and at the same time to improve the channels of ongoing consultation between government and concerned interest groups."[100]

At a distance, Abacha's path of coercive, outward-oriented development appears to be a modified version of the authoritarian East Asian or Pinochet's Chilean strategies of development, albeit with a much weaker domestic business sector. Some members of Vision 2010 have expressed their attraction to such models and have even visited East Asia and Chile. Like Africa 2020, Vision 2010 gives Abacha an open-ended role as an overseer of reform. The appearance of groups such as Fourth Force—headed by Patrick Ani, the finance minister's brother—and Shehudeen Adesina's National Youth Movement have supported calls for Abacha to abandon the planned transition to an elected civilian rule.

But a closer look at the political pressures facing Abacha's regime suggests a greater likelihood that he will continue to pursue a political strategy closer to the warlord politics model described in this book, a model designed to address the political threats that develop in unsustainable patrimonial politics as state institutions weaken. Abacha's divide-and-rule policies, both among civilian elites and within his own military, treat factions as self-interested, to be played off one another. Ultimately, Abacha's fear of bureaucrats, especially technocrats, reflects the impact of the deep roots of patronage networks in Nigeria's political economy. The autonomy of one group, especially one that can generate or divert resources independent of the direct authority of a ruler, threatens to undermine a regime that bases its power on the manipulation of economic opportunity.

Herein lies the contradiction of Vision 2010. Abacha will reasonably suppose that he and his regime cannot survive the opening up of new centers of accumulation, since even committed technocrats will likely cultivate the support of enterprising strongmen to implement and generate support for programs. Thus, Vision 2010 will not become a technocratic core of reform as were the free market Chicago boys in Pinochet's Chile in the 1970s or the Berkeley mafia in Suharto's Indonesia in the 1960s.

Abacha will likely rely more heavily on nonbureaucratic methods. External aspects of his policies will look like economic liberalization insofar as they will seek to attract foreign investors who can be depended on to control centers of accumulation as Abacha deals with internal rivals. But Abacha's policies will likely include significant aspects of patronage politics. He and his clique will continue to control rivals and rogue strongmen through direct regulation, tribunals, and applications of violence—even if they become more savvy about how to do so without raising criticism from outsiders. Abacha and his followers will continue to build political authority on their capacity to control commercial opportunity inside Nigeria, which they translate into political resources.

But Abacha will continue to face serious internal security threats. Nigeria is too urbanized, its economy too commercialized—with multitudes of links to regional and global markets—and its people too expectant to easily impose a politics that excludes large numbers of people or denies citizens the benefits from revenues. One might see hope in this civil society Abacha rejects. But to the extent that Abacha successfully represses unified groups and manipulates factions, especially in ways that promote narrow ethnic or sectional agendas, his failure will likely clear the field for ethnic entrepreneurs who can transform their positions in Abacha's system of internal control into independent personal advantage.

This scenario repeats some of the "Mobutu or chaos" themes in Chapter 5. Yet Mobutu's defeat and Kabila's arrival did not dissolve Congo. In Nigeria, however, the geographic concentration of one resource—oil—will be a pole of conflict (as it was during the Biafran War in 1967–1970 when separatists in the oil region sought to leave the federation). This scenario makes unlikely any kind of divisible sovereignty of the Congolese type. The fact that Nigeria's economy is so sophisticated by regional standards and its bureaucracy so extensive raises the prospect of more numerous and intense efforts to preserve group position if Abacha should fail. One could take this as an argument for supporting Abacha against disorder. It would be more accurate, however, to say that the longer Abacha holds power (and the longer the social raw materials of warlord politics accumulate), the more difficult it will be for successors to chart an alternative political course of institutional accountability.

NOTES

1. Muyiwa Akintunde, "Abacha's Terror Tribunals," *Theweek,* 31 May 1996, 3.

2. Wole Soyinka, *The Open Sore of a Continent* (New York: Oxford University Press, 1996), 14–15.

3. Julius Ihonvbere and Olufemi Vaughan, "Nigeria: Democracy and Civil Society," in John Wiseman, ed., *Democracy and Political Change in Sub-Saharan Africa* (New York: Routledge, 1995), 71–91.

4. Richard Joseph, *Democracy and Prebendal Politics in Nigeria* (Lagos: Spectrum, 1991), 181.

5. Figures are from Keith Panter-Brick, *Soldiers and Oil: The Political Transformation of Nigeria* (London: Frank Cass, 1978), 27; Ben Naanen, "Oil Producing Minorities and the Restructuring of Nigerian Federalism: The Case of the Ogoni People," *Journal of Commonwealth and Comparative Politics* 33:1 (March 1995), 52–53.

6. Peter Lewis, "End Game in Nigeria?" *African Affairs* 93:372 (July 1994), 323.

7. Soyinka, *Open Sore,* 6. See also, Julius Ihonvbere, "Are Things Falling Apart? The Military and the Crisis of Democratization in Nigeria," *Journal of Modern African Studies* 34:2 (June 1996), 193–225; Peter Lewis, "From Prebendalism to Predation: The Political Economy of Decline in Nigeria," *Journal of Modern African Studies* 34:1 (March 1996), 79–103.

8. For example, Samuel Ikoku, *Fourth Coup d'État: Options for Modern Statehood* (Lagos: Ofada Printers, 1995); Niyi Oniororo, *Moneycrazy for the Third Republic* (Ibadan: Ororo Publications, 1993); Adebayo Lamikanra, *Wake Me Up in the Year 2000* (Lagos: Amka and Allied Services, 1994); "Thank You Abacha, Your Administration Listens," *ThisDay,* 16 Oct. 1995; "The Nigerian Dream," *Vanguard,* 1 June 1995.

9. "New Ventures," *African Business,* July 1988, 14; Tony Hawkins, "The Pressures for Stabilization Grow," *Financial Times,* 7 March 1988; S. O. Uniamikogbo, ed., *Issues in Privatisation and Commercialisation of Public Enterprises in Nigeria* (Ibadan: Kraft Books, 1995), 123–125.

10. Interview with creditor official in Nigeria, 12 Aug. 1991.

11. Tokoya 'Yomi, *General IBB: A Patriotic Leader of Our People* (Lagos: People's Publishing, 1988), 73.

12. Sayre Schatz, "Pirate Capitalism and the Inert Economy of Nigeria," *Journal of Modern African Studies* 22:1 (March 1984), 45–57.

13. Thomas Forrest, *Politics and Economic Development in Nigeria* (Boulder: Westview, 1995), 82–89, 134.

14. S. Egite Oyovbaire, "The Context for Democracy in Nigeria," S. Egite Oyovbaire, ed., *Democratic Experiment in Nigeria* (Lagos: Academy Press, 1987), 1–19.

15. Thomas Imobighe, ed., *The Politics of the Second Republic* (Kuru: National Institute for Policy and Strategic Studies, 1992).

16. Soyinka, *Open Sore,* 65–74.

17. Francis Nzeribe, *Nigeria: Seven Years After Shehu Shagari* (London: Kilimanjaro Publishing, 1990).

18. On institutional engineering, see Peter Koehn, "Competitive Transition to Civilian Rule: Nigeria's First and Second Experiments," *Journal of Modern African Studies* 27:3 (Sept. 1989), 401–430; for a skeptical view, see Ayogu Eze, "Old Game, New Players," *Newswatch,* 5 Aug. 1991, 38–40.

19. Rofimi Suberu, "The Travails of Federalism," *Journal of Democracy* 4:4 (Oct. 1993), 39–53.

20. Lindsay Barrett, *Agbada to Khaki: Reporting a Change of Government in Nigeria* (Enugu: Fourth Dimension, 1985), 40–42.

21. See Thomas Forrest, *The Advance of African Capital: The Growth of Nigerian Private Enterprise* (Edinburgh: Edinburgh University Press, 1994); "Nigeria II: One North, One People," *Africa Confidential,* 9 Sept. 1994.

22. "Nigeria: The Butchers of Bauchi," *Africa Confidential,* 17 April 1991.

23. Jonathan Beatty and S. C. Gwynne, *The Outlaw Bank* (New York: Random House, 1993), 190–194.

24. The Rigar Kaya section of *Gaskiya Ta Fi Kwabo,* a Kano daily newspaper, provides information about Dasuki's and Tukur's backgrounds, various issues, 1989–1991. See also Bala Takuya and Sonne Gwanle Tyoden, *The Kaduna Mafia* (Jos: Jos University Press, 1987).

25. Nyaknno Osso, ed., *Who's Who in Nigeria* (Lagos: Newswatch Communications, 1990).

26. Demola Oguntayo, "Business on Fire," *African Concord,* 4 Feb. 1991; H. R. Zayyad, *Economic Democratisation* (Kaduna: Technical Committee on Privatisation, 1992), 32.

27. Erim Anim, "Neither Friend nor Foe," *Newswatch,* 26 Nov. 1990, 15–20.

28. "Nigeria: More Machiavelli than Maradona," *Africa Confidential,* 20 Dec. 1991.

29. Richard Robison, "Authoritarian States, Capital-Owning Classes and the Politics of Newly Industrializing Countries: The Case of Indonesia," *World Politics* 41:1 (Oct. 1988), 52–74.

30. World Bank, *World Tables 1991* (Baltimore: Johns Hopkins University Press, 1991), 436–439.

31. Central Bank of Nigeria, *Economic and Financial Review* (Lagos: Central Bank of Nigeria, 1993), A19.

32. Nigerian Deposit Insurance Corporation, *Annual Report 1991,* (Lagos: Central Bank of Nigeria, 1991).

33. Dapo Olorunyomi et al., "The Unseen Hands," *African Concord,* 16 March 1992, 32–39. For more general discussion, see Peter Lewis, "Shifting For-

tunes: The Political Economy of Financial Liberalization in Nigeria," *World Development* 25:1 (1997), 5–22.

34. William Reno, "Old Brigades, Money Bags, New Breeds and the Ironies of Reform in Nigeria," *Canadian Journal of African Studies* 27:1 (April 1993), 66–87.

35. Joseph Ebhodaghe, *How the Fraudsters Do It* (Abuja: Nigerian Deposit Insurance Corporation, no date); *Customer Protection in the Nigerian Banking System* (Lagos: D.E.R., 1995).

36. Joseph Ode, "Bankers Behind Bars," *Newswatch*, 11 March 1996, 25.

37. Peter Lewis, "Economic Statism, Private Capital and the Dilemmas of Accumulation in Nigeria," *World Development* 22:3 (March 1994), 437–451.

38. Thomas Callaghy, "Political Passions and Economic Interests: Economic Reform and Political Structure in Africa," in Thomas Callaghy and John Ravenhill, eds., *Hemmed In: Responses to Africa's Economic Decline* (New York: Columbia University Press, 1993), 492–493.

39. For guides to the banking industry, see *Nigeria's Major 500 Companies: Fourth Edition 1994/95* (Lagos: Goldstar Media, 1995); Economic Community of West African States, *ECOWAS Financial Directory*, 2d ed. (Lagos: D.E.R., 1996).

40. Moffatt Ekoriko, "295 Million Naira Riddle," *Newswatch*, 5 June 1995, 27–28.

41. Joseph Ode, "Bankers Behind the Bar," *Newswatch*, 11 March 1996, 16–25.

42. Moffatt Ekoriko, "Haven for Fraudsters," *Newswatch*, 13 Feb. 1995, 27–30.

43. "Agitating for Redress," *Tempo*, 1 April 1996.

44. Wale Oladepo, "A Can of Worms," *Newswatch*, 23 Jan 1995; "Traditional Ruler in Court," *Daily Times*, 12 Aug. 1996.

45. "Banking in Nigeria: Surviving the Turbulent Times, *West Africa*, 1 Feb. 1993, 148.

46. Tony Hawkins, "Survey of Nigeria," *Financial Times*, 26 May 1995; Federal Office of Statistics, *Review of the Nigerian Economy* (Lagos: Federal Office of Statistics, 1994), 21.

47. Paul Adams, "Abacha Fails Test on Reforms," *Financial Times*, 5 Jan. 1994.

48. "Nigeria: Juju Economics," *Africa Confidential*, 18 Feb. 1994; Lewis, "From Prebendalism to Predation."

49. Wale Adedayo, "Poor Life at the Barracks," *Guardian* (Lagos), 24 July 1994.

50. "Nigeria: The Khalifa's Coup," *Africa Confidential*, 3 Dec. 1993.

51. Kayode Soyinka, *Diplomatic Baggage—MOSSAD and Nigeria: The Dikko Story* (Ikeja [Lagos]: Newswatch Books, 1995).

52. "Over a Barrel," *Africa Confidential*, 17 March 1995; Moffat Ekoriko, "The Goose Is Sick," *Newswatch*, 1 May 1995, 18–23. On continuing Chagouri connections, see "Nigeria: The General's Labyrinth," *Africa Confidential*, 4 July 1997.

53. "The Oil Hostage," *Africa Confidential*, 29 Aug. 1997.

54. Rashid Faruqee, "Nigeria: Ownership Abandoned," in Ishrat Husain and Rashid Faruqee, eds., *Adjustment in Africa: Lessons from Country Case Studies* (Washington, D.C.: World Bank, 1994), 238–285.

55. "Nigeria: Booming and Bombing," *Africa Confidential*, 17 Jan. 1997.

56. Some informal reports indicate a 200 percent increase. See Jonah Achema, "Nightmare," *Newswatch*, 28 Nov. 1994, 13–18.

57. World Bank, *World Debt Tables, 1995* (Washington, D.C.: World Bank, 1995).

58. Nats Agbo, "Rumbles of Politics," *Newswatch,* 2 Oct. 1995, 10–16; "Nigeria: Booming."

59. "Nigeria: Booming"; Dotun Oladipo, "State of Insecurity," *Newswatch,* 29 April 1996, 15–17; Emmanuel Ugwu, "Under Siege," *Newswatch,* 19 Feb. 1996, 8–10.

60. Imo State Government, *Government White Paper: Enquiry into the Disturbances at Oguta* (Owerri: Imo State Government, 1994); Sam Olukoya, "Law Keepers, Law Breakers," *Newswatch,* 12 Dec. 1994, 21–22.

61. Sam Olukoya, "Street Corner Gangs," *Newswatch,* 5 April 1994.

62. U.S. Department of State, Bureau of International Narcotics and Law Enforcement Affairs (BINLEA), *International Narcotics Control Strategy Report* (Washington, D.C.: BINLEA, 1995); Agbo, "Rumbles."

63. Economist Intelligence Unit, *Nigeria,* 1st quarter, 1996.

64. Noted in James Jukwey, "Nigerian Ruler Wins Some Accolades for Reforms," *Reuters Financial Service,* 28 Nov. 1996.

65. Alhaji Maman Kolo Zugurma on behalf of Alhaji Ibrahim Dasuki, "Swear in Abiola" (mimeo, no date); Emmanuel Ado, "End of the Sultan's Honeymoon with Abacha?" *Theweek,* 15 July 1996.

66. "Nigeria: Speechless," *Africa Confidential,* 13 Oct. 1995. See also, "Nigeria: Army Arrangements," *Africa Confidential,* 2 July 1993.

67. Emmanuel Ado, "Foreign Minister's Future in Doubt," *Theweek,* 27 May 1996.

68. "Atuwase II Sued by Regulatory Authorities over Failed Bank," *Daily Times,* 12 May 1996.

69. "House Cleaning at Failed Banks," *Guardian* (Lagos), 24 June 1996.

70. "Battle for the Banks," *Africa Confidential,* 23 June 1995.

71. Interviews by the author with Nigerian bank officials, 14 Oct. 1996, 6 Nov. 1996.

72. Quoted in "Dynamic Partnership," *Africa Economic Digest,* 22 May 1995, 8.

73. Muyiwa Akintunde, "Abacha's Terror Tribunals," *Theweek,* 2 June 1996.

74. Wale Akin Aina, "Pandora's Box," *Newswatch,* 16 Jan. 1995, 8–14.

75. Yusuph Olaniyonu, "Does Abacha Plan to Exit in 1998?" *Theweek,* 15 July 1996, 8.

76. Mark Richard, Deputy Assistant Attorney General, Department of Justice, "Nigerian White Collar Crime," Testimony before the House International Relations Committee on Nigerian White Collar Crime, U.S. Congress, Washington, D.C., 11 Sept. 1996; "Nigeria: The Cocaine Trail," *Africa Confidential,* 22 March 1991.

77. Robert Rotberg, "They Slip out of Nigeria and Drug the World," *Christian Science Monitor,* 24 Sept. 1996.

78. Olukoya, "Where the Cash Is"; Agbo, "Rumbles of Politics"; Observatoire Géopolitique des Drogues, *The Geopolitics of Drugs* (Boston: Northeastern University Press, 1996), 14.

79. Bayo Ohu, "Bamaiyi Vows to Prevent Drug Barons from Politics," *Guardian* (Lagos), 11 July 1996.

80. Emmanuel Ado, "Judgement Day for the Rich," *Theweek,* 7 June 1996.

81. "States Have Firms to Collect Revenues," *Guardian* (Lagos), 9 July 1996.

82. Larry Diamond, "Preventative Diplomacy for Nigeria," Testimony before the House International Relations Committee, Sub-Committee on Africa, U.S. Congress, Washington, D.C., 12 Dec. 1995.

83. Sam Olukoya, "Why They Seethe," *Newswatch,* 18 Dec. 1995, 11.

84. Discussion with Professor Claude Ake, Helsinki, 9 Oct. 1996.

85. Human Rights Watch—Africa, *Nigeria: Permanent Transition* (New York: Human Rights Watch, 27 Sept. 1996); Soyinka, *Open Sore,* 145–153. Civil Liberties Organisation, *Ogoni: Trials and Travails* (Lagos: Civil Liberties Organisation, 1996).

86. Peter Ishaka, "Brothers at War," *African Concord,* 11 April 1994, 19.

87. Ibid., 20.

88. Human Rights Watch, *Permanent Transition,* 41.

89. Udenna Biriye, "Gang Warfare Terrorizes Area," *Guardian* (Lagos), 28 July 1996.

90. Human Rights Watch, *Permanent Transition,* 50.

91. Paul Lewis, "Nigeria's Deadly Oil War," *New York Times,* 13 Feb. 1996; ibid., 50–51.

92. Forrest, *Politics and Economic Development,* 134.

93. Lucy Komisar, "The People Who Peddle Nigeria," *Nation,* 25 Dec. 1995, 829.

94. Glenn Frankel, "Nigeria Mixes Oil and Money," *Washington Post,* 24 Nov. 1996.

95. Wale Akin Aina, "Back on the Beat," *Newswatch,* 17 July 1995, 17.

96. Sani Abacha, "Vision 2010" (mimeo, 27 Nov. 1996).

97. "Nigeria at 36: Economics of Political Expediency," *Nigeria Now* 5:7 (Sept.–Oct. 1996), 5.

98. "Abacha Wins," *Economist,* 9 Nov. 1996, 46.

99. "Coleur kaki?" *Lettre du Continent,* 1 Feb. 1996.

100. Joan Nelson, "The Politics of Economic Transition: Is Third World Experience Relevant in Eastern Europe?" *World Politics* 45:3 (April 1993), 459.

7

▼ ▼ ▼ ▼ ▼

WARLORDS IN THE GLOBAL SYSTEM OF STATES

Dear W. Gladstone . . . We want our country to be governed by British Government. We are tired of governing this country ourselves, every dispute leads to war, and often to great loss of lives, so we think it is [the] best thing to give up the country to you British men who no doubt will bring peace, civilization, and Christianity in the country.
—*King Bell and King Acqua of the Cameroons River, 6 Nov. 1881*[1]

The weakest states in Africa and elsewhere in the world have received increasing attention in recent years. In his article, "The Coming Anarchy," Robert Kaplan wrote that

Sierra Leone is a microcosm of . . . the withering away of central governments, the rise of tribal and regional domains, the unchecked spread of disease, and the growing pervasiveness of war . . . and an interior that, owing to violence, volatility and disease, is again becoming "blank" and "unexplored."[2]

Kaplan's vision of a Malthusian dystopia predicted omnipresent disorder and violence. He identified a frightening breakdown of government and society, confirming long-held suspicions by some officials in strong states that rulers in weak states face insurmountable problems that are a consequence of their mismanagement of, and incapacity to regulate, their physical and biological environments.[3] Kaplan also wrote that collapse is not confined to Africa; Mexico also shows signs of disintegration as the intensified pressures of modernization and demographic expansion have overwhelmed state rulers.[4] Some analysts have cited those fears to justify the intervention of groups such as Executive Outcomes in Sierra Leone and Angola to restore order.[5] Although such firms may quell violence against civilians, we saw how firms such as Executive Outcomes have played an important part in the transition of

217

weak states to the market-based tactics and nonbureaucratic organization of warlord politics.

Rather than simply showing the failure of conventional states, the
four case studies in this book explain how jettisoning bureaucracies, abjuring pursuit of a broad public interest, and militarizing commerce are
rational responses in a setting in which very weak states have become
unsustainable. Thus, the primary causes of those changes are twofold—
the internal unsustainability of old patronage politics, and new external
limits on support for weak states combined with new commercial opportunities for rulers who are willing and able to innovate. The prior weakness of state institutions has considerable bearing on whether a weak-
state ruler will pursue a warlord strategy. Rulers may rationally fear
rivals who use their hold on state offices to build personal power bases
and threaten rulers' rule. This is especially true in states that have had
scant popular legitimacy from the start, such as many of Africa's postcolonial states, which began their existence as foreign-imposed military
dictatorships barely a century ago and have little or no history of extensive accountability to popular interests.

But history does not absolve warlord politicians. A number of scholars have documented the growth of vigorous independent commercial
classes in Central Africa that could have become the core constituency
of reformist regimes.[6] Much of Sierra Leone's history shows colonial and
postcolonial governments limiting the unwanted political power of Krio
businesspeople, a policy pursued by systematically undermining the independent commercial power of Krio entrepreneurs.[7] Nigeria's still substantial commercial class and numerous broad-based societal groups indicate that a different kind of politics that would receive popular
backing may yet be possible there.

Why do rulers abjure these alternative paths, beyond the risks associated with basing authority on possibly (but not inevitably) unreliable
bureaucracies? It is not the mere absence of "civil society" that makes
the crucial difference. Rather, a partial answer lies in the capacity of organized groups to force rulers to heed their demands. John Harbeson
has averred that "civil society is a hitherto missing key to sustained political reform, legitimate states and government, improved governance, viable state-society and state-economy relationships and prevention of the
kind of political decay that undermined new African governments a gen-
eration ago."[8]

I argue, however, that societal groups were never missing (except
perhaps in scholarly eyes). Rather, warlord politics is in part about those
groups' lack of capacity to make rulers listen. In Congo, for example, vigorous organizing by citizens was insufficient to wean (or force) Mobutu
away from a reliance on essentially private exploitation of resources in

alliance with foreigners to bolster his authority. Kabila shows no signs of change, except to perform in an outwardly more efficient manner.

The problem for Congolese is not necessarily the weakness of their organizations or their demands but that their rulers have been able to dominate the country's abundant natural resources and to call on a wide array of outsiders to help them do so. The economics of resource exploitation has played a pivotal role in insulating rulers from societal demands in Liberia and Sierra Leone as well. The exploitation of oil in Nigeria has given Nigerian rulers an alternative to the arduous and dangerous task of building a nationwide constituency of supporters on the basis of the efficient provision of government services.

The globalization of new economic partners and opportunities appears to be increasing the attractiveness to rulers of a reliance on commercial exploitation as a quick way to solve problems of political authority. In Africa, the transmutation of old security networks into private security firms that team up with small, flexible mining ventures is the most obvious such development. To the extent that IMF and World Bank reform programs stress marketization of weak states' resources, rulers reap an additional bonus for using foreign firms to help them deal with their internal security problems.

These changes are also taking place in relatively stronger states. In Colombia, for example, Defense Systems Limited (DSL) has reportedly taken an active role in training anti-insurgency forces in that country since the company arrived in 1992 to protect British Petroleum and its employees from rebel assaults. Like Executive Outcomes, DSL has roots in Cold War state security services. The firm is staffed primarily with former British Special Air Service troops who now offer their skills to private industrial and state clients in twenty-six countries in which DSL provides military training, intelligence operations, and hostage rescue in addition to guard services.[9]

Outsiders' concerns about instability in troubled countries will likely make the synergy between foreign firm security and the privatization of weak-state regime security more palatable to global society. In Nigeria, for example, domestic critics of the regime, international nongovernmental human rights organizations, and officials in the U.S. State Department's Office of Human Rights may protest the Abacha regime's violent repression of civic organizations. But at the same time, the U.S. ambassador to Nigeria must balance U.S. government concerns that Nigerian troops will continue to constitute the main contingent of ECO-MOG and enforce recent peace agreements in Liberia. U.S. Treasury Department officials are doubtlessly more worried about the impact sanctions or some other disruption of Nigeria's oil imports would have on global oil prices and U.S. inflation. U.S. Drug Enforcement Agency officials may place their highest priority on retaining the NDLEA's cooperation in drug interdiction efforts.

THE CREATION OF NEW POLITICAL COALITIONS

In each case I found that the recent appearance of warlord tactics in the politics of Africa's weakest states owed much to the prior context of those states' relations with outsiders. State-to-state relations among these regimes before the end of the Cold War had already concentrated on propping up weak-state rulers' capacity to act personally as patrons, rather than build the capacity of state bureaucracies to administer. The major impetus for change that forced rulers to innovate and extended opportunity to enterprising strongmen lay in shifts in the relative distribution of resources. In most cases, bureaucratic state collapse was already fairly advanced. In Sierra Leone, President Stevens's privatization of the country's diamond resources as a basis for his exercise of power was largely complete by 1980. Mobutu made great strides in gutting state institutions in Congo when he destroyed commercial agriculture as a consequence of the 1973 "Zairianization" that transferred private enterprises and state assets to regime cronies.

The loss of aid from superpower allies and the end of preferential treatment by multilateral creditors undermined internal patronage networks in the very weakest states. In Nigeria, even limited political and economic reforms worked insofar as they promoted enterprise (even if fraudulent) and raised popular demands for an end to the old patronage politics. At the same time, outsiders' insistence that the ruler further dismantle state institutions reduced the ruler's direct administrative control over patronage. The specter of political competition and market reforms seemed an invitation for further fragmentation of politics as officials pursued their own interests at the expense of the ruler's control over resources. It is as if a great tidal wave swept away key elements of an established political accommodation and social control, bringing in its wake new resources and opportunities strongmen could more easily appropriate than weak-state rulers could immediately control.

I argue that the broad-based external changes, the end of most external patronage, and the rise of new commercial actors and opportunities set into motion the creation of new political coalitions in weak states. I take into account the rational interests of internal actors in serving material interests and maximizing autonomy to act. The appearance of a novel political arrangement, the warlord political authority, is explained by the nature of new political accommodations that develop as they respond to changing conditions. This reflects the fact that some individuals are better placed to capitalize on their improved relative posi-

tions and to change old political arrangements in pursuit of their interests, whereas others discover that the bases of their old privilege have
disappeared.

Even within a warlord context, the outcome of such realignments is
not a foregone conclusion. We saw how Mobutu responded in a way
sufficient to sustain elements of old patrimonial strategies by manipulating the opportune rise of French diplomatic interest in a conflict in
neighboring Rwanda in 1994. This instance also points to the role of ac-
cidents and luck. Mobutu did his best to aggravate local ethnic conflicts,
but he could not have predicted that French officials would respond so
favorably—especially after the official hostility toward him personally
and pronouncements about a general disengagement from African dic-
tators. Ignorance or lack of information also plays a role. Strasser, for
example, appeared unaware of the Executive Outcomes option until
foreign firm officials took the initiative and found outside protection
for their own sites. Different rates of learning and discounting of alternatives also influence outcomes. For example, Bio, Strasser's anti-insurgency military commander, was more aggressive at building ties with
mercenaries once they had arrived in the country, a relationship he used
to his advantage when he removed the president in a coup. Such enterprising behavior places a premium on immediate success and calls for
risky but decisive strategies, especially when the penalty for failure is
death.

In short, warlord politics does not merely reflect the preferences of
the most powerful individuals in weak states. The calculus of information,
risks, threatening rivals, new arrivals, accident, and luck plays out in a
process of political bargaining and conflict. Furthermore, different types
of arrangements in one place exert competitive pressure on neighbors.
For example, the appearance of RUF in Sierra Leone because of its connections to Taylor's NPFL was decisive in forcing first Momoh and then
Strasser to address the fragmentation of the previous ruler's patronage
network. Strongmen in Congo's provinces have struggled to find ways to
fend off interventions by other political cliques. The case of Taylorland,
which survived as a separate political authority up to Taylor's election as
president of the globally recognized Republic of Liberia in July 1997, also
shows that a nonsovereign warlord arrangement has at times been a viable contender, or at least a serious threat, to its weak-state neighbors.

By acknowledging this variation in outcomes, I could more accurately identify the causes of change without merely affirming that state
institutions have collapsed in some places more than others. This preci-
sion allowed me to account for specific variables that favored some
strategies over others.

First, I discovered that from a systemic perspective, political leaders
who combined warlord techniques with global recognition of existing

state sovereignty were better able to attract newcomers such as foreign firms and mercenaries. They did so because of material advantages de jure sovereignty—distinct from control on the ground—could still offer partners, both foreign and domestic. This advantage gave rulers new power to regulate conflict through those alliances despite the sovereign state's loss of strategic importance and access to entitlements from outside patrons. Sovereignty has remained a resource to seal new political bargains, since it gives private actors access to credit, a place in international forums, legitimation of wholesale privatization of state assets, immunity from serious outside scrutiny of internal affairs, access to foreign aid, and the capacity to offer more convincing contracts to foreign firms.

Second, de jure sovereignty proved an efficient means of reincorporating old partners, such as officials from strong states and creditors, in a new political alignment. As with foreign aid during the Cold War, those associations have given rulers of weak states the means with which to address internal security challenges.

Now, however, instead of offering diplomatic or strategic alignment to a superpower patron, rulers are offering promises of stability and their status as rulers of a recognizable sovereign state who can speak for internal matters that are of global interest, such as drug trafficking. Thus, a warlord's ability to lay claim to the mantle of sovereignty matters more to the outside world than his actual conduct of politics, even if that conduct violates the norms of territoriality or internal hegemony that characterize most states. It is thus significant that Charles Taylor had maintained throughout the war in Liberia that his goal was to become the recognized president of the Republic of Liberia and that Congo's ethnic strongmen abjured outright secession. The global society of states accepts warlords-as-state-leaders, as it did rulers of quasi-states during the Cold War. But warlord politics diverges from the continuum of strong to weak states, as it jettisons almost entirely many internal components of conventional states, such as bureaucratic hierarchies, or any autonomous definition of an interest of state that has characterized even very weak states.

Furthermore, recognition of the importance of foreign firms, mercenaries, and other outsiders to weak-state rulers' and warlords' internal strategies points to the significance of success or failure to those rulers' capacity to tailor and contextualize state sovereignty to the needs of their increasingly externalized political accommodations. Thus, whereas Kaplan mistakenly identified the cause of warlord politics as a failure of governments to cope with the tasks global economies and politics thrust on them, it would also be a mistake to identify the survival of recognizable states in Sierra Leone, Nigeria, and Congo as evidence that Weberian ideal notions of bureaucratic states are more workable in the African context. For as we saw in each case, the disruption of patronage networks and the political realignments that occurred made conventional state-building strategies highly dangerous for threatened rulers and rewarding for enterprising strongmen. At the same time, the disruptions placed even more of a premium on controlling the facade of a sovereign state that could be manipulated for the private gain of the new political coalition.

The heightened importance of external members of the political coalition highlights my broader theoretical point that in the study of governance in warlord and weak-state political authorities, distinctions between internal politics and international relations are analytically integral to each other. Whereas scholars have long recognized that external actors influence internal political calculations, the cases show that warlord politics creates new ways in which internal and external politics interact. The expansion of clandestine economies and the perception of a growing global problem of law and order by some in strong states are concerns rulers can translate into partnerships with a growing roster of global actors. This reality has an important impact on conditions faced by officials in other states. One of the central points of this book is that warlord politics should be understood in terms of Africa's reintegration into global markets, largely as a consequence of the reconfiguration and further externalization of the old Cold War patron-client political accommodation. Furthermore, the single-mindedness with which creditors and many officials in strong states have supported market autonomy and deregulation will complicate efforts to regulate African weak-state and warlord entry into global commerce.

WARLORDISM AND COMPETITION IN A GLOBAL ECONOMY

Is the growing intensity of external market pressures on weak-state patron-client politics primarily responsible for the changing character of very weak states? But elements of post–Cold War warlord strategies such as local partnerships with buccaneering foreign investors appeared in the Cold War quasi-state. Sierra Leone's rulers, for example, have a recent history of using Iranian commercial networks for political leverage. In the early 1980s, Sierra Leone's president Stevens used outside pressure to privatize state-controlled commerce and thus give himself and an ethnic Lebanese business partner exclusive control over oil imports into the country. Stevens manipulated official currency regulations to boost the partnership's profitability, and his partner funneled aid to Iranian-backed Lebanese factions in Lebanon's civil war.[10] In 1976 Mobutu signed an agreement with West Germany's Orbital Transport and

Rocket AG, giving the firm nearly unrestricted control of a 150,000-square-kilometer area of Congo.[11]

Neorealists assert that such instances of interdependence take place within the continuing norms and rules of a state system that is not bound or diminished by those relationships. This may be correct insofar as sovereignty becomes a resource for managing the relationships. Nonetheless, the post–Cold War strategic shift and subsequent loss of patronage from outside states did not necessarily weaken the power of local strongmen as much as it did that of rulers. It was then that the political economic variable of foreign firms and clandestine opportunities assumed autonomous importance as causal variables, as rulers (and strongmen) radically quickened their pace of innovation. As Taylor demonstrated, strongmen who could not lay claim to a globally recognized sovereign state could reach accommodations with outsiders who promised access to foreign exchange and wider markets. Similarly, in Somalia General Mohamed Farah Aideed, Siad Barre's former defense minister, worked with the U.S. firm Dole to operate a banana plantation in territory under his control, the sale of which helped to finance the estimated $40,000 weekly expense of maintaining the general's militia.[12]

The shift in strategic relations—the commercialization of patron-client ties—thus promoted a shift in the structure of Africa's state system. A useful question for neorealists in this regard is: Can weak-state rulers who adopt internal warlord strategies but who (mostly) conform to minimal external standards of sovereign state behavior later pursue a more conventional state-building project? The difficulty in such a reversal lies in its lack of external support. Indeed, external factors mitigate against it. How will creditors greet the diversion of debt payments to a state-building project? Will more established firms tolerate greater demands from a revenue-poor regime desperate to invest in social amenities? Where will rulers find the resources needed to simultaneously fend off rivals and buy popular support while financing the construction of a state administration? How will creditors and officials in other states greet those actions, which contradict their advice to trim bureaucracies and minimize government tasks? Meanwhile, buccaneering firms will not disappear and may even offer services to the reformer's rivals. Disorder in neighboring states may keep up the pressure to deal with short-term security rather than long-term development tasks.

The mimicry of warlord politics by weak-state rulers also reflects an effort on the part of the weak-state ruler to join the competitive advantages of partnerships with new foreign commercial partners to the prerogatives of globally recognized sovereignty. In doing so, weak-state rulers can manipulate sovereign status itself to further their material and political aims. Foreign firm partners such as Executive Outcomes and IDAS expand rulers' range of operation, freeing them from the constraints of frontiers in their pursuit of market control, as clandestine operators are either attracted to or banished from market networks as a result of the more competitive firm's presence. Diplomacy can also be privatized, as we saw in the Congo case with Mobutu's use of firms such as Pat Robertson's African Development Company to lobby the U.S. government. Firms also provide greater speed in decisionmaking. When Strasser faced rebel forces at the edges of Freetown in April 1995, calls to Executive Outcomes set a campaign into motion that within two weeks had secured the regime's hold on power and within two months controlled the country's diamond fields.

Most important for weak-state rulers, foreign firm partnerships are flexible, which gives rulers capabilities and access to resources they would otherwise find difficult to obtain. New foreign firm partners in each case in this book permitted rulers to quickly jettison threatening clients and bureaucracies and to rework relations with others on new terms. A primary advantage of the new partnership lies in the lack of rigid functional definitions of commercial operations. In Liberia, for example, UN and creditor proposals to contract out port and airport operations to a foreign firm in mid-1997 could be used for one or more of the following: to collect revenue, deny access to specific individuals, selectively limit criminal behavior, provide contacts to other firms, and abolish a bureaucracy, along with other innovative functions.

The flexibility of action for nonstate global actors, coupled with the warlord strategy of market control, creates economic warfare in which those who can occupy a commercial terrain will win. This is why considerable creative effort and innovation are being used to extend the range, speed, and flexibility of warlord politics. Innovation of this sort creates its own markets, as vulnerable rulers of the weakest states have to cope with both the by-products of those strategies—such as strengthened clandestine commercial networks—and the global partnerships they create.

As the addition of outside commercial-military syndicates to weak-state political accommodations shows, warlord politics is not just a retreat to past communal conflicts or a popular reaction to marginalization. Qualitative changes in commerce, warfare, and governance in weak states have come relatively recently, especially since the fading of Africa's Cold War strategic position by the mid-1980s, although they have built on elements long present. The changes came as the Cold War system of quasi-states started its terminal decay. Meanwhile, a new kind of foreign firm developed out of the dismantling of communism and apartheid in other states. The new political accommodation incorporates the latest technology and new anti-insurgency strategic thinking and is at the forefront of economic ideas that stress deregulation and flexible firm adaptation, bringing all to bear on the political problems of building authority in weak states that lack bureaucratic institutions. When this happens, the old balance of power among a ruler, local societies, and the position of weak states in global society is shattered. This is a rare, profound revolutionary change.

In this regard, warlord politics, as with the breakdown of feudal states in Europe, sweeps away old political forms. In the latter, external conditions permitted the creation of centralized political alliances that benefited political and commercial elites through regulation and promotion of a territorially defined market. Warlord politics, on the other hand, creates new externalized political accommodations as it destroys old internal alliances of elites. The consequent partnerships are well suited to profitable operation in a global economy. The structure of warlord politics described earlier more closely resembles the decentralized subcontracting structure of a successful global firm such as Nike than an inefficient, centrally organized, mammoth firm such as General Motors, which laid off 90,000 workers—a quarter of its workforce in 1992—in hopes of matching its competitors' efficiency.[13]

The external partners of Cold War–era African rulers tended to be other states that were committed to a rigid ideological or diplomatic agenda. Partners also included large firms that were well equipped for the physical demands of investing in difficult places but were constrained in their ability to interfere in internal politics for fear that a highly activist role would expose them to criticism from other host governments. Executive Outcomes and other firms studied here resemble newer, more efficient firms elsewhere that use specialized subcontractors, flexibility in their investment strategy, specialization in niche markets, adaptation to customer needs, service to an increasingly diverse market, and a global reach without extensive bureaucratic encumbrances. This form of commercial organization is especially well suited for doing business in places where top-down concentrated linear firms are ineffective, such as a nonbureaucratic weak-state environment.

As with firms, size has also become less important for nonbureaucratic political units engaged in warlord politics. Large organizations can be pecked to death by private operators, as Babangida discovered with his reforms in Nigeria. Rulers of slimmed-down political networks, unconstrained by popular or bureaucratic opinion, can make decisions quickly and reverse course with relatively little encumbrance.

Ironically, Africa's increased participation in global markets has promoted change that undermines the efficacy of the efforts of strong states to regulate that change. Sovereign state rulers' involvement in clandestine and criminal trade helps to create a problem of law and order on a global scale as long as warlord manipulation of conventional norms of sovereignty continues. Furthermore, the notions of market autonomy and deregulation to which creditors and many strong-state officials are ideologically committed will complicate efforts to regulate African weak-state innovations in a global market.

In fact, from this perspective those who fear the criminalization of the state will likely call for further deregulation and globalization. Executive Outcomes' success as a commercial enterprise and a political partner is in part a result of the absence of action by a hegemonic state or states to impose a standard of internal political behavior as a condition for recognition of sovereignty. Indeed, officials in stronger states appear increasingly willing to tolerate novel internal arrangements so long as they permit weak-state rulers to at least seem to fulfill the external obligations of sovereignty at local expense. For example, the political defeat of former U.S. president Bush's New World Order thus added to the functional autonomy of firms such as Executive Outcomes. Further, the financial strains (and politically remote prospect) of directly aiding conventional state-building enterprises, either directly or through significant debt relief, prompt this alignment of partners.

Warlord politics incorporates a new form of wealth creation that is not restricted to Africa. One can see state organizations managing similar changes in places such as Peru. There, in one of the most effective anti-insurgency campaigns against Shining Path guerrillas, Peruvian brigadier general Alberto Arciniega controlled drug production and trafficking to give peasants an attractive material alternative to rebel trafficking operations. Recognizing that Peru lacked effective bureaucratic means of dealing with the rebel threat, the officer accomplished his goal by directly manipulating what appeared to outsiders who focus on state institutions to be an unregulated private market.[14]

One can argue that the Peruvian official was doing what states should do—define an independent public interest (in this case, security) and mobilize citizens around that project. In the comparable situation in Sierra Leone, the army dissolved into private syndicates (sobels) to gather diamonds in a fashion almost indistinguishable from that of the rebels. Once the old Cold War quasi-state system of political and economic patronage of very weak states was disrupted in Africa, the almost total lack of existing autonomous state organizations made it more attractive for rulers to absorb those modes of accumulation into what are now essentially private syndicates. Truly, something new is always coming out of Africa.

NOTES

1. Cited in Michael Doyle, *Empires* (Ithaca: Cornell University Press, 1986), 162.

2. Robert Kaplan, "The Coming Anarchy," *Atlantic Monthly* 273:2 (Feb. 1994), 48.

3. Robert Chase, Emily Hill, and Paul Kennedy, "Pivotal States and U.S. Strategy," *Foreign Affairs* 75:1 (Jan.–Feb. 1996), 33–51.

4. Robert Kaplan, "History Moves North," *Atlantic Monthly* (Feb. 1997), 14–18.

5. Elizabeth Rubin, "An Army of One's Own," *Harper's Magazine* 294:1761 (Feb. 1997), 44–55; Kareem Pech and Yusuf Hassan, "Sierra Leone's Faustian Bargain," *Mail and Guardian,* 30 May 1997.

6. Janet MacGaffey, ed., *The Real Economy of Zaire* (Philadelphia: University of Pennsylvania Press, 1991); Tom de Herdt and Stefaan Marysee, *L'économie informelle au Zaire* (Paris: Harmattan, 1996).

7. Akintola Wyse, *The Krio of Sierra Leone* (Freetown: Okrafo-Smart, 1989).

8. John Harbeson, "Civil Society and Political Renaissance in Africa," in John Harbeson, Donald Rothchild, and Naomi Chazan, eds., *Civil Society and the State in Africa* (Boulder: Lynne Rienner, 1994), 1–2.

9. Michael Sean Gillard and Melissa Jones, "BP's Secret Soldiers," *Mail and Guardian,* 4 July 1997.

10. Stephen Ellis, "Les prolongements du conflit israélo-arabe en Afrique noire: le cas du Sierra Leone," *Politique Africaine* 30 (June 1988), 69–75.

11. Christopher Clapham, *Africa and the International System* (New York: Cambridge University Press, 1996), 252.

12. "Investment Crucial to Somalia's Revitalization," *Soomaaliya Maanta,* 17 Nov. 1994; Moyiga Nduru, "No End in Sight for Banana War," *Mail and Guardian,* 3 May 1996.

13. On Nike, see Michael Donagu and Richard Barff, "Nike Just Did It: International Subcontracting and Flexibility in Athletic Footwear Production," *Regional Studies* 24:6 (Dec. 1990), 537–552; on General Motors, see William Tabb, *The Postwar Japanese System* (New York: Oxford University Press, 1995), 119.

14. José Gonzales, "Guerrillas and Coca in the Upper Huallaga Valley," in David Scott Palmer, ed., *Shining Path of Peru* (New York: St. Martin's Press, 1994), 123–143.

▼ ▼ ▼ ▼ ▼ ▼ ▼ ▼ ▼ ▼ ▼ ▼ ▼ ▼

ACRONYMS

ADB	African Development Bank
ADC	African Development Company
ADF	Alliance of Democratic Forces
ADK	Association des Diamantaires du Kwango
AFDL	Alliance des Forces Démocratiques pour la Libération
AFL	Armed Forces of Liberia
AMCL	African Mining Consortium Limited
AMF	American Mineral Fields
APC	All People's Congress
APROFIM	Agence Promotion et Financement Immobiliers
BCCI	Bank of Credit and Commerce International
CRC	Central Revolutionary Committee
CIA	Central Intelligence Agency
CODEKOR	Conference for the Development of Kasai Oriental
COMIEX	Compagnie Mixte d'Import-Export
CSO	Central Selling Organisation
DSL	Defense Systems Limited
DSP	Division Spéciale Présidentielle
ECOMOG	ECOWAS Monitoring Group
ECOWAS	Economic Community of West African States
ENPLA	Equatorial People's Liberation Army
EO	Executive Outcomes
FDA	Forestry Development Authority
FLEC	Frente de Liberação do Enclave do Cabinda
GNP	gross national product
GSA	General Services Administration
GSG	Gurkha Security Guards
HCR	Haut consiel de la Republique
IDAS	International Defense and Security
IDCC	Industrial Development Coordination Committee
IGNU	Interim Government of National Unity
IMF	International Monetary Fund

INPFL	Independent National Patriotic Front of Liberia
LAFTRACO	Lebanese African Finance and Trading Company
LAMCO	Liberian American Mining Company
LIAT	Hebrew acronym for LIAT Finance and Construction
LIMCO	Liberian Iron Mining Company
LPC	Liberian Peace Council
LPMC	Liberian Produce Marketing Corporation
LPRC	Liberian Petroleum Refining Corporation
LRA	Lord's Resistance Army
MIBA	Miniére de Bakangwa
MOSOP	Movement for the Salvation of Ogoni People
MPRI	Military Professional Resources, Inc.
NADECO	National Democratic Coalition
NDLEA	Nigerian Drug Law Enforcement Agency
NGO	nongovernment organization
NICON	National Insurance Company of Nigeria
NIMCO	Nimba County Iron Ore Mining Company
NNPC	Nigerian National Petroleum Corporation
NPFL	National Patriotic Front of Liberia
NPFL-CRC	NPFL–Central Revolutionary Committee
OIC	Organisation of the Islamic Conference
OKIMO	state-run diamond mining firm (Congo)
OMPADEC	Oil Mineral Producing Areas Development Commission
OPEX	Operating Experts
PERDIC	Public Enterprise Reform and Divestiture Committee
PLO	Palestine Liberation Organization
PRP	Parti de la Revolution Populaire
RENAMO	Mozambique National Resistance Movement
RPF	Revolutionary Patriotic Front
RUF	Revolutionary Unity Front
SCIPA	Hebrew acronym for SCIPA Finance, Inc.
SFEM	Second Tier Foreign Exchange Market
SIEROMCO	Sierra Leone Ore and Metal Company
SPLA	Sudan People's Liberation Army
SSI	Specialist Services International
SSS	State Security Service
SWIPCO	Swiss Procurement Company
TCPC	Technical Committee for Privatisation and Commercialisation
UDPS	Union pour la démocratie et le progrès social
UFERI	Union des Federalistes et Republicains Independants

ULIMO	United Liberation Movement of Liberia for Democracy
ULIMO-J	ULIMO-Johnson
ULIMO-K	ULIMO-Kromah
UNITA	Uniõ Nacional para a Independencia Total do Angola
WAIC	War Against Indiscipline and Corruption
WNBF	West Nile Bank Front

▼ ▼ ▼ ▼ ▼ ▼ ▼ ▼ ▼ ▼ ▼ ▼ ▼

BIBLIOGRAPHY

An alphabetical listing of the newspapers and news journals referenced in the notes appears at the end of this bibliography.

Abacha, Sani. 1996. "Vision 2010." 27 Nov., photocopy.

Adedeji, Adebayo. 1996. *South Africa and Africa: Within or Apart?* Atlantic Highlands, N.J.: Zed.

Africa Watch. 1990. *Liberia: Flight from Terror. Testimony of Abuse in Nimba County.* New York: Africa Watch.

African Rights. 1995. "Humanitarianism Unbound? Current Dilemmas Facing Multi-Mandate Relief Operations in Political Emergencies." London: African Rights discussion paper.

Ake, Claude. 1995. "The New World Order: A View from Africa." In Hans Henrick-Holm and Gregory Srensen, eds. *Whose World Order? Uneven Globalization and the End of the Cold War.* Boulder: Westview, 19–42.

Alliance des Forces Democratiques pour la Libération. No date. "Le Commissariat general a l'Economie et aux Finances aux Compagnies 'amies.'" Photocopy.

Arlacchi, Pino. 1986. *Mafia et Compagnies: L'éthique mafieusse et l'esprit du capitalisme.* Grenoble: Presses Universitaires de Grenoble.

Armstrong, Robert. 1996. *Ghana Country Assistance Review.* Washington, D.C.: World Bank.

Aron, Raymond. 1973. *Peace and War: A Theory of International Relations.* New York: Anchor Press.

Atkinson, Philippa. 1997. *The War Economy in Liberia: A Political Analysis.* Relief and Rehabilitation Network Paper No. 22. London: Overseas Development Institute.

Austin, Kathi. 1994. *Invisible Crimes: U.S. Private Intervention in the War in Mozambique.* Washington, D.C.: Africa Policy Information Center.

Ayoade, John. 1988. "States without Citizens." In Donald Rothchild and Naomi Chazan, eds. *The Precarious Balance: State and Society in Africa.* Boulder: Westview, 100–118.

Ayoob, Mohammed. 1995. *The Third World Security Predicament: State-Making, Regional Conflict, and the International System.* Boulder: Lynne Rienner.

Bank of Sierra Leone. (various issues). *BSL Bulletin.* Freetown: BSL Printer and Rogers TPI.

———. (various issues). *Economic Review.* Freetown: Bank of Sierra Leone.

———. (various issues). *Economic Trends.* Freetown: Bank of Sierra Leone.

———. (various issues). *Statistical Report.* Freetown: Government Printer.

Banque du Zaire. (various issues). *Bulletin Trimestriel.* Kinshasa: Banque du Zaire.

———. (various issues). *Rapport Annuel.* Kinshasa: Banque du Zaire.

Barrett, Lindsay. 1985. *Agbada to Khaki: Reporting a Change of Government in Nigeria.* Enugu: Fourth Dimension.

Barrett-Brown, Michael, and Pauline Tiffen. 1992. *Short-Changed: Africa and World Trade.* Boulder: Pluto Press.

Bates, Robert. 1981. *Markets and States in Tropical Africa.* Berkeley: University of California Press.

Bayart, Jean-François. 1989. *L'État en Afrique.* Paris: Fayard.

———. 1990. "France-Afrique: La fin du pacte colonial." *Politique Africaine* 39, 47–53.

———. 1993. "Une criminalisation de l'economie?" In Fariba Adelkhah, Jean-François Bayart, and Olivier Roy, eds. *Thermidor en Iran.* Paris: Éditions Complexe, 40–41.

———, ed. 1994. *La réinvention du capitalisme.* Paris: Fayard.

Beatty, John. 1993. *The Outlaw Bank: A Wild Ride into the Secret Heart of BCCI.* New York: Random House.

Beinart, Peter. 1994. "Out of Africa." *New Republic* 26 (Dec.), 16–18.

Berkeley, Bill. 1986. *Liberia: A Promise Betrayed.* New York: Lawyers Committee for Human Rights.

———. 1992. "Liberia's Warring Currencies." *Institutional Investor* (Sept.), 224–225.

Berry, Sara. 1989. "Social Institutions and Access to Resources." *Africa* 59:1, 40–55.

Bienen, Henry, and Jeffrey Herbst. 1996. "The Relationship Between Political and Economic Reform in Africa." *Comparative Politics.* 29:1 (Oct.), 23–42.

Biggart, Nicole. 1989. *Charismatic Capitalism: Direct Selling Organizations in America.* Chicago: University of Chicago Press.

Blumenthal, Erwin. 1982. "Zaire: rapport sur sa credibilité financière internationale." *La Revue Nouvelle* 77:11 (Nov.), 360–378.

Bond, Patrick. 1996. "Neoliberalism Comes to South Africa." *Multinational Monitor* 17:5 (May), 8–14.

Boyne, Jean. 1997. "The White Legion: Mercenaries in Zaire." *Jane's Intelligence Review* 9:6 (June), 278–281.

Braeckman, Colette. 1992. *Le dinosaure: Le Zaire de Mobutu.* Paris: Fayard.

———. 1995. "Le Zaire de Mobutu, 'parrin' des Grands Lacs." André Guichaoua, ed. *Les crises politiques au Burundi et au Rwanda (1993–1994).* Paris: Karthala, 387–394.

———. 1997. "Zaire at the End of a Reign." *New Left Review.* 222 (June), 129–138.

Braudel, Fernand. 1980. *On History.* Translated by Sarah Matthews. Chicago: University of Chicago Press.

Bull, Hedley. 1977. *The Anarchical Society: A Study of Order in World Politics.* New York: Columbia University Press.

———, ed. 1984. *The Expansion of International Society.* New York: Oxford University Press.

Callaghy, Thomas. 1984. "Africa's Debt Crisis." *Journal of International Affairs* 38:1 (Summer), 61–79.

———. 1984. *The State-Society Struggle: Zaire in Comparative Perspective.* New York: Columbia University Press.

———. 1993. "Political Passions and Economic Interests: Economic Reform and Political Structure in Africa." In Thomas Callaghy and John Ravenhill, eds. *Hemmed In: Responses to Africa's Economic Decline.* New York: Columbia University Press, 463–519.

Callaghy, Thomas, and John Ravenhill. 1993. "How Hemmed In?" In Thomas Callaghy and John Ravenhill, eds. *Hemmed In: Responses to Africa's Economic Decline.* New York: Columbia University Press, 520–563.

Campbell, Bonnie. 1996. "Débats actuels sur la reconceptualisation de l'État par les organismes de financement multilatéraux et l'USAID." *Politique Africaine* 61 (March), 18–28.

Carim, Xavier. 1995. "Illegal Migration to South Africa." *Africa Insight* 25:4, 221–223.

Central Bank of Nigeria. 1993. *Economic and Financial Review.* Lagos: Central Bank of Nigeria.

Chabi, Maurice. 1994. *Banqueroute: Mode d'emploi.* Porto Novo: Éditions Gazette Livres.

Charlton, Roger, and Roy May. 1989. "Warlords and Militarism in Chad." *Review of African Political Economy* 45–46 (Winter), 12–25.

Chase, Robert, Emily Hill, and Paul Kennedy. 1996. "Pivotal States and U.S. Strategy." *Foreign Affairs* 75:1 (Jan.–Feb.), 33–51.

Chazan, Naomi. 1983. *An Anatomy of Ghanaian Politics: Managing Political Recession, 1969–1982.* Boulder: Westview.

Civil Liberties Organisation. 1996. *Ogoni: Trials and Travails.* Lagos: Civil Liberties Organisation.

Clapham, Christopher. 1989. "Liberia." In Donal B. Cruise O'Brien, John Dunn, and Richard Rathbone, eds. *Contemporary West African States.* New York: Cambridge University Press, 99–111.

———. 1996. *Africa and the International System.* New York: Cambridge University Press.

Clower, Robert W. 1966. *Growth without Development.* Evanston, Ill: Northwestern University Press.

Collins, Carole. 1996. "Zaire Remains Africa's Heart of Darkness." *National Catholic Reporter* 32:15 (Feb.), 9–14.

Contamin, Bernard, and Yves-A Fauré. 1990. *La Bataille des enterprises publiques en Côte d'Ivoire: L'histoire d'un ajustement.* Paris: Karthala.

Coquery-Vidrovitch, Catherine. 1972. *Le Congo au temps des grandes compagnies concessionaires.* Paris: Mouton.

Crawford, James. 1978. "The Criteria for Statehood in International Law." *The British Yearbook of International Law, 1976–1977,* Vol. 48. Oxford: Oxford University Press. 111–159.

Crocker, Chester. 1985. "Recent Developments in Liberia." Testimony before the Subcommittee on Africa, Senate Foreign Relations Committee, U.S. Senate. Washington, D.C., 10 Dec.

Cruise O'Brien, Donal, John Dunn, and Richard Rathbone, eds. 1989. *Contemporary West African States.* 2d ed. New York: Cambridge University Press.

David, Steven. 1991. "Explaining Third World Alignment." *World Politics* 43:2 (Jan.), 233–256.

Davidson, Basil. 1992. *The Black Man's Burden.* New York: Times Books.

De Boeck, Filip. 1996. "Postcolonialism, Power and Identity: Local and Global Perspectives from Zaire." In Richard Werbner and Terence Ranger, eds. *Postcolonial Identities in Africa.* Atlantic Highlands, N.J.: Zed Books, 75–106.

De Herdt, Tom, and Stefaan Marysee. 1996. *L'économie informelle au Zaire.* Paris: Harmattan.

De Montclos, Michel. 1996. "Liberia: des predateurs aux ramasseurs de miettes." In François Jean and Jean-Christophe Rufin, eds. *Economie des guerres civiles.* Paris: Hachette, 137–159.

Department of State. 1997. *Sierra Leone Country Report on Human Rights Practices for 1996*. Washington, D.C: Department of State.

D.E.R. 1995. *Customer Protection in the Nigerian Banking System*. Lagos: D.E.R.

De Waal, Alex. 1996. "Contemporary Warfare in Africa." *IDS Bulletin* 27:3 (July), 6–16.

Dia, Mamadou. 1994. "Indigenous Management Practices: Lessons for Africa's Management in the '90s." In Ismail Serageldin and June Taboroff, eds. *Culture and Development in Africa*. Washington, D.C.: World Bank, 165–180.

———. 1996. *Africa's Management in the 1990s and Beyond*. Washington, D.C.: World Bank.

Diamond, Larry. 1995. "Preventative Diplomacy for Nigeria." Testimony before the Subcommittee on Africa, House International Relations Committee, U.S. Congress. Washington, D.C., 12 Dec.

Donagu, Michael, and Richard Barff. 1990. "Nike Just Did It: International Subcontracting and Flexibility in Athletic Footwear Production." *Regional Studies* 24:6 (Dec.), 537–552.

Doyle, Michael. 1986. *Empires*. Ithaca: Cornell University Press.

Dungia, Emmanuel. 1992. *Mobutu et l'argent du Zaire*. Paris: Harmattan.

Dunn, D. Elwood, and S. Byron Tarr. 1988. *Liberia: A National Polity in Transition*. Metuchen, N.J.: Scarecrow Press.

Dzaka, Théophile, and Michel Milandou. 1994. "L'entrepreneuriat congolais à l'épreuve des pouvoir magiques." *Politique Africaine* 56 (Dec), 108–118.

Ebhodaghe, Joseph. No date. *How the Fraudsters Do It*. Abuja: Nigerian Deposit Insurance Corporation.

Economic Community of West African States. 1996. *ECOWAS Financial Directory*. 2d ed. Lagos: D.E.R.

Economist Intelligence Unit. 1995. *F and T Risk Advisor*. London: Economist Intelligence Unit.

———. 1996. *South Africa: Country Profile, 1995*. London: Economist Intelligence Unit.

Economist Intelligence Unit Country Report (various issues). *Ghana, Sierra Leone, Liberia* (to 1992), *Guinea, Sierra Leone, Liberia* (from 1993). London: Economist Intelligence Unit.

——— (various issues). 1988–1996. *Nigeria*. London: Economist Intelligence Unit.

——— (various issues). *Zaire, Rwanda, Burundi* (to 1992), *Zambia, Zaire* (from 1993). London: Economist Intelligence Unit.

Ellis, Stephen. 1988. "Les prolongements du conflit israélo-arabe en Afrique noire: le cas du Sierra Leone. *Politique Africaine* 30 (June), 69–75.

———. 1995. "Liberia 1989–1994: A Study of Ethnic and Spiritual Violence." *African Affairs* 94:375 (April), 165–97.

Ellis, Stephen, and Janet MacGaffey. 1997. "Le commerce international informel en Afrique sub-saharienne." *Cahiers d'Études Africaines* 37:1, 11–37.

Emizet, Kisangani. 1996. "Zaire After Mobutu: A Potential Case of Humanitarian Emergency." Paper for the World Institute for Development Economics Research Seminar. Helsinki, 6–8 Oct.

Epstein, Joshua, and Robert Axtell. 1996. *Growing Artificial Societies: Social Science from the Bottom Up*. Cambridge: MIT Press.

Evans, Peter, Dietrich Rueschemeyer, and Theda Skocpol, eds. 1985. *Bringing the State Back In*. New York: Cambridge University Press.

Faruqee, Rashid. 1994. "Nigeria: Ownership Abandoned." In Ishrat Husain and Rashid Faruqee, eds. *Adjustment in Africa: Lessons from Country Case Studies*. Washington, D.C.: World Bank, 238–285.

Federal Office of Statistics. 1994. *Review of the Nigerian Economy.* Lagos: Federal Office of Statistics.

Fleischman, Janet. 1993. "An Uncivil War." *Africa Report* (May–June), 56–59.

———. 1995. "U.S. Policy on Liberia." Testimony before the Subcommittee on Africa, Foreign Relations Committee, U.S. Congress. Washington, D.C., 21 Sept.

Foccart, Jacques. 1995. *Foccart parle: entretiens avec Philippe Gaillard.* Paris: Fayard.

Foltz, William. 1995. "Reconstructing the State in Chad." In I. William Zartman, ed. *Collapsed States: The Disintegration and Restoration of Legitimate Authority.* Boulder: Lynne Rienner, 15–32.

Forrest, Thomas. 1994. *The Advance of African Capital: The Growth of Nigerian Private Enterprise.* Edinburgh: Edinburgh University Press.

———. 1995. *Politics and Economic Development in Nigeria.* Boulder: Westview.

Fyle, C. Magbaily. 1994. "The Military and Civil Society in Sierra Leone: The 1992 Coup d'état." *Africa Development* 18:2, 17–30.

Fyle, C. Magbaily, ed. 1993. *The State and Provision of Social Services in Sierra Leone Since Independence, 1961–91.* Dakar: Codesira.

Gagnon, V. P., Jr. 1994–1995. "Ethnic Nationalism and International Conflict: The Case of Serbia." *International Security* 19:3 (Winter), 130–166.

Gelb, Stephen. 1997. "South Africa's Post-Apartheid Political Economy." In Larry Swatuck and David Black, eds. *Bridging the Rift: The New South Africa in Africa.* Boulder: Westview, 41–69.

Gershoni, Yekutiel. 1989. "Liberia and Israel." *Liberian Studies Journal* 14:1, 34–50.

Geschiere, Peter. 1992. "Kinship, Witchcraft and 'the Market': Hybrid Patterns in Cameroonian Society." In Roy Dilley, ed. *Contesting Markets: Analyses of Ideology, Discourse and Practice.* Edinburgh: Edinburgh University Press, 82–97.

Giddens, Anthony. 1981. *A Contemporary Critique of Historical Materialism: Power, Property and the State.* Berkeley: University of California Press.

———. 1985. *The Nation-State and Violence.* Berkeley: University of California Press.

Global Witness. 1996. *Thai-Khmer Rouge Links and the Illegal Trade in Cambodia's Timber.* London: Global Witness.

Gonzales, José. 1994. "Guerrillas and Coca in the Upper Huallaga Valley." In David Scott Palmer, ed. *Shining Path of Peru.* New York: St. Martin's Press, 123–143.

Goody, Jack. 1971. *Technology, Tradition and the State in Africa.* London: Hutchinson.

Gould, David. 1980. *Bureaucratic Corruption and Underdevelopment in the Third World: The Case of Zaire.* New York: Pergamon.

Gould, Stephen Jay. 1980. *The Panda's Thumb: More Reflections on Natural History.* New York: W. W. Norton.

Government of Liberia. 1974. *National Housing and Population Census.* Monrovia: Ministry of Planning and Economic Affairs.

———, Land Reform Commission. 1981. *Guidelines for Drafting of Land Tenure Decree.* Monrovia: Government Printer.

———, Ministry of Commerce and Industry. 1989. *Liberian Trade Directory, 1989–1990.* Monrovia: Unity Printing Press.

Government of South Africa. 1995. *Commission of Inquiry into Alleged Arms Transactions Between One Eli Wazan and Other Related Matters* (Cameron Commission). Pretoria: Government of South Africa.

———. 1996. *Commission of Inquiry into the Alleged Trade in Ivory and Rhinoceros Horn in South Africa* (Kumleben Commission). Pretoria: Government of South Africa.

———. 1996. *Interim Truth Commission Report.* Pretoria: Government of South Africa.

Griffiths, Sir Percival. 1974. *A License to Trade: The Histories of English Chartered Companies.* London: Ernest Benn.

Grindle, Merilee. 1996. *Challenging the State: Crisis and Innovation in Latin America and Africa.* New York: Cambridge University Press.

Guilbert, F. 1993. "Les dangers de l'homo-economicus Khmer Rouge." *Défense Nationale* 50, 133–150.

Handelman, Stephen. 1995. *Comrade Criminal: Russia's New Mafiya.* New Haven: Yale University Press.

Harbeson, John. 1994. "Civil Society and Political Renaissance in Africa." In John Harbeson, Donald Rothchild, and Naomi Chazan, eds. *Civil Society and the State in Africa.* Boulder: Lynne Rienner, 1–29.

Hardin, Blaine. 1990. *Africa: Dispatches from a Fragile Continent.* New York: Norton.

Harding, Jeremy. 1997. "The Mercenary Business: 'Executive Outcomes.'" *Review of African Political Economy* 24:71 (March), 87–97.

Harvey, Charles. 1996. "Constraints on Sustained Recovery from Economic Disaster in Africa." In Charles Harvey, ed. *Constraints on the Success of Structural Adjustment Programmes in Africa.* London: Macmillan, 130–151.

Hawkins, Tony. 1994. *The New South Africa: Business Prospects and Corporate Strategies.* London: Economist Intelligence Unit.

Hayward, Fred. 1989. "State Consolidation, Fragmentation and Decay." In Donal Cruise O'Brien, John Dunn, and Richard Rathbone, eds. *West African States.* 2d ed. New York: Cambridge University Press, 165–180.

Hayward, Fred, and Jimmy Kandeh. 1987. "Perspectives on Twenty-Five Years of Elections in Sierra Leone." In Fred Hayward, ed. *Elections in Independent Africa.* Boulder: Westview, 25–59.

Henrick-Holm, Hans, and Gregory Srensen, eds. 1995. *Whose World Order? Uneven Globalization and the End of the Cold War.* Boulder: Westview.

Herbst, Jeffrey. 1990. "War and the State in Africa." *International Security* 14:4 (Spring), 117–139.

———. 1993. *The Politics of Reform in Ghana, 1982–1991.* Berkeley: University of California Press.

Holsti, Kalevi. 1996. *The State, War, and the State of War.* New York: Cambridge University Press.

Hooper, Jim. 1996. "Sierra Leone—the War Continues." *Jane's Intelligence Review* 8:1 (Jan.), 41–45.

———. 1997. "Peace in Sierra Leone: A Temporary Outcome?" *Jane's Intelligence Review* 9:1 (Jan.), 91–93.

Howe, Herb. 1996. "South Africa's 9-1-1 Force." *Armed Forces Journal* 134:3 (Nov.), 38–39.

Human Rights Watch—Africa. 1994. *Liberia: Human Rights Abuses by the Liberian Peace Council and the Need for International Oversight.* New York: Human Rights Watch.

———. 1996. *Nigeria: Permanent Transition.* New York: Human Rights Watch.

———. 1996. *Zaire: Forced to Flee: Violence Against the Tutsis in Zaire.* New York: Human Rights Watch.

————. 1997. *Zaire: Attacked by All Sides: Civilians and the War in Eastern Zaire.* New York: Human Rights Watch.

Human Rights Watch—Arms Project. 1995. *Rwanda/Zaire: Rearming with Impunity.* Washington, D.C.: Human Rights Watch.

————. 1996. *Angola, Between War and Peace: Arms Trade and Human Rights Abuses Since the Lusaka Protocol.* New York: Human Rights Watch Arms Project.

Hunter, Tom. 1997. "Russia's Mafiyas: The New Revolution." *Jane's Intelligence Review* 9:6 (June), 247–254.

Huntington, Samuel. 1968. *Political Order in Changing Societies.* New Haven: Yale University Press.

Hyden, Goran. 1983. *No Shortcuts to Progress.* Berkeley: University of California Press.

————. 1992. "Governance and the Study of Politics." In Goran Hyden and Michael Bratton, eds. *Governance and Politics in Africa.* Boulder: Lynne Rienner, 1–26.

Hyden, Goran, and Michael Bratton, eds. 1992. *Governance and Politics in Africa.* Boulder: Lynne Rienner.

Hyland, Paul. 1990. *The Black Heart: A Voyage into Central Africa.* New York: Paragon House.

Ikoku, Samuel. 1995. *Fourth Coup d'État: Options for Modern Statehood.* Lagos: Ofada Printers.

Ilori, Segun, ed. 1995. *Nigeria: Who's Who in Business.* Lagos: Mednet.

Imo State Government. 1994. *Government White Paper: Enquiry into the Disturbances at Oguta.* Owerri: Imo State Government.

Imobighe, Thomas, ed. 1992. *The Politics of the Second Republic.* Kuru: National Institute for Policy and Strategic Studies.

Independent National Patriotic Front of Liberia. 1990. "INPFL Forever." Monrovia. Video.

Inegbedion, E. John. 1994. "ECOMOG in Comparative Perspective." In Timothy Shaw and Julius Emeka Okolo, eds. *The Political Economy of Foreign Policy in ECOWAS.* London: Macmillan, 218–244.

Ingram, Gregory, and Christine Kessides. 1994. "Infrastructure for Development." *Finance and Development* 31:3 (Sept.), 18–21.

International Monetary Fund. 1988. "1988 Article XIV Consultations." Sierra Leone. Mimeo.

————. 1990. *International Financial Statistics Yearbook.* Washington, D.C.: International Monetary Fund.

————. 1990. EBS/89/233, "Sierra Leone: Staff Report for the 1989 Article IV Consultation." Mimeo.

————. 1996. *International Financial Statistics.* Washington, D.C.: International Monetary Fund.

Isilonyonyi, Anzuluni Bembe. 1996. "Le Haut Consiel de la Republique Parlement de Transition, Resolution sur la Nationalité." Kinshasa. Mimeo.

Ihonvbere, Julius. 1996. "Are Things Falling Apart? The Military and the Crisis of Democratization in Nigeria." *Journal of Modern African Studies* 34:2 (June), 193–225.

Ihonvbere, Julius, and Olufemi Vaughan. 1995. "Nigeria: Democracy and Civil Society." In John Wiseman, ed. *Democracy and Political Change in Sub-Saharan Africa.* New York: Routledge, 71–91.

Jackson, Robert. 1990. *Quasi-States: Sovereignty, International Relations, and the Third World.* New York: Cambridge University Press.

James, Alan. 1986. *Sovereign Statehood: The Basis of International Society.* London: Allen and Unwin.

Jewsiewicki, Bogumil. 1992. "Jeux d'argent et de pouvoir au aire: la 'bindomonie' et le crépuscule de la Deuxieme Republique." *Politique Africaine* 46 (June), 55–70.

Joseph, Richard. 1991. *Democracy and Prebendal Politics in Nigeria.* Lagos: Spectrum.

Kabwegyere, Tarsis. 1996. *The Politics of State Formation and Destruction in Uganda.* Kampala: Fountain.

Kaké, I. Baba. 1987. *Sékou Touré: Le héros et le tryan.* Paris: Jeune Afrique.

Kamara, A. K. 1996. *Sierra Leone: The Agony of Independence.* Freetown: Tarus Communications.

Kandeh, Jimmy. 1996. "What Does the 'Militariat' Do When It Rules? Military Regimes in The Gambia, Sierra Leone and Liberia." *Review of African Political Economy.* 69, 387–404.

Kaplan, Robert. 1994. "The Coming Anarchy." *Atlantic Monthly* 273:2 (Feb.), 44–76.

———. 1996. *The Ends of the Earth.* New York: Random House.

———. 1997. "History Moves North." *Atlantic Monthly* 279:2 (Feb.), 14–18.

Karimu, John. 1995. *Government Budget and Economic and Financial Policies for the Fiscal Year, 1995/96.* Freetown: Government Printer.

Karny, Yo'av. 1987. "Byzantine Bedfellows: What Israel Does for Itself—and for Us." *New Republic* 196 (2 Feb.), 23–28.

Kerry, Senator John. 1992. "Trip to Thailand, Cambodia, and Vietnam." Report to the Committee on Foreign Relations. Washington, D.C.: U.S. Senate, 30 Sept.

Khripunov, Igor. 1995. "Conventional Weapons Transfers." *Comparative Strategy* 14:4, 453–466.

Kieh, George. 1989. "An Analysis of Israeli Re-penetration of Liberia." *Liberian Studies Journal* 14:2, 117–129.

Klein, Axel. 1994. "Trapped in the Traffick: Growing Problems of Drug Consumption in Lagos." *Journal of Modern African Studies* 32:4 (Dec.), 657–677.

Knight-Ridder Financial/Commodity Research Bureau. (various issues). *The CRB Commodity Yearbook.* New York: John Wiley.

Knoll, Arthur J. 1991. "Firestone's Labor Policy, 1924–1939." *Liberian Studies Journal* 16:2, 49–75.

Koehn, Peter. 1989. "Competitive Transition to Civilian Rule: Nigeria's First and Second Experiments." *Journal of Modern African Studies* 27:3 (Sept.), 401–430.

Komisar, Lucy. 1995. "The People Who Peddle Nigeria." *Nation* 25 (Dec.) 829.

Kpundeh, Sahr John. 1994. "Limiting Administrative Corruption in Sierra Leone." *Journal of Modern African Studies* 32:1 (March), 139–157.

———. 1994. *Politics and Corruption in Africa: A Case Study of Sierra Leone.* Lanham, Md.: University Press of America.

Krasner, Stephen. 1984. "Approaches to the State: Alternative Conceptions and Historical Dynamics." *Comparative Politics* 16:2 (Jan.), 223–246.

Kryshtanovskaia, Olga. 1996. "Illegal Structures in Russia." *Russian Social Science Review* 37:6 (Nov.–Dec.), 44–64.

Kynoch, Gary. 1996. "The 'Transformation' of the South African Military." *Journal of Modern African Studies* 34:3 (Sept.), 441–457.

Lamikanra, Adebayo. 1994. *Wake Me Up in the Year 2000.* Lagos: Amka and Allied Services.

Lane, Frederic. 1973. *Venice: A Maritime Republic.* Baltimore: Johns Hopkins University Press.

———. 1979. *Profits from Power: Readings in Protection Rent and Violence Controlling Enterprises.* Albany: State University of New York Press.

Lautier, Bruno, Claude de Miras, and Alain Morice. 1991. *L'État et l'informel.* Paris: Harmattan.

Ledeen, Michael. 1994. "African Scenarios: The Future of Zambia, Zimbabwe and Zaire." Paper presented at Cobalt 94: Opportunities, Problems and Survival Strategies. Vienna, Va., 2–4 Nov.

Lewis, Peter. 1994. "Economic Statism, Private Capital and the Dilemmas of Accumulation in Nigeria." *World Development* 22:3 (March), 437–451.

———. 1994. "End Game in Nigeria?" *African Affairs* 93:372 (July), 323–340.

———. 1996. "From Prebendalism to Predation: The Political Economy of Decline in Nigeria." *Journal of Modern African Studies* 34:1 (March), 79–103.

———. 1997. "Shifting Fortunes: The Political Economy of Financial Liberalization in Nigeria." *World Development* 25:1, 5–22.

Liebenow, J. Gus. 1987. *Liberia: The Quest for Democracy.* Bloomington: Indiana University Press.

Luke, David, and Stephen Riley. 1989. "The Politics of Economic Decline in Sierra Leone." *Journal of Modern African Studies* 27:1 (March), 133–142.

Luling, Virginia. 1997. "Come Back Somalia? Questioning a Collapsed State." *Third World Quarterly.* 18:2 (June), 287–302.

Lyon, Peter. 1993. "The Rise and Fall and Possible Revival of International Trusteeship." *Journal of Commonwealth and Comparative Politics* 31:1 (March), 96–110.

Maasdorp, Gavin. 1996. *Can South and Southern Africa Become Globally Competitive Economies?* Basingstoke: Macmillan.

Maass, Peter. 1996. *Love Thy Neighbor: A Story of War.* New York: Knopf.

MacGaffey, Janet. 1987. *Entrepreneurs and Parasites: The Struggle for Indigenous Capitalism in Zaire.* New York: Cambridge University Press.

———, ed. 1991. *The Real Economy of Zaire.* Philadelphia: University of Pennsylvania Press.

MacKenzie, Sibyl. 1994. "Rent-a-Gurkha." *Soldier of Fortune* 19:3 (March), 30–31.

———. 1995. "Death of a Warrior." *Soldier of Fortune* 20:7 (July), 36–41.

Mamdani, Mahmood. 1996. *Citizen and Subject.* Princeton: Princeton University Press.

Marishane, Jeffrey. 1991. "Prayer, Profit and Power: U.S. Religious Right and Foreign Policy." *Review of African Political Economy* 52, 73–117.

Massaquoi, Siaka. 1992. "Sierra Leone: The April 29 Revolution." Freetown. Mimeo.

Mazrui, Ali. 1995. "The Blood of Experience." *World Policy Journal* 12:1 (Spring), 28–33.

Mbembe, Achille. 1992. "Pouvoir, violence et accumulation." In Jean-François Bayart, Achille Mbembe, and Comi Toulabor, eds. *Le politique par le bas en Afrique noire.* Paris: Karthala, 233–256.

McCoy, Alfred. 1991. *The Politics of Heroin: CIA Complicity in the Global Drug Trade.* New York: Lawrence Hill Books.

Metz, Steven. 1994. *Disaster and Intervention in Sub-Saharan Africa: Learning from Rwanda.* Carlisle Barracks, Pa.: U.S. Army War College.

Michaels, Marguerite. 1993. "Retreat from Africa." *Foreign Affairs* 72:1 (Jan.–Feb.), 93–108.

Migdal, Joel. 1988. *Strong Societies and Weak States.* Princeton: Princeton University Press.

———. 1994. "The State in Society: An Approach to Struggles for Domination." In Joel Migdal, Atul Kohli, and Vivienne Shue, eds. *State Power and Social Forces.* New York: Cambridge University Press, 7–34.

Migdal, Joel, Atul Kohli, and Vivienne Shue, eds. 1994. *State Power and Social Forces.* New York: Cambridge University Press.

Minter, William. 1994. *Apartheid's Contras.* Johannesburg: Witwatersrand University Press.

Misser, François, and Olivier Vallée. 1997. *Les Gemmocraties: l'economie politique du diamant Africain.* Paris: Desclée de Brouwer.

Mommsen, Wolfgang, and Jurgen Osterhammel, eds. 1986. *Imperialism and After: Continuities and Discontinuities.* Boston: Allen and Unwin.

Moore, Barrington. 1966. *Social Origins of Dictatorship and Democracy.* Boston: Beacon Press.

Morice, Alain. 1987. "Guinée 1985: État, corruption et traffics." *Les Temps Modernes* 487 (Feb.), 97–135.

Mortimer, Robert. 1996. "ECOMOG, Liberia, and Regional Security in West Africa." In Edmond Keller and Donald Rothchild, eds. *Africa in the New International Order.* Boulder: Lynne Rienner, 149–164.

Mpandajila, Joseph Ngalulu. 1981. "Lettre ouverte au Citroyen Président Fondateur du Movement Populaire de la Révolution." *Politique Africaine* 3 (Sept.), 94–140.

Mwissa, Kuyu. 1993. "La privatisation de la violence institutionnalisée." In Etienne le Roy and Trutz von Trotha, eds. *La violence et l'état: formes et évolution d'un metropole.* Paris: Harmattan, 165–181.

Naanen, Ben. 1995. "Oil Producing Minorities and the Restructuring of Nigerian Federalism: The Case of the Ogoni People." *Journal of Commonwealth and Comparative Politics* 33:1 (March), 46–78.

National Bank of Liberia. 1989. *Annual Report of Operations.* Monrovia: Government of Liberia.

———. (various issues). *Statistical Bulletin.* Monrovia: National Bank of Liberia.

Naughton, Barry. 1995. *Growing Out of the Plan.* New York: Cambridge University Press.

Nelson, Joan. 1993. "The Politics of Economic Transition: Is Third World Experience Relevant in Eastern Europe?" *World Politics* 45:3 (April), 433–463.

Nigerian Deposit Insurance Corporation. 1991. *Annual Report 1991.* Lagos: Central Bank of Nigeria.

Nigeria Now. 1996. "Nigeria at 36: Economics of Political Expediency." *Nigeria Now* 5:7 (Sept.–Oct.), 4–7.

Nigeria's Major 500 Companies: Fourth Edition 1994/95. 1995. Lagos: Goldstar Media.

Nolutshungu, Sam. 1996. *Limits of Anarchy: Intervention and State Formation in Chad.* Charlottesville: University of Virginia Press.

Nzeribe, Francis. 1990. *Nigeria: Seven Years After Shehu Shagari.* London: Kilimanjaro Publishing.

Observatoire Géopolitique des Drogues. 1996. *The Geopolitics of Drugs.* Boston: Northeastern University Press.

Ogunleye, Bayo. 1995. *Behind Rebel Line: Anatomy of Charles Taylor's Hostage Camps.* Enugu: Delta.

Omara-Otunnu, Amii. 1995. "The Dynamics of Conflict in Uganda." In Oliver Furley, ed. *Conflict in Africa.* London: I. B. Tauris, 223–236.

Oniororo, Niyi. 1993. *Moneycrazy for the Third Republic.* Ibadan: Ororo.

Opala, Joseph. 1994. "Ecstatic Renovation: Street Art Celebrating Sierra Leone's 1992 Revolution." *African Affairs* 93:371, 195–218.

Osso, Nyaknno, ed. 1990. *Who's Who in Nigeria.* Lagos: Newswatch Communications.

Owoeye, Jide. 1994. "What Can Africa Expect from a Post-Apartheid South Africa?" *Africa Insight* 24:1, 44–46.

Owusu, Maxwell. 1996. "Tradition and Transformation: Democracy and the Politics of Popular Power in Ghana." *Journal of Modern African Studies* 34:2 (June), 307–343.

Oyovbaire, S. Egite. 1987. "The Context for Democracy in Nigeria." In S. Egite Oyovbaire, ed. *Democratic Experiment in Nigeria.* Lagos: Academy Press.

Pabanel, Jean-Pierre. 1993. "Conflits locaux et stratégie de tension Nord-Kivu." *Politique Africaine* 52 (Dec.), 132–134.

Panter-Brick, Keith. 1978. *Soldiers and Oil: The Political Transformation of Nigeria.* London: Frank Cass.

Péan, Pierre. 1988. *L'argent noir: corruption et sous-devellopement.* Paris: Fayard.

Pfaff, William. 1995. "A New Colonialism?" *Foreign Affairs* 74:1 (Jan.–Feb.), 2–6.

Price, Robert. 1991. *The Apartheid State in Crisis.* New York: Oxford University Press.

Prunier, Gerard. 1995. *The Rwanda Crisis.* New York: Columbia University Press.

———. 1997. "The Great Lakes Crisis." *Current History* (May), 193–199.

Raghaven, Sudarsan. 1996. "Africa Puts Its Money Where Its Fear Is." *Business Weekly* (15 July), 52–54.

Reeve, Ross, and Stephen Ellis. 1995. "An Insider's Account of the South African Security Forces' Role in the Ivory Trade." *Journal of Contemporary African Studies* 13:2, 213–233.

Reeves, Mollai, and Michel Moulard. 1993. *Postwar Strategy for Forestry Development and Environmental Management in Liberia.* Monrovia: Ministry of Planning and Economic Affairs.

Reno, William. 1993. "Old Brigades, Money Bags, New Breeds and the Ironies of Reform in Nigeria." *Canadian Journal of African Studies* 27:1 (April), 66–87.

———. 1995. *Corruption and State Politics in Sierra Leone.* New York: Cambridge University Press.

Richard, Mark. 1996. "Nigerian White Collar Crime." Testimony before the House International Relations Committee on Nigerian White Collar Crime, U.S. Congress. Washington, D.C., 11 Sept.

Richards, Paul. 1994. "Video and Violence in the Periphery: Rambo and War in the Forests of Sierra Leone—Liberia." *IDS Bulletin* 25:2 (April), 88–93.

———. 1995. "Rebellion in Liberia and Sierra Leone: A Crisis of Youth?" In Oliver Furley, ed. *Conflict in Africa.* London: I. B. Tauris, 134–170.

———. 1996. *Fighting for the Rainforest: War, Youth and Resources in Sierra Leone.* Portsmouth, N.H.: Heinemann.

Riley, Stephen. 1996. *Liberia and Sierra Leone: Anarchy or Peace in West Africa?* London: Research Institute for the Study of Conflict and Terrorism.

———. 1997. "Sierra Leone: The Militariat Strikes Again." *Review of African Political Economy* 72 (June), 287–292.

Riley, Stephen and Max Sesay. 1995. "Sierra Leone: The Coming Anarchy?" *Review of African Political Economy* 63 (March), 121–126.

Roberts, Wess. 1989. *Leadership Secrets of Attila the Hun.* New York: Warner.

Robison, Richard. 1988. "Authoritarian States, Capital-Owning Classes and the Politics of Newly Industrializing Countries: The Case of Indonesia." *World Politics* 41:1 (Oct.), 52–74.

Rodney, Walter. 1982. *How Europe Underdeveloped Africa.* Washington, D.C.: Howard University Press.

Rosenau, James. 1990. *Turbulence in World Politics: A Theory of Change and Continuity.* Princeton: Princeton University Press.

Rosenau, James and Mary Duffee. 1995. *Thinking Theory Thoroughly.* Boulder: Westview.

Roy, Olivier. 1994. "En Asie centrale: kolkhoziens et entreprenants." In Jean-François Bayart, ed. *La réinvention du capitalisme.* Paris: Fayard, 73–86.

———. 1994. *The Failure of Political Islam.* Cambridge: Harvard University Press.

———. 1995. *Afghanistan: From Holy War to Civil War.* Princeton: Darwin Press.

Rubin, Barnett. 1995. *The Fragmentation of Afghanistan: State Formation and Collapse in the International System.* New Haven: Yale University Press.

Rubin, Elizabeth. 1997. "An Army of One's Own." *Harper's Magazine* 294:176 (Feb.), 44–55.

Ruggie, John. 1993. "Territoriality and Beyond: Problematizing Modernity in International Relations." *International Organization* 47:1 (Winter), 139–174.

Sandbrook, Richard. 1993. *The Politics of Africa's Economic Recovery.* New York: Cambridge University Press.

Sawyer, Amos. 1992. *The Emergence of Autocracy in Liberia.* San Francisco: Institute for Contemporary Studies.

Schatz, Sayre. 1984. "Pirate Capitalism and the Inert Economy of Nigeria." *Journal of Modern African Studies* 22:1 (March), 45–57.

———. 1994. "Structural Adjustment in Africa: A Failing Grade So Far." *Journal of Modern African Studies* 32:4 (Dec.), 679–692.

———. 1996. "The World Bank's Fundamental Misconception in Africa." *Journal of Modern African Studies* 34:2 (June), 239–248.

Schatzberg, Michael. 1988. *The Dialectics of Oppression in Zaire.* Bloomington: Indiana University Press.

———. 1991. *Mobutu or Chaos: The United States and Zaire.* Lanham, Md.: University Press of America.

Schwartz, Herman. 1994. *States Versus Markets: History, Geography and the Development of the International Political Economy.* New York: St. Martin's Press.

Serageldin, Ismail, and June Taboroff, eds. 1994. *Culture and Development in Africa.* Washington, D.C.: World Bank.

Sesay, Max. 1995. "State Capacity and the Politics of Economic Reform in Sierra Leone." *Journal of Contemporary African Studies* 13:2, 165–191.

Sesay, Max, Charles Alao, and Samuel Kofi Woods, eds. 1996. *The Liberian Peace Process 1990–1996.* London: Conciliation Resources.

Shoumikhin, Andrei. 1995. "The Weapon Stockpiles." *Comparative Strategy* 14:2, 201–211.

Sierra Leone Government. 1993. *White Paper on the Report of the Justice Beccles-Davies Commission of Inquiry.* 2 vols. Freetown: Government Printer.

———. 1993. *White Paper on the Report of the Mrs. Justice Laura Marcus-Jones Commission of Inquiry.* Freetown: Government Printer.

———, Government Gold and Diamond Office. 1989. *1988: Annual Report.* Freetown: Government Gold and Diamond Office.

————. Ministry of Agriculture, Natural Resources and Forestry file. 1990. "Proposed Joint Venture Agreement for Management and Control of Fishing Rights in Sierra Leone's Territorial Waters." Freetown: Ministry of Agriculture.

————, Ministry of Finance. 1990. "Review and Revitalisation of the Mining Economy." Freetown: Ministry of Finance. Mimeo.

————, Ministry of Mines. 1989. "Report of the Inspector of Mines." Freetown: Ministry of Mines. Mimeo.

Sigo, John. 1995. *Political Jesus.* Enugu: Snaap Press.

Simons, Anna. 1995. *Somalia: Networks of Dissolution.* Boulder: Westview.

Singh, Ravinder Pal, and Pieter Wezeman. 1996. "South Africa's Arms Production and Exports." In *SIPRI Yearbook, 1995.* New York: Oxford University Press, 441–457.

Smith, Stephen, and Antoine Glasser. 1992. *Ces Messieurs Afrique: Le Paris-Village du continent noire.* Paris: Calmann-Levy.

Soyinka, Kayode. 1995. *Diplomatic Baggage—MOSSAD and Nigeria: The Dikko Story.* Ikeja: Newswatch Books.

Soyinka, Wole. 1996. *The Open Sore of a Continent.* New York: Oxford University Press.

Spruyt, Hendrik. 1995. *The Sovereign State and Its Competitors.* Princeton: Princeton University Press.

Stevenson, Burton. 1967. *The Home Book of Quotations.* 10th ed. New York: Dodd, Mead.

Stille, Alexander. 1995. *Excellent Cadavers: The Mafia and the Death of the First Italian Republic.* New York: Pantheon.

Stopford, John, and Susan Strange. 1991. *Rival States, Rival Firms: Competition for World Market Shares.* New York: Cambridge University Press.

Suberu, Rofimi. 1993. "The Travails of Federalism." *Journal of Democracy* 4:4 (Oct.), 39–53.

Swaray, John. 1995. "Debt Reduction Programme." Freetown: Bank of Sierra Leone. Mimeo.

Tabb, William. 1995. *The Postwar Japanese System.* New York: Oxford University Press.

Takuya, Bala, and Sonne Gwanle Tyoden. 1987. *The Kaduna Mafia.* Jos: Jos University Press.

Tarr, S. Byron. 1993. "The ECOMOG Initiative in Liberia: A Liberian Perspective." *Issues* 21:1–2, 74–83.

Thomson, Janice. 1994. *Mercenaries, Pirates, and Sovereignties: State-Building and Extra-Territorial Violence in Early Modern Europe.* Princeton: Princeton University Press.

Tilly, Charles. 1985. "War Making and State Making as Organized Crime." In Peter Evans, Dietrich Rueschemeyer and Theda Skocpol, eds. *Bringing the State Back In.* New York: Cambridge University Press, 169–191.

————. 1992. *Coercion, Capital and European States, 990–1990 A.D.* New York: Blackwell.

Tilly, Charles and Wim Blockmans, eds. 1994. *Cities and the Rise of States in Europe, A.D. 1000 to 1800.* Boulder: Westview.

Toulabor, Comi. 1995. "Le capitaine Strasser croque le pouvoir au pays des diamants." *Politique Africaine* 57 (March), 149–154.

Truell, Peter, and Larry Gurwin. 1992. *False Profits: The Inside Story of BCCI, the World's Most Corrupt Financial Empire.* New York: Houghton Mifflin.

Turner, Thomas. 1997. "Zaire: Flying High Above the Toads: Mobutu and Stalemated Democracy." In John Clark and David Gardinier, eds. *Political Reform
in Francophone Africa.* Boulder: Westview.

Twaddell, William. 1996. "Foreign Support for Liberian Factions." Testimony before the International Relations Committee, U.S. House of Representatives.
Washington, D.C., 26 June.

Uniamikogbo, S. O., ed. *Issues in Privatisation and Commercialisation of Public
Enterprises in Nigeria.* Ibadan: Kraft Books.

United Nations. (various issues). *International Trade Statistics Yearbook.* New
York: United Nations.

United Nations Conference on Trade and Development. (various issues). *Commodity Yearbook.* New York: United Nations.

United Nations General Assembly. 1990. "18.51 Protection of Mount Nimba,
Guinea." New Resolutions. New York: United Nations General Assembly.

U.S. Arms Control and Disarmament Agency. 1995. *World Military Expenditures
and Arms Transfers, 1993–1994.* Washington, D.C.: U.S. Government Printing
Office.

U.S. Department of State. 1997. "Liberia Country Report on Human Rights
Practices for 1996." Washington, D.C.: Department of State.

———, Bureau of International Narcotics and Law Enforcement Affairs
(BINLEA). 1995 and 1997. *International Narcotics Control Strategy Report.*
Washington, D.C.: BINLEA.

U.S. District Court of Massachussetts. 1984. "Charges Against Charles A. Taylor."
Magistrate's Docket No. 84-1251-R.

Van der Kraaij, F.P.M. 1983. *The Open Door Policy of Liberia.* Bremen: Bremer
Afrika Archiv.

Van de Walle, Nicolas. 1993. "The Politics of Non-Reform in Cameroon." In
Thomas Callaghy and John Ravenhill, eds. *Hemmed In: Responses to Africa's
Economic Decline.* New York: Columbia University Press, 357–397.

Van Wolferen, Karel. 1990. *The Enigma of Japanese Power: People and Politics in
a Stateless Nation.* New York: Vintage Books.

———. 1990. "The Japan Problem Revisited." *Foreign Affairs* 69:4 (Fall),
42–55.

Venter, Al J. 1995. "Not RUF Enough." *Soldier of Fortune* 20:12 (Dec.), 32–37.

———. 1995. "Sierra Leone's Mercenary War Battle for the Diamond Fields."
International Defense Review 28:11 (Nov.), 61–66.

———. 1996. "Executive Outcomes' Mercs and MiGs Turn Tide in Angola." *Soldier of Fortune* 21:1 (Jan.), 31–36.

———. 1996. "Gunships for Hire." *Flight International* (21 Aug.).

———. 1996. "Mercenaries Fuel Next Round in Angolan Civil War." *International Defense Review* 29:3 (March), 63–67.

Volman, Daniel. 1996. "Arming Liberia's Factional Gangs." *African Policy Report,* No. 5, 15 Aug.

Vwakyanakazi, Mukohya. 1982. *African Traders in Butembo, Eastern Zaire
(1960–1980).* Ph.D. dissertation. Madison: University of Wisconsin.

Wahab, Indra. 1995. "Structural Adjustment and Government Consumption:
Sub-Saharan and Industrialized Countries Compared." In David Simon et al.
eds. *Structurally Adjusted Africa.* Boulder: Pluto Press, 178–198.

Wallerstein, Immanuel. 1984. *The Politics of the World Economy.* New York:
Cambridge University Press.

Waltz, Kenneth. 1979. *Theory of International Relations.* New York: McGraw-
Hill.

———. 1986. "Reflections on *Theory of International Politics:* A Response to Its Critics." In Robert Keohane, ed. *Neorealism and Its Critics.* New York: Columbia University Press, 325–349.

Weber, Max. 1948. *The Protestant Ethic.* London: Allen and Unwin.

———. 1961. *General Economic History.* New York: Collier Books.

———. 1964. *The Theory of Social and Economic Organization.* New York: Free Press.

Wendt, Alexander. 1987. "The Agent-Structure Problem in International Relations Theory." *International Organization* 41:3 (Summer), 335–370.

Werber, Richard, and Terence Ranger, eds. 1996. *Postcolonial Identities in Africa.* Atlantic Highlands, N.J.: Zed.

Willame, Jean-Claude. 1986. *L'épopée d'Inga.* Paris: Harmattan.

———. 1991. "Zaire: Années 90." *Cahiers du CEDAF* 1:4–5 (entire issue).

———. 1994. *Governance et Pouvoir: Essai sur trois trajectoires africaines.* Paris: Harmattan.

Winternitz, Helen. 1987. *East Along the Equator: A Journey up the Congo and into Zaire.* New York: Atlantic Monthly Press.

Wiseman, John. 1993. "Leadership and Personal Danger in African Politics." *Journal of Modern African Studies* 31:4 (Dec.), 657–660.

Wonkeryor, Edward. 1985. *Liberia Military Dictatorship: A Fiasco "Revolution."* Chicago: Strugglers' Community Press.

Woodward, Susan. 1995. *Balkan Tragedy: Chaos and Dissolution After the Cold War.* Washington, D.C.: Brookings Institute.

World Bank. 1989. *Sub-Saharan Africa: From Crisis to Sustainable Growth.* Washington, D.C.: World Bank.

———. 1991. *World Tables 1991.* Baltimore: Johns Hopkins University Press.

———. 1992. *1992 World Development Report.* New York: Oxford University Press.

———. 1993. *The East Asian Miracle.* New York: Oxford University Press.

———. 1993. *Ghana 2000 and Beyond.* Washington, D.C.: World Bank, Africa Regional Office.

———. 1994. *Adjustment in Africa.* New York: Oxford University Press.

———. 1994. *World Development Report, 1994.* New York: Oxford University Press.

———. 1995. *Bureaucrats in Business.* Washington, D.C.: World Bank.

———. 1995. "Côte d'Ivoire Private Sector Assessment." Report No. 14112.

———. 1995. "Mali Public Expenditure Review." Report No. 13086.

———. 1995. *World Debt Tables, 1995.* Washington, D.C.: World Bank.

———. 1996. *World Debt Tables, 1996.* Washington, D.C.: World Bank.

———. 1996. *World Development Report, 1996.* New York: Oxford University Press.

Wyse, Akintola. 1989. *The Krio of Sierra Leone.* Freetown: Okrafo- Smart.

'Yomi, Tokoya. 1988. *General IBB: A Patriotic Leader of Our People.* Lagos: People's Publishing.

Young, Crawford. 1994. "Zaire: The Shattered Illusion of the Integral State." *Journal of Modern African Studies* 32:2 (June), 247–264.

Young, Crawford, and Thomas Turner. 1985. *The Rise and Decline of the Zairian State.* Madison: University of Wisconsin Press.

Zack-Williams, A. B. 1995. *Tributors, Supporters and Merchant Capital: Mining and Underdevelopment in Sierra Leone.* Aldershot: Avebury Press.

Zartman, I. William. 1995. "Introduction: Posing the Problem of State Collapse." In I. William Zartman, ed. *Collapsed States: The Disintegration and Restoration of Legitimate Authority.* Boulder: Lynne Rienner, 1–11.

Zartman, I. William, ed. 1995. *Collapsed States: The Disintegration and Restoration of Legitimate Authority.* Boulder: Lynne Rienner.
Zayyad, H. R. 1992. *Economic Democratisation.* Kaduna: Technical Committee on Privatisation.
Zhao, Quansheng. 1996. *Japanese Policymaking: The Politics Behind Politics.* New York: Oxford University Press.
Zolberg, Aristide. 1980. "Strategic Interactions and the Formation of Modern States: France and England." *International Social Science Journal* 32, 687–716.

NEWSPAPERS AND NEWS JOURNALS

Africa Confidential (London)
Africa Economic Digest (London)
Africa Energy and Mining (Paris)
Africa Recovery (New York)
African Concord (Lagos)
Boston Globe (Boston)
Business Mail (Johannesburg)
Christian Science Monitor (Boston)
La Cité (Brussels)
Concord Times (Freetown)
Daily Telegraph (London)
Daily Times (Lagos)
Defense News (London)
Economist (London)
Elima (Kinshasa)
Expo Times (Freetown)
Financial Times (London)
For Di People (Freetown)
Gaskiya Ta Fi Kwabo (Kano)
Gazette Times (Freetown)
Guardian (Lagos)
Guardian (Manchester)
Horoya (Conakry)
L'Independent (Conakry)
Indian Ocean Newsletter (Paris)
Inquirer (Monrovia)
Institutional Investor (New York)
International Herald Tribune (Paris)
Jane's Defense Weekly (London)
Jeune Afrique (Paris)
Le Jour (Abidjan)
Lettre du Continent (Paris)
Los Angeles Times (Los Angeles)
Mail and Guardian (Johannesburg)
Marchés Tropicaux (Paris)
Mining Journal (London)
Le Monde (Paris)
Le Monde-Diplomatique (Paris)
Monrovia Daily News (Monrovia)
National (Freetown)

New African (London)
New Democrat (Monrovia)
New Nation (Freetown)
New Patriot (Monrovia)
New York Times (New York)
Newswatch (Lagos)
Patriot (Gbarnga)
Sierra Leone Gazette (Freetown)
Le Soft (Kinshasa)
Soomaaliya Maanta (Mogadishu)
Tempo (Lagos)
Theweek (Lagos)
Third World Week (Hanover, N.H.)
Times (London)
Vanguard (Lagos)
La Voie (Abidjan)
Wall Street Journal (New York)
Washington Post (Washington, D.C.)
We Yone (Freetown)
West Africa (London)

▼ ▼ ▼ ▼ ▼ ▼ ▼ ▼ ▼ ▼ ▼ ▼ ▼ ▼

INDEX

251

▼ ▼ ▼ ▼ ▼ ▼ ▼ ▼ ▼ ▼ ▼ ▼ ▼

ABOUT THE BOOK

The dramatic reconfigurations of political authority taking place in Africa—what many term warlordism or state failure—call for an exploration of the origins of those changes, the likelihood of their durability, and their implications for the continent's regional system of states.

Reno argues that the end of the Cold War as a particular configuration of the international state system changed, by definition, the nature of sovereignty in Africa. Rulers cut off from overseas largesse are vulnerable to threats from strongmen; enterprising strongmen are joining with marginalized groups to exploit regime weakness; opposing groups are trafficking in illegal drugs, weapons, and natural resources and are even forging foreign commercial partnerships.

Focusing on the examples of Liberia, Nigeria, Sierra Leone, and Congo (formerly Zaire), Reno demonstrates how rulers hold on to power amid cutoffs of foreign aid, collapsing economies, and disappearing bureaucracies. In his tightly argued book, he analyzes the emergence of a diversity of forms of political authority and the effect of their appearance on relations between states in the region; he also considers how the international system accommodates a growing variety of constitutive entities.

The evidence presented contradicts the conventional wisdom that Africa's worst-off states are those increasingly marginal to the world economy. Ironically, closer integration of those states into global markets promotes warlord politics, not the bureaucratic forms of administration most studies of reform in Africa prescribe.

WILLIAM RENO is associate professor of political science at Florida International University.